Reimagining Journalism and Social Order in a Fragmented Media World

This book examines journalism's ability to promote and foster cohesive and collective action while critically examining its place in the intensifying battle to maintain a society's social order.

From chapters discussing the challenges journalists face in covering populism and Donald Trump, to chapters about issues of race in the news, intersections of journalism and nationalism, and increased mobilities of audiences and communicators in a digital age, *Reimagining Journalism and Social Order in a Fragmented Media World* focuses on the pitfalls and promises of journalism in moments of social contestation. Rich with perspectives from across the globe, this book connects journalism studies to critical scholarship on social order and social control, nationalism, social media, geography and the function of news as a social sphere.

In a fragmented media world and in times of social contestation, *Reimagining Journalism and Social Order in a Fragmented Media World* provides readers with insights as to how journalism operates in order to highlight—and enhance—elements and actions that bring about order. This book was originally published as a special issue of *Journalism Studies* and a special issue of *Journalism Practice.*

Robert E. Gutsche, Jr. is Senior Lecturer in Critical Digital Media Practice at Lancaster University, UK. His research focuses on issues of intersections of journalism, geography and power, and appears in *Journalism Studies, Journalism Practice*, and *Journalism and Mass Communication Quarterly*. He is editor of *The Trump Presidency, Journalism, and Democracy* (Routledge, 2018).

Kristy Hess is Associate Professor in Communication at Deakin University, Australia. She studies journalism and its relationship to social connection and place-making, often through a lens of media power. Her work appears in leading international journalism and media journals, she is the author of two monographs and she is the Associate Editor of *Digital Journalism*.

Reimagining Journalism and Social Order in a Fragmented Media World

Edited by
Robert E. Gutsche, Jr. and Kristy Hess

Routledge
Taylor & Francis Group
LONDON AND NEW YORK

First published 2020
by Routledge
2 Park Square, Milton Park, Abingdon, Oxon, OX14 4RN

and by Routledge
52 Vanderbilt Avenue, New York, NY 10017

Routledge is an imprint of the Taylor & Francis Group, an informa business

British Library Cataloguing in Publication Data
A catalogue record for this book is available from the British Library

ISBN13: 978-0-367-36605-6

Typeset in Myriad Pro
by Newgen Publishing UK

Publisher's Note
The publisher accepts responsibility for any inconsistencies that may have arisen during the conversion of this book from journal articles to book chapters, namely the inclusion of journal terminology.

Disclaimer
Every effort has been made to contact copyright holders for their permission to reprint material in this book. The publishers would be grateful to hear from any copyright holder who is not here acknowledged and will undertake to rectify any errors or omissions in future editions of this book.

Contents

Citation Information

The following chapters were originally published in *Journalism Studies*, volume 19, issue 4 (2018). When citing this material, please use the original page numbering for each article, as follows:

Introduction
Contesting Communities: The problem of journalism and social order
Robert E. Gutsche Jr. and Kristy Hess
Journalism Studies, volume 19, issue 4 (2018), pp. 473–482

Chapter 1
Journalism and the "Social Sphere": Reclaiming a foundational concept for beyond politics and the public sphere
Kristy Hess and Robert E. Gutsche Jr.
Journalism Studies, volume 19, issue 4 (2018), pp. 483–498

Chapter 2
From Control to Chaos, and Back Again: Journalism and the politics of populist authoritarianism
Brian McNair
Journalism Studies, volume 19, issue 4 (2018), pp. 499–511

Chapter 3
Populism, Journalism, and the Limits of Reflexivity: The case of Donald J. Trump
Michael McDevitt and Patrick Ferrucci
Journalism Studies, volume 19, issue 4 (2018), pp. 512–526

Chapter 4
Migration Maps with the News: Guidelines for ethical visualization of mobile populations
Paul C. Adams
Journalism Studies, volume 19, issue 4 (2018), pp. 527–547

Chapter 5
Veritable Flak Mill: A case study of Project Veritas and a call for truth
Brian Michael Goss
Journalism Studies, volume 19, issue 4 (2018), pp. 548–563

Chapter 6

Re-Thinking Trust in the News: A material approach through "Objects of Journalism"
Nikki Usher
Journalism Studies, volume 19, issue 4 (2018), pp. 564–578

Chapter 7

Community Repair through Truce and Contestation: Danish legacy print media and the Copenhagen shootings
Henrik Bødker and Teke Ngomba
Journalism Studies, volume 19, issue 4 (2018), pp. 579–593

Chapter 8

Diverging Projections of Reality: Amplified frame competition via distinct modes of journalistic production
Curd Benjamin Knüpfer
Journalism Studies, volume 19, issue 4 (2018), pp. 594–611

The following chapters were originally published in *Journalism Practice*, volume 12, issue 2 (2018). When citing this material, please use the original page numbering for each article, as follows:

Chapter 9

Using the Elaboration Likelihood Model to Explain to Whom "#Black Lives Matter" … and to Whom it Does not
Lanier Frush Holt
Journalism Practice, volume 12, issue 2 (2018), pp. 146–161

Chapter 10

Coverage of the Surgical Strike on Television News in India: Nationalism, journalistic discourse and India–Pakistan conflict
Sushmita Pandit and Saayan Chattopadhyay
Journalism Practice, volume 12, issue 2 (2018), pp. 162–176

Chapter 11

Please Follow Us: Media roles in Twitter discussions in the United States, Germany, France, and Russia
Svetlana S. Bodrunova, Anna A. Litvinenko, and Ivan S. Blekanov
Journalism Practice, volume 12, issue 2 (2018), pp. 177–203

Chapter 12

And Deliver Us to Segmentation: The growing appeal of the niche news audience
Jacob L. Nelson
Journalism Practice, volume 12, issue 2 (2018), pp. 204–219

Chapter 13

Nurturing Authority: Reassessing the social role of local television news
Tanya Muscat
Journalism Practice, volume 12, issue 2 (2018), pp. 220–235

Chapter 14

"Tightening the Knots" of the International Drugs Trade in Brazil: Possibilities and challenges for news media to acquire social capital through in-depth reporting
Alice Baroni and Andrea Mayr
Journalism Practice, volume 12, issue 2 (2018), pp. 236–250

Notes on Contributors

Paul C. Adams is Professor of Geography at the University of Texas at Austin, USA, and also holds a four-year Associate Professor II appointment at the University of Bergen, Norway.

Alice Baroni is an MSCA Seal of Excellence @UNIPD research fellow in the Department of Political Science, Law and International Studies, University of Padova, Italy.

Ivan S. Blekanov is Associate Professor in the Faculty of Applied Mathematics and Control Processes, St. Petersburg State University, Russia.

Henrik Bødker is Associate Professor in the Department of Media and Journalism Studies, Aarhus University, Denmark.

Svetlana S. Bodrunova is Professor and Doctor of Political Science at the School of Journalism and Mass Communications, St. Petersburg State University, Russia.

Saayan Chattopadhyay is Assistant Professor and Head of the Department of Journalism and Mass Communication, Baruipur College, India.

Patrick Ferrucci is Assistant Professor of Journalism and the Associate Chair for Graduate Studies at the College of Media, Communication and Information, University of Colorado Boulder, USA.

Brian Michael Goss teaches and conducts research in the Department of Communication, Saint Louis University–Madrid, Spain.

Robert E. Gutsche, Jr. is Senior Lecturer in Critical Digital Media Practice at Lancaster University, UK.

Kristy Hess is Associate Professor in Communication at Deakin University, Australia.

Lanier Frush Holt is Assistant Professor at the School of Communication, The Ohio State University, USA.

Curd Benjamin Knüpfer is Assistant Professor of Political Science at the John F. Kennedy Institute, Freie Universität Berlin, Germany.

Anna A. Litvinenko is a researcher at the Institute for Media and Communications Studies, Freie Universität Berlin, Germany.

Andrea Mayr is Lecturer in the College of Media and Communication Science, Zayed University, UAE.

Michael McDevitt is Professor of Journalism and Media Studies at the College of Media, Communication and Information, University of Colorado Boulder, USA.

Brian McNair is Professor of Journalism, Media, and Communication at the Creative Industries Faculty, Queensland University of Technology, Australia.

Tanya Muscat teaches in the Department of Media, Music, Communication and Cultural Studies, Macquarie University, Australia.

Jacob L. Nelson is Assistant Professor at the Walter Cronkite School of Journalism and Mass Communication, Arizona State University, USA.

Teke Ngomba is Associate Professor of Media Studies in the Department of Media and Journalism Studies, Aarhus University, Denmark.

Sushmita Pandit is Assistant Professor in the Department of Media Studies, Future Media School, India.

Nikki Usher is Associate Professor at the College of Media, University of Illinois Urbana-Champaign, USA.

INTRODUCTION—CONTESTING COMMUNITIES

The problem of journalism and social order

Robert E. Gutsche Jr. and **Kristy Hess**

This introductory chapter provides an overview of some of the key contemporary approaches to studying journalism and social order discussed throughout this book. It argues the need to step beyond a functionalist framework when considering the news media's central role in shaping social connections, community and cohesion. To advance our understandings of social order, our paper suggests a greater emphasis of the significance of journalism's relationship to the wider social sphere along with three other key considerations, including (1) a critical focus on the relationship between media, politics and social order, especially in defining and/or negotiating "anti-social" practices and social disintegration; (2) a more refined focus on the "imagined" and geographic boundaries of news audiences in digital spaces; and (3) the changing relationship to norms and conventions of journalism practice from trust and legitimacy to the role of journalists as arbiters and connectors across social spaces.

Introduction

When it comes to social order, media scholars and sociologists have celebrated the humble ant as a triumph of collective action and sociability (see e.g. Hechter and Horne 2009; Marshall 2016). Ants learn to coordinate activities in remarkable unison, forming organized highways and bridges with their living bodies to carry food and build shelter. Using refined communication techniques, they can organize the building of underground passageways and towering hills all with amazing efficiency and order.

These skills are attractive to social and political scholars in discussing human social organization, yet what theorists often omit is the dark side of the ant world. Ants recognize and react to those within their "colony" by odour—if one smells "wrong" it will be forced out. Ant queens—the highest of the social order—are also under constant threat from their subjects; a swarm will attack those that do not produce large broods for the colony, biting and spraying acid in a contest of ultimate natural selection (Keller and Ross 1998). Amazon slave ants, meanwhile, are indoctrinated into a life of inequality, learning to follow in the footsteps of their sisters who do the drudge work for their masters, from nest-building to foraging for prey (Moffett 2010).

Functionalist accounts of news media can view journalists in much the same way social theorists position the ant. Reporters are socialized by peers within an organizational structure and draw on the interpretive community's norms and values. Using their own set of advanced communication practices, they are expected to gather and share information that should not be seen to benefit themselves as individuals but contribute to the success of a broader collective whole. Yet journalism, too, is not immune from issues of power and inequality, especially in a digital world where competing media practices and platforms have become integral to our social lives (Couldry and Hepp 2016). Journalists, for example, have marched quickly to exclude or contest practices of those who either do not belong or who challenge traditional norms and values that may (re)shape the field. In some instances, metaphorically speaking, they have begun to spit acid at the new queens of the media world such as Google and Facebook to re-assert their centrality to "truth" seeking and the shaping of core societal values (Hess and Gutsche 2017). Outside the journalistic field, boundary work also looms large as nations on both sides of the globe threaten to erect their own "walls" highlighted by movements such as Brexit and the contentious rise of Donald Trump. In these contexts, boundary work functions as a practice of power and coercion.

The focus on who and what makes a journalist in these changing times, therefore, cannot be fully addressed until we consider the more complex role journalism plays, or is expected to play in the wider social spaces they serve. Scholars must balance considerations of context, power and control alongside cohesion, collective identity, connections and sociability. This volume calls for a re-assessment of the relationship between journalism and social order as it relates to theory and practice. Scholars draw on a kaleidoscope of complementary lenses from cultural studies to political communication, critical cartography and philosophy, to consider the problem of social order. Such an approach is vital for examining changing legacy and established new media in an increasingly fragmented world of journalism.

To advance our understandings of social order and control, this essay recommends alterations to dominant perspectives on the role of journalism in the maintenance of social order. We begin by emphasizing the significance of journalism's relationship to the wider social sphere along with three other key considerations, including (1) a critical focus on the relationship between media, politics and social order, especially in defining and/or negotiating "anti-social" practices and social disintegration; (2) a more refined focus on the "imagined" and geographic boundaries of news audiences in digital spaces; and (3) the changing relationship to norms and conventions of journalism practice from trust and legitimacy to the role of journalists as arbiters and connectors across social spaces. Articles in this volume address, to varying degrees, elements of this realignment and surround how journalists identify—or imagine—their audiences, their needs, and the ability (and legitimacy) of journalism to satisfy those standards.

Journalism and Social Order

Social order is widely understood as the necessity of people to maintain collective stability or a status quo. Early social theorists, from Durkheim (1889), de Tocqueville (1945) and Weber (1947) have examined how individuals and societies come together in the interests of something bigger than themselves and leads to extensive literature simply too large in scope to canvas here. Work on media and its relationship to community and social integration certainly evolved through the Chicago School via, among others, scholars such as George Mead (1934), Charles Cooley (1909) and Robert Park (1922). More contemporary scholarship has examined the ritualistic function of news (see especially Carey 1989; Sumiala 2013) and the role of media events (and media power) in uniting people in time and/or place (Turner 1974; Anderson 1983; Dayan and Katz 1992 ; Rothenbuhler 1998; Couldry 2003). There, too, has been extensive studies on the relationship between news media and concepts such as social capital, civic and public journalism (see e.g. Glasser and Craft 1998; Putnam 2000; Merritt 2009; Haas 2012; Leupold, Kilnger, and Jarren 2016).

Importantly some media theorists who examine what we say and do around media and its relationship to the social distance themselves from the functionalist dimensions of social order and/or the very idea that the concept is "contained" to nations or societies in the digital era (see especially Couldry and Hepp 2016). It is our contention that journalism studies cannot completely disentangle itself from either of these dimensions given its deep symbiotic relationship with the societ(ies) and/or the communities of interest that news media is seen to "serve". There is a need, nonetheless, to position journalism studies against a backdrop of power to identify issues of coercion and control, to embrace the everyday use of news media in shaping our everyday social lives and community integration, and to challenge key concepts, norms and understandings of journalism that may inhibit more comprehensive research in this space.

In this volume, Michael McDevitt and Patrick Ferrucci (2017) draw on James Carey to highlight that "the public" is much like a "god term", which without, the enterprise of how and why journalism operates "fails to make sense" (Carey 1989, 5). That journalism, then, is viewed as a public service seemingly negates its elements of abuses of power or its potential to negatively influence our social lives. Some news media practices—or even social media practices that attract journalistic attention—can indeed foster sociability and connections between individuals, but others exert influence and control. News media can play an active role in community maintenance and repair, connecting people during times of crisis and enhancing people's sense of place. In everyday spaces, meanwhile, citizens armed with cell phone cameras and YouTube accounts patrol social and cultural boundaries, catching out those who engage in anti-social or immoral behaviour and reinforced via coverage in news media.

Contestation is captured too within the news media beyond overt forms of surveillance and ideological control through journalistic norms and practices. They can be evident in the more banal aspects of everyday life—from obituaries to wedding announcements in news media—all of which reinforce ritualistic practices and behaviours but which can also impose a form of symbolic violence on those who do not conform to certain societal expectations and values.

Another important dimension of social order that is often overlooked in journalism studies is the very significance of the "social realm". We set a tone in this volume to re-position the social sphere as a key foundational concept for journalism scholars. In turn, we argue that too often the significance of the social is subsumed by a focus on news media's relationship to the public sphere, or more recently, on the role of social media. While the Latin word "com" has been embedded in many words that express deep ties of togetherness (communicate, commune, commiserate) (see Goss 2017), the increasing focus on the tools and technology afforded in the digital era that provide real-time communication and complex, data-driven visualizations, suggest the social is now more readily equated with ".com". A critical approach to social media and journalism is needed in the context of social order.

In this volume, Svetlana S. Bodrunova, Anna A. Litivnenko, Anna S. Smolyarova, Ivan S. Blekanov, and Alexey I. Maksimov (2017) critically engage with the (journalistic) role of Twitter, posing questions about journalism's processes of performance via the social networking platform in the United States, Germany, France and Russia. Here, the authors combine network and content analysis of news coverage during times of crisis to evaluate the social forces at play in creating both journalistic community and a sense of ideological and physical collectivity via performance. From strictly providing information via Twitter to enticing (or inviting) audiences to "follow" the news outlet across social and traditional platforms, the authors argue that Twitter has become a normalized news tool and platform in a cross-continent fashion during times of contestation. The authors also found, however, that despite technological advancement in networking, tabloid and mainstream media in each of these countries remained committed to media traditions of geographic markets in building and maintaining legitimacy among audiences.

Critically Engaging with Media, Politics and the Challenge to Social Order

While we attempt to set the social sphere as something distinct but complementary to the public sphere, the importance of the political realm to social order is of central concern to scholars in this volume. The rise of digital spaces and its relationship to the public sphere is discussed by Brian McNair (2017) in his thoughtful essay on social order in a time of "cultural chaos". McNair reassesses his theory to highlight that while "cultural chaos" can empower minorities, digital platforms are also utilized with great effect by opponents of liberal democracy, whether they be extreme factions within faith groups, reactionaries and populists within the democratic countries, or in authoritarian polities. It is necessary to consider, according to McNair, if "cultural chaos" has emerged as a driver of ideological conflict in addition or in opposition to cultural democratization.

The very acknowledgement of "anti-social" practices suggests that who we turn to in order to help to identify and negotiate socially acceptable or unacceptable media practices in a given context speaks to issues of media legitimacy in digital spaces. This resonates with the work of Brian Michael Goss (2017) who explores the manipulation of "flak" in the changing news environment. At a time when there is indeed an abundance of news and information across a range of platforms, Goss refers to "flak" as a type of deliberate political harassment that erodes community sensibilities and trust. In an era of fake news, he contends outdated journalistic norms of objectivity and fact-checking limit what the profession might become in the interests of serving community and building cohesion.

The traditional role of "fact-checking", Goss suggests, does more harm than good. Scrupulous organizations are more vulnerable to flak stunts because they will perform due diligence and investigate even dubious claims of wrongdoing that ultimately breed heightened cynicism and mistrust among audiences. Examining bad faith political discourses simply by fact-checking, he argues, is "akin to pursuing financial fraudsters for parking tickets even as the fraudsters hold the economy hostage". The key for Goss is a more ambitious pursuit of truth within the field of journalism.

The clear relationship between politics and media in the shaping of the social is also evident in the work of Sushmita Pandit and Saayan Chattopadhyay (2017) who analyse journalism in India in regards to that nation's 2016 "surgical strike" against Pakistan. They show that news media largely presented the attack through patriotic, militaristic and nationalistic language aimed at normalizing tensions. Focusing on television coverage in an age of digital real-time demands, the authors argue that journalists employed a "Foxification" of news stories, relying on emotional and aggressive language of othering that enhanced Indian nationalism. Their work aligns journalism (as practice)—in this case the role of journalists in using sometimes personalized language to describe military action and conflict—with "patriotism". This work suggests that sometimes it is not the "story" that is reported but how it is presented through vocal tone, personification, personal narratives, and collective identification that requires more attention from journalism scholars.

Henrik Bødker and Teke Ngomba's (2017) work in this issue offers a different yet complementary approach to journalists' response to national crisis in their study of news discourse in the aftermath of a gunman's deadly rampage in Copenhagen in 2016. They demonstrate how the attacks promoted a range of discourses at the intersection of social control with religious freedom, immigration and ideas of national community. Here, the challenge for mainstream journalism was to reassert national relevance while acknowledging the diversity of its audience. Indeed, Bødker and Ngomba highlight the broader process and stages of community repair from stories of condemnation, demonstrations of unity, resilience and resolve, along with instances of contestation. The case also highlights the fractious and symbiotic relationship between media and politics during such media moments. They cite a clear truce period in discourse around blame and conflict between elite groups to allow time for community repair before coverage shifted to avenues of action and responsibility that brought about ideological and cultural tensions.

The "Imagined" Audience and Shifting Boundaries in Changing Digital Spaces

Journalism's relationship to social order requires not only a rethinking of Anderson's (1983) "imagined communities", but signals a need for greater journalistic reflexivity in terms of the how their perceived idea of the "imagined audience" matches reality. In this issue, McDevitt and Ferrucci (2017), for instance, draw on the recent US election to argue that the way journalists imagine their audiences led to an acceptance of punitive populism as a strain of anti-intellectualism. They argue that journalists, commentators and academics failed to understand the public on its own terms and that journalism's anti-intellectualism is often not subject to reflexivity in professional awareness.

McDevitt and Ferrucci also contend the role of journalism, moving forward, is not to engage the public mood but to engage the best ideas of candidates towards policy coherence. Journalism and journalism studies advocate misguided reform when they perceive the election as a failure of the press to affirm populist frustration, they write. To McDevitt and Ferrucci, a journalism of expertise—an "elite" journalism without apology—would have better captured the substantive concerns of rural America. They highlight that the entrenched journalistic norm of objectivity is most evidently challenged during periods of war and situations rich in cultural resonance, when journalists show allegiance to binding beliefs.

From scholarship that appears in these issues, it is clear that greater emphasis is also needed on how social and cultural factors influence audience understandings of credible news sources during media events that seek to enact social change. Lanier Holt (2017) asks how audience perceptions of race and the #BlackLivesMatter influence their response to news coverage of police shootings of African Americans in the United States based on the expertise (or experience) of the sources used to explain, in this case, resistance to racialized police action. From his work, Holt identifies issues of ideological control that likely may reduce interest or understanding of both audiences and journalists of race-related injustice as journalists turn to select sources of expertise in matters of race that hold varying levels of credibility among both diverse (read, non-white) audiences.

Journalism's relationship to the patrolling of social and geographic boundaries means acknowledging the importance of physical territory and borders in shaping people's connection to place via journalism. Paul Adams (2017), for instance, calls for journalism scholars to consider the richness of critical cartography to examine the visual representation of the communities and nation states we imagine and the people who make up these ideals. News articles on refugees, asylum seekers and immigrants entering Europe, Adams writes, are often illustrated with eye-catching maps featuring brightly coloured arrows converging on Europe from various directions, scaled to represent aggregated human flows—a thousand people coming by one route, several tens of thousands via another route. Adams, therefore, highlights how news maps reflect choices on what to include and exclude and promote biases that influence dangerous social policies and acts against populations and individuals (see also Gutsche 2014).

This issue also incorporates discussions of tensions between digital and legacy news outlets, production, and audience interactions and understandings of the changes occurring within a fragmented, and evolving, news ecosystem. Jacob L. Nelson (2017), for instance, conducts an analysis of the journalistic interpretive community of mainstream legacy journalism in the United States and nonprofit news. Using Chicago as his case, Nelson turns to interviewing journalists at the *Chicago Tribune* and the nonprofit City Bureau to examine the processes of identifying news audiences and the needs of both audience members and the journalistic outlet. Specifically, Nelson examines how journalists address perceptions of audiences that news outlets remain "objective" or "balanced" while nonprofit news outlets are seen to approach journalism through a sense of "public service". Moreover, Nelson examines how *Chicago Tribune* journalists engage with audiences in ways that maintain journalistic autonomy, but bring in audience perceptions of the news, to shape local journalism.

The Changing Relationship to Norms and Conventions of Journalism Practice

Some researchers in this special issue have called for a reconsideration of traditional norms and conventions that guide journalism practice, from a renewed emphasis on "truth" over objectivity to the importance of journalistic reflexivity. In being reflexive of our own practices, for example, we acknowledge that a shortcoming of this particular collection is the emphasis on advanced liberal democracies. Studies of social order should promote a shift from western-centric models to consider the interdependency of a range of political, religious and media systems that either possess power to influence (or attempt to exert) the maintenance of norms and values within a given "community". It is our hope that this collection can guide scholars in this manner.

Relevant across the globe, however, is the role of trust in journalism, a core concept that has preoccupied journalism scholars in a digital era—especially given the rise of fake news. Here, Nikki Usher (2017) sets out a convincing argument that trust in journalism is a critical mechanism in social cohesion, yet journalism's conceptual understanding of trust is broken. She highlights scholarship that demonstrates trust in the news across many western democracies is at an all-time low, but that trust is too often measured in terms of news consumption rather than it being a relational construct involving journalists, audiences, sources and other social actors, including the "objects of journalism". Usher invokes the material turn in journalism as a way to move beyond this dichotomy. Hard and soft objects of journalism, such as the influence of physical news buildings or digital news products like software, inspire new ways of thinking about trust.

There are also growing expectations that journalists play a much greater connector role in the communities they serve, especially in the local context, due to the rise in journalistic adoptions of social media. Tanya Muscat (2017), in her study of local news audiences in Australia, for example, analyses perceptions of authority of local news production in Sydney. Her work is based on interviews with local television news audiences that not only recognizes how journalists present stories of the everyday to audiences, but also suggests that journalists perform surveillance over social conditions and actors. Audience members reported that journalists' self-branding as "local" arbiters of the everyday served as both a community-building effort, but also one that then advances published notions of "bad neighborhoods" or "good citizens" based on the self-authority that journalists ascribe to themselves in the news they cover. In other words, Muscat argues, journalists hold the authority with audiences that they say they have, despite audience interpretations that they operate at a distance from citizens' everyday experiences that provide alternative meanings and interpretations to social conditions.

Alice Baroni and Andrea Mayr (2017), meanwhile, adopt the same theory of mediated social capital as deployed by Muscat to encourage a greater emphasis and appreciation of journalists' own social capital and networks during investigative reporting of Brazil's drug trade. They examine the power of habitus as a form of cultural capital both inside and outside the journalistic field. Importantly, this research also provides insight into the way journalists engage elites in discussions that ultimately inform policy on the drugs trade.

Of course, in a desire to rethink normative ideals of journalism, there must also be scope to provide improved analytical frameworks for understanding journalism in the digital era. This leads to an enriching article by Curd Benjamin Knüpfer (2017), who argues that the rising use of concepts such as echo chambers or filter bubbles does not account for a coherent analytical framework or provide scope to consider the overlap or feedback between competing projections of reality. He proposes a model through which frame competition via different modes of journalistic production might be systematically observed. Knüpfer contends that political communication scholars, for example, are increasing likely to encounter stark differences in public perception and knowledge stocks and argues that his model provides a baseline measure to gauge the degrees of overlap and difference of mediated output. Only by acknowledging similarities between various types of news production, he writes, is it possible to highlight the actual degree to which they may differ in their output.

Conclusion

The relationship between news media and social order can be viewed and examined through a variety of theoretical lens and contexts, but our aim here—above all—is to reposition the value of and journalism's ordering role within the social realm. In a fragmented media world, it is also imperative that we gather the fragmented dimensions of social order as it relates to journalism studies and piece together a more nuanced approach to this area of inquiry—one which acknowledges journalism's ability to promote and foster cohesive and collective action, but which also considers its place in the intensifying battle to control the social. The ways in which journalism subtly and overtly shapes the expectations we have of others and patrols and shapes social, geographic and cultural boundaries deserves attention, particularly in times when scholarship—and social networks—lead to a view of utopian society and ignore institutional desires for control.

ACKNOWLEDGEMENTS

We would like to thank other journalism scholars from Australia, the United States, the United Kingdom and throughout Latin America who have collaborated with us as individuals on key conceptual ideas and approaches to journalism extended here. They include Associate Professor Lisa Waller, Dr Julie Rowlands, Dr Kathryn Bowd and Professor Ian Richards.

DISCLOSURE STATEMENT

No potential conflict of interest was reported by the authors.

REFERENCES

Adams, Paul. 2017. "Migration Maps with the News Guidelines for Ethical Visualization of Mobile Populations." *Journalism Studies* 16: 1–21. doi:10.1080/1461670X.2017.1375387.

Anderson, Benedict. 1983. *Imagined Communities : Reflections on the Origin and Spread of Nationalism*. London: Verso.

Baroni, Alice, and Andrea Mayr. 2017. "'Tightening the Knots' of the International Drugs Trade in Brazil: Possibilities and Challenges for News Media to Acquire Social Capital through In-Depth Reporting." *Journalism Practice*. doi:10.1080/17512786.2017.1397528.

Bodrunova, Svetlana S., Anna A. Litivnenko, Anna S. Smolyarova, Ivan S. Blekanov, and Alexey I. Maksimov. 2017. "Please Follow Us: Media Roles in Twitter Discussions in the USA, Germany, France and Russia." *Journalism Practice*. doi:10.1080/17512786.2017.1394208.

Bødker, Henrik, and Teke Ngomba. 2017. "Community Repair Through Truce and Contestation: Danish Legacy Print Media and the Copenhagen Shootings." *Journalism Studies* 5: 1–15. doi:10.1080/1461670X.2017.1386584.

Carey, James. 1989. *Communication as Culture*. Boston: Unwin Hyman.

Cooley, Charles. 1909. *Social Organisaton: A Study of the Larger Mind*. New York: Charles Scribner's Sons.

Couldry, Nick. 2003. *Media Rituals: A Critical Approach*. London: Routledge.

Couldry, Nick, and Andreas Hepp. 2016. *The Mediated Construction of Reality*. London: Polity.

Dayan, Daniel, and Elihu Katz. 1992. *Media Events: The Live Broadcasting of History*. Cambridge, MA: Harvard University Press.

de Tocqueville, A. 1945. *Democracy in America*. New York: Knopf.

Durkheim, Émile. 1889. "Tönnies, F., Gemeinschaft und Gesellschaft." *Revue philosophique* 27: 416–433.

Glasser, Theodore, and Stephanie Craft. 1998. "Public Journalism and the Search for Democratic Ideals." In *Media Ritual and Identity*, edited by Tamar Liebes, and James Curran, 203–218. London: Routledge.

Goss, Brian. 2017. "Veritable Flak Mill: A Case Study of Project Veritas and a Call for Truth." *Journalism Studies*: 1–16. doi:10.1080/1461670X.2017.1375388.

Gutsche Jr., Robert E. 2014. "News Place-Making: Applying "Mental Mapping" to Explore the Journalistic Interpretive Community." *Visual Communication* 13 (4): 487–510.

Haas, Tanni. 2012. *The Pursuit of Public Journalism: Theory, Practice Criticism*. Oxon: Routledge.

Hechter, Michael, and Christine Horne. 2009. *Theries of Social Order*. Stanford: Stanford University Press.

Hess, Kristy, and Robert E. Gutsche Jr. 2017. "Journalism and the "Social Sphere": Reclaiming a Foundational Concept for Beyond Politics and the Public Sphere." *Journalism Studies* 5: 1–16. doi:10.1080/1461670X.2017.1389296.

Holt, Lanier. 2017. "Using the Elaboration Likelihood Model to Explain to Whom "#Black Lives Matter" … And to Whom it Does Not." *Journalism Practice*: 1–16. doi:10.1080/17512786.2017.1370974.

Keller, Larent, and Kenneth Ross. 1998. "Selfish Genes: A Green Beard in the Red Fire Ant." *Nature* 394: 573–575.

Knüpfer, Curd Benjamin. 2017. "Diverging Projections of Reality: Amplified Frame Competition via Distinct Modes of Journalistic Production." *Journalism Studies*. doi:10.1080/1461670X.2017.1387072.

Leupold, Anna, Ulrike Kilnger, and Otfried Jarren. 2016. "Imagining the City: How Local Journalism Depicts Social Cohesion." *Journalism Studies* 6: 1–23. doi:10.1080/1461670X.2016.1245111.

Marshall, David. 2016. "Introduction." In *Contemporary Publics: Shifting in New Media, Technology and Culture*, edited by D. Marshall, Glen D"Cruz, Sharyn McDonald, and Katya Lee, 1–15. Basingstoke: Palgrave.

McDevitt, Michael, and Patrick Ferrucci. 2017. "Populism, Journalism, and the Limits of Reflexivity: The Case of Donald J. Trump." *Journalism Studies* 11: 1–15. doi:10.1080/1461670X.2017.1386586.

Mead, George. 1934. *Mind Self and Society*. Chicago: University of Chicago Press.

Merritt, Davis. 2009. *Public Journalism and Public Life: Why Telling the News is not Enogh*. 2nd ed. New York: Routledge.

Moffett, Mark. 2010. *Adventures Among Ants: A Global Safari with a Cast of Trillions*. Los Angeles: University of California Press.

Muscat, Tanya. 2017. "Nurturing Authority: Reassessing the Social Role of Local Television News." *Journalism Practice* 32: 1–16. doi:10.1080/17512786.2017.1377630.

McNair, Brian. 2017. "From Control to Chaos and Back Again: Journalism and the Politics of Populist Authoritarianism." *Journalism Studies*. doi:10.1080/1461670X.2017.1389297.

Nelson, Jacob. 2017. "And Deliver us to Segmentation: The Growing Appeal of the Niche News Audience." *Journalism Practice*. doi:10.1080/17512786.2017.1378588.

Pandit, Sushmita, and Saayan Chattopadhyay. 2017. "Coverage of the Surgical Strike on Television News in India: Nationalism, Journalistic Discourse and India-Pakistan Conflict." *Journalism Practice*. doi:10.1080/17512786.2017.1397529.

Park, Robert. 1922. *The Immigrant Press and its Control*. New York: Harper and Brothers.

Putnam, Robert. 2000. *Bowling Alone: The Collapse and Revival of American Community*. New York: Simon & Schuster.

Rothenbuhler, Eric. 1998. *Ritual Communication: From Everyday Conversation to Mediated Ceremony*. Thousand Oaks: Sage.

Sumiala, Johanna. 2013. *Media and Ritual: Death, Community and Everyday Life*. London: Routledge.

Turner, Victor. 1974. *The Ritual Process*. Ithaca: Cornell University Press.

Usher, Nikki. 2017. "Re-thinking Trust in the News: A Material Approach through "Objects of Journalism"." *Journalism Studies*. doi:10.1080/1461670X.2017.1375391.

Weber, Max. 1947. *The Theory of Social and Economic Organisation*. New York: Free Press.

JOURNALISM AND THE "SOCIAL SPHERE"

Reclaiming a foundational concept for beyond politics and the public sphere

Kristy Hess and **Robert E. Gutsche Jr.**

This article realigns the field of journalism studies to acknowledge within itself the multiple dimensions of social life and, as well, to provide greater clarity on the social and cultural forms and functions of journalism. It reclaims the importance of the "social sphere" as a key foundational concept for journalism studies with its links to collective identity, sociability, social honour, and soft coercion. We argue the relevance of the social sphere has been subsumed over time by the dominance of the "public sphere" and, most recently, has been considered synonymous with the rise of social networking platforms and tools. Here, we recommend that scholarship shifts from the dominant influence of political theory in explanations of journalism's societal function to the value of critical cultural sociology, which reconciles power with the basic human desire for social order within individual–institutional–cultural interactions informed by and through journalism.

Introduction

When homeowners plan extensive renovations in Australia, there is a term surveyors refer to as "re-stumping." It is where the structural footings of a building are assessed and work is needed to remove or strengthen supports that have rotted or weathered. The rationale for re-stumping is clear: there is no point in advancing the structure's integrity without a solid foundation. When it comes to understanding journalism's relationship to social life—or, indeed, social order, as this special issue seeks to address—we argue that foundational work is required to provide a stronger foothold for scholars in this space. Specifically, we excavate an integral key concept for journalism studies: that of social sphere(s).

Our call for evaluating—or re-evaluating—the role of social spheres in journalism studies might seem superfluous given the increased attention to "the social" that scholars have applied to advancements in journalistic uses and influences of social media (Garcia de Torres and Hermida 2017; Goode 2009; Hill and Lashmar 2014; Phillips 2012; Singer 2015). It is our contention, however, that the real potential of social spheres as a foundational concept has not been fully illuminated by those well placed to light the scholarly runway for journalism studies. In fact, we argue, the flurry of scholarship that emerges in massive progressions of media technologies and alterations to business models sustaining news all leads to diffused understandings of just what is occurring in practical and theoretical developments of journalism. In this movement, ironically, the richness of what the "social sphere" offers journalism studies has become slighted.

Social sphere(s) are not new. As we highlight, the concept is as old as social theory itself (Arendt 1958; Bourdieu 1989, 1990; Durkheim 1958; Sennett 1977, 2012; Weber 1947, 1968). Yet, theoretically speaking, our full appreciation of the "social" has largely been subsumed by a term that has become almost synonymous with journalism: the *public* sphere. A key argument in this paper is that the dominance of the public sphere in journalism studies—with its emphasis on political action and participation, democracy, deliberation, and public opinion—overshadows the importance of the wider social sphere. Habermas (1974, 49) himself, for example, reminds us that the public sphere is just *one dimension* of the social—"a realm of social life in which something approaching public opinion can be formed."[1]

Misunderstanding or equating the political and social realms, we know, is not restricted to the journalistic field alone. Across disciplines, confusion relating to the delineation between social and public worlds "is as old as the translation of Greek terms into Latin and their adaption to Roman and Christian thought" (Arendt 1958, 28). This article, therefore, is designed to realign the field to acknowledge within itself the multiple dimensions of social life and, as well, to reaffirm the social and cultural forms and functions of journalism. In turn, we define social spheres as the realm of our everyday within which our social lives help us make sense of who we are as individuals and ultimately as collectives. It is within these spheres where we construct connections to others beyond our intimate lives and where appropriate, meaningful behaviour and practices are negotiated.

Certainly, these actions appear in an array of social environments and situations, including those that are mediated through journalism. News media plays a distinct role in establishing social norms which function as forms of social control and order, maintaining approved standards of daily life, institutional structures and practices, and dominant explanations of the world around us. Indeed, as Goffman (1959) argues, journalism serves as a "front stage" in which social norms are presented through setting and performance and addressed by audiences through the reflectivity of internalized norms and expectations for behaviour. Therefore, to explore the multifaceted context of social spheres further, we suggest scholarship shift from the influence of political theory in explanations of journalism's societal function to the value of critical cultural sociology and theory (Lichterman 2016; Turner 2009), which reconciles power with the basic human desire for social order within individual–institutional–cultural interactions and to complicate issues of social class, honour and disadvantage.

Underpinned by the battle to uphold a common good rather than a "public good" (see Hess 2017), the social sphere becomes a permeable shell through which journalism scholars can better probe ideas of collectivity, virtue and vice, ritual, myth, sociability, social honour, and control. Such existing scholarship in journalism studies appears scattered within rank-and-file debates about methodology, empirical inquiry, and town-and-gown divides between scholars, practitioners, and citizens—divides that will continue to occur until addressed through integration with critical and cultural theory. As a result, the public sphere as a foundational concept is not entirely equipped to build understanding around such dimensions of journalism and journalistic influence. A complementary construct that rotates on a broader philosophical axis is needed.

To position our arguments, this paper is divided into two main sections. We begin by highlighting the importance of salvaging "the social" from the tsunami of scholarship on digital tools, connectivity, and social media. We argue that in an era when social networking and social media are now part of the everyday lexicon of both journalism practice and studies, there has never been a more important time to reassess the notion and value of the "social."

Our next challenge is to separate clearly and distinguish understandings of the public sphere from social spheres. It is not our intention to discount the importance of matters political and participatory from journalism studies, rather we wish to ensure there is an accessible complementary framework for scholars exploring the social dimensions of news. We tease out the significance of the social sphere through four key dimensions: the common good, collective identity through performance of ritual and mythical practice, sociability, and social coercion and control.

Subsuming the Importance of the Social in Journalism Studies

In journalism studies, dominant understandings of the social is shifting into dangerous territory. Increasingly, the idea of the social is considered synonymous with social media and social networking, in which the public writ large is engaged (or is invited to engage) in a mediated sphere of public meaning (Dutton and Dubois 2015). Terms such as social journalism (Hermida 2012), social news (Goode 2009), and the sociability of news (Phillips 2012) have been coined to explore how social networking is shaping journalism, from its celebrated fifth estate function (Jerico 2012) to audience and journalistic engagement and participation, and perceptions of digital platforms (Holton, Lewis, and Coddington 2016). Phillips (2012, 669), for example, positions "sociability" in journalism as news produced in a form that is capable of spreading virally. Others, such as Correia (2012, 99), seek to clarify the conditions for an effective public sphere in relation to online journalism, emphasizing the desire for "reason without coercion" and "reciprocity between participants in collective debate."

It is our contention, however, that the significance of structure/agency over rational action, the role of subtle and/or blatant coercion in digital journalism practice, and its relationship to power deserve attention. What is often overlooked in studies that examine the relationship between journalism practice and social media tools is the very significance of the social and cultural life worlds that drive demand for these new platforms.

We acknowledge that inroads have been made in exploring the relationship between social media and journalism in mobilizing collective action and challenging established political institutions that reinforce social order. Events such as the "Arab Spring"—dubbed the Twitter revolution—demonstrate the way in which media systems and communication networks have complexly conditioned and facilitated such uprisings (Cottle 2011; Issawi and Cammaerts 2015). Yet still, a focus on historical revolts and their relationship to journalism inadvertently sidesteps the significance of our everyday social practices around news media that reinforce moral norms and shapes social order (see Goffman 1963).

The importance of balancing journalism's power to shape social order both in moments of political and apolitical crisis and in negotiating the banality of the everyday is what renders the social sphere necessary to journalism studies. Too often scholarship addressing news platforms and processes of participation in digital spaces emphasizes the desire for a utopian "public sphere" of involvement and open and free communication guided by a media-centric and politically literate engaged and empowered citizenry. The public sphere—which "comes into being in every conversation in which private individuals assemble [freely] to form a public body" (Habermas 1974, 49), is one of the most widely accepted, discussed, and critiqued concepts in journalism studies (i.e. Allan 2005; Lunt and Livingston 2013; McNair, Flew, and Harrington 2017; Simpson 2014).

A review of scholarship in two leading journalism journals (*Journalism Studies* and *Journalism: Theory, Practice and Criticism*) highlights that the "public sphere" along with "politics" have been among the 10 most-frequently adopted keywords in discussions about journalism between 2007 and 2013 (see Steensen and Ahva 2015). Since the appearance of Habermas' major texts from the 1960s (for full discussion, see Hansen 2014), the public sphere has been both adopted and challenged as a framework to discuss the relationship between media and democracy. That the social sphere in journalism studies has been overshadowed by the more politically oriented idea of the public sphere is of no surprise. Propagated by Western ideals and socio-political globalization, journalism is celebrated for its democratic, Fourth Estate function, for lubricating wheels of democracy, keeping the powerful accountable, and serving as a conduit of information that helps people connect and deliberate about public affairs.

While it is not our intention to provide an extensive review or critique (see especially Fraser 1990) of the public sphere, we recognize that its dominance—coupled with the emergence of social media—increasingly obscures the conceptual significance of the social and its relationship to journalism studies. Inherent in these realms are challenges to sovereignty of collectives and individuals to operate freely in society without mandated compliance with dominant social norms and expectations of behaviour.

(Un)masking the Social: Excavating Foundations of Social Spheres

Our emphasis on social spheres complements and extends scholarship that reinforces the importance of the social and apolitical dimensions of the news media (Couldry, Livingstone, and Markham 2007; Couldry 2012; Dahlgren 2009; Ettema 2005; Hanitzch and Vos 2016). While scholars tease out the mediated role of everyday thoughts, conversations, and activities, they are not always explored specifically through a journalism studies lens and the objective is often to examine the preconditions for effective democratic politics. Couldry, Livingstone, and Markham (2007), for instance, lay solid foundations for journalism and social spheres in their research on the "mediated public connection," which highlights the importance of theoretical models beyond deliberative democracy to detail the mediating role of everyday thoughts, conversation, and activities that may, under certain conditions, bridge the private and public spheres (Livingstone 2005).

At the root of much work on social life, Bourdieu's (1989, 1990) work on *social spaces* or *fields* can explicate how journalism both shapes and is shaped by society and embodied practices associated with news (i.e. Benson and Neveu 2005; Hess and Waller 2017; Robinson 2017). Journalism studies scholars—even Bourdieu himself (see Bourdieu 1998)—often focus on the relationship between journalists and other elite actors or the internal logics of the journalistic field (Benson and Neveu 2005; Schultz 2007; Willig 2012). While Bourdieu's reference to capital, habitus, and practice serves as a complementary set of tools to examine social spheres (beyond that of sites of competition), there remains limitations within his articulations when it comes to analysing intersections and relationships between news and everyday audiences.[2]

In advocating for social spheres, we also move beyond the "grand dichotomy" between public and private spheres explored in wider scholarship where the focus is on the blurring of boundaries between the world of family, intimacy, and personal life versus the public and the political. Some social theorists (Arendt 1958; Hansen 1997; Lii 1998; Wolfe 1997) and media scholars (see especially Papacharissi 2010) contend that the emergence of the social is neither private nor public and that there are problems and gaps created when the public and the private are treated as exclusive dimensions of the social world. Papacharissi (2010) suggests the value of studying the "trichotomy" (see also Wolfe 1997) when exploring questions about society and digital media—our aim here to emphasize the significance and rebuild the social as a key foundational concept for journalism studies.

Of course, the importance of social spheres stretches beyond contemporary discussions around the technological distortion of public–private boundaries. From Durkheim's (1958) functionalist account of the reproduction of social structures to Weber's (1968) emphasis on symbolic domination in social life, early philosophical thought has perhaps always positioned the social sphere as something distinct from the political. Notions of collectivity, community, ritual, and myth were explored, albeit critically, by Habermas himself (see also Bertland 2000), but take a backseat in journalism theory to political participation in the public sphere.

An important distinction between the social and public sphere to journalism is that while the public sphere tends to emphasis reason and language in its operation, the social sphere stresses sense, body, time, and performance (Lii 1998). The social sphere, in this articulation, represents a shared living context in which sensual perceptions of each individual member of a collective are articulated and from which a social fabric among members is developed. The role of performance (as a presupposition to practice), for example, enables individuals to advance and reassess what journalism is and stands for, particularly in the digital age, by both expressing, affirming, reproducing, and transforming it (Warde 2015).

Below, we examine the role of "the social" within journalism in the following sections which express (1) journalism as a custodian of the common good, (2) the function of journalism in forming notions of collective identities, (3) journalistic processes of sociability, and (4) the action of journalism as soft coercion.

Curating the "Common Good": Journalism as Moral Compass

In journalism studies, the public sphere has largely been aligned with understandings of the public good and public interest. It is our contention that the social sphere is underpinned by the common good (Hess 2017). Here, morality and civility take a much more pronounced position along with the battle over "good versus evil," right from wrong, notions of "community," virtue, and collective identity (Drakard 2010; Gutsche and Salkin 2016). The common good—a universal idea constantly challenged and re-negotiated in certain social contexts—offers a deliberate shift from normative democratic models of journalism (Hutchins Commission 1947; Siebert, Peterson, and Schramm 1956) and categorizes aspects of society beyond issues of politics and governance, towards ideas (and ideals) of justice, social life, liberty, and culture (Hollenbach 2002; Riordan 2008).[3]

Habermas argued that individuals within an ideal public sphere could rise above oppressive forms of social and political power to reach or debate a "common good." A key distinction here is to align understandings of the common good with Bourdieu's position on universalism. Here our understanding of journalism moves beyond rational action and deliberation to contend that society expects certain individuals and institutions to reinforce powerful *doxic* attitudes, placing those who are seen as central to generating and negotiating their meaning in given contexts in a position of symbolic power, such as journalists (Bourdieu 1990; Hess 2017). When it comes to producing everyday news, for instance, reporters work according to core values and pressures from within the journalistic field, but when core values in society are threatened, journalists switch to presenting a cultural narrative that moves the public mind back towards the dominant cultural order (i.e. Nossek and Berkowitz 2007).

The rise of new digital media spaces and the emergence of "fake news" highlight the importance of certain institutions which society expects to perform the role of monitoring and mediating acceptable behaviour, language, and values in social life. Journalism as performance is never fully determined by accumulated history but is the re-appropriation of a habitus and a cultural repertoire in a new and uncertain situation (Rao 2010). Performances of "journalism" can be judged correct or incorrect in that they are assessed in terms of their acceptability within society.

Consider the contentious relationship between Facebook, Google, and traditional mainstream journalism. As competition to control the social intensifies, the newer players on the block now face regular criticism by the press for failing to take moral and social responsibility for content, especially in "good versus evil" discourse around terrorism, paedophilia, and prostitution. Headlines and editorials such as "Time for Facebook and Google to Act Against Terror," "News Blasts Facebook," and "Fighting Evil in Cyberspace" increasingly appear in global mainstream news content. In this way, news media adopt the performative role of civic custodian as a point of distinction—not just in terms of individual ethical practice but in what the very essence of journalism represents and stands for in regards to a perceived common good. Cultural arbitration is a resource of power and, in this analysis, serves in direct opposition to the "objective" bystander role widely adopted in journalism practice. We acknowledge that dominant cultural standards of any social order are fundamentally arbitrary and stem from the activities and interests of particular elites who possess the power to shape reality (Schwartz 1997). This means we must also place greater emphasis on reflexivity in journalism practice—encouraging those in the media to interrogate their own social location and disentangle how issues of power shape their individual and professional interpretations of a situation being covered in the news (Behar 1996; Hobart 2010).

Journalism and Collective Identity: Boundaries via Myth and Ritual

The ability of people to create a shared common world through news media should not be narrowed to the deliberation of matters of political concern; rather, this ability depends on members interacting with each other through various forms of performance, meetings, and everyday practices, ultimately creating a social fabric (Lii 1998). This, we contend, is exemplified through boundary work and understandings of news myth and ritual.

Constructions of "community" and of collective identity (for both journalists and audiences) are largely perceived within journalism studies as a public resource. But these notions of togetherness do not evolve in the public sphere, instead they are formed within the realm of the social. Habermas is frequently criticized for his theories relating to community being constructed according to an unduly narrow construal of legitimate argumentation and democratic participation (Elliott 2009). Also there remain tensions between interpretations and articulations of collectivity, functionalism, and the maintenance and expanding of organizational power, especially in the context of media (Couldry 2003a; Curran 2002). Ideas of community and collectivity are socially constructed and "imagined" (Anderson 1983) or powerful attitudes that news media is well documented as serving an integral function.

Journalistic boundary work helps to explore the role of journalism in shaping centre–periphery relations, and the patrolling, maintenance, and changing performative nature of journalism in constructing socially constructed boundaries (Gutsche 2014a, 2014b). Too often, however, boundary work is adopted within journalism studies to provide an inward-looking approach around the norms and conventions shaping the journalistic profession. For example, boundary work is used to explore how journalists cement their professional standing from others who "claim" to be journalists (Carlson and Lewis 2015; Davidson 2013). While understanding journalists' interactions with news norms is relevant, boundary work can also be particularly useful when examining journalists' interactions with wider social spaces and the relationship to social order, especially at the intersection with the public sphere—for example, the role and expectations of journalism in shaping understandings of "us" and "them" in geopolitical and cultural contexts (i.e. journalism and the relationship to nationalism/localism in Western democracies such as Brexit and the rise of Donald Trump). Relatedly, a concept such as "community" has for too long been a taken-for-granted assumption in journalism research, especially at the local level (Gutsche and Salkin 2016; Hess and Waller 2017), as though the idea operates within single interpretations of geographic territory or a single homogenous group. In the end, this approach provides little scope to acknowledge unevenness, diversity, and contestation inherent in practices and inquiries of boundary work.

Concepts of myth and ritual position the value of time, place, and context within the social sphere (Carey 1989; Lule 2001; McDevitt, Briziarelli, and Klocke 2013). Myth and ritual are not new, grand revelations to journalism studies, but highlighting their significance is necessary in re-positioning the significance of the social sphere. Journalists draw on mythical explanations and archetypes to perform a powerful meaning-making function in which to reinforce values, beliefs, and behaviours in a given context (Gutsche and Salkin 2016) and make sense of news events and experiences that are difficult to explain (Ettema 2005). Yet at times within journalism studies, this cultural function tends to be situated in the shadows of a more widely adopted normative set of news values within professional journalism practice as applied to matters of public interest (i.e. Galtung and Ruge 1981). Habermas (1984) rightfully highlights that mythical reinforcement by social elites can impede innovative and critical thought and yet this aspect of his work has been largely overlooked in journalism studies. Consider the myth of motherhood that fails in news coverage of infanticide to acknowledge the hegemony of maternal expectations of women (Barnett 2011), the role of deviance in inexplicable hatred, such as school shootings of innocents, and racialized policing and social policies through mythical explanations of social conditions and behaviours (Gutsche 2017).

Likewise, ritual analysis—emphasized by Carey (1989) as media's role in maintaining society in time and celebrating, creating, and representing shared beliefs—enables us to tease out ways in which journalism serves as the legitimate centre of our social lives in a period of apparent digital disruption. Non-functionalist accounts of media and ritual have developed in scholarship and are particularly relevant here as they put media power front and centre of the discussion related to social spheres (Cottle 2006; Couldry 2003b, 2012; Sumiala 2013). News media have always performed an important role in legitimating social, cultural, and religious rituals and milestones, such as the appearance of birth, death, and marriage columns, for instance, or determining who in a given social context will be remembered for their contribution to civic and social life in the "news" pages under obituaries—paid and otherwise. Yet the relationship between news and everyday social order via "banal" news items remains a largely under-explored aspect of journalism studies.

Journalism, Sociability, and Connection

Despite well-established links between collective identity and news media, the role of journalism in actively forming opportunities and guiding everyday sociability has struggled to find its place in journalism theory. The social sphere illuminates the space between the formation of social bonds that serve as a precondition for democratic, political action (Putnam 2000) and the levels of sociability (Simmel 2009) that shape our everyday encounters. Our degree and desire to be "sociable," after all, is not a new phenomenon that has suddenly emerged with the advent of Facebook and Twitter. There is significant advantage that comes to those institutions and individuals who help guide our "playful" or apolitical levels of sociability—as evidenced by the popularity of Facebook. Indeed, social networking has pushed journalism to the periphery when it comes to accessing certain types of basic information (Peters and Broersma 2017). Consider, for example, the changing nature of Facebook "buy, sell and swap" pages that serve geographic areas across the globe. Many of these pages have come to resemble digital versions of early twentieth-century newspapers (Hess and Waller 2017), providing a platform not only for individuals to sell their wares, but to feature a variety of posts from those desperately searching for lost animals and objects, to messages of thank you, acknowledging random acts kindness among strangers, or announcing births and marriages. Such "news" content is often given short shrift within the journalism academy, yet this communication highlights the value that the social dimension of news plays in our everyday lives and the role journalism might reassess or re-assert in the digitial age. "Banal" types of information (Williams and Harte 2016)—from traffic reporting to weather stories—ground basic social order via interpretation guided by dominant ideologies as a normalized function of the legitimizing and authorizing of social institutions. Positioning journalists as performing the role of social connector through concepts such as mediated social capital (Hess 2013) further provides scope to acknowledge the active connecting capacity of journalists as a resource of power.

Of course, there are times when our level of sociability and connection with strangers is required in the interests of immediate social order, such as in times of natural disaster. In the lead up to Hurricane Irma, which devastated parts of the United States in 2017, there were reports of dozens of "fake news" stories on social media providing misinformation about the storm, highlighting the increasing importance of and need for legitimate channels to guide our actions during times of crisis (Rannard 2017). Social actions of individuals and collectives—the where to go and what to do in times of disaster—coupled with stories of survival and hardship may be mistakenly positioned within the public sphere. Yet, as Lii (1998, 117) argues, the public sphere "rises above any private view in order to reach a common mind" while the social sphere creates a shared living context in which the sensual perceptions of individual members are articulated and a "social bond amongst strangers is formed." A sense of place and *communitas*, the latter well noted by social scientists, often occur in human societies during times of natural disaster where people consciously ritualize and mythologize their actions through media, creating an expanded sense of self, and a purpose that can leave may survivors with a sense of undergoing a profoundly meaningful experience (Jencson 2001; Turner 1969). Journalist's ability to reinforce and appeal to sense of place was evidenced by BuzzFeed in the wake of Hurricane Irma with the story "The Only Place Worse Than Florida is Everywhere Else," where reporter Orin Heidelberg wrote: "among those who can leave but choose not to, most do so out of a very Floridian mixture of hubris and sense of place. There is a deep sense of pride among us Floridians ... Floridians would rather go down with the ship than have to live anywhere else" (Heidelberg 2017). Such moments of confusion, contestation, and clarity, however, also become trademark moments of meaning-making for journalists to align audiences with institutional authority and explanation (Robinson 2009; Schudson 1995). We discuss this element of social spheres in relationship to journalism next.

Soft Coercion in Journalistic Construction of Reality

It is the social sphere—not the public sphere—in which our lives are characterized by informal rules and fluid negotiation, as compared with the more formal legal and political structures of the public. Sets of collective and approved social beliefs and behaviours expressed through journalism function as hegemonic tools of maintaining the status quo (Bourdieu 1991; Goffman 1963).

There are variables at play when it comes to journalism's role in reinforcing acceptable behaviour. One variable is the notion of social honour and approval (Goffman 1963), a form of soft coercion that reinforces moral codes and social rules against which approved acts receive applause while others are cast as sinister (see also Bourdieu 1991; Weber 1947). In Durkheim's view, for instance, the social realm provides a space for private people to concentrate together, often for celebration—a view that resonates with Carey's (albeit functionalist account) of media and ritual. News media, with its established symbolic power to shape and determine "what is good" or worthy of applause, creates in the social sphere a "type of consciousness which supersedes the isolated, private individual" (Lii 1998, 129). Consider news media's tendency to place "centre stage" those who exemplify virtuous behaviour in its many forms—from stories of everyday heroes, courage, to random acts of bravery or celebrating the commitment of long-serving volunteers. The flipside to this, of course, means certain individuals are always subconsciously excluded or made "invisibile" in given social contexts.[4]

The other variable at play in the function of order via journalism is the consequences for individuals and collectives of failing to uphold the rule (Goffman 1963). In the very same crime reporting that depicts particular acts as devious, journalists juxtapose rules of law against which the crime (and criminal) is judged. For example, the practice of media shaming—the performance of a powerful cultural practice of publically ostracizing individuals for intolerable social or cultural behaviour—positions news media as the modern-day symbolic pillory (Noelle-Neumann 1993; Petley 2013; Waller and Hess 2014). While ordinary individuals are now armed with mobile phones or other devices and quick to expose the wrongdoings of others—a process known as souseveillance (Gutsche 2017), journalists continue to perform the role of "arbiters of shame" (Heo and Park 2017; Hess and Waller 2017).

Of course, the difficulty in this conversation is examining the degree to which something is truly "right," "wrong," or "virtuous." As these moral codes fluctuate across collectives and over time, operating outside the judgement of a single moment's sensibilities, journalism serves not only to position social acts within an analysis of sensibilities but within an overarching, dominant ideological system of mores. This power can be too intense for some journalists and yet is rarely discussed in textbooks on "how to practise" journalism. One American reporter, for example, in a reflexive piece for *The Guardian* wrote "Why I Quit: Local Newspapers Can Needlessly Ruin Lives for Empty Clicks" (Pauli 2017). She continues:

> As the sole crime reporter at a daily paper in Butte, Montana in charge of putting out the daily blotter, I found the process for deciding which poor residents of my city to shame completely arbitrary ... we blow small crimes out of proportion and ruin people's lives for pennies, all while missing the big picture. (Pauli 2017)

News practices that align conduct within social spheres function as well to banish undesirables not only from social and public spheres, but from dominant, journalistic storytelling and explanation of social and cultural life (Nichols and McChesney 2005). As journalistic values and norms of information-gathering, assessment, and production operate in conjunction with fellow social institutions of power maintenance (i.e. government, police, entertainment and popular culture enterprise, faith communities), those with counter-narratives risk being funnelled out of dominant discourse. What remains, then, in journalistic work—in part because of pressures of newswork, in part because of issues of power—are voices and perspectives of a select few who maintain acceptable social practices and positions. These voices, therefore, boost fallacies of "community" in a given context in which discourse and contestation appear, but which also exudes elite, dominant articulations of public life that represent idealistic views of journalistic functions of democratic speech and involvement.

Conclusion

The aim of this article has been to excavate the social sphere and to reclaim its foundational importance to journalism studies. For too long the dominance of the public sphere has cast a shadow over its philosophical bedfellow, and it is now critical to reclaim such an historically rich concept before it is accepted as some new phenomena attached to social networking platforms. It is our contention that the philosophical origins of the social realm and its importance to journalism existed long before Mark Zuckerberg and the rise of Facebook as a news and "community" platform. Peters and Broersma (2017, 13) argue that in the changing media environment, we need to study new everyday news habits, along with "de-ritualisations and re-ritualisations" if we want to understand what journalism is or, more to the point what it might be, in the changing media environment.

Moving forward, we suggest that there is much work to be conducted at the intersection between the social and public spheres, where issues of power—both the ability to suppress and emancipate—are most apparent and prevalent. Social control and surveillance are amplified, for example, where social and political power intersect. Such a layered approach also places emphasis on the knowledge-seeker or scholar-interpreter as observing and interacting from a position of power. Indeed, the frequent lack of such reflexivity and the inward-looking observations in journalism studies scholarship that seek social justice and change through increased citizen participation and public involvement in communication hinder the ability of scholarship and journalism itself to hold open court for creating a just society.

Our intention here is to provide a foundational framework that journalism scholars can relate to and juxtapose—one that acknowledges the power of media to shape collective identity, perform boundary maintenance, guide sociability, and play a role in soft coercion as it relates to social order and our everyday lives.

DISCLOSURE STATEMENT

No potential conflict of interest was reported by the authors.

NOTES

1. Habermas (1974, 49) defined the public sphere as: "A realm of our social life in which something approaching public opinion can be formed [and] access is guaranteed to all citizens. Citizens behave as a public body when they confer in an unrestricted fashion—that is, with the guarantee of freedom of assembly and association and the freedom to express and publish their opinions—about matters of general interest."
2. Scholars such as Couldry (2003a, 655) suggest that field theory does not take into account the role of "ordinary" people who do not compete for resources necessarily or belong to any particular field. He contends: "field-based research … avoids both a general account of the impacts of media representations on social space and a detailed account of media audiences. Its explanatory dynamics are located entirely in the internal workings of the journalistic field or in the specific connections between those internal workings and the operations of other fields that come into contact with it" (655).
3. In this article we do not join the debate about the specific types of virtuous practices or character traits we expect of journalists, or how a truly moral journalist might behave, rather we highlight the value of the common good as a universal idea negotiated in context-specific situations.
4. For example, couples in long-standing *de facto*, or non-traditional relationships are rarely celebrated in the news nor is the single mother holding three jobs to support a family commended for her courage in the "news."

REFERENCES

Allan, Stuart. 2005. *Journalism: Critical Issues*. London: Open University Press.

Anderson, Benedict. 1983. *Imagined Communities: Reflections on the Origin and Spread of Nationalism*. London: Verso.

Arendt, Hannah. 1958. *The Human Condition*. London: University of Chicago Press.

Barnett, Barbara. 2011. "Medea in the Media: Narrative and Myth in the Newspaper Coverage of Women Who Kill Their Children." In *Cultural Meanings of News*, edited by Dan Berkowitz, 285–300. Thousand Oaks, CA: Sage.

Behar, Ruth. 1996. *The Vulnerable Observer: Anthropology That Breaks Your Heart*. Boston, MA: Beacon.

Benson, Rodney, and Erik Neveu. 2005. *Bourdieu and the Journalistic Field*. London: Polity.

Bertland, Alexander. 2000. "Habermas and Vico on Mythical Thought." In *Perspectives on Habermas*, edited by Lewis Edwin Hahn, 71–88. Chicago: Open Court Publishing.

Bourdieu, Pierre. 1989. "Social Space and Symbolic Power." *Sociological Theory* 7: 14–25.

Bourdieu, Pierre. 1990. *The Logic of Practice*. Cambridge: Polity.

Bourdieu, Pierre. 1991. *Language and Symbolic Power*. Cambridge: Polity.

Bourdieu, Pierre. 1998. *On Television*. New York: The New Press.

Carey, James. 1989. *Communication as Culture*. Boston: Unwin Hyman.

Carlson, Matt, and Seth C. Lewis. 2015. *Boundaries of Journalism: Professionalism, Practices and Participation*. London: Routledge.

Correia, Joao Carlis. 2012. "Online Journalism and Civic Life." In *The Handbook of Global Online Journalism*, edited by E. Siapera, and A. Veglis, 99–118. Oxford: Wiley-Blackwell.

Cottle, Simon. 2006. "Mediatised Rituals: Beyond Manufacturing Consent." *Media Culture and Society* 28 (3): 411–432.

Cottle, Simon. 2011. "Media and the Arab Uprisings of 2011: Research Notes." *Journalism: Theory Practice Criticism* 12 (5): 647–659.

Couldry, Nick. 2003a. "Media Meta-Capital: Extending Bourdieu's Field Theory." *Theory and Society* 32 (5/6): 653–677.

Couldry, Nick. 2003b. *Media Rituals: A Critical Approach*. London: Routledge.

Couldry, Nick. 2012. *Media, Society World: Social Theory and Digital Media Practice*. Cambridge: Polity Press.

Couldry, Nick, Sonia Livingstone, and Tim Markham. 2007. *Media Consumption and Public Engagement: Beyond the Presumption of Attention, Consumption and Public Life*. New York: Palgrave Macmillan.

Curran, James. 2002. *Media and Power*. London: Routledge.

Dahlgren, Peter. 2009. *Media and Political Engagement: Citizens, Communication and Democracy*. Cambridge: Cambridge University Press.

Davidson, Roei. 2013. "Two Sides of the Same Coin: The Role of Boundary Work and Isomorphism in the of Financial Journalism in Israel." *Journalism Studies* 14 (3): 440–455.

Drakard, M. 2010. "Media Language: Serving the Common Good." In *Media and the Common Good: Perspectives on Media, Democracy and Responsibility*, edited by C. Mwita, and L. Franceschi, 151–161. Kenya: Law Africa Publishing.

Durkheim, Emile. 1958. *The Rules of Sociological Method*. Glencoe: Free Press.

Dutton, William, and Elizabeth Dubois. 2015. "The Fifth Estate: a Rising Force of Pluralistic Accountability." In *Handbook of Digital Politics*, edited by Stephen Coleman, and Deen Freelon, 51–66. Northampton: Edward Elgar Publishing.

Elliott, Brian. 2009. "Theories of Community in Habermas, Nancy and Agamben: A Critical Evaluation." *Philosophy Compass* 4 (6): 893–903.

Ettema, James. 2005. "Crafting Cultural Resonance: Imaginative Power in Everyday Journalism." *Journalism: Theory, Practice, and Criticism* 6 (6): 131–152.

Fraser, Nancy. 1990. "Rethinking the Public Sphere: A Contribution to the Critique of Actually Existing Democracy." *Social Text* 25: 56–80.

Galtung, Johan, and Mari Holmboe Ruge. 1981. "Structuring and Selecting News." In *The Manufacture of News: Social Problems, Deviance and the Mass media*, edited by S. Cohen, and J. Young, 52–63. Beverly Hills: Sage.

Garcia de Torres, Elvira, and Alfred Hermida. 2017. "The Social Reporter in Action: An Analysis of the Practice and Discourse of Andy Carvin." *Journalism Practice* 11 (2/3): 177–194.

Goffman, Erving. 1959. *The Presentation of Self.* New York: Anchor Books.

Goffman, Erving. 1963. *Behaviour in Public Places: Notes on the Social Organisation of Gatherings.* New York: The Free Press.

Goode, Luke. 2009. "Social News, Citizen Journalism and Democracy." *New Media and Society* 11 (8): 1287–1305.

Gutsche Jr., Robert E. 2014a. *A Transplanted Chicago: Race, Place and the Press in Iowa City.* Jefferson, NC: McFarland.

Gutsche Jr., Robert E. 2014b. "News Place-Making: Applying "Mental Mapping" to Explore the Journalistic Interpretive Community." *Visual Communication* 13 (4): 487–510.

Gutsche Jr., E. Robert. 2017. *Media Control: News as an Institution of Power and Social Control.* New York: Bloomsbury.

Gutsche Jr., Robert E., and Erica R. Salkin. 2016. "Who Lost What? An Analysis of Myth, Loss, and Proximity in News Coverage of the Steubenville Rape." *Journalism: Theory, Practice, and Criticism* 17 (4): 456–473.

Habermas, Jurgen. 1974. "The Public Sphere: An Encyclopaedia Article." *New German Critique* 3: 49–55.

Habermas, Jurgen. 1984. *The Theory of Communicative Action*. Boston: Beacon Press.

Hanitzch Thomas, and Tim Vos. 2016. "Journalism Beyond Democracy: A New Look into Journalistic Roles in Political and Everyday Life." *Journalism: Theory, Practice, and Criticism*. doi: 10.1177/1464884916673386.

Hansen, Karen. 1997. "In Antebellum New England and the Limits of the Public/Private Dichotomy." In *Public and Private in Thought and Practice*, edited by J. Weintraub, and K. Kumar, 268–289. Chicago: University of Chicago Press.

Hansen, Ejvind. 2014. "The Positive Freedom of the Public Sphere: The Need for Courageous Truth-Tellers." *Journalism Studies* 16 (6): 767–781.

Heidelberg, Orin. 2017. "The Only Thing Worse than Florida is Everywhere Else." *Buzzed News*, September 14. https://www.buzzfeed.com/orinheidelberg/the-only-thing-worse-than-florida-is-everywhere-else?utm_term=.kx42gDd3k#.nnrKwmq16.

Heo, Mansup, and Jaeyung Park. 2017. " Shame and Vicarious Shame in the News: A Case Study of the Sewol Ferry Disaster." *Journalism: Theory Practice, Criticism*. doi: 10.1177/1464884916688928.

Hermida, Alfred. 2012. "Social Journalism: Exploring how Social media is Shaping Journalism." In *The Handbook of Global Online Journalism*, edited by E. Siapera, and A. Veglis, 309–328. Oxford: Wiley-Blackwell.

Hess, Kristy. 2013. "Tertius Tactics: Mediated Social Capital as a Resource for Traditional Commercial News media." *Communication Theory* 23 (2): 112–130.

Hess, Kristy. 2017. "Shifting Foundations: Journalism and the Power of the Common Good." *Journalism: Theory Practice Criticism*. doi:10.1177/1464884915627149.

Hess, Kristy, and Lisa Waller. 2017. *Local Journalism in a Digital World*. London: Palgrave McMillan.

Hill, Steve, and Paul Lashmar. 2014. *Online Journalism: The Essential Guide*. London: Sage.

Hobart, Mark. 2010. "What do we Mean by 'media Practices?'" In *Theorising media and Practice*, edited by Brigid Brauchler, and John Postill, 55–74. New York: Berghan Books.

Hollenbach, David. 2002. *The Common Good and Christian Ethics*. Cambridge: Cambridge University Press.

Holton, Avery, Seth Lewis, and Mark Coddington. 2016. "Interacting with Audiences: Journalistic Role Conceptions, Reciprocity and Perceptions About Participation." *Journalism Studies* 17 (7): 849–859.

Hutchins Robert M. 1947. *A Free and Responsible Press: Report of the Commission on Freedom of the Press*. Chicago: University of Chicago Press.

Issawi, Fatima el, and Bart Cammaerts. 2015. "Shifting Journalistic Roles in Democratic Transitions: Lessons From Egypt." *Journalism: Theory Practice Criticism* 17 (5): 549–566.

Jencson, Linda. 2001. "Disastrous Rites: Liminality and Communitas in a Flood Crisis." *Anthropology and Humanism* 61 (1): 46–58.

Jerico, Greg. 2012. *The Rise of the Fifth Estate: Social Media and Blogging in Australian Politics*. Melbourne: Scribe Publications.

Lichterman, Paul. 2016. "Civic Culture at the Grassroots." In *Blackwell Companion to the Sociology of Culture*, edited by Mark Javons, and Nancy Weiss Hanrahan, 383–397. West-Sussex: Wiley-Blackwell.

Lii, Ding-Tzann. 1998. "Social Spheres and Public Life: A Structural Origin." *Theory, Culture and Society* 15 (2): 115–135.

Livingstone, Sonia. 2005. *Audience and Publics: When Cultural Engagement Matters for the Public Sphere*. Chicago: University of Chicago Press.

Lule, Jack. 2001. *Daily News, Eternal Stories: The Mythological Role of Journalism*. New York and London: The Guilford Press.

Lunt, Peter, and Sonia Livingston. 2013. "Media Studies' Fascination with the Concept of the Public Sphere: Critical Reflections and Emerging Debates." *Media Culture Society* 35 (1): 87–96.

McDevitt, Michael, Marco Briziarelli, and Brian Klocke. 2013. "Social Drama in the Academic-media Nexus: Journalism's Strategic Response to Deviant Ideas." *Journalism: Theory Practice Criticism* 14 (1): 111–128.

McNair, Brian, Terry Flew, and Stephen Harrington. 2017. *Politics, media and Democracy in Australia: Public and Producer Perceptions of the Political Sphere*. London: Routledge.

Nichols, John, and Robert W McChesney. 2005. *Tragedy and Farce: How the American Media Sell Wars, Spin Elections, and Destroy Democracy*. New York and London: The New Press.

Noelle-Neumann,, Elizabeth. 1993. *The Spiral of Silence*. 2nd ed. Chicago: University of Chicago Press.

Nossek, Hillel, and Dan Berkowitz. 2007. "Mythical Work as Journalistic Practice in Crisis." *Journalism Studies* 5 (7): 691–707.

Papacharissi, Zizi. 2010. *A Private Sphere: Democracy in a Digital Age*. Cambridge: Polity.

Pauli, Hunter. 2017. "Why I Quit: Local Newspapers Can Needlessly Ruin Lives for Empty Clicks". *The Guardian*, August 9. https://www.theguardian.com/media/2017/aug/08/local-news-crime-reporting-quitting-journalism.

Peters, Chris, and Marcel Broersma. 2017. *Rethinking Journalism Again: Societal Role and Public Relevance in a Digital age*. New York: Routledge.

Petley, Julian. 2013. *Media and Public Shaming: Drawing the Boundaries of Disclosure*. London and New York: I.B. Tauris and Co.

Phillips, Angela. 2012. "Sociability, Speed and Quality in the Changing News Environment." *Journalism Practice* 6 (5/6): 669–679.

Putnam, R. 2000. *Bowling Alone: The Collapse and Revival of American Community*. New York: Simon and Schuster.

Rannard, Georgina. 2017. Hurricane Irma: No Such Thing as a Category Six Storm. BBC Trending. http://www.bbc.com/news/blogs-trending-41187164

Rao, Ursula. 2010. "Embedded/Embedding media Practices and Cultural Production." In *Theorising media and Practice*, edited by Brigid Brauchler, and John Postill, 147–170. New York: Berhahn books.

Riordan, Patrick. 2008. *A Grammar of the Common Good*. London: Continuum International Publishing Group.

Robinson, Sue. 2009. "'We Were all There:' Remembering America in the Anniversary of Hurricane Katrina." *Memory Studies* 2 (2): 235–253.

Robinson, Sue. 2017. *Networked News, Racial Divides: How Power and Privilege Shape Public Discourse in Progressive Communities*. Cambridge: Cambridge University Press.

Schudson, M. 1995. *The Power of News*. Cambridge, MA: Harvard University Press.

Schultz, Ida. 2007. "The Journalistic gut Feeling, Journalistic Doxa, News Habitus and Orthodox News Values." *Journalism Practice* 1 (2): 190–207.

Schwartz, David. 1997. *Culture and Power: The Sociology of Pierre Bourdieu*. Chicago: University of Chicago Press.

Sennett, Richard. 1977. *The Fall of Public Man*. Knopt: New York.

Sennett, Richard. 2012. *Together: The Rituals, Pleasures and Politics of Cooperation*. Boston: Yale University Press.

Siebert, Fred, Peterson, Theodore and Schramm, Wilbur. 1956. *Four Theories of the Press: The Authoritarian, Libertarian, Social Responsibility and Soviet Communist of What the Press Should be and Do*. Urbana: University of Illinois Press.

Simmel, George. 2009. *Inquiries Into the Construction of Social Forms*. Translated by A. J. Blasi, A. Jacobs and M. Kanjiranthinkal, vol. 1, Leiden, The Netherlands: Brill.

Simpson, Edgar. 2014. *News Public Affairs and the Public Sphere in a Digital Nation*. London: Lexington Books.

Singer, Jane. 2015. "Out of Bounds: Professional Norms as Boundary Markers." In *Boundaries of Journalism: Professionalism, Practices and Participation*, edited by Matt Carlson, and Seth Lewis, 21–36. Abigdon, Oxon: Routledge.

Steensen, Steen and Laura Ahva. 2015. "Theories of Journalism in a Digital Age: An exploration and introduction." *Digital Journalism* 3 (1): 1–18.

Sumiala, Johanna. 2013. *Media and Ritual: Death, Community and Everyday Life*. London: Routledge.

Turner, Victor. 1969. *The Ritual Process: Structure and Anti-Structure*. New Jersey: Transaction Publishers.

Turner, Richard. 2009. *The New Blackwell Companion to Social Theory*. West Sussex: Wiley-Blackwell.

Waller, Lisa, and Kristy Hess. 2014. "The Digital Pillory: Media Shaming of "Ordinary' People for minor Crimes." *Continuum* 28 (1): 101–111.

Warde, Allan. 2015. *The Practice of Eating*. Polity Press: Cambridge.

Weber, Max. 1947. *The Theory of Social and Economic Organistion*. New York: Free Press.

Weber, Max. 1968. *Economy and Society: An Outline of Interpretive Sociology*. New York: Bedminster Press.

Williams, Andy, and Dave Harte. 2016. "Hyperlocal News." In *Sage Handbook of Digital Journalism*, edited by Tamara Witschge, C. W. Anderson, David Domingo, and Alfred Hermida, 280–295. London: Sage.

Willig, Ida. 2012. "Newsroom Ethnography in a Field Perspective." *Journalism Theory Practice and Criticism* 14 (3): 372–387.

Wolfe, Alan. 1997. "Public and Private in Theory and Practice: Some Implications of an Uncertain Boundary." In *Public and Private in Thought and Practice*, edited by J. Weintraub, and K. Kumar, 182–203. Chicago: University of Chicago Press.

FROM CONTROL TO CHAOS, AND BACK AGAIN
Journalism and the politics of populist authoritarianism

Brian McNair

With the advent of the internet it had appeared to many that the traditional, normative, pro-democratic functions of journalism as critical scrutineer, Fourth Estate and source of common knowledge for the public sphere would be strengthened. Today, however, digital platforms are being utilized with great effect by the opponents of liberal democracy, whether extreme factions within Islam, reactionaries and populists within the democratic countries, or in authoritarian polities such as Russia and China. This article considers if cultural chaos and the digital tools which fuel it have now emerged as drivers of ideological conflict in addition, or opposition, to cultural democratization.

Introduction

We inhabit a *globalized public sphere*, characterized by unprecedented turbulence and volatility in the communication space. This digitized, globally networked system (Volkmer 2014) has brought into being what we can call a *chaotic* communication environment (McNair 2006, 2016), very different in structure from the relative order and informational stability of the analogue era. Digital news culture enables an ecology in which journalistic information moves faster and reaches further than at any time in human history, and with fewer constraints on its capacity to cross boundaries of time and space. As the impact of an organization such as Wikileaks has demonstrated, in this digitally networked environment (Castells 2009, 2015) nation states have lost much, if not all, of their capacity to regulate or control the flow of information within their geographical borders (if they wish to do so). The news media environment confronted by every individual member of the public in a digitally networked society, should he or she wish to access it, comprises national, transnational and global outlets in print, broadcast and online platforms.

At the same time, given the participatory and interactive affordances of digital technology, publics have gained the capacity to engage in public speech through social media, blogging and online commentary posted on the websites of news media. User engagement with journalism in the analogue age was limited to letters to the editor, of which even a relatively spacious print publication such as the London *Times* might produce 20 or so in a given day. Now, articles in many online publications routinely receive thousands of comments, sent from anywhere on the planet where readers are located.

I have previously termed this development as the onset of *cultural chaos* (McNair 2006), arguing that it represents a democratization of the public sphere, which has at least the potential (not necessarily fulfilled in practice) to empower hitherto marginalized voices and communities by granting them new forms of access to the means of communication and public discourse. In democratic polities this has produced new possibilities for social organization and collective action, such as Get Up and Indigenous X in Australia, and the Occupy movements in the United States and elsewhere. In transitional and authoritarian societies, it has generated challenges to dictatorial and despotic rule, as seen in the Arab Spring movement of 2011 (Bebawi 2014; Bossio 2014). To that extent, cultural chaos can be seen as underpinning not just a globalization, but a progressive evolution of the public sphere, where progress is defined by social movement towards improved or better public outcomes (such as the increased representation of communities previously excluded from media production; extensions of human rights to ethnic, sexual and other minorities).

However, digital tools are also available for use by anti-social elements on the twenty-first-century global stage. They are being utilized with great effectiveness by the opponents of liberal democracy, whether they be coming from extreme factions within Islam, reactionary populists in the United States and many other countries, or authoritarian regimes in Russia and elsewhere. The article considers if cultural chaos and the digital tools which fuel it have now emerged as drivers of ideological conflict in addition to cultural democratization and the global expansion of human rights.

I begin by describing the *chaos paradigm* of communication, contrasting it with the *control paradigm* which traditionally dominated critical journalism studies, and assess the implications of a chaotic communication model for the understanding of how journalism impacts on how power is exercised, challenged and maintained in contemporary societies.

The Long Peace

This special issue appears at a time of unusual global turbulence, as compared to the experience of recent decades. As of this writing, although the pace of events indicates no room for complacency in our speculations as to the future direction of inter-state relations, the world had experienced no major power conflicts since the end of the Second World War, and remained in what has been called the Long Peace (Pinker 2011). Of course there have been many more minor conflicts of great destructiveness since 1945: civil wars as in the former Yugoslavia; wars by proxy of the type conducted by the rival superpowers during the Cold War in such locations as Angola, Mozambique, Indonesia and Central America; ethnic conflicts and pogroms in Rwanda, the Soviet Union and the Middle East, where the Israeli–Arab dispute over the future of Palestine has regularly broken out into full-blown military conflict. But there has been no "total" or world war in the post-Second World War era, and the rate of deaths in conflict has been, per capita, at historically low levels by comparison with previous centuries (Marshall and Cole 2014; Roser 2015). Even in the era of Islamic State (ISIS) and what is, in effect, a transnational civil war within Islam affecting millions in the Middle East, Africa and Asia, we continue to live by this measure in the most peaceful period of human civilization to date. In the Middle Ages in Europe, one in six people would expect to die a violent death. Today, the figure is closer to one in 1000, and many of those, as in the United States, will be deaths resulting from criminal behaviour and legally held firearms. For all that, the globalized public sphere is regularly flooded with images of grotesque violence and destruction, the great majority of the world's population are wealthier, healthier and less exposed to violent death than any previous generation.

But the world's governments and populations are now confronted with a resurgence of violent conflict. If, as suggested above, we date the onset of cultural chaos to the attack on New York in September 2001, which came 10 years after the formal dissolution of the Soviet Union and the end of the New Cold War, we are as of this writing 16 years into an era characterized by the:

- realignment of ideological and political boundaries;
- erosion of time–space distantiation (such that events in one part of the world are much more quickly the stuff of journalism and politics in another);
- resurgence of long-suppressed conflicts between and within human societies founded on competing categories of religion, ethnicity and national identity.

In relation to the journalistic media, the emergence of the internet from the mid-1990s has provided a technological infrastructure which, on the one hand, democratizes and diversifies the globalized public sphere—indeed brings a globalized public sphere into being for the first time in human history, making possible new forms of transnational community and global social action—but on the other hand, has caused the collapse of traditional media structures and the professional, ethical, moderating practices which they fostered. Big "legacy" media have been widely and justifiably critiqued from many directions in the last century (not least from scholars of journalism studies) for bias towards elites and dominant groups, excessive centralization of cultural power and other presumed evils. The internet has permitted cultural democratization, as noted above, but has also allowed the rise of unconstrained hate speech and extremism on a scale unseen since the 1930s in Europe. Extreme Islam has been one beneficiary of this tendency, as has been the response to it amongst the nativist, populist right in Europe, the United States and Asia.

In addition, the decentralizing, networked power of the internet has enabled the critics of elite media to simply route around them, forming what have been called "echo chambers" and "filter bubbles" of like-minded, ideologically conformist audiences and users. As a growing body of research is finding (Lazer et al. 2017), the internet encourages an ideological environment in which people tend to avoid opponents and "dissonant" public speech in favour of material which confirms their pre-existing beliefs. In the digital era, voices who believe (or claim to) that 9/11 was a Central Intelligence Agency-staged hoax, or that the 2012 Sandy Hook Massacre of schoolchildren never happened, become mainstream and influential merely by declaring their non-eliteness. The Sandy Hook conspiracy theory was popularized by figures such as Alex Jones and his Infowars website, which became a leading outlet of pro-Trump influence in the 2016 presidential election. Trump, indeed, declared that Infowars was one of his favourite news sources, while BuzzFeed has gone so far as to suggest that Jones had "won" the 2016 election for Trump (Warzel 2017).

We see in many societies the internet-fuelled rise of populist demagogues who break with conventional political discourse, most obviously Donald Trump, who uses Twitter to partially bypass mainstream media and communicate directly with his followers (Oborne 2017). The Philippines' Rodrigo Duterte uses social media to call for the murder of three million drug users in his country, proudly compares himself to Hitler and encourages his soldiers to rape with impunity. Europe has witnessed the rise of far right and nationalist parties in many countries including France, Austria, Germany and the Scandinavian states. These populist political movements utilize social media platforms to mobilize angry masses who appear to yearn for strong leaders and easy solutions to complex problems, notably the relationship of Islam to secular democratic nation states. The United Kingdom's referendum vote to leave the European Union in 2016 was, like Donald Trump's electoral victory, a dramatic example of the phenomena. Both took "elites", including mainstream media elites, almost completely by surprise.

This is a world of a kind not observed since the Second World War. Some declare the imminent demise of liberal democratic political cultures, and the return of fascistic, authoritarian politics of the kind which dominated the early twentieth century. Others see grounds for optimism in the defeat of the far right in the Austrian presidential elections in 2016, and the victory of Emmanuel Macron over Marine Le Pen in 2017. The direction of travel is not linear, then, and every country and local political culture has its specificities and exceptions. But that we live in dangerous and volatile times for liberal democracy is not in doubt. How they will be resolved in the interests of a common humanity is the great question of our time, urgent for the planet as a whole in an increasingly globalized, boundary-less political environment. No one doubts that journalists and their organizations will play a key role in that resolution.

The Control Paradigm

Let us think of the globalized public sphere now inhabited by politicians and publics in every digitally networked country as something like the cosmos, and define the moment of Singularity, or communicative Big Bang which started it all, as the explosion of mass reproducible information which accompanied the invention of the printing press and brought into being what has been called the Gutenberg Galaxy, about 550 years ago. Following Gutenberg's revolutionary invention in Mainz, Germany, printing technology allowed human beings to undertake the mass reproduction of texts and images for the first time. Production and consumption of those texts was restricted to wealthy, educated elites, and remained so until the development of mass print media in the nineteenth century—newspapers, magazines, paperback books, which democratized cultural consumption. For the next five centuries and more, information flowed downwards from centralized, industrialized locations financed and largely controlled by Big Capital—from the few to the many.

Those who consumed this information had few opportunities to reply to it, or to challenge it directly at source. Control of the information and communication system was relatively easy to maintain, and in the nineteenth century Karl Marx famously developed his theory of dominant ideology to explain its role in the reproduction of capitalist societies. Ruling classes, argued Marx and the tradition he inspired, controlled the media by various means—coercive or hegemonic—and thus secured the consent of their subordinate, exploited masses to the status quo. Thus, even in conditions of gross social inequality societies reproduced themselves over time, albeit subject to periodic shocks from revolutionary groups and internal challengers. Lenin famously remarked that bombs were more dangerous than bullets, and that whoever commanded the radio channels—the only electronic media platform of his era—commanded a society.

This is the *control paradigm* for understanding the relationship between communication and power in which information travels in a linear, predictable fashion, under elite control. Control was never absolute of course, and even in the most authoritarian societies of left and right there were dissidents and subversive voices. But they could be easily shut down. The Soviet Communists had their gulags; the Nazis had their concentration camps.

As electronic media expanded in the twentieth century, the control paradigm remained dominant. Big television and radio networks in every industrialized society joined newspapers as channels of mass communication, disseminating information in the same top-down manner. The Gutenberg Galaxy grew, but remained by its vertically structured nature relatively manageable. Great state enterprises, such as the Soviet Union's Gostelradio or the United Kingdom's BBC, largely monopolized the means of communication. In the capitalist world, commercial corporations became broadcasters too, and companies such as Silvio Berlusconi's MediaSet and Rupert Murdoch's News Corporation built global empires of print and broadcast media, which they often used—and still do, if with diminishing impacts—to disseminate information functional for the maintenance of the status quo. Big Media in this era were assumed to be powerful forces in public opinion management and ideological control.

The fields of critical media and journalism studies were largely framed by this control paradigm, and the related theory of dominant ideologies. The failure of socialist revolution in the twentieth century was attributed by many scholars in the media and communications fields—from Antonio Gramsci (1971) to Jurgen Habermas (1989) to Louis Althusser (1970)—to the ideological control exerted by elites over the allegedly oppressed masses. Nominally socialist revolutions that did occur, as in Cuba, North Korea and China, used the media to secure the rule of Marxist–Leninist authoritarian parties, and prevent the emergence of opposition. Against "bourgeois objectivism" they enforced media conformity to the ideas of new ruling elites.

The Chaos Paradigm

And so it went, more or less, through world wars and anti-colonial movements and the rotation of elites in democratic polities, until the end of the 1980s. The collapse of the Soviet Union in 1991, the Tienanmen Square massacre of 1989, the fall of the Berlin Wall—all signalled the onset of a new era, and a new communicative paradigm, which I have called a *competitive* or *chaos* paradigm, or *cultural chaos* for short (McNair 2006). Thinking in terms of a chaos paradigm helps us to understand the unpredictable, radical transformations now occurring in the state of many societies; processes of *phase transition*, to use the language of chaos science, in which systems suddenly and without warning move out of order into chaos, and then back into a new kind of order (as in the transition from water to ice, or molten lava to hard volcanic rock) (Gleick 1996). After seven decades of apparent stability, the Soviet Union fell apart within the space of a few short years, reforming into a new stability. Yugoslavia broke apart, and the Ceauşescu dynasty fell in Romania. Many of the dictatorships of the Middle East, having survived for decades in some cases, collapsed in the chaos of the Arab Spring.[1]

What had changed to cause these phase transitions within authoritarian social systems, which brought with it the end of the Cold War and the beginning of a *New World Order* (as the first President Bush optimistically called it)? New information and communication technologies, first—the fax, the video recorder, the satellite news channel.

These technological innovations began to break down the political and cultural boundaries which had enabled elite control in many societies for decades (such as the Soviet Union). They made public access to potentially destabilizing information easier, and elite control of unwanted information harder. They made oppression visible on the global stage, as it was happening.

The fall of the Berlin Wall, and the Moscow coup attempt, were watched by the whole world. Tienanmen's Tank Man became a global symbol of resistance. People in the Soviet Union and other authoritarian societies began to access information from abroad which challenged the propaganda of the Party, and thus its legitimacy. In 1970, American musician and civil rights activist Gil Scott-Heron wrote a song called "The Revolution Will Not Be Televised". He was wrong. Not only was it televised, it was on transnational 24-hour news channels, round the clock.

Authoritarian states fell like dominoes in Europe, but have survived in China, North Korea and Cuba. The onset of cultural chaos did not, and still does not, guarantee radical transformation of a society in a democratic direction. As we have seen with growing certainty since 1989, it does not mean that social progress is inevitable. However, this expanding, increasingly globalized public sphere makes the mechanisms of power and control unprecedentedly transparent. The Tienanmen Square massacre stopped the student movement for democratic control, but hugely damaged the global image of China. To this day, those events remain a prohibited topic in Chinese media, although they are discussed by at least some Chinese on social media and the internet (King, Pan, and Roberts 2013).

The Inflationary Public Sphere

Which brings us to a key moment in the evolution of cultural chaos—the phase of *inflationary expansion*, when the internet became a mass medium. For the sake of argument we can date this moment to the launch of Netscape in 1995, which made the internet user-friendly and accessible to ordinary people for the first time. Like the cosmologists' theory of the expanding universe after the Big Bang, the massification of the internet begins the phase of extremely rapid, inflationary expansion of the global communication space—the first, truly globalized public sphere.

From the Singularity of Gutenberg's printing press five centuries ago, and slow, gradual expansion over five centuries thereafter, global culture moved virtually overnight (in historical time-scales) to the vast infosphere of Google, Apple, social networks and user-generated content on a scale never previously imagined. Societies entered a communicative environment characterized by participatory, interactive social media, where anyone on the planet with a networked device had the potential to be an actor who not only consumes information but produces it, shares it and has the capacity to make it known to anyone else in the world. The Tiananmen Square massacre was televised by the BBC, CNN and other global news organizations, and given massive, if still limited coverage on transnational 24-hour news channels. The 2015 Tianjin explosions, by contrast, were recorded on a million smartphones, uploaded to social media and made visible to the entire planet within minutes (McNair 2016). This is a communicative environment in which information moves along and through network hubs and spokes, relatively uncensorable, and where Big Media are joined by a myriad sources of alternative and ideologically diverse voices, uniquely empowered to challenge elite power (Freedman 2014; Volkmer 2014).

While this emerging chaos of communication involves hundreds of millions, indeed billions of individual, largely anonymous voices across the planet, there are some well-known agents of chaos. Wikileaks has for more than a decade been subverting elite authority and information control with its data dumps of sensitive military, diplomatic and commercial communication. Views differ as to whether the data-dumping activities for which Wikileaks is best known are rightly considered journalism, or a source of information for the more conventional media outlets which turn the raw data into news, such as the UK *Guardian*. Edward Snowden exposed the hitherto clandestine surveillance activities of the US National Security Agency (and the National Security Agency's counterparts in many other countries). The International Consortium of Investigative Journalists, with its coverage of the Panama Papers, exposed the scale of global elite tax avoidance, and embarrassed many governments, from Iceland to the United Kingdom to China and Malaysia.

Leaks, exposés and subversions of information which elites would rather keep hidden are not unique to the internet era, of course. Watergate was 45 years ago. But the ease with which they are undertaken and communicated at the speed of light to global publics most certainly is unprecedented. Media storms and frenzies blow up with no warning, like typhoons in the ocean. They wreak havoc on the image and authority of political elites long used to more or less undiluted control of the information environment. The Big Media of the analogue era still exist—indeed, they are getting bigger in the digital age, as we were reminded in 2016 with the announced merger of AT&T and Time Warner. But they have lost much of their political power as dominant sources of news and opinion. In 2006 Rupert Murdoch declared that "power is moving away from the old elite in our industry—the editors, the chief executives and, let's face it, the proprietors" (quoted in McNair 2009, 52). The election of Donald Trump, and the loss of the British Conservatives' majority in the UK general election of 2017, both went against the grain of mainstream media coverage.

The Consequences of Chaos: Positives

The communicative consequences of chaos have been in key respects beneficial, facilitating social reform movements and campaigns for political change that were hitherto marginalized in their access to public speech. While there can be no cause and effect relationship between "cultural chaos" and progressive social change, the existence of digital media and its participatory affordances at a minimum permits new channels of global publicity for, and enhanced visibility of, such phenomena as human rights abuses and other forms of elite corruption. For example, in 2009, pro-democracy reformers in Tehran were attacked by pro-regime snipers, leading to the death of one young female protester, Neda Agha-Soltan. Because of the availability of globally connected smartphones and social media even in the authoritarian climate of revolutionary Iran, Neda Agha-Soltan's agonizing death was recorded and uploaded to the globalized public sphere as a YouTube video. One source describes it as "probably the most widely witnessed death in human history".[2] As a consequence, the regime was exposed across the world as oppressive and brutal. It won the election in 2009 regardless, but Iran became, as a result, even more obviously a global pariah in the field of human rights. The death of Neda Agha-Soltan was a global news story within hours. There, and increasingly everywhere, social media users have provided global news media outlets with graphic and disturbing evidence of the anti-democratic nature of many regimes.

Two years later, in the course of the pro-democracy movements that came to be known as the Arab Spring (Ahy 2014; Bruns and Highfield 2014; Lynch 2014), digital technology was again at the forefront of social protest in many countries in the region. Although analysts and observers have disagreed on the impact of the social media in the outcomes of these movements (Shirky 2011; Brym et al. 2013), no-one disputed that they, alongside 24-hour news channels such as Al Jazeera, have brought into existence an Arab public sphere of a genuinely new type, able to articulate anti-authoritarian political ideas to an extent impossible in the analogue era of top-down media.

Chaos and Democratic Governance

In democratic polities, cultural chaos presents different challenges. Given the possibilities for journalists and others such as WikiLeaks to uncover hitherto hidden sources of secret and even classified information, communicative openness and information transparency associated with cultural chaos have been found to be nearly always better for democratic governance than closure and opacity (we note the controversy around Wikileaks' involvement in the 2016 US election, in which Julian Assange facilitated the leaking of Hillary Clinton campaign information allegedly in collusion with the Russians). Not everything to do with governance and politics can or should be public, of course, but only genuine concerns such as national defence and individual privacy should justify the keeping of secrets from the public in the digital age. In the digital era information always leaks out, somewhere in the globalized public sphere, and so does power, if it is judged complicit in keeping secrets from digitally empowered citizens. This rule applies to all forms of governance, from democratic through transitional to authoritarian. China was required by the nature of the coverage which accompanied it to display unfamiliar transparency around the Tianjin incident. Russia has tried unsuccessfully to hide the truth about its role in Ukraine and the shooting down of Malaysia Airlines Flight MH17 (Wilson 2014; Pomerantsev 2015; Sutyagin 2015). It is clear which regime is the more respected internationally in 2016.

Negatives

These, one might suggest, are among the positive consequence of chaos. More scrutiny of power elites, whether democratic or authoritarian; more visibility for protesters and dissidents when they confront power, must be, other things remaining equal, a good thing. The efforts of Russian reformist Alexei Navalny to mobilise protest against Vladimir Putin have been high on the global news agenda, even as he and his supporters are regularly silenced by imprisonment and worse. Such movements now have a global media platform of a kind denied previous generations of campaigners.

At the same time, however, there are movements which seek to turn the clock back on social progress and democracy, and they too have access to the globalized public sphere. During the Arab Spring, the Muslim Brotherhood in Egypt fought for a fundamentalist Islam of the type which, once in government, began to institute religious rather than secular authoritarianism. While they and other islamist movements challenged incumbent dictators, their goals were not "democratic". Rather, they sought imposition of theocratic regimes hostile to women's rights, gay liberation and other achievements of secular liberal democracy. To repeat the point made above—the democratizing tendencies of the globalized public sphere can readily be employed by political actors who in their objectives are not in fact democratic (or for whom democratic reform is simply a vehicle for the imposition of a different, perhaps even more oppressive, authoritarianism).

The decentralization, diversification and democratization of communication, to repeat, are not guarantees of social progress. The same digital tools as were employed by the Umbrella Revolution in Hong Kong can be utilized by reactionary social movements violently opposed to democracy and human rights, notably ISIS. US research published in 2015 (Berger and Morgan 2015) showed that ISIS and its affiliates had at that time control of some 40,000 Twitter accounts, and the world has witnessed all too often the communicative power of Islamic terrorism disseminated to the globalized public sphere on socially networked video (beheading videos, mass shootings of civilians, the murder of homosexuals thrown off rooftops in ISIS-controlled territory, for example). As noted above, the use of social media can provide relatively small, resource-poor groups, such as ISIS, influence and impact far beyond an objective calculation of their size.

The Return to Control—Populism and the Challenge to Liberal Journalism

In *Cultural Chaos* (McNair 2006), I suggested that the trend towards erosion of elite control of information might be reversed—or the attempt made at the least—by one or more of several developments. These included a global crisis of capitalism, the resurgence of great power conflict, or some other unforeseen catastrophe such as environmental collapse. In 2008, many of the largest capitalist economies were thrown into crisis by the global financial crisis. In recent years both Russia and China have emerged as global powers capable of challenging Western authority in Europe and Asia; and the failure of Western efforts to defeat or contain global jihad after 9/11 have made the "clash of civilizations" foreseen by some in the 1990s a greater threat to world peace and stability than could have been imagined even in the aftermath of that atrocity.

The effectiveness of asymmetric warfare pursued by ISIS and other Islamic fundamentalist groups, which led in turn to vastly destructive civil conflicts in Syria, Libya and Iraq, and consequent waves of mass migration into Europe, is arguably a major cause of the reactionary populism which propelled Donald Trump into the US presidency, pulled the United Kingdom out of the European Union and led to the recent rise of extreme right-wing political parties in a number of European countries. When the heartbreaking photograph of a young boy lying dead on a Mediterranean beach went around the world in September 2015, it deepened what was already a political crisis for the European Union—a perceived loss of control of borders through mass migration from the Middle East (McNair 2016). In the United Kingdom, this crisis merged with the EU referendum of June 2016 to produce Brexit—representing the rise of extreme nationalist, populist sentiments and the vote to leave the European Union. There is some polling evidence to suggest that the fear of the loss of control of UK borders was an important factor in driving many "Leave" voters (many of them traditionally Labour-supporting working-class voters alarmed by a perceived influx of migrants and refugees—real or not—into their already economically struggling communities). Digital media and the globalized public sphere generated a heightened sense of crisis (McNair 2016), delegitimized the established elites of both Britain and the European Union, and pulled the United Kingdom out of the 28-country alliance. The result has been genuine chaos in UK government, seen most recently in the outcome of the 8 June 2017 election.

The rise of Donald Trump, similarly, is agreed by many US observers to reflect a sense of loss amongst a certain proportion of the US electorate. Perceived loss of border control, loss of manufacturing jobs to the Asian economies, fear of Islamist terror and much else are widely accepted to be the drivers of the Trump ascendancy. Trump used social media aggressively to fight his populist campaign, and has sought to delegitimize the entire system of American democracy, including the mainstream media, since his election in November 2016. Millions of his supporters genuinely believe established institutions of liberal democracy to be "rigged" against them. The "elite", represented in 2016 by Hillary Clinton and the mainstream Republican and Democratic establishments, are regarded by this sizeable group as discredited and corrupt. This disillusionment has been fuelled also by the aggressive information warfare campaigns of Vladimir Putin's Russian government, seen also in the French presidential election of 2017 and other democratic processes in recent times.

As a consequence, a form of nativist populism now occupies the Executive branch of the US government, and digital media—Twitter, obviously, Breitbart.com and the "alt-right" online commentariat—have played an important role in its emergence and spread. Moreover, as the results of the 2016 election came in, the mainstream media in the United States and around the world demonstrated their inability to cope with the challenge of a president Trump within the conventional paradigms of journalistic objectivity, balance and fairness; or, rather, to cope without normalizing the most conspicuously overt racism, sexism and proto-fascism ever heard from the mouth a serious candidate for president.

As street protests broke out in Portland, Oregon in the days after the election, for example, BBC World noted the police definition of the events as a "riot", in response to what it coyly described as "some racist remarks" made by Donald Trump during his campaign. A man whose comments were denounced even by his own party chief Paul Ryan as "textbook racism", and whose references to "grabbing pussy", "a nasty woman", "Miss House Keeping" and other indicators of what most reasonable commentators would regard as unabashed misogyny, horrified millions in the United States across the party spectrum, was now president. For the BBC, henceforth, criticism of even the most outlandish and offensive remarks—when judged by the standards of recent decades—would be severely muted, if not excluded. Suddenly, rather can call a spade a spade in coverage of Trump's hate-mongering campaign, his ascendancy to office had legitimized those views, and the process of normalization had begun.

The mainstream media have largely followed suit in this approach to Trump's victory, bestowing a new respectability on what before election day had been generally reported as absurdly offensive statements and policies. One can without too much imagination foresee Ku Klux Klan chief David Duke becoming an expert commentator on CNN or MSNBC (or at least on Fox News). In News Corp outlets all over the world, from Sky News and *The Australian* to Fox in the United States, commentators and pundits were to the fore in constructing legitimacy around his policies, insofar as anyone really knew what they were.

This descent into normalization of the hitherto unacceptable, occasioned by Trump's democratically endowed seizure of political power as of 8 November, is very similar to the rise of Hitler and the Nazis in 1930s Germany. Hitler's ascent, and all that came from it, was a product of free choices made in ballot boxes, and of free media coverage which moved to the extreme right with the ruling party. Then, as now, a demagogic populist exploited perceptions of victimhood and "anti-elitism", targeting ethnic and religious minorities as "the enemy". No-one forced national socialism on the German people, or on their media, nor on the many Western media such as the *Daily Mail* in the United Kingdom that spoke out in his favour. Since 8 November, the mainstream media have shown their inability to engage with the enormity of what is happening in Western and global politics within conventional paradigms of objectivity. Left to them, the slide into fascism will simply become another news story, another "he said, she said" performance of balance, legitimized by the fact that this is what democracy has delivered.

Conclusions

Journalists and media freedom are under assault all over the world as this special edition goes to press (Karlekar and Dunham 2013). Not only in Russia, China and other authoritarian states where press freedom has never existed (or only briefly, in the post-Soviet Yeltsin era for Russia). In the United States too, the fake news discourse has led to regular assaults on the objectivity and honesty of the mainstream media. "Fake news" more generally has become a source of instability for those media, as they struggle to find ways of distinguishing truth from falsity which can satisfy publics of diverse political and ideological affiliations (Ball 2017; D'Ancona 2017; Davis 2017). The propensity of the primary definer in chief, the US president himself, to lie and dissemble, or to spread "facts" which are verifiably false, has generated debate about the limits of objectivity in the post-truth era. Going forward, as these processes unfold and deepen, journalists in liberal democracies must hope for two things: (1) that they are defended in their efforts to maintain critical scrutiny in the face of the populist assault on their competence and integrity—that they are empowered to resist the attempt seen in so many countries to restore control; and (2) that tools and mechanisms can be found which enable media organizations to more effectively sift and assort the wheat from the chaff in the globalized public sphere. As they struggle to maintain trust and credibility in the face of these challenges, both of these goals will be crucial.

DISCLOSURE STATEMENT

No potential conflict of interest was reported by the author.

NOTES

1. The Chinese state survived Tienanmen Square, and remains intact, but only by adopting an increasingly anachronistic strategy of cultural control and economic freedom. The Chinese Communist Party seeks to maintain its monopoly of political control, but also wishes to promote a growing economy. For the latter, it needs a media-literate population, at ease with digital tools and how to use them. But digital media are inherently leaky and hard to control. Images of the Tianjin explosions of 2015 came out through social media over which the Party had relatively little control, and the government had to respond with an unprecedented degree of openness and transparency to ease the anxieties of its people. In other situations—such as the publication of damaging information in the Panama Papers, or of scandalous books by Hong Kong publishers about corruption amongst the Party elite—it behaves in the old-fashioned way, censoring information and locking people up. A censorship apparatus of some 10,000 people, costing some \$10 billion a year, keeps watch over the internet and social media. Faced with the Umbrella

Revolution in Hong Kong, meanwhile—staged by young people armed with smart devices and global reach—the Tienanmen Square response of 1989 was not tenable. There was no massacre in Hong Kong in 2014. Bolstered by a rapidly growing economy and the delivery of major material improvements for its people (hundreds of millions have been lifted out of poverty since the 1980s), the Chinese model remains as of this writing balanced delicately between order and chaos.

2. See https://en.wikipedia.org/wiki/Death_of_Neda_Agha-Soltan.

REFERENCES

Ahy, M. Hanska. 2014. "Networked Communication and the Arab Spring, Linking Broadcast and Social Media." *New Media and Society* 18: 99–116.

Althusser, Louis. 1970. "Ideology and Ideological State Apparatuses." In *Lenin and Philosophy and Other Essays*, London: Verso.

Ball, James. 2017. *Post-Truth, How Bullshit Conquered The World*. New York: Biteback Publishing.

Bebawi, Saba. 2014. "A Shift in Media Power, The Mediated Public Sphere during the 'Arab Spring'." In Bebawi and Bossio, eds, 123–138.

Berger, J. M., and Jonathon Morgan. 2015. *The ISIS Twitter Census, Defining and Describing the Population of ISIS Supporters on Twitter*. New York: Brookings Institute.

Bossio, Diana. 2014. "Journalism during the Arab Spring, Interactions and Challenges." In Bebawi and Bossio, eds. 11–32.

Bruns, Axel, and Tim Highfield. 2014. "The Arab Spring on Twitter, Language Communities in #egypt and #libya." In S. Bebawi, D. Bossio, eds., 33–55.

Brym, Robert, Melissa Godbout, Andreas Hoffbauer, Gabe Menard, and Tony Huiquan Zhang. 2013. "Social Media in the 2011 Egyptian Uprising." *British Journal of Sociology* 65 (2): 266–292.

Castells, Manuel. 2009. *Communication Power*. London: Macmillan.

Castells, Manuel. 2015. *Networks of Outrage and Hope*. Cambridge: Polity.

D'Ancona, Michael. 2017. *Post Truth, The New War on Truth and How to Fight Back*. London: Ebury Press.

Davis, Edward. 2017. *Post-Truth, Why We Have Reached Peak Bullshit and What We Can Do About It*. New York: Little Brown.

Freedman, Des. 2014. *The Contradictions of Media Power*. London: Bloomsbury.

Gleick, James. 1996. *Chaos, the Amazing Science of the Unpredictable*. London: Minerva.

Gramsci, Antonio. 1971. *Selections From the Prison Notebooks*. New York: International Publishers.

Habermas, Jurgen. 1989. *The Structural Transformation of the Public Sphere*. Cambridge: Cambridge University press.

Karlekar, Karin Deutsch, and Jennifer Dunham. 2013. *Press Freedom in 2012, Middle East Volatility and Global Decline*. Washington, DC: Freedom House.

King, Gary, Jennifer Pan, Margaret E. Roberts. 2013. "How Censorship in China Allows Government Criticism But Silences Collective Expression." *American Political Science Review* 107 (2): 326–343.

Lazer, David, Matthew Baum, Nir Grinberg, Lisa Friedland, Kenneth Joseph, Will Hobbs, and Carolina Mattsson. 2017. *Combating Fake News, an Agenda for Research and Action*. Harvard: Harvard Kennedy School.

Lynch, Marc. 2014. "Media, Old and New." In *The Arab Uprisings Explained*, edited by M. Lynch, 93–110. New York: Columbia University Press.

Marshall, Monty G., and Benjamin R. Cole. 2014. *Global Report 2014, Conflict, Governance and State Fragility*. Vienna, VA: Centre For Systemic Peace.

McNair, Brian. 2006. *Cultural Chaos, Journalism, News and Power in a Globalized World*. London: Routledge.

McNair, Brian. 2009. *News and Journalism in the UK*. 5th ed. London: Routledge.

McNair, Brian. 2016. *Communication and Political Crisis, Media, Politics and Governance in a Globalized Public Sphere*. New York: Peter Lang.

Oborne, Pete. 2017. *How Trump Thinks, his Tweets and the Birth of a new Political Language*. London: Head of Zeus.

Pinker, Steven. 2011. *The Better Angels of our Nature, how Violence Declined*. New York: Viking.

Pomerantsev, Peter. 2015. *Nothing Is True and Everything Is Possible, Adventures in Modern Russia*. New York: Faber.

Roser, Michael. 2015. *War and Peace after* 1945, ourworldindata.org. http://ourworldindata.org/data/war-peace/war-and-peace-after-1945/2014

Shirky, Clay. 2011. "The Political Power of Social Media." *Foreign Affairs* 90: 28–41.

Sutyagin, Igor. 2015. "Russian Forces in Ukraine." *Briefing Paper*, London: Royal United Services Institute.

Volkmer, Ingrid. 2014. *The Global Public Sphere, Public Communication in the Age of Reflective Interdependence*. Cambridge: Polity Press.

Warzel, C. 2017. "Alex Jones Will Never Stop Being Alex Jones." *Buzzfeed*, May 4 2017. https://www.buzzfeed.com/charliewarzel/alex-jones-will-never-stop-being-alex-jones?utm_term=.vjVBWpjyb.

Wilson, Andrew. 2014. *Ukraine Crisis, What it Means for the West*. New Haven: Yale University Press.

POPULISM, JOURNALISM, AND THE LIMITS OF REFLEXIVITY

The case of Donald J. Trump

Michael McDevitt and **Patrick Ferrucci**

This study considers how punitive populism as a strain of anti-intellectualism is condoned in the ways that US journalists imagine audiences. A disregard for intellect is nevertheless antithetical to journalism's understanding of its contribution to an informed electorate. This contradiction between the representation of public antipathy and reason-based reporting leads to an appraisal of how journalists critiqued their work in the rise of presidential candidate Donald J. Trump. To identify boundaries of reflexivity, we compare the near-instant commentaries of scholars to the interpretations of journalists following the startling election of 2016. Textual analysis of news and news commentary documents a form of reflexivity in which practice is not so much justified to the public as the public is imagined in ways that justify problematic practice. Scholars viewed the rise of Trump as predictable when considering long-established routines of the press and journalists' misunderstanding of populism. We suggest that reform of campaign coverage is contingent on the recognition of journalists that their work is shaped by audiences they imagine.

Introduction

The specter of populism during election campaigns constitutes both a threat to reason-based reporting and an opportunity for journalism to manage public attention in ways reminiscent of the pre-digital era. Anti-intellectualism is typically characterized as a diffusive and latent sentiment (Claussen 2004; Rigney 1991), but it is periodically mobilized when populist rhetoric opposes virtues of "the people" against privileges of the ruling elite (Krämer 2014). The sectors of digital and legacy media that produce quality journalism doubtlessly motivate grassroots movements in an oppositional sense (e.g., the Tea Party). Journalism nevertheless obtains a central role in media politics when it provokes attention back toward itself and when it enhances its relevance by affirming populist alienation toward the complexities of issue-based politics (Mazzoleni, Stewart, and Horsfield 2003).

Toward the end of the twentieth century, journalists in Western democracies "detached themselves from the 'political' (i.e., choices facing political leaders), representing public opinion not so much as the *content* of what the public believed" but more as an "*attitude* toward the performance of powerful institutions" (Kunelius and Reunanen 2016, 374). Applied to populist climates, journalism in this interpretation represents audiences in a limited, plebiscitary respect—in depicting the emotive forces of resentment and suspicion.

Against the backdrop of the US 2016 presidential campaign and its aftermath, this study seeks to illuminate dark matter of political journalism, a subsistent anti-intellectualism that structures observable content but is generally not subject to reflexivity in professional awareness. Populist anti-elitism is rationalized (so to speak) in journalism's view of itself as tribune of the people. When journalists imagine an agitated public, the reified resentment is no more real than the fiction of omnipotent citizens in democratic theory. The demos is portrayed as holding intellect accountable, and journalism's complicity remains muddled in an imagined public.

A disregard for intellect, experts, and expertise is nonetheless antithetical to journalism's understanding of its contribution to an informed electorate. This contradiction between the representation of public emotion and reason-based reporting leads to an appraisal of how journalists critiqued their work in the rise of Donald J. Trump. To identify boundaries of reflexivity, we take advantage of a rare opportunity to compare the near-instant analysis of media scholars to the interpretations of journalists following a startling election. Textual analysis documents how journalists articulate concerns about campaign reporting, their audiences, and most importantly the relationship between journalism and the public. Looking to future election cycles, we suggest that reform of campaign coverage is contingent on the recognition of journalists that their work is shaped by audiences they imagine.

The Pure People and the Imagined Audience

In the cultural history of Richard Hofstadter, anti-intellectualism is endemic to American society, inseparable from its democratic ethos.

> The common strain that binds together the attitudes and ideas which I call anti-intellectual is a resentment and suspicion of the life of the mind and of those who are considered to represent it; and a disposition constantly to minimize the value of that life. (Hofstadter 1963, 7)

Anti-intellectualism extends beyond politics and takes forms such as instrumentalism in higher education, unreflective hedonism in popular culture, and religious fundamentalism. The present analysis focuses on punitive populism as a particular type of antipathy periodically at play in campaign politics. We consequently work from a modified version of Hofstadter's definition of anti-intellectualism to recognize that populism is evident in both latent and active expressions and that it seeks retribution when mobilized. A punitive populism encompasses elements of anti-rationalism and anti-elitism—an instinct to protect core beliefs from systemic probing coupled with mistrust of intellectuals, a social class viewed as haughty and highbrow.

Populist anti-elitism resonates with news values at deep levels of professional conviction. Gans (1980) argued that US journalism should be understood as a "paraideology" to distinguish an assemblage of partially thought-out values from an integrated set of values typically defined as ideology. He documented eight enduring values that underscore a vision of the good society. Among these, small-town pastoralism, ethnocentrism, moderatism, and respect for social order readily play into a narrative of the people naturally aligned against cultural elites.

A comprehensive explication of the connections between journalism and populism is beyond our scope, but Trump's success in exploiting a *zeitgeist* of media-centered politics implies a symbiotic relationship. Block and Negrine propose that while news media are not solely responsible for the advance of anti-elitist sentiment in the United States, the United

Kingdom, and Venezuela, contemporary populism relies on a distinctive style of political communication:

> The populist style has deeper roots associated with identity and culture, a specific style of rhetoric, and savvy use of various communication channels (that mainly involves the media but not exclusively the media) through which populists connect with the political feelings, aspirations, and needs of those who feel disenchanted, excluded, aggrieved, and/or disadvantaged by conventional center-ground politics or by social advances that threaten their ways of life. (Block and Negrine 2017, 179)

In 2016, the eventual Republican nominee for president received "free" and mostly favorable coverage from Fox News but also institutions in the elite press, including *The New York Times* and *The Washington Post* (Patterson 2016). Neither Trump's poll numbers nor fundraising ability explains the level of attention. "Journalists seemed unmindful that they and not the electorate were Trump's first audience" (5). With no credentials and no constituency, Trump understood instinctively that respectable media would cooperate. The elite press apparently imagined a populist response to Trump as a precursor to actual evidence of widespread public support. In this view, populist sentiment takes on a looking-glass quality in news work, existing as a narrative template because reporters and editors—along with those adept at press manipulation—anticipate its activation.

Trump's exploitation of news media implies a link between reified populism in news work and Anderson's (1987) "imagined communities." Nations exist in the minds of their members in imagined communities. While these social constructs are philosophically impoverished, a horizontal comradeship is deeply felt in the rise and spread of nationalism. Contemporary theory understands imagined communities as unstable depending on macro-level conditions such as social norms and micro-level factors such as motivations of message senders and recipients (Litt 2012).

Journalists evoke "the public" in language at once celebratory and obeisant, a dynamic captured by James Carey (1987, 5): "The god term of journalism—the be-all and end-all, the term without which the enterprise fails to make sense, is the public." The public is "totem and talisman, and an object of ritual homage." The god of Romans 12 ("Vengeance is mine … ") comes to mind for how journalists might view sectors of the citizenry when the press is viewed by many as an enemy of the people. Journalists presumably protect or enhance their credibility as attention brokers when they echo the style of populism and condone its grievance.

The problem with anticipation of a punitive public is the way this mindset shapes the management of public attention. In the pre-digital era, journalistic representations provided the primary, day-to-day proxy for public opinion. Kunelius and Reunanen (2016) contend that the coordination of public attention persists as a powerful resource in a diffusive and networked media environment. Leaving aside the possibility that news media might misread public opinion—and taking anti-elitist sentiment as an authentic feature of audience engagement—the representation of widespread disaffection is advantageous to journalism in a tactical sense. In "strategic ritual" as originally proposed by Tuchman (1972), the balancing of opinions, reliance on official sources, and other routines associated with objectivity ward off partisan attacks. Contemporary elaborations of strategic ritual portray journalism as adaptive and often reflexive in practices such as paradigm repair (Cecil 2002), paradigm change (Hindman 2005), and boundary work (Frank 2003).

Routines in the objectivity paradigm are put aside during periods of war and other situations rich in cultural resonance, when journalists show allegiance to binding beliefs (Taylor 2014). The emergence of a punitive populism in how journalists portray audiences constitutes another type of crisis, one internal to representative democracy. Populism considers society "to be ultimately separated into two homogeneous and antagonistic groups, 'the pure people' versus 'the corrupt elite'" (Mudde 2004, 543). Journalism's indulgence in the imaginary of the *volonté générale* (general will) is consequently both defensive and opportunistic as the news sustains a mesmerizing message in the countdown to Election Day.

Boundaries of Reflexivity

Journalists, for their part, are increasingly willing to criticize their work in digital media, signifying a shift from objectivity to transparency in the discourse of legitimation (Kunelius and Reunanen 2016). Professional reflexivity refers to "journalists' capacity for self-awareness; their ability to recognize influences and changes in their environment, alter the course of their actions, and renegotiate their professional self-images as a result" (Ahva 2012, 791).

Anti-intellectualism, however, is rarely up for discussion in newsrooms or classrooms where the profession is taught:

> news media have rarely covered intellectuals *as intellectuals* or even employed the word "anti-intellectual." Its relatively recent coining aside, mass media surely have been unlikely to use such a clearly negative-sounding word to label themselves, their readers, their advertisers or their news sources. (Claussen 2004, 23)

While reflexivity allows journalists to negotiate the boundaries of responsible practice, transparency is itself subject to boundaries for the types of critiques that become salient (Frank 2003).

Notwithstanding journalists' resistance to a critique of their work as anti-intellectual, commodified information influences the public's capacity for critical thinking, tolerance for complexity, and receptivity to new ideas (Rigney 1991). Still, anti-intellectualism as overt practice is difficult to conceptualize and to operationalize because it entails opportunities not taken, context not provided, ideas otherwise not engaged. The problem persists as a murky presence in journalism as an interpretive community, rarely recognized in metajournalistic discourse, not readily subject to measurement, and difficult to isolate from other forces.

News commentators, to be sure, are more likely to allude to anti-intellectualism with the advent of conservative populism in the modern presidency, beginning with Dwight D. Eisenhower (Shogan 2007). In the fall of 2015, CNBC moderator John Harwood asked Trump if he were running a "comic-book version" of a presidential campaign. Reporters and editors doubtlessly recognize anti-intellectualism in their audiences when it flares up. Following the "comic-book" question, no one missed the positive feedback Marco Rubio received from the audience when he quipped: "We need more welders than philosophers."

Conditions that compromise news work periodically induce paradigm repair, although not necessarily in ways that embrace professional responsibility, as when "pack journalists bash pack journalism" (Frank 2003). As a theoretical perspective, paradigm repair itself seems problematic if the public is viewed as more moralistic than deliberative. The textual analysis below anticipates articulations of reflexivity in which practice is not so much justified to the public as the public is imagined in ways that justify problematic practice.

We consequently apply *professional realism* to account for reflexivity when audiences are viewed from a populist prism. Klocke and McDevitt (2013) introduced professional realism as a modification of paradigm repair for circumstances in which journalists lower expectations for the public and their news organizations. Professional realism refers not to repair of normative or deviant practice but to a retreat from principles of deliberation. Journalists insist on realistic boundaries for what is possible in ideologically charged climates. The public, not the press, is in need of repair in this form of reflexivity. If professional realism is an accurate scheme in the context of Trump coverage, we should not expect much effort to defend news work to audiences but to instead focus on limitations of those same audiences.

Methods

We have outlined a rationale for why journalists would not acknowledge their complicity in the representation and legitimation of a punitive populism during the 2016 presidential campaign. The confrontational style of populist discourse, its thin ideology, and the election outcome might nevertheless prompt reflexivity on factors that influenced problematic aspects of campaign coverage. We conducted a textual analysis of metajournalistic discourse to identify boundaries of reflexivity on the relationship between campaign reporting and the rise of Trump.

Through metajournalistic discourse, actors within and outside media challenge assumptions for what is desirable and realistic. This form of pragmatic discourse delineates journalism as cultural practice and strikes "a subjunctive tone about what the news should be" (Carlson 2016, 350). Practices that produce news content, the news itself, and conditions for audience reception are critiqued in ways that ensure the provisional status of journalism as knowledge work. Routines of journalism are nonetheless anchored by doxic news values: unspoken norms such as newsworthiness not subject to dispute (Schultz 2007). Gut feeling guides reporters and editors as they align incidents and circumstances with what they perceive will appeal to public interest.

A comparison of the discourse of scholars and journalists provides leverage for tracing limits of reflexivity. Our intent is to map the regions of *possible* themes—those articulated by scholars plus journalists—and then compare those viable interpretive schemes to those *actually* articulated by journalists. For commentary of scholars, we analyzed *US Election Analysis 2016: Media, Voters and the Campaign*, a volume produced by Bournemouth University in the United Kingdom (Lilleker et al. 2016). The tight timeframe and brevity of analyses required for inclusion in the subtitled "Early Reflections from Leading Academics" were not conducive to theory-laden perspectives, putting journalists and academics to some extent on the same footing in making sense of the Trump victory.

> The aim of this publication is to capture immediate thoughts, reflections and early research of leading academics in media and politics in the United States and around the globe; and in this way contribute to public understanding of the contest whilst it is fresh in the memory and help shape the path ahead. (Lilleker et al. 2016, 6)

Four editors from communication disciplines at Bournemouth invited 82 scholars "in the US and around the globe" to comment on journalistic performance; campaign rhetoric; policy platforms of Trump and Democratic nominee Hillary Clinton; diversity and division in identity politics; social media in campaign strategy; popular culture and populism; and global perspectives on the reputation of US electoral politics. Entries were submitted within 10 days of the election outcome. We examined commentary of both the editors and the invited authors ($N = 86$).[1]

For discourse produced by journalists, we used a convenience sample of 212 articles published in the 35 most-circulated newspapers in the United States. The timeframe—November 9–28—extends beyond the deadline given to scholars (November 18). The additional 10 days allows for a larger sample of text while recognizing that the deadline constraints of news work require more time for reflexivity to crystalize. A larger corpus from journalists is also needed given the inclusion of news stories ($N = 121$) as well as commentary ($N = 91$). We anticipated that a relatively small amount of news about the election would be sufficiently interpretive and evaluative to warrant comparisons with academic discourse on the same topics. We conducted a Factiva search using the following terms: "Trump," "journalism," "media," "journalist," "populism," and "election." These parameters netted more than 8000 articles, but only the 212 that discussed journalism's role in the election were subject to textual analysis.[2]

Findings

Journalistic discourse generally asserted that Trump's victory occurred due to media illiteracy in the public; social media propagation of fake news and allowance of filter bubbles; and failure of the press to understand the depth of voter anger. Scholars viewed the rise of Trump as predictable, when considering long-established routines of the press; journalists' misunderstanding of both the public and populism; and the dire economics of legacy journalism.

Discourse from Journalists

Journalists argued fairly consistently that much of the public ignored respectable news outlets—those that value truth and accuracy—and instead sought out fake news that fit ideological preferences. Many media consumers did not understand the difference between authentic and fraudulent news, according to this perspective. A columnist wrote:

> One of my great sadnesses of this past election cycle is the villainization of the press corps. I chafe at the insistence, even in my own social circles, that the great and evil media are out to get the "other" side. I also object to the idea that if a story doesn't appear in someone's social media feed, then clearly the mainstream media are ignoring it. Readers and consumers vote with every mouse click. News organizations have a duty to provide balanced and complete coverage, but consumers have a duty to seek it out, which means reading and subscribing. (Trower Doolittle 2016)

In a similar interpretation, Trump supporters relied on "news" from conspiracy theorists such as Alex Jones. One story quoted former Trump advisor Roger Stone:

> I think he's emerged as the single most powerful voice on the right. Elitists may laugh at his politics (but) Alex Jones is reaching millions of people, and they are the foot soldiers in the Trump revolution. (Haberman 2016)

The article noted that Jones forged his reputation by disseminating fake news such as the #Pizzagate story. A *New York Times* reporter suggested that audiences weighted fake news the same as mainstream, quality news. "Major news organizations, household names trusted for decades, lost a great deal of ownership over audiences" (Herrman 2016). Respectable news sources were reduced to noise "among many contributors in infinite feeds."

This lament cautioned against giving into a mobilized irrationalism. The columnist Dana Milbank wrote:

> This is a time of self-flagellation in the media, as we scold ourselves for being out of touch with the anger in the country and failing to hear the beleaguered white working class. But this is both misleading and potentially harmful. (Milbank 2016)

Journalists targeted social media, Facebook in particular. In this retelling of the election, the public fell prey to a technology conglomerate that cared only for profits. Journalists posited that Facebook disseminated fake news; the public did not understand the content was fake; and the result was Trump's victory. A journalist explained that a purveyor of fake news "illustrates how websites can use Facebook to tap into a surging ideology, quickly go from nothing to influencing millions of people and make big profits in the process" (McCoy 2016). Facebook knew it was publishing fake news and chose not to act. Twenty-five of the 35 newspapers sampled quoted Mark Zuckerberg after the election. When the CEO spoke at a press conference, a correspondent condescendingly applauded him for acknowledging Facebook's role. "It was heartening to hear, especially after his earlier assertion that it was 'crazy' to believe that misinformation on Facebook had affected the presidential election in any real way—despite copious evidence that it was disturbingly in the mix" (Rutenberg 2016b).

While 18 reporters and columnists emphasized Facebook's profit-driven decision to not remove fake news, others blamed the platform for allowance of filter bubbles and echo chambers:

> The problem with Facebook's influence on political discourse is not limited to the dissemination of fake news. It's also about echo chambers. The company's algorithm chooses which updates appear higher up in users' newsfeeds and which are buried. (Tufekci 2016)

Explicit criticism of the social media giant tended to excuse its users as bystanders not expected to understand the nuances of News Feed. "The most influential sources of political misinformation on Facebook are not Macedonian fake-news sites or satirical pages but the thousands of partisan news outlets, pages and blogs that derive their traffic from News Feed" (Dwoskin, Dewey, and Timberg 2016).

Slightly more than 88 percent of the articles we examined did not address the role of the press, although some journalists observed that news media did little to understand middle America. A public editor detailed a group in North Carolina after Election Day to illustrate the problem:

> There is a group of 10 friends in Charlotte, N.C., all women, all in their 50s, all white. They're college educated with successful careers, and they have a message for *The New York Times*: "Come visit us." (Spayd 2016)

Media columnist Jim Rutenberg (2016a) wrote that reporters failed "to capture the boiling anger of a large portion of the American electorate that feels left behind by ... establishment Washington, Wall Street and the mainstream media."

In other instances, journalists argued that the press overestimates its cultural authority and comprehension of public sentiment. In the words of one *USA Today* contributor, "The media ideologically aligned itself not just against Donald Trump but with the demographic groups that made up its audience" (Wolff 2016). Some journalists proposed that their colleagues misread of the public could be traced to overreliance on polls (e.g., Toff 2016). One columnist characterized mainstream journalism as elitist and "unbearably smug" for how it covered the election (Kelly 2016). The overall theme seemed to be that "journalism took a hit" on Election Day "and rightly so" (Cillizza 2016).

Discourse from Academics

A striking difference between journalists and academics concerns normative practice as part of the solution or the core problem. Newspaper reporters and columnists often contended that journalism failed to adhere to principles, including a commitment to understand the public on its own terms. Scholars asserted that news media, in fact, followed routines of professionalization established in the early twentieth century. In the media studies view, journalists gather and report news in a specific manner, using specific routines that did not translate well in 2016. Massive attention devoted to Trump "is not the fault of the mainstream media, nor of their journalists, who are simply applying the professional codes and practices with which they have been raised" (McNair 2016, 12). Journalists, in fact, were loyal to tradition as they adhered to "a set of institutionally defined values, procedures and practices" (Ottovordemgentschenfelde 2016, 77).

Trump relied on news media to spread messages initially sent only to supporters (Hermida 2016). Thus, journalists would return a news subsidy with a campaign subsidy —the favor of newsworthy oddities would be rewarded with amplification and diffusion of Trump's messages. Twitter posts "were information subsidies for the global media—free content that is accessible and easy to reuse" (Marland 2016, 71). Candidate Trump appeared to turn the appeal of soft news against journalism itself by luring campaign reporters out of their comfort zone, the realm of undisputed facts and analysis.

While journalists acknowledged that they failed to understand the heartland *in 2016*, scholars emphasized that the quality press had for many decades shown little interest in rural communities. Journalists were consequently ill-equipped to comprehend the power of populism once mobilized (Van Aelst 2016). Political scientist Lance Bennett explained:

> Most of the press and party elites missed the scale of angry emotion aimed at them by white working and middle class Americans. Indeed, the cosmopolitan press had long rendered these folk nearly invisible, brushing off the early warning signs of the Tea Party as a minor disturbance. And so, most media experts and party insiders engaged in knowing discussions of how impossible it would be for anyone to be elected with Trump's combination of inexperience, shady business dealings, and inability to manage his emotions and stay on script. (Bennett 2016, 98)

Lacking empathy for the concerns of disenchanted voters, reporters failed to adequately confront Trump on policy details: "his candidacy became an ill-defined canvas onto which disgruntled and fearful voters could project their hopes and assuage their anxieties" (Bucy 2016, 32).

Still, most academic discourse seemed to assume that US political journalism could be remedied. The dissent of Lewis and Carlson was thus sober in its uncertainty:

> Much of the post mortem criticism now being levelled at the news media assumes that basic terms like "news" have some shared understandings attached to them, some agreed-upon normative expectations for journalism in public life. We shouldn't be so sure anymore. (Lewis and Carlson 2016, 78)

Much of the academic analysis proposed a connection between public antipathy toward the press and disruption of the news industry caused by economic turmoil. The press could not produce insightful content because "newspapers, shrunken by the onslaught of the digital revolution on their revenues, with fewer journalistic resources and in a constant scramble for 'hits' and 'eyeballs,' amplify 'news' without troubling with time-consuming verification" (Muller 2016, 17). Rural America, in particular, suffers from the gutting of newsrooms:

> newspapers that served as key community institutions have been hollowed out, much like the factories and church pews, and the print-to-digital shift has only accelerated the concentration of power to coastal news elites—the same elites who mostly responded to Trump and his ilk with snark and scorn, either explicitly on Twitter or implicitly in their framing of news coverage. (Lewis and Carlson 2016, 78)

Hermida (2016, 76) placed most of the blame for superficial coverage on cable news, arguing that the "news" in that term is a "misnomer" and that "these networks are not in the business of evidence-based reporting."

> They are in the emotion business. And emotion sells. Ratcheting up anger and outrage on cable makes business sense. (Hermida 2016, 76)

Media studies scholar Geoffrey Baym (2016, 15) argued that reporters wrote about Trump incessantly, especially during the Republican primaries when the volume of coverage was not warranted, because Trump recognized the "mutual interests" of his campaign and a struggling news industry.

Discussion

This study was motivated in part by recognition of the 2016 election as an opportunity to identify emergent forms of journalistic resistance to punitive populism. With journalism's celebrated suspicion of political elites in mind, we would expect reporters to show more willingness to recognize crude populism in speechmaking than to acknowledge this sentiment in the public itself. Still, the ritualistic homage to the public that Carey (1987) paints is difficult to reconcile with journalistic experiences covering Trump. Reporters took stock of episodes such as being scolded to "Tell the truth!" as they were herded into pens at rallies. Efforts of journalists to distance themselves from an abrasive populism could signify productive reflexivity in how professionals think about audiences. Alternatively, evaluation of news work might be interpreted as a calculated defense of tainted news, particularly the disproportionate attention to Trump in the pre-primary season, when media coverage is so valuable to anti-establishment candidates (Patterson 2016).

The earthquake election prompted both journalists and scholars to focus on problematic aspects of reporting and citizen participation in media-centered politics. Perhaps not surprisingly, reporters and columnists preferred to emphasize limits of audience engagement in the election period. Academics, by contrast, proposed connections between the nature of an angry electorate and campaign reporting. Many journalists implicitly argued that the rise of anti-elitist populism and Trump's victory were aided by media illiteracy of citizens unable to resist or even detect fake news as fake. This sector of the electorate presumably voted for fake news and against respectable journalism.

Academics and journalists overlapped to some extent in criticism of the press as elitist. The "snark and scorn" described by Lewis and Carlson implies a need to better connect with disenchanted citizens. If we grant, however, that anti-intellectualism is a growing problem in politics, the remedy for journalism is not to infuse its style and interpretive schemes with a down-home sensitivity. In our view, both journalism and journalism studies advocate misguided reform when they perceive the problem of 2016 as a failure of the press to affirm public frustration. A journalism of expertise—an "elite" journalism without apology—would better capture the substantive concerns of rural America.

Boundaries of reflexivity observed are in some respects an artifact of this study's narrow timeframe and the content sampled. Findings from a future textual analysis would offer more nuance and probably a wider range of perspective from both journalists and academics on the 2016 election. The current study is, nevertheless, focused on limits of reflexivity. We sought to capture journalistic thinking in the moment, to reveal how the public imagined shapes both the news created and how journalists rationalize their work.

Reliance on large-circulation newspapers prevented a comparison with perspectives of journalists working in rural and small-town communities. Our textual analysis of journalists is also confined to audience-facing critiques. Metajournalistic discourse broadly conceived (Carlson 2016) includes not just front-stage criticism of the news with readers as consumers, but back-stage perspectives in which reporters and editors are sometimes more critical of their work (Klocke and McDevitt 2013). Front-stage reflexivity, in a tactical sense, could be quite subtle. A dynamic in which journalists are unlikely to expose themselves and their readers as anti-deliberative implies a third-person effect. Journalists in this scenario would explain that Americans (OTHER Americans) are non-newspaper readers unable to distinguish real news from fake news.[3]

Dark Side of Reflexivity

News media are consequential in political discourse in the classification of ideas in spheres of full legitimacy, partial legitimacy, implicit deviance, or explicit deviance (Hallin 1994; Taylor 2014). Journalists appeared to place Trump and his supporters in the realm of deviance. Academics, by contrast, indirectly advanced the view that journalists did not simply characterize Trump as deviant; they widened legitimate debate to include the ideology of a punitive populism.

Much is at stake in how journalists make sense of their contribution to Trump's success. Katz and Liebes (2007) argue that while cynicism, disenchantment, and audience fragmentation explain a retreat from ceremonial "media events," news media and anti-establishment agents are now invested in disruptive events. They are, in a sense, co-producers of these sustained and riveting events. Did US news media co-produce the Trump campaign? Did they co-produce a crisis of deliberative democracy in the condoning of anti-intellectual discourse? Katz and Liebes warn that while journalists benefit from audience engagement in periods of crisis, they can lose control of coverage to anti-establishment actors. The lavish attention to Trump during the presidential primaries was apparently less threatening to journalism's self-image under the assumption that he would never actually occupy the White House.

This scenario points to a dark side of reflexivity. As discussed earlier, professional realism departs from paradigm repair in the perception that news work must adjust to limitations of the public. Deviance is located in imagined audiences rather than in professional practice. Journalists, for example, repeatedly referenced the public's appetite for fake news. Downplaying of expectations for the public is accompanied by a foreclosing on the aspirations of deliberative journalism. Reform of campaign reporting is consequently contingent on recognition of journalists that their work is shaped by audiences they imagine.

We are quick to add, however, that our evidence for how journalists imagine the public is indirect, reliant on textual analysis. On the other hand, reflexivity in normative theory is viewed as accountability through transparency, and thus meaningful reflexivity must manifest in what the press expresses openly to its readers. Textual analysis in this respect generates evidence for how journalists, in their own words, view the public's receptivity to deliberative news.

Future research on how journalists might reify public sentiment is vital in the wake of the 2016 election. Subjunctive sentiment becomes consequential to the extent that it finds a voice, a rationale, and a medium for mobilization (Cottle 2006). The question at hand is the extent to which journalism condoned a punitive populism such that the news became a medium for unfocused anger. The rise of Trump would ideally prompt sustained reflexivity on how the epistemology of news work shapes how audiences are imagined. If newsworthiness as a doxic value is resistant to reflexivity (Schultz 2007), and newsworthiness orients journalists to the perceived feelings of audiences, the perception of an agitated and incompetent public constitutes a crisis for both journalism and democracy.

The 2016 campaign should nevertheless encourage researchers to identify how professionals resist populist ideology. A devotion to editorial autonomy is indeed observable in hostile climates. Independence is evident in a narrative technique used by reporters to distance themselves from tainted stories. By *disdaining the news*, journalists seek to resolve the dilemma created by a personal desire to not report when competitive pressures induce a need to join the fray (Levy 1981). Evidence of *disdaining the publisher* goes back to the dawn of media sociology with Breed's (1955) "Social Control in the Newsroom":

> ... the reporters had fashioned a kind of underground and subversive pattern of ironic mocking of Hearst policy. Patriotic events would have speakers "proclaiming," and doing it "boldly"—not just "saying"—or "proudly clasping a flag to his heart." (quoted in Reese and Ballinger 2001, 652)

Disdaining the public is also plausibly interpreted as an assertion of intellectual independence. Literature in political communication has investigated autonomy—or lack thereof—in relationship to elite actors (e.g., Entman 2003), but we know less about how journalists distance themselves from popular sentiment. That said, practices such as mocking of a publisher also target pomposity of a flag-waving public.

Against Representation

Journalism embodies a cultural contradiction of democracy: political inclusiveness at the expense of deliberative coherence. In its heyday of mass media—coinciding with the decline of political parties (Patterson 1993)—journalism arguably carried the burden of inclusiveness of public sentiment. Developments in interactive media should encourage journalists to rethink whether the serious sectors of news media must still accept the responsibility of representative politics. A punitive populism draws motive power from many sources, and while it fluctuates in strength across election cycles, it will persist without the help of journalism. The affordance of an inclusive, democratic media system is also an opportunity to promote an idea-centered journalism. Mass media, the blogosphere, and social media mobilize collective sentiment and solidarities, and journalism should chronicle the ferment. Journalism's epistemological capacity is constrained, however, when the profession conflates representing social action in a descriptive mode with representing the populace in a political mode. Journalists should not internalize a duty to represent the public against cultural elites. Political scientists recognize that news media are miscast in campaign communication, incapable of organizing elections in a coherent fashion in a system characterized by weak political parties and entrepreneurial candidates (Patterson 2016). Journalism is also miscast when it views itself as tribune of the people.

A journalism that views itself as an organ of direct democracy risks collusion with irrationalism. In *The Open Society and its Enemies*, Karl Popper (1945, 439) observed: "The irrationalist insists that emotions and passions rather than reason are the mainsprings of human action." To be sure, journalists recognized audience deficits, but they did not acknowledge how the press may have exploited those deficits by affirming political disaffection. While scores of journalists were undoubtedly repulsed by Trump on the campaign trail, the "earned" media that he benefited from suggests that they were fascinated by a perceived wellspring of populist support.

DISCLOSURE STATEMENT

No financial interests or benefits arise directly from publication of this study.

NOTES

1. Most of the contributors work at universities in the United Kingdom and the United States. Here is the breakdown: United States (43), United Kingdom (21), Australia (4), Belgium (3), Canada (3), Russia (2), Greece (2), Croatia (2), Czech Republic (1), Italy (1), Ireland (1), China (1), Slovenia (1), and Norway (1).
2. We removed duplicate articles from wire services, then culled articles not about the election. Finally, we read through the remaining content and removed articles that did not include any reflections about the election. This left us with 212 articles.
3. We thank an anonymous reviewer of this study for the insight on a third-person dynamic applied to metajournalistic discourse.

REFERENCES

Ahva, Laura. 2012. "Public Journalism and Professional Reflexivity." *Journalism* 14 (6): 790–806.

Anderson, Benedict. 1987. *Imagined Communities: Reflections on the Rise and Spread of Nationalism*. London: Verso.

Baym, Geoffrey. 2016. "Trump and Mediatization." In *US Election Analysis 2016: Media, Voters and the Campaign: Early Reflections From Leading Academics*, edited by Darren Lilleker, Daniel Jackson, Einar Thorsen, and Anastasia Veneti, 15. Bournemouth: Bournemouth University Press.

Bennett, W. Lance. 2016. "Democracy Trumped." In *US Election Analysis 2016: Media, Voters and the Campaign: Early Reflections From Leading Academics*, edited by Darren Lilleker, Daniel Jackson, Einar Thorsen, and Anastasia Veneti, 98. Bournemouth: Bournemouth University Press.

Block, Elena, and Ralph Negrine. 2017. "The Populist Communication Style: Toward a Critical Framework." *International Journal of Communication* 11: 178–197.

Breed, Warren. 1955. "Social Control in the Newsroom: A Functional Analysis." *Social Forces* 33 (4): 326–335.

Bucy, Erik P. 2016. "Image Bites, Voter Enthusiam, and the 2016 Presidential Election." In *US Election Analysis 2016: Media, Voters and the Campaign: Early Reflections From Leading Academics*, edited by Darren Lilleker, Daniel Jackson, Einar Thorsen, and Anastasia Veneti, 32–33. Bournemouth: Bournemouth University Press.

Carey, James W. 1987. "The Press and Public Discourse." *The Center Magazine* 20 (2): 4–32.

Carlson, Matt. 2016. "Metajournalistic Discourse and the Meanings of Journalism: Definitional Control, Boundary Work, and Legitimation." *Communication Theory* 26 (4): 349–368.

Cecil, Matthew. 2002. "Bad Apples: Paradigm Overhaul and the CNN/*Time* 'Tailwind' Story." *Journal of Communication Inquiry* 26 (1): 46–58.

Cillizza, Chris. 2016. "How Hillary Clinton Won." *The Washington Post*, November 10.

Claussen, Dane. 2004. *Anti-intellectualism in American Media: Magazines and Higher Education*. New York: Peter Lang.

Cottle, Simon. 2006. "Mediatized Ritual: Beyond Manufacturing Consent." *Media, Culture & Society* 28 (3): 411–432.

Dwoskin, Elizabeth, Caitlin Dewey, and Craig Timberg. 2016. "Facebook, Google Take Steps to Fight Fake News." *The Washington Post*, November 16.

Entman, Robert M. 2003. "Cascading Activation: Contesting the White House Frame After 9/11." *Political Communication* 20 (4): 415–432.

Frank, Russell. 2003. "'These Crowded Circumstances': When Pack Journalists Bash Pack Journalism." *Journalism* 4 (4): 441–458.

Gans, Herbert J. 1980. *Deciding What's News: A Study of CBS Evening News, NBC Nightly News, Newsweek and Time*. New York: Vintage/Random House.

Haberman, Maggie. 2016. "Alex Jones, Host and Conspiracy Theorist, Says Donald Trump Called to Thank Him." *The New York Times*, November 17.

Hallin, Daniel C. 1994. *We Keep America on Top of the World: Television Journalism and the Public Sphere*. London: Routledge.

Hermida, Alfred. 2016. "Trump and the Triumph of Affective News When Everyone is the Media." In *US Election Analysis 2016: Media, Voters and the Campaign: Early Reflections From Leading Academics*, edited by Darren Lilleker, Daniel Jackson, Einar Thorsen, and Anastasia Veneti, 76. Bournemouth: Bournemouth University Press.

Herrman, John. 2016. "An Election Ill Timed for Media in Transition." *The New York Times*, November 9.

Hindman, Elizabeth B. 2005. "Jayson Blair, *The New York Times*, and Paradigm Repair." *Journal of Communication* 55 (2): 225–241.

Hofstadter, Richard. 1963. *Anti-intellectualism in American Life*. New York: Alfred A. Knopf.

Katz, Elihu, and Tamar Liebes. 2007. "'No More Peace': How Disaster, Terror and War Have Upstaged Media Events." *International Journal of Communication* 1: 157–166.

Kelly, Jack. 2016. "The Press Lost Too; Mainstream Journalists Are Totally Out of Touch." *The Pittsburgh Post-Gazette*, November 20.

Klocke, Brian, and Michael McDevitt. 2013. "Foreclosing Deliberation: Journalists' Lowering of Expectations in the Marketplace of Ideas." *Journalism Studies* 14 (6): 891–906.

Krämer, Benjamin. 2014. "Media Populism: A Conceptual Clarification and Some Theses on its Effects." *Communication Theory* 24 (1): 42–60.

Kunelius, Risto, and Esa Reunanen. 2016. "Changing Power of Journalism: The Two Phases of Mediatization." *Communication Theory* 26: 369–388.

Levy, Mark R. 1981. "Disdaining the News." *Journal of Communication* 31 (3): 24–31.

Lewis, Seth C., and Matt Carlson. 2016. "The Dissolution of News: Selective Exposure, Filter Bubbles, and the Boundaries of Journalism." In *US Election Analysis 2016: Media, Voters and the Campaign: Early Reflections From Leading Academics*, edited by Darren Lilleker, Daniel Jackson, Einar Thorsen, and Anastasia Veneti, 78. Bournemouth: Bournemouth University Press.

Lilleker, Darren, Daniel Jackson, Einar Thorsen, and Anastasia Veneti, eds. 2016. *US Election Analysis 2016: Media, Voters and the Campaign: Early Reflections From Leading Academics*. Bournemouth: Bournemouth University Press.

Litt, Eden. 2012. "Knock, Knock. Who's There? The Imagined Audience." *Journal of Broadcasting & Electronic Media* 56 (3): 330–345.

Marland, Alex. 2016. "Trying to Avoid Trump: A Canadian Experience." In *US Election Analysis 2016: Media, Voters and the Campaign: Early Reflections From Leading Academics*, edited by Darren Lilleker, Daniel Jackson, Einar Thorsen, and Anastasia Veneti, 71. Bournemouth: Bournemouth University Press.

Mazzoleni, Gianpietro, Julianne Stewart, and Bruce Horsfield. 2003. *The Media and Neo-Populism: A Contemporary Analysis*. Westport, CT: Praeger.

McCoy, Terrence. 2016. "For the 'New Yellow Journalists,' Opportunity Comes in Clicks and Bucks." *The Washington Post*, November 21.

McNair, Brian. 2016. "After Objectivity." In *US Election Analysis 2016: Media, Voters and the Campaign: Early Reflections From Leading Academics*, edited by Darren Lilleker, Daniel Jackson, Einar Thorsen, and Anastasia Veneti, 12. Bournemouth: Bournemouth University Press.

Milbank, Dana. 2016. "Trump's Campaign Made It Safe to Hate Again. Will He Turn That Around?" *The Washington Post*, November 16.

Mudde, Cas. 2004. "The Populist Zeitgeist." *Government and Opposition* 39 (4): 542–563.

Muller, Denis. 2016. "Trump, Truth and the Media." In *US Election Analysis 2016: Media, Voters and the Campaign: Early Reflections From Leading Academics*, edited by Darren Lilleker, Daniel Jackson, Einar Thorsen, and Anastasia Veneti, 17. Bournemouth: Bournemouth University Press.

Ottovordemgentschenfelde, Svenja. 2016. "Tweeting the Election: Political Journalists and a New Privilege of Bias." In *US Election Analysis 2016: Media, Voters and the Campaign: Early Reflections From Leading Academics*, edited by Darren Lilleker, Daniel Jackson, Einar Thorsen, and Anastasia Veneti, 77. Bournemouth: Bournemouth University Press.

Patterson, Thomas E. 1993. *Out of Order: How the Decline of the Political Parties and the Growing Power of the News Media Undermine the American Way of Electing Presidents*. New York: Alfred A. Knopf.

Patterson, Thomas E. 2016. "Pre-Primary News Coverage of the 2016 Presidential Race: Trump's Rise, Sanders' Emergence, Clinton's Struggle." Harvard Kennedy School Working Paper No. 16-023, June 20. https://ssrn.com/abstract=2798258.

Popper, Karl. 1945. *The Open Society and its Enemies*. Princeton: Princeton University Press.

Reese, Stephen D., and Jane Ballinger. 2001. "The Roots of a Sociology of News: Remembering Mr. Gates and Social Control in the Newsroom." *Journalism & Mass Communication Quarterly* 78 (4): 641–658.

Rigney, Daniel. 1991. "Three Kinds of Anti-Intellectualism: Rethinking Hofstadter." *Sociological Inquiry* 61 (4): 434–451.

Rutenberg, Jim. 2016a. "A 'Dewey Defeats Truman' Lesson for the Digital Age." *The International New York Times*, November 9.

Rutenberg, Jim. 2016b. "Mark Zuckerberg and Facebook Must Step Up to Defend Truth." *The New York Times*, November 21.

Schultz, Ida. 2007. "The Journalistic Gut Feeling: Journalistic Doxa, News Habitus and Orthodox News Values." *Journalism Practice* 1 (2): 190–207.

Shogan, Colleen J. 2007. "Anti-Intellectualism in the Modern Presidency: A Republican Populism." *Perspectives on Politics* 5 (2): 295–303.

Spayd, Liz. 2016. "One Thing Voters Agree On: Better Coverage Needed." *The New York Times*, November 20.

Taylor, Ian. 2014. "Local Press Reporting of Opposition to the 2003 Iraq War in the UK and the Case for Reconceptualizing the Notions of Legitimacy and Deviance." *Journal of War & Culture Studies* 7 (1): 36–53.

Toff, Benjamin. 2016. "Polls May Be Making Voters Worse at Predicting Elections." *The Washington Post*, November 18.

Trower Doolittle, Tara. 2016. "During Farewell, A Lament for Public Discourse's Sad Spiral." *The Austin American-Statesman*, November 13.

Tuchman, Gaye. 1972. "Objectivity as Strategic Ritual: An Examination of Newsmen's Notions of Objectivity." *American Journal of Sociology* 77 (4): 666–679.

Tufekci, Zaynep. 2016. "Mark Zuckerberg Is in Denial." *The International New York Times*, November 15.

Van Aelst, Peter. 2016. "The 2016 Election and the Success of Fact Free Politics." In *US Election Analysis 2016: Media, Voters and the Campaign: Early Reflections From Leading Academics*, edited by Darren Lilleker, Daniel Jackson, Einar Thorsen, and Anastasia Veneti, 16. Bournemouth: Bournemouth University Press.

Wolff, Michael. 2016. "Media Has Itself to Blame for Such an Epic Election Fail; Botched Coverage Similar to that of '07 Financial Meltdown." *USA Today*, November 14.

MIGRATION MAPS WITH THE NEWS
Guidelines for ethical visualization of mobile populations

Paul C. Adams

Maps showing immigration into Europe are a potential source of journalistic bias. Limited time and funding to create maps of migration can lead to dependence on data from institutions dedicated to controlling migration, in effect promoting a logic of surveillance directed at immigrants rather than a logic of hospitality based on respect for human rights. There are organizational and logistical barriers to overcome if migration is to be portrayed in ways that support thoughtful, democratic, rights-based deliberation but efforts need to be made to map migration in ways that reveal the geographical experiences of individual immigrants including their movement paths and the risks they face. This article examines unusual maps of migration, drawing on examples from news media as well as from non-governmental organizations, research teams, book authors, private companies, and entertainment media based in several European countries. The examples provide a foundation for concrete recommendations regarding the responsible use of cartographic visualization as a component of immigration news.

Introduction

> "If there is one thing certain about the EU, it is that there will be many more maps in many more colours, with many more lines." (Manners 2011, 254)

News articles on refugees, asylum seekers and immigrants entering Europe are often illustrated with eye-catching maps featuring brightly colored arrows converging on Europe from various directions, scaled to represent aggregated human flows—a thousand people coming by one route, several tens of thousands via another route. These representations play a vital role within the larger body of news about migration, rendering migration visible in certain ways, directing attention toward selected aspects of migration, and reinforcing particular understandings of migrants. Graphic representations of migration, henceforth indicated as "migration maps," necessitate cartographic choices. The choices that are made not only present different facts, they also resonate with different emotional responses to migration. Through these differences, migration maps in the news play an important political role. In a time when the issue of migration has become a political lightning rod there is an ethical imperative to critically examine this role. Maps in the news can act insidiously to perpetuate social marginalization, discrimination and exclusion (Vujaković 2002, 188). In response, this article critically examines the task of visualizing migration and suggests ways to overcome common types of cartographic bias.

The objectives of this article are simultaneously practical and ethical. I offer concrete suggestions regarding the creation of maps that counterbalance existing journalistic biases. The suggestions are driven by the question of how to look not only *at* migrants but also *with* migrants, attending to their individual experiences, motivations and risks. I also consider how to encourage public participation in, and engagement around, questions of migration through concrete guidelines for more ethical cartographic approaches to migration. The maps used to illustrate the guidelines are drawn from a range of sources within and beyond news media and point to the potential for news media to draw from the cartographic innovations of nongovernmental organizations (NGOs), research teams, book authors, private companies, and entertainment media. In various ways, each of these sources employs a unique perspective on migration with clear potential to guide journalistic cartography. The article proceeds from a theoretical section exploring how ideology operates through maps, to guidelines for mapping that avoid the biases of conventional migration maps, and concludes with a reflection on the role of alternative migration maps in relation to the functions of journalism within civil society.

Visual Media and the Power of Maps

Every map reflects choices regarding what to include and exclude, what scale and orientation to adopt, what symbols and colors to employ, and so forth. Any given approach to map-making inevitably promotes certain biases. The maps accompanying newspaper and television reports are often quite simple, with their information pared-down and focused to capture attention, to expedite the sending of messages, and to avoid reader confusion. However, the simpler the map the more it leaves out of the story. As information is excluded sources of potential bias are introduced. There is consequently a need for critical reflection on maps that accompany the news, particularly insofar as maps in the news are a critical component of what we could call "news place-making" (Gutsche 2014a, 2014b) including constructions of the nation as a place of individual and collective identity, and news stories are the most important media genre in which maps are encountered (Monmonier 1989, 19).

In a prominent analysis of framing, Entman argues that there are inherent connections between the salience of phenomena, ways of defining problems, presumptions of causality, moral judgments, and recommended treatments (1993, 52). In a later work, he links this argument to visual representation and action, arguing that images have the power to affect judgments after only a single viewing (2004, 6). Visuals in the news do not merely direct a way of looking, a *gaze*, they also shape judgments regarding what should be done with regard to policy. Coleman confirms this link (2009, 240), arguing that visuals in the news demonstrate "Entman's four functions: defining problems, assigning blame, declaring right or wrong, and fixing them." Her survey of research on visual agenda setting and framing highlights a key insight: if a news story is constructed so that the "visual message is different from the verbal message, people's impressions tend to go with the information conveyed by the visual."

Maps are similar to other news genres in that they contribute to framing, agenda setting, and priming (Scheufele 1999; Weaver 2007; Protess and McCombs 2016). Starting with frames, these are "interpretations that lead to evaluations" (Entman 2004, 26) and they manifest as "schemes for both presenting and comprehending news" (Scheufele 1999, 106). Functionally, frames create connections between journalists and audiences which can be thought of as the lines along which journalists organize reality in order to be understood by audiences and the lines audiences follow to trace the meanings of the news they encounter (Gamson and Modigliani 1989). While these lines are metaphorical in the case of verbal representations (i.e., lines of reasoning), they are literal when we consider cartographic representations. That is, lines on paper or onscreen represent borders and human movements, and as seemingly straightforward as a line may be, its color, weight, orientation, and scale all speak to both structure and agency, order and disorder, the footprint of state power and the traces of human lives. Cartographic elements act as what D'Angelo calls "framing devices" (2002, 881), telling stories and making arguments. Just as the notion of framing can be applied to cartography, agenda setting is also present in maps. The agenda setting power of cartography in the news works at two levels: the first shows what issues are worth paying attention to, directing attention to certain phenomena as relevant, and the second establishes how issues are actually defined (Coleman 2009, 251). The second level would, for example, emphasize attributes of a particular place (e.g., the island of Lampedusa) once that place has been designated as relevant to the story of migration. The power of framing and agenda setting to affect public opinion is referred to as priming. Priming is notoriously difficult to measure because it works cumulatively over a long period of time through multiple media encounters and feedback loops, and journalists respond to public opinion even as they shape it. Rather than belabor the distinctions between framing, agenda setting, and priming, the interest here is on cataloguing alternative mapping strategies which can intervene in all three of these processes.

Visual representations, including maps, lay claim to objectivity through their seeming transparency, as they "frame what can be seen, thought and said" (Bleiker 2015, 874). Objectivity has been criticized as a "god trick," an attempt to see the world in a way that distances "the knowing subject from everybody and everything in the interests of unfettered power" (Haraway 1988, 581). Migration maps adopt such an omniscient angle, what Thomas Nagel (1989) called a "view from nowhere," seemingly objective but performing a kind of surveillance. This way of visually organizing the world benefits from and reinforces what Gunnar Olsson calls "cartographic reason," the habit of thinking of reason itself in terms of mapping (Olsson 2007), and it fosters the imperialist notion that whoever employs Western style mapping has the right to control and dominate territory (Cosgrove 2001). Maps do of course come from somewhere, in both a literal and a figurative sense, serving particular political, economic and social interests of those who have made them (Harley 1988, 1989; Woodward 1992).

Among the most common visualizations of migration are maps showing human movements as various sized arrows superimposed on national outlines—a map genre which is easy to create and immediately recognizable by news consumers (Figures 1–2). Such maps portray refugees, asylum seekers and immigrants (henceforth indicated collectively as migrants) in a way that is impersonal, static, and selective, but it is so familiar as to seem natural and unquestionable. These maps contribute to the processes of agenda setting, framing, and priming, and their ideological and political power merits careful consideration for theoretical, practical, and ethical reasons.

As Thompson notes, ideology is "*meaning in the service of power*" (1990, 7, emphasis in original). In the case of immigration, dominant ideologies construct immigrants as economic refugees who depend on welfare while taking jobs from the local population, persons do not belong and need to be sent back to their country of origin (Foss 2004, 239). While such frames are readily apparent in verbal texts it is somewhat trickier to see how they

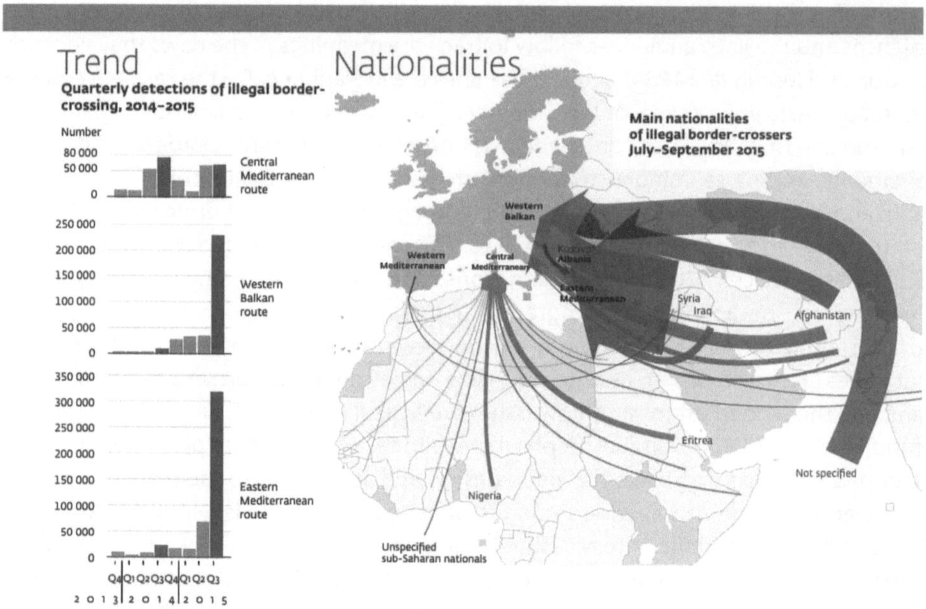

FIGURE 1

Map of immigration to the Europe, aggregated to show migration flow volumes as scaled arrows in different shades of red entering Europe by four access routes and returning by one route. Europe is rendered in blue with faint internal borders. Source: "Illegal border crossings by source and route in the third quarter of 2015" Frontex Risk Analysis Unit (January 2016). *FRAN Quarterly*, Quarter 3, July–September 2015, p. 9. Warsaw, Poland. Copyright Frontex, reference number: 20617/2015

operate in visual texts like photographs and maps. Representations adopted or accepted with little thought to their intersection with power relations can misinform people and contribute to exclusionary forces acting in and through public discourses, impairing journalism's vital democratic functions including information dissemination and the fostering of inclusionary debate (Strömbäck 2005). The challenge is to enhance sensitivity to ways in which the "little tacit theories about what exists, what happens, and what matters" (Gitlin 1980, 6) are at work behind the scenes in processes of cartographic representation. It is in the spirit of counterbalancing the ideologies implicit in "default" migration maps that the body of this article proposes some alternatives to the common migration maps and their surveillant gaze (Vukov and Sheller 2013).

Critiques of mapping therefore draw on broader concerns with objectivity and representation, arguing that each map stakes out a position. This positioning is particularly evident in maps of migration which speak with authority about who "should be here" and who "belongs elsewhere"—a complex process of *bordering* and *ordering* (Van Houtum and Van Naerssen 2002). As the borders of European states and the "external" borders of Europe, that is, the Schengen Area, are foregrounded by news reports of immigration, what is pushed to the background and treated as neutral and natural are the state borders, including the "arrogant partitioning" (Monmonier 2010, 4) imposed by colonial powers without regard for pre-existing linguistic, religious, and ethnic geographies which set the stage for political instability and international conflict in the twentieth and

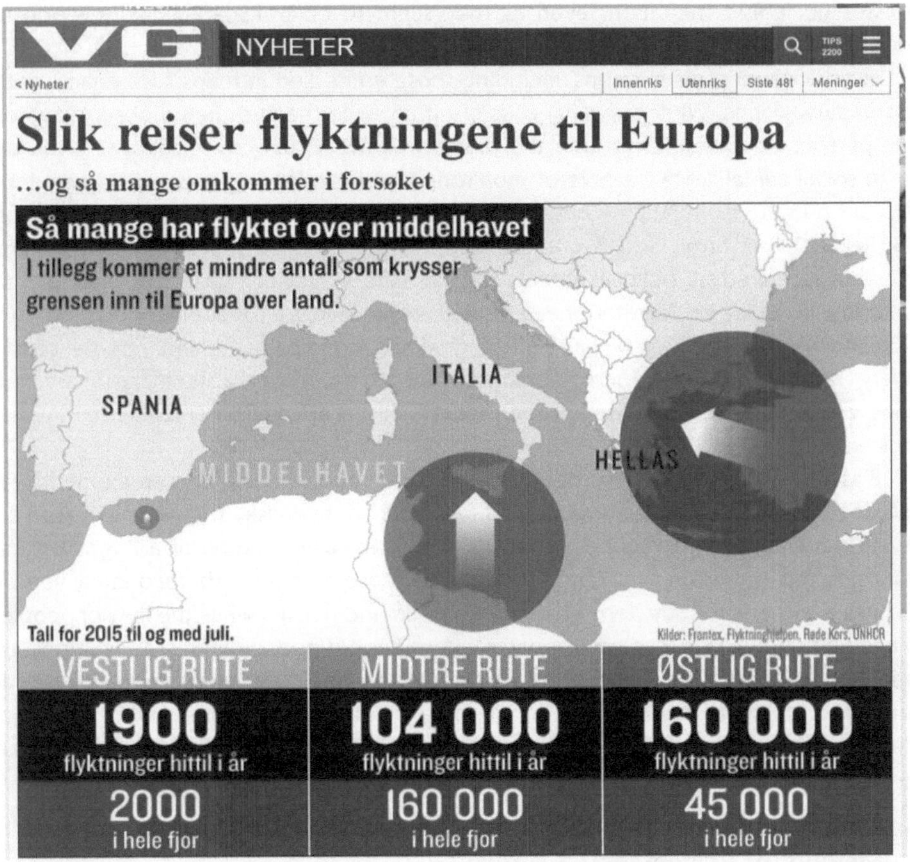

FIGURE 2

Map of migration flows across the Mediterranean in the first three quarters of 2015, aggregated with three scaled circles in yellow, blue and red, for the western, central and eastern routes, respectively. Europe is rendered in tan with gray internal borders. Source: "Så mange har flyktet over Middelhavet" [So many have fled across the Mediterranean] by Tom Byermoen accompanying the article "Slik reiser flyktningene til Europa ... og så mange omkommer i forsøket" [How refugees travel to Europe ... and so many die in the attempt]. *Verdens Gang,* August 25, 2015. Online file at: http://www.vg.no/nyheter/utenriks/flyktningkrisen-i-europa/slik-reiser-flyktningene-til-europa/a/23511730/ (accessed 18 May 2017)

twenty-first centuries. Human flows are juxtaposed on borders which seem to be "given" but in fact reinforce perceptions of borders as: natural (instead of created), equivalent (since they are represented on all sides of every country with the same kind of line), and linear (although the forces that maintain borders are anchored at many points far away from borders), while disguising the border's role as a "power container" (Sack 1986; Vujaković 2014). Therefore migration maps promote "a quest to become inhospitable" (Balch 2016, 2), resonating with state propaganda and nationalism (Pickles 1992) as "veiled racial acts" (Gutsche 2014a, 12). Thus, the features on the map become objectively real *through* the understandings people have when they appropriate cartographic representations for individual and collective purposes, and maps are implicated in historical processes (including migration) even as they seem to be transparent windows on the world.

Exclusionary representations, including those embodied in maps, also enact various forms of surveillance. While surveillance is often taken to mean targeted observation of a single person, for example through the tapping of telephone conversations, it can also refer to social surveillance—a host of monitoring and cataloguing practices applied to a group or an entire population (Foucault 1976, 1978; Hartley 2008; Houen 2008; Mbembe 2008; Reid 2008; Morton and Bygrave 2008b). In the context of migration maps, alien bodies are rendered as political threats through the surveillant gaze. For example, the monitoring of Europe's Mediterranean border zone involves "real-time mapping" with the "technological eyes" of ocean patrols guided by radio, radar and remote sensing imagery (Tazzioli 2016, 571). Such mappings have both exclusionary and inclusionary implications, depending on the biases of map makers and map readers (Tazzioli 2016; Casas-Cortes et al. 2017).

Bias can result simply from decisions like which color to use for map elements. Red and orange are semiotically tied to all sorts for bad, negative, risky things while green and blue are generally used for good or neutral things. A naïve reading of a migration map juxtaposing red arrows on a cool or neutral colored base map (as with the original versions of Figures 1 and 2) is that the territorial order is good and normal while the flow of people is bad and dangerous. This reading resonates with maps of floods, wildfires, infestations, epidemics and invasions. The shape of the arrows and the way they penetrate the boundaries of the state (or multi-state territory in the case of the EU) resonates with exclusionary discourses which associate foreigners with narratives of contamination, pollution and rape (Ó Tuathail and Agnew 1992, 200–201; Keskinen 2016).

Methods of Cartographic Critique

Distinct methodologies are required so journalistic maps can be reconsidered in accordance with an ethics of hospitality (Dikeç 2002; Silverstone 2007; Horsti and Nikunen 2013; Jansson 2017). This presents a challenge because of the contrast between verbal and visual communication. While the potential to critique visual representations has been demonstrated within various critical frameworks such as cluster criticism, feminist criticism, metaphor criticism and generic criticism (Foss 2004), the majority of rhetorical criticism still centers on written and spoken texts. Methods targeting terminology have been demonstrated abundantly in studies of verbal accounts of migration (Gitlin 1980; Pan and Kosicki 1993; Kurtz and Snowden 2003; Ibrahim 2005; Vliegenthart and Roggeband 2007; Balch and Balabanova 2011; Helbling 2014). For example, tabloids are more likely than broadsheets to characterize migrants as "spongers," "gangsters," "criminals," and "fanatics" (Gabrielatos and Baker 2008, 29). Guidelines for interpreting frames in visual representations are less common although a valuable summary is provided by Coleman (2009) who also highlights the reasons why frames are hard to identify in maps. While visual images are usually processed "peripherally," meaning that audiences do not pay as much attention to news images as to the words, images elicit more emotional responses which contribute to the meaning of the whole text via "emotional lamination" (Coleman 2009, 239).

This lamination means images do not argue in discrete units analogous to words, nor do their elements interrelate via rules as rigid or easily defined as the rules of grammar. This elusive quality accounts for the rhetorical power of visual media, however, because a message is more likely to be accepted at face value when one is unsure how to argue with it. Recalling Coleman's model, maps are particularly powerful when included with the news because they simultaneously show audiences what to look at (first level agenda setting) and how to look at things (second level agenda setting). In addition, there is a gap between the banal and utilitarian language of mapping and the more artful forms of visual communication such as painting, photography, sculpture, and architecture (Foss 2004, 78–93, 168–181, 205–218, 325–331). This gap exacerbates the taken-for-grantedness of the messages embedded in maps, making them less amenable to critique. Maps are also rather peculiar among visual media in that they are expected to carry substantive meaning—facts rather than impressions. This makes the "emotional lamination" of cartographic discourse particularly surreptitious. A map is given the weighty responsibility to explain, analyze, and elucidate the accompanying verbal arguments, so its emotional impact can be easily overlooked.

To give a specific example, to show the difference in the number of migrants entering Europe via the Canary Islands and the number of migrants entering via the Aegean Sea, a common strategy would make the latter arrow proportionally wider, trying to match the ratio in arrow widths to the numbers of immigrants taking each route. This "default" method of using scaled arrows to show differences in flow almost inevitably leads to bias because the ratio is over 1:80, forcing the wider arrow to read (if erroneously referenced to the map's scale) as hundreds of kilometers wide. A naïve reading of the map therefore produces the impression that an impossibly huge number of people is flooding across the borders of Europe, an impression which resonates with news frames operating at various scales and contexts to create the xenophobic frame Gutsche in a very different context describes as "encroachment of *others* into *our* spaces" (Gutsche 2014a, 6).

The techniques of critical cartography help respond to the peculiarities of maps. Insight is found, for example, in works such as Mark Monmonier's *Maps with the News* (1989) which takes a historical and descriptive approach to journalistic mapping practices, *How to Lie with Maps* which takes a more pragmatic approach to cartography's fraught relationship with the truth (Monmonier 2014), and *No Dig, No Fly, No Go* (Monmonier 2010) which focuses on the exclusionary practices concretized in maps. There is insight as well in the foundational works of critical cartography which showed maps as cultural products reflecting social, spatial and historical contexts (Harley 1988, 1989; Pickles 1992; Woodward 1992), and in the large body of geographic work that continues to cite these scholars, especially in the journals *Cartographica, The Cartographic Journal,* and *ACME*. Such contributions analyze, interpret and contextualize cartography as a social practice, but their insights have yet to be systematically applied to migration-related news (although see Tazzioli 2016; Casas-Cortes et al. 2017).

Alternatively, maps can offer the progressive "capacity to imagine places anew" (Nikunen 2016, 165). An innovative map offers avenues to question the rigid social and geographical order and take a proactive position within the ongoing "combat of cartographies" (Casas-Cortes et al. 2017, 28). It can be hospitable to marginalized groups and co-opt the surveillant gaze. Ways of doing this become clearer in conjunction with concrete cartographic guidelines.

Guidelines for Mapping Migration

The following section introduces four guidelines to counterbalance habits of cartographic representation that are inherently inhospitable and are tied in to social surveillance practices. Each cartographic strategy will be explained, illustrated with one or two sample maps, and linked to broader theoretical issues. Recommendations are guided by D'Angelo's (2002) model of framing as multiple flows. The maps reference any or all of the affected groups: refugees, asylum seekers and immigrants, so I simplify by employing the term "migration map." Each example is followed by relevant theories. While some of the examples are not from news media, they all indicate practices that could be adopted to the needs of journalism.

Guideline 1

Map the paths taken by particular refugees, asylum seekers, and immigrants before, during, and after the period of relocation. This type of mapping can involve, for example, tracing initial moves between countries in the Middle East or Africa, the locations of entry into Europe (i.e., the Schengen Area or the EU), personal movements between European countries (for example seeking asylum in a country with relatively hospitable laws), and personal movements within European countries (for example relocation between various camps and detention facilities). Maps of this type reveal aspects of immigration that are normally invisible in maps, news stories, and daily life more generally (Casas-Cortes et al. 2017, 14).

To appreciate this guideline, we must reflect for a moment on the politics of personalization. Photographic images accompanying Australian news stories about immigration were found to perpetuate what Bleiker et al. (2013, 413) described as a "pattern of anonymous masses." Photographers and editors favored images of medium to large groups as opposed to images of individuals or small groups. The "category of images that is most likely to evoke compassion in viewers—a single refugee with clearly recognisable facial features" accounted for only two percent of such images (Bleiker et al. 2013, 405). This obsession with anonymous masses and avoidance of the individual portrayal supports viewing "the 'imagined refugee' as a distant being" (Lenette 2016, np.) while casting immigrants as a kind of swarm that endangers territorial integrity.

What group photos are to photography, straight arrows are to cartography. Arrows showing migration as an aggregate flow or flows (see Figures 1 and 2) resonate with the same defensive emotions as maps of storm movements, troop advances or epidemic disease outbreaks, and as such "contribute to further dehumanizing refugees, and erase their humanity or biographies" (Lenette 2016, np.). In relation to this guideline we also must note the peculiarities of representing Europe, where territorial integrity is associated most often with the outside boundaries of the EU/Schengen countries and "migration is not covered in the media as an exclusively national issue; instead, it is socially constructed as a European problem" (e.g., Horsti 2012, 298). For example, nine maps used by the BBC to represent "'Key Migrant routes from Africa to Europe' … limited their depictions to the Europe–Africa border, without depicting the complicated, winding routes the migrants took prior to reaching Europe or after their arrival. The arrows pointed from Africa to points of entry into Europe: Canary Islands, Ceuta, Melilla, Lampedusa and Malta" (Horsti 2016, 10–11). These oversimplified trajectories present immigrants as a threat, evoking "powerful metaphors of war and invasion" (Horsti 2016, 10–11).

To counterbalance this "interpretive package" (Gamson and Modigliani 1989, 3), line details as well as line type and color can differentiate individual modes of immigrant transport (water, land, air) and conditions of travel (foot, private vehicle, public transit, smuggler-supplied vehicle, hidden compartment, etc.). Figure 3 is a map of the migration paths of Nidal and Salah, two brothers from Syria. Salah and his family were selected for admission by lottery while Nidal took the risk of entering Europe uninvited, crossing the Aegean Sea in a small boat then making a sinuous crossing through seven or eight European countries, in order to reunite with his brother. The map is part of a multimedia NRK documentary incorporating written story, photos, videos, and another map.

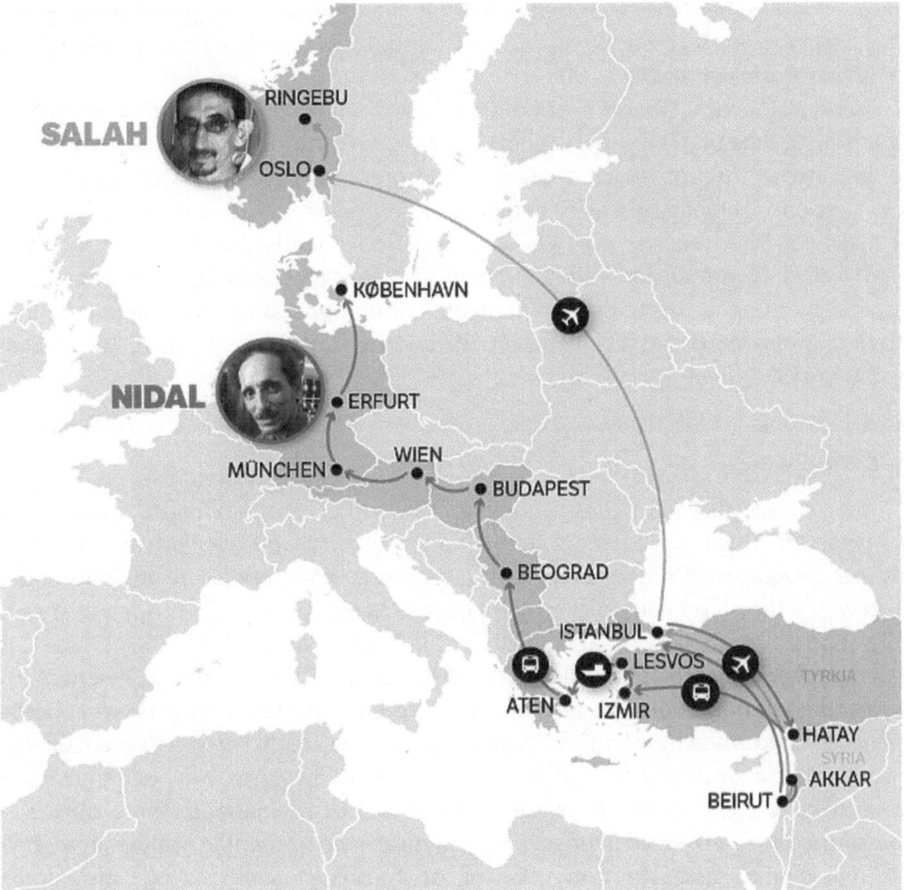

FIGURE 3
Map of the migration paths of two brothers, Salah and Nidal, as blue and red lines. The former is shown traveling directly to Norway by air while the latter's trajectory goes more indirectly by land. European and non-European countries are rendered in the same shade of gray with white borders. Source: Mari Grafsrønningen, untitled map with the article "Ble da brødrene flyktet" [When the brothers fled] NRK, 11-24-2015. Online file at: https://www.nrk.no/dokumentar/xl/ble-da-brodrene-flyktet-1.12667811 (accessed 18 May 2017)

This map is instructive because it is both particular and general, in the sense that the brothers' journeys are biographically accurate but also typify divergent experiences of arrival in Europe. It is common for irregular immigrants to make repeated efforts to cross certain borders within Europe; the typical path of a refugee or asylum seeker is convoluted and idiosyncratic, with multiple stages entailing particular risks and uncertainties, encumbered with twists, turns, returns, and delays (motivated for example by the Dublin Regulation, EU 2013). While it is impossible to capture a large number of complex trajectories on a single map, the reduction of immigrant movements to broad arrows as in Figures 1 and 2 masks several important things: it masks the personal experience of each migrant, including challenges encountered along the way; it masks the junctures where a migrant's destination is uncertain; it masks strategic relocation within Europe; and finally it masks the long-distance ties to family and relatives who have remained at home or who have become separated as a result of migration. To map an individual immigrant's trajectory is to create what one newcomer to Europe insightfully called a "tabu map" (Casas-Cortes et al. 2017, 14).

To break the tabu what is needed is a different relationship to the production of the map, acquiring data that is normally ignored or purged from migration maps. To depict personal trajectories through space depends on biographical data that is difficult to access unless a reporter actually talks with migrants, sitting down with one or more migrants to hear their stories. A reporter may need to hear from friends and family, as well, if the migrant trajectory in question ended in death. Theoretically speaking, then, this guideline is justified by the need to transcend norms of cartographic production dependent on a "pattern of anonymous masses" (Foucault 1976, 1978; Morton and Bygrave 2008a; Bleiker et al. 2013, 413).

Guideline 2

Map the risks faced by people who are traveling to Europe as refugees, asylum seekers, and immigrants. This intervention is closely tied to the first and responds to the fact that there is a geographical organization to the risks that drive people to migrate and the risks to which they are exposed during migration. Geographers refer to the initial causes of migration as "push factors" and "pull factors" (Dorigo and Tobler 1983; O'Lear 1997) and geographers have long considered the distribution of such factors as essential to an understanding of migration. The risks encountered en route to Europe's external borders, risks encountered while traveling to a destination country within Europe, risks encountered upon arrival at a destination country, and risks faced by those who undergo forcible removal back to their country or region of origin can all be mapped. These risks matter because they threaten wellbeing, security, physical health, mental health, social status, autonomy, dignity, and life itself, as well as "pushing" and "pulling" on migrants. Mapping makes such risks visible, joining in broader strategies of visualization which counter a logic of surveillance with "humanitarian visibility" (Tazzioli 2016), rendering at-risk lives more easily protected while enriching "qualitative understandings of [migrants'] lived experiences [in order] to effect social change, expose issues, and raise public awareness" (Lenette 2016, np). Maps of risks to migrants therefore counterbalance conventional migration maps which frame newcomers as a risk to society.

Figure 4 shows a map from *Le Monde Diplomatique*, "Des morts par milliers aux portes de l'Europe" [Deaths by the thousands on the doorstep of Europe] designed by

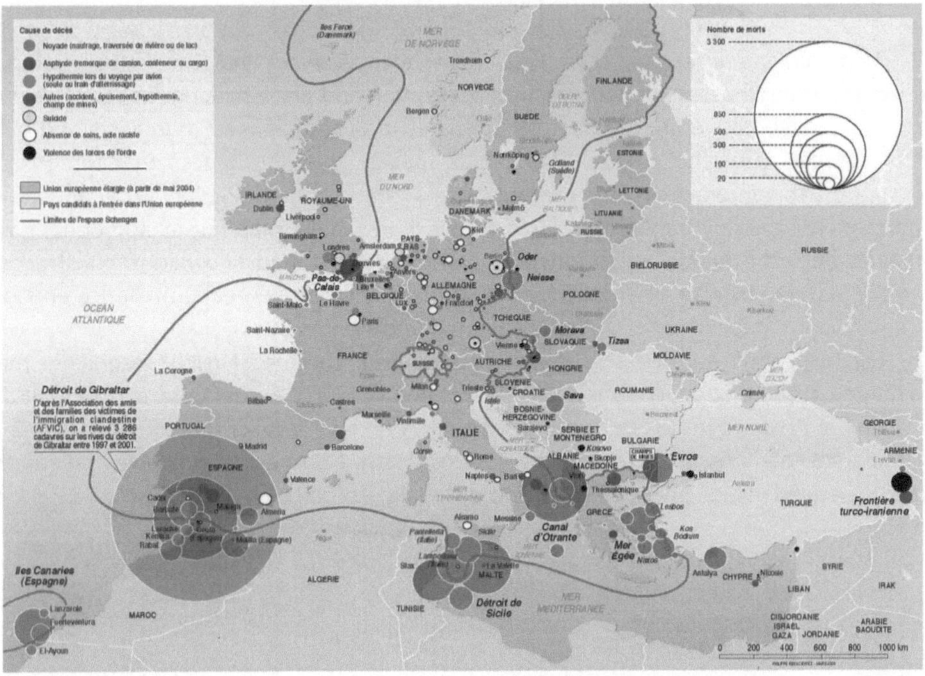

FIGURE 4

Map of deathplaces of immigrants and refugees occurring in the years 1993 to 2006 inclusive, with aggregated counts shown as scaled circles juxtaposed the boundaries of both the Schengen area and the European Union. EU countries are light green and internal borders are white. Deaths are shown with circles colored blue, purple, orange, dark green, yellow, white and black. Source: Olivier Clochard and Philippe Rekacewicz "Des morts par milliers aux portes de l'Europe" [Deaths by the thousands on the doorstep of Europe]. *Le Monde Diplomatique,* March 2004. Online file at: http://www.monde-diplomatique.fr/cartes/mortsauxfrontieres (accessed 18 May 2017)

Olivier Clochard and Philippe Rekacewicz (http://www.monde-diplomatique.fr/cartes/mortsauxfrontieres). The map locates deaths of immigrants, classifying them by cause: drowning, asphyxiation, hypothermia, suicide, lack of medical care, violence and "other." When representing people, it is easy to fall into stereotypes, marking certain persons as "out of place" and implying that others are "in place" (Cresswell 1996). This symbolic Othering (Van Houtum and Van Naerssen 2002), is one of the primary ways in which visualization perpetuates power relations. To create a different type of map that does not engage in Othering changes what is visible and hence it changes the frame construction flow (D'Angelo 2002).

Visualizing personal risks therefore co-opts an Othering process that imposes greater risks on certain people. The intertwinement over hundreds of years between "sending" and "receiving" regions (political, economic, and environmental aspects of colonial and postcolonial relations) falls out of the story when it is illustrated with a standard migration map but it is precisely this history that has created the risks faced now by immigrants. Maps of risks faced by migrants can therefore help expose the geography of personal risk that is obscured by the surveillant gaze.

Guideline 3

Map immigration in ways that invite audience involvement and participation. Journalism takes part in processes of geographical perception and place-making that are, over the long term, collaborative and interactive, "a shared process between journalists and their official sources" (Gutsche 2014b, 494). Digital media have affordances that foreground and support this interactivity, for example maps employing JavaScript. A dynamic map requires a considerably greater time investment than a static map but its additional functionalities alter the relationships between computer users and knowledge construction since the act of exploring an interactive digital graphic prompts greater audience engagement with the complexities of an issue (Gynnild and Adams 2013).

Figures 5 and 6 suggest a couple of possibilities in this area. First, an interactive map and graphic created under the auspices of the Human Costs of Border Control (HCBC) at the University of Amsterdam (www.borderdeaths.org) employs JavaScript, permitting users to filter migrant fatalities according to the year of death. Numbers of migrant fatalities are shown as scaled circles juxtaposed on the approximate place of death, and these circles

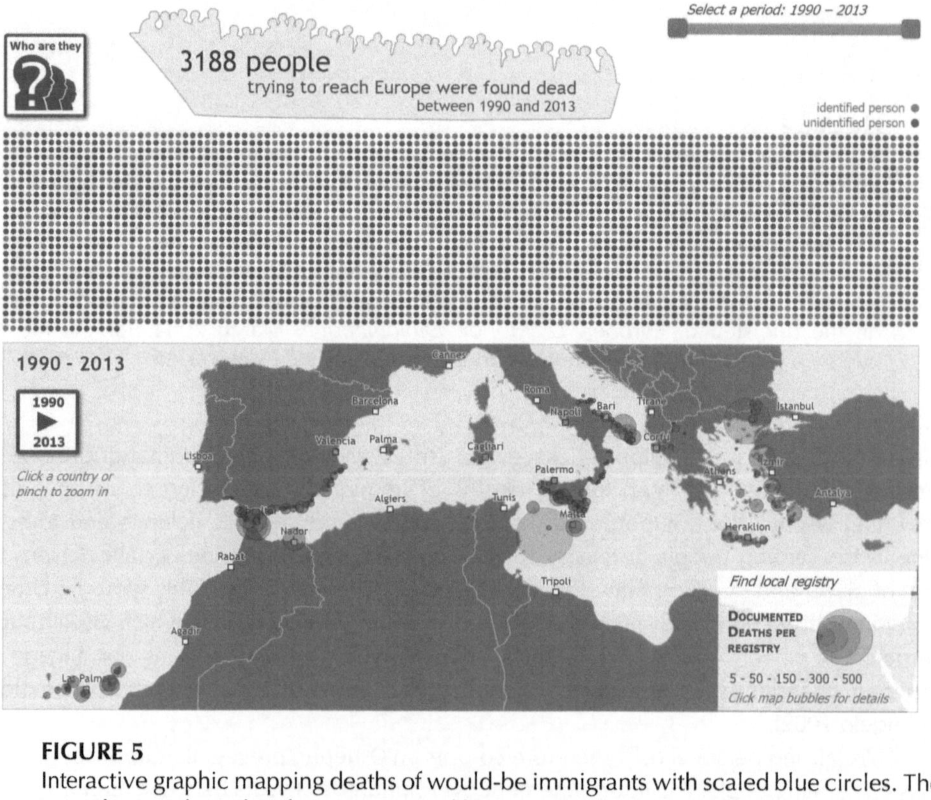

FIGURE 5

Interactive graphic mapping deaths of would-be immigrants with scaled blue circles. The map alters to show data from any interval between 1990 and 2013. Individual deaths are represented by a grid of 3188 dots. Clicking on "Who are they" reorganizes these dots by category: age, origin, and cause of death, while sex is indicated by the color of the dot. Source: Dutch Data Design (visualization) and the Human Costs of Border Control (HCBC) project at the University of Amsterdam, "Deaths at the Borders of Southern Europe." Online file at: http://www.borderdeaths.org/ accessed 5-18-2017

FIGURE 6
A dynamic, interactive map of country-to-country movement patterns as comet-like symbols moving between sending countries outside the Schengen area and receiving countries inside the Schengen area, with each comet representing 25 to 50 refugees "depending on device characteristics." Countries are rendered in black with gray borders, but scrolling over the map shows sending countries in purple and receiving countries in green. Source: Lucify https://www.lucify.com (designed by Ville Saarinen and Juho Ojala). Online file at: https://www.lucify.com/the-flow-towards-europe/) accessed 5-19-2017

change size depending on a user-selected time period, which is set with sliders at the top of the image. Migrant deaths are shown as dots, organized in a block pattern and can be classified in different ways, including age, sex, region of origin and cause of death.

Second, a sophisticated digital representation created by the web design firm Lucify (https://www.lucify.com/the-flow-towards-europe/) renders migration as streams of white comet-like objects moving from source countries in Africa, Central Asia and the Middle East toward European countries. The graphic starts in June 2012 and progresses to the present, but users can jump forwards or backwards in time. In addition, hovering the cursor over a particular country filters the data to show only the streams of migrants to or from that country. Countries are shaded according to the number of immigrants or emigrants, and destination countries also tally immigration with vertical bars. Below the map one finds other informative graphics. All of this constitutes the most sophisticated interactive immigration graphic available—but one with room for improvement since one cannot see immigration and emigration from the same country and return migration is not indicated.

Turning to theoretical arguments for interactivity, framing results in part from the reception of media by audiences, through what D'Angelo calls "framing effects flow" (2002). User involvement with a visual image is the first step toward involvement with whatever is portrayed in the image. In essence, interactivity affects awareness: people resistant to learning about certain problems, risks, or conditions are more receptive if they feel they are actively discovering something—even if they are aware that digital interactivity may be designed to steer them toward certain conclusions (Gynnild and Adams 2013, 55–56). Such interactive graphics are also suited to innovations that support "collective mapping" (Casas-Cortes et al. 2017), understood as a collaborative effort uniting immigrants with local participants. The potential importance of controversial messages is more likely to be recognized if these messages are embedded in interactive websites than if they are encountered passively through watching videos (Adams and Gynnild 2013, 124).

Interactive visual representations are a relatively new phenomenon, and their affordances mark one of the ways in which digital media enable audience appreciation for the complex issues around migration. This argument assumes that cartographic framing of migration is a process of political socialization, open to co-optation, even as it is also a system of cognitive associations open to negotiation (D'Angelo 2002).

Guideline 4

Map the non-geographic spaces that refugees, asylum seekers and immigrants must navigate on the way toward becoming full citizens. Between the inside and the outside of the nation-state there exists a mazelike terrain of opportunity that is neither here nor there, "an open space affected by but not restricted to state boundaries" (Casas-Cortes et al. 2017, 19). These spaces include the bureaucratic maze that confronts immigrants on the way from outsider (non-citizen) to insider (citizen) status. Different status designations have implications for what one can do at any given time, for example open a bank account, attend school, travel abroad, access legal counsel, or receive medical care. There is a *structure of opportunities* between variously empowered states of citizenship: refugee, asylum seeker, unaccompanied child, paperless person, holder of residence permit, holder of work permit, guest worker, economic immigrant, resident of state-supported housing, resident of detention center, inmate of jail or prison, person awaiting forcible return, person preparing for voluntary return, newly-admitted citizen with foreign family members, and so on. These categories overlap to various degrees and are related to each other in particular ways, not only as higher or lower positions in a hierarchical social structure but also as points of passage through a space of different types and degrees of personhood. Maps of spaces of status and opportunity join the personalization strategies described in Guidelines 1 and 2, counterbalancing habitual modes of visualization that "contribute to further dehumanizing refugees," and disrupting the taken-for-grantedness of visualizations that erase the "humanity or biographies" of less-powerful border-crossers (Lenette 2016, 3).

Figure 7 shows one way of rendering visible the nonphysical spaces navigated by refugees and asylum seekers. The Norwegian radio channel P3, which is operated by the Norwegian Broadcasting Corporation (NRK) has an affiliated website, and on that site there appeared a story linked to the radio documentary "Norges lengste kø" [Norway's longest queue] along with an interactive map. This remarkable map showed various stages of the immigration process along with corresponding status shifts, spatializing the complex terrain an immigrant must navigate between outsider and insider.

Theoretical defense of this kind of visualization depends on the argument that maps of people with contested status in a given society are most often created by and for those with less contested status, and this difference between Us and Them is written into many "normal" maps. Political scientist Ian J. Manners puts the case in the starkest terms: "The standard EU map serves as a multilingual icon of who is in and who is out" (2011, 254). By mapping the maze of in-between status designations and how they relate to each other a news story about immigration can help readers move beyond naïve understandings of migrant experiences. Here again the migration map intervenes in the framing effects

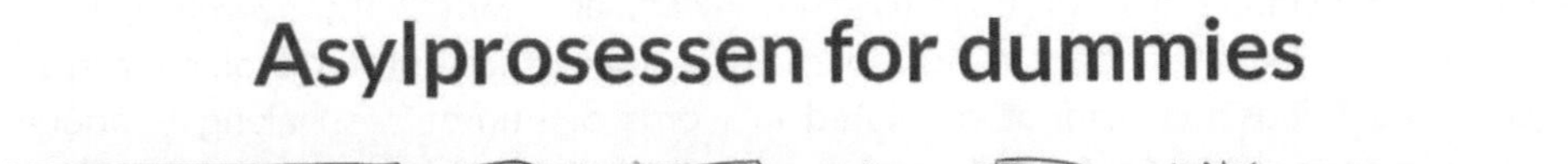

FIGURE 7
A map-like graphic "Asylprosessen for dummies" (Asylum process for dummies) accompanying the article "Norges lengste kø" (Norway's longest waiting line) by Mari Aftret Mørtvedt, published 9-9-2015 on the P3 website, a radio station affiliated with NRK, the Norwegian national broadcasting company. The graphic shows various status designations for persons seeking citizenship. Scrolling over a region highlights the region and clicking produces a popup window with supplemental information. Online file at: http://p3.no/dokumentar/norges-lengste-ko/ accessed 5-19-2017

flow (D'Angelo 2002)—reframing migration by altering the audience's relationship to information and knowledge.

Conclusion

If typical migration maps frame migrants as faceless masses, with flame colored arrows smashing through pristine linear borders, the ethical response offered here supplements such maps with alternative visualizations that emphasize migrant movements, experiences and risks at the personal level, and encourages audiences to discover some of the complex spaces of immigration on their own. This builds sympathy and constitutes priming for more constructive public responses to immigration. Alternative mappings of migration promote visualization of the terrains of in-between status navigated by people whose citizenship is in transition, a framing strategy that helps co-opt dominant ideologies. Furthermore, user involvement in interactive discovery of the many facets of migration can be fostered with participatory cartography to set an agenda in which inclusionary public engagement revitalizes the democratic process.

Care and reflection are needed in order to make cartographic visualizations that relate positively to multiculturalism, where justice is "a public and collective effort to achieve political parity among all social perspectives (along with the interests associated with them), including, especially, the perspectives (and interests) of systematically disenfranchised individuals and groups" (Glasser, Awad, and Kim 2009, 62–63). Migration maps enter into debates about ethical journalism, surveillance and technology in special ways, saying things that cannot be stated in words or numbers, speaking a language that is tremendously powerful yet poorly understood by most journalists and readers. It is incumbent on those who design and produce the news to be aware of the implicit biases of standard, default migration maps. There are ideological implications to treating immigration as an aggregate, faceless and impersonal flow, while simultaneously treating the audience as passive witnesses rather than active participants in the meaning-making process; this "official package" is an ethically questionable starting point for addressing immigration (Gamson and Modigliani 1989, 7).

Migration maps in the news can alternatively help to individualize immigrants and extend rights and ordinary social obligations to them, support interactive exploration of data, and map the invisible spaces of "in between" statuses that assist audiences in negotiating the insider/outsider distinction. Within the overall mission of journalism to provide actionable information regarding democratic procedures and political choices (Strömbäck 2005), alternative cartographic visualizations enhance the role of journalism because they assist in avoiding the trap of lending de-facto support to dominant power blocks. They facilitate the dialogic processes of civil society. To reconceive how immigrants are represented by engaging in "counter-mapping" (Peluso 1995) is to avoid foreclosing debates about immigration. This representational "challenger package" (Gamson and Modigliani 1989, 8) promotes inclusive dialogue rather than exclusionary habits.

Journalism professionals must ask of each migration map what it does: how it intervenes, to what purpose, and in support of what interests. This article has shown that the answers to such questions are not as obvious as they seem at the outset, nor are maps as simple as they at first appear. Drawing on D'Angelo's (2002) nomenclature, when it comes to the mapping of migration, frame construction, frame effects and frame definition can all be addressed in more constructive ways by redesigned migration maps.

DISCLOSURE STATEMENT

No potential conflict of interest was reported by the author.

FUNDING

Funding for this research was provided by the Ann-Marie and Gustaf Anders Foundation for Media Research, Karlstad, Sweden (Anne-Marie and Gustaf Anders Stiftelse för mediaforskning), the Research Council of Norway (Norges Forskningsråd [Prosjektnr. 247721/O70]), and the College of Liberal Arts at the University of Texas at Austin.

REFERENCES

Adams, Paul C., and Astrid Gynnild. 2013. "Environmental Messages in Online Media: The Role of Place." *Environmental Communication: A Journal of Nature and Culture* 7 (1): 113–130. doi:0.1080/17524032.2012.754777.

Balch, Alex. 2016. *Immigration and the State: Fear, Greed and Hospitality*. London: Palgrave Macmillan.

Balch, Alex, and Ekaterina Balabanova. 2011. "A System in Chaos? Knowledge and Sense-Making on Immigration Policy in Public Debates." *Media, Culture & Society* 33 (6): 885–904. doi:10.1177/0163443711411007.

Bleiker, Roland. 2015. "Pluralist Methods for Visual Global Politics." *Millennium: Journal of International Studies* 43 (3): 872–890. doi:10.1177/0305829815583084.

Bleiker, Roland, David Campbell, Emma Hutchison, and Xzarina Nicholson. 2013. "The Visual Dehumanisation of Refugees." *Australian Journal of Political Science* 48 (4): 398–416. doi:10.1080/10361146.2013.840769.

Casas-Cortes, Maribel, Sebastian Cobarrubias, Charles Heller, and Lorenzo Pezzani. 2017. "Clashing Cartographies, Migrating Maps: Mapping and the Politics of Mobility at the External Borders of E.U.rope." *ACME: An International E-Journal for Critical Geographies* 16 (1): 1–33.

Coleman, Renita. 2009. "Framing the Pictures in Our Heads: Exploring the Framing and Agenda-Setting Effects of Visual Images." In *Doing News Framing Analysis: Empirical and Theoretical Perspectives*, edited by Paul D'Angelo and Jim A. Kuypers, 233–261. London: Routledge.

Cosgrove, Denis. 2001. *Apollo's Eye: A Cartographic Genealogy of the Earth in the Western Imagination*. Baltimore: The Johns Hopkins University Press.

Cresswell, Tim. 1996. *In Place-Out of Place: Geography, Ideology, and Transgression*. Minneapolis: University of Minnesota Press.

D'Angelo, Paul. 2002. "News Framing as a Multiparadigmatic Research Program: A Response to Entman." *Journal of Communication* 52 (4): 870–888.

Dikeç, Mustafa. 2002. "Pera, Peras, Poros: Longing for Spaces of Hospitality." *Theory, Culture and Society* 19: 227–247. doi:10.1177/026327640201900111.

Dorigo, Guido, and Waldo Tobler. 1983. "Push-Pull Migration Laws." *Annals of the Association of American Geographers* 73 (1): 1–17.

Entman, Robert M. 1993. "Framing: Toward Clarification of a Fractured Paradigm." *Journal of Communication* 43 (4): 51–58.

Entman, Robert M. 2004. *Projections of Power: Framing News, Public Opinion, and U.S. Foreign Policy*. Chicago, IL: University of Chicago Press.

EU. 2013. "Regulation (EU) No. 604/2013 of the European Parliament and of the Council of 26 June 2013 Establishing the Criteria and Mechanisms for Determining the Member State Responsible for Examining an Application for International Protection Lodged in one of the Member States by a Third-Country National or a Stateless Person (Recast)". Official Journal of the European Union. L (180/31). 29 June 2013.

Foss, Sonja K. 2004. *Rhetorical Criticism: Exploration & Practice*. Third ed. Long Grove, Il: Waveland Press, Inc.

Foucault, Michel. 1976. *La Volonté du Savoir*. Paris: Gallimard.

Foucault, Michel. 1978. *The History of Sexuality, vol. 1: The Will to Knowledge*. London: Penguin.

Gabrielatos, Costas, and Paul Baker. 2008. "Fleeing, Sneaking, Flooding: A Corpus Analysis of Discursive Constructions of Refugees and Asylum Seekers in the UK Press, 1996-2005." *Journal of English Linguistics* 36 (1): 5–38. doi:10.1177/0075424207311247.

Gamson, William A., and Andre Modigliani. 1989. "Media Discourse and Public Opinion on Nuclear Power: A Constructionist Approach." *American Journal of Sociology* 95 (1): 1–37. doi:10.1086/229213.

Gitlin, Todd. 1980. *The Whole World is Watching: Mass Media in the Making and Unmaking of the New Left*. Berkeley: University of California Press.

Glasser, Theodore L., Isabel Awad, and John W. Kim. 2009. "The Claims of Multiculturalism and Journalism's Promise of Diversity." *Journal of Communication* 59 (1): 57–78. doi:10.1111/j.1460-2466.2008.01404.x.

Gutsche, Robert E. Jr. 2014a. *A Transplanted Chicago: Race, Place and the Press in Iowa City*. Jefferson, NC: McFarland & Company, Inc.

Gutsche, Robert E. Jr. 2014b. "News Place-Making: Applying 'Mental Mapping' to Explore the Journalistic Interpretive Community." *Visual Communication* 13: 487–510. doi:10.1177/1470357214541754.

Gynnild, Astrid, and Paul C. Adams. 2013. "Animation, Documentary or Interactive Gaming? Exploring Communicative Aspects of Environmental Messaging Online." *International Symposium on Online Journalism* 3 (1): 39–60. http://www.isoj.org/journal/volume-3-issue-1/.

Haraway, Donna. 1988. "Situated Knowledges: The Science Question in Feminism and the Privilege of Partial Perspective." *Feminist Studies* 14 (3): 575–599. http://www.jstor.org/stable/3178066.

Harley, J. B. 1988. "Maps, Knowledge and Power." In *The Iconography of Landscape: Essays on the Symbolic Representation, Design and Use of Past Environments*, edited by Denis Cosgrove and Stephen Daniels, 277–312. Cambridge: Cambridge University Press.

Harley, J. B. 1989. "Deconstructing the Map." *Cartographica: The International Journal for Geographic Information and Geovisualization* 26: 1–20. doi:10.3138/E635-7827-1757-9T53.

Hartley, Lucy. 2008. "War and Peace, or Governmentality as the Ruin of Democracy." In *Foucault in an Age of Terror Essays on Biopolitics and the Defence of Society*, edited by Stephen Morton and Stephen Bygrave, 133–151. Houndmills, Basingstoke, UK: Palgrave MacMillan.

Helbling, Marc. 2014. "Framing Immigration in Western Europe." *Journal of Ethnic And Migration Studies* 40 (1): 21–41. doi:10.1080/1369183X.2013.830888.

Horsti, Karina. 2012. "Humanitarian Discourse Legitimating Migration Control: FRONTEX Public Communication." In *Migrations: Interdisciplinary Perspectives*, edited by Michi Messier, Ruth Wodak and Renée Schroeder, 297–308. Vienna: Springer Science & Business Media.

Horsti, Karina. 2016. "Visibility Without Voice: Media Witnessing Irregular Migrants in BBC Online News Journalism." *African Journalism Studies* 37 (1): 1–20. doi:10.1080/23743670.2015.1084585.

Horsti, Karina, and Kaarina Nikunen. 2013. "The Ethics of Hospitality in Changing Journalism: A Response to the Rise of the Anti-Immigrant Movement in Finnish Media Publicity." *European Journal of Cultural Studies* 16 (4): 489–504. doi:10.1177/1367549413491718.

Houen, Alex. 2008. "Sovereignty, Biopolitics and the Use of Literature: Michel Foucault and Kathy Acker." In *Foucault in an Age of Terror Essays on Biopolitics and the Defence of Society*, edited by Stephen Morton and Stephen Bygrave, 63–87. Houndmills, Basingstoke, UK: Palgrave MacMillan.

Ibrahim, Maggie. 2005. "The Securitization of Migration: A Racial Discourse." *International Migration* 43 (5): 163–187. doi:10.1111/j.1468-2435.2005.00345.x.

Jansson, André. 2017. "Critical Communication Geography: Space, Recognition, and the Dialectic of Mediatization." In *Communications/Media/Geographies*, edited by Paul C. Adams, Julie Cupples, Kevin Glynn, André Jansson and Shaun Moores, 95–131. New York, NY: Routledge.

Keskinen, Suvi. 2016. "Borders of the Finnish Nation: Media Politics and Rape by 'Foreign' Perpetrators." In *Media in Motion: Complexity and Migration in the Nordic Region*, edited by E. Eide and K. Nikunen, 107–124. London: Routledge.

Kurtz, Cynthia F., and David J. Snowden. 2003. "The New Dynamics of Strategy: Sense-Making in a Complex and Complicated World." *IBM Systems Journal* 42 (3): 462–483. doi:10.1147/sj.423.0462.

Lenette, Caroline. 2016. "Writing with Light: An Iconographic-Iconologic Approach to Refugee Photography." *Forum Qualitative Sozialforschung / Forum: Qualitative Social Research* 17 (2), article 8, np. http://nbn-resolving.de/urn:nbn:de:0114-fqs160287

Manners, Ian. 2011. "Symbolism in European Integration." *Comparative European Politics* 9 (3): 243–268. doi:10.1057/cep.2010.11.

Mbembe, Achille. 2008. "Necropolitics." In *Foucault in an Age of Terror Essays on Biopolitics and the Defence of Society*, edited by Stephen Morton and Stephen Bygrave, 152–182. Houndmills, Basingstoke, UK: Palgrave MacMillan.

Monmonier, Mark. 1989. *Maps with the News: The Development of American Journalistic Cartography*. Chicago, IL: University of Chicago Press.

Monmonier, Mark. 2010. *No Dig, No Fly, No Go: How Maps Restrict and Control*. Chicago, IL: University of Chicago Press.

Monmonier, Mark. 2014. *How to Lie with Maps*. Chicago, IL: University of Chicago Press.

Morton, Stephen, and Stephen Bygrave, eds. 2008a. *Foucault in an Age of Terror: Essays on Biopolitics and the Defence of Society*. Houndmills, Basingstoke, UK: Palgrave MacMillan.

Morton, Stephen, and Stephen Bygrave. 2008b. "Introduction." In *Foucault in an Age of Terror: Essays on Biopolitics and the Defence of Society*, edited by Stephen Morton and Stephen Bygrave, 1–13. Houndmills, Basingstoke, UK: Palgrave MacMillan.

Nagel, Thomas. 1989. *The View From Nowhere*. Revised ed. Oxford, UK: Oxford University Press.

Nikunen, Kaarina. 2016. "Hopes of Hospitality: Media, Refugee Crisis and the Politics of a Place." *International Journal of Cultural Studies* 19 (2): 161–176. doi:10.1177/1367877914530314.

O'Lear, Shannon. 1997. "Migration and the Environment: A Review of Recent Literature." *Social Science Quarterly* 78 (2): 606–618. http://www.jstor.org/stable/42864357

Olsson, Gunnar. 2007. *Abysmal: A Critique of Cartographic Reason*. Chicago, IL: The University of Chicago Press.

Ó Tuathail, Gearoid, and John Agnew. 1992. "Geopolitics and Discourse: Practical Geopolitical Reasoning in American Foreign Policy." *Political Geography* 11 (2): 190–204.

Pan, Zhongdang, and Gerald M. Kosicki. 1993. "Framing Analysis: An Approach to News Discourse." *Political Communication* 10: 55–75.

Peluso, Nancy L. 1995. "Whose Woods are These? Counter-Mapping Forest Territories in Kalimantan, Indonesia." *Antipode* 27 (4): 383–406.

Pickles, John. 1992. "Text, Hermeneutics and Propaganda Maps." In *Writing Worlds: Discourse, Text and Metaphor in the Representation of Landscape*, edited by Trevor J. Barnes and James S. Duncan, 193–230. New York, NY: Routledge.

Protess, David L., and Maxwell McCombs, eds. 2016. *Agenda Setting: Readings on Media, Public Opinion, and Policymaking*. London: Routledge.

Reid, Julian. 2008. "Life Struggles: War, Discipline and Biopolitics in the Thought of Michel Foucault." In *Foucault in an Age of Terror Essays on Biopolitics and the Defence of Society*, edited by Stephen Morton and Stephen Bygrave, 14–42. Houndmills, Basingstoke, UK: Palgrave MacMillan.

Sack, Robert D. 1986. *Human Territoriality: Its Theory and History*. Cambridge, UK: Cambridge University Press.

Scheufele, Dietram A. 1999. "Framing as a Theory of Media Effects." *Journal of Communication* 49 (1): 103–122. doi:10.1111/j.1460-2466.1999.tb02784.x.

Silverstone, Roger. 2007. *Media and Morality: On the Rise of the Mediapolis*. Cambridge, UK: Polity Press.

Strömbäck, Jesper. 2005. "In Search of a Standard: Four Models of Democracy and Their Normative Implications for Journalism." *Journalism Studies* 6 (3): 331–345. doi:10.1080/14616700500131950.

Tazzioli, Martina. 2016. "Eurosur, Humanitarian Visibility, and (Nearly) Real-Time Mapping in the Mediterranean." *ACME: An International Journal for Critical Geographies* 15 (3): 561–579.

Thompson, John B. 1990. *Ideology and Modern Culture*. Stanford, CA: Stanford University Press.

Van Houtum, Henk, and Ton Van Naerssen. 2002. "Bordering, Ordering and Othering." *Tijdschrift voor Economische en Sociale Geografie* 93 (2): 125–136. doi:10.1111/1467-9663.00189.

Vliegenthart, Rens, and Conny Roggeband. 2007. "Framing Immigration and Integration Relationships Between Press and Parliament in the Netherlands." *The International Communication Gazette* 69 (3): 295–319. doi:10.1177/1748048507076582.

Vujaković, Peter. 2002. "Mapping the War Zone: Cartography, Geopolitics and Security Discourse in the UK Press." *Journalism Studies* 3 (2): 187–202. doi:10.1080/14616700220129964.

Vujaković, Peter. 2014. "The State as a 'Power Container': The Role of News Media Cartography in Contemporary Geopolitical Discourse." *The Cartographic Journal* 51 (1): 11–24. doi:10.1179/1743277413Y.0000000043.

Vukov, Tamara, and Mimi Sheller. 2013. "Border Work: Surveillant Assemblages, Virtual Fences, and Tactical Counter-Media." *Social Semiotics* 23 (2): 225–241. doi:10.1080/10350330.2013.777592.

Weaver, David H. 2007. "Thoughts on Agenda Setting, Framing, and Priming." *Journal of Communication* 57 (1): 142–147. doi:10.1111/j.1460-2466.2006.00333.x.

Woodward, David. 1992. "Representations of the World." In *Geography's Inner Worlds: Pervasive Themes in Contemporary American Geography*, edited by Ronald F. Abler, Melvin G. Marcus and Judy M. Olson, 50–76. New Brunswick, NJ: Rutgers University Press.

http://prcid.org./0000-0002-9303-0027

VERITABLE FLAK MILL

A case study of Project Veritas and a call for truth

Brian Michael Goss

Flak may be concisely defined as political harassment and is detrimental to community for its strained ethical posture, cynicism, and corrosive impact on social and political bonds of trust. Following conceptualization of flak that differentiates it from scandal and activism, this investigation focuses on Project Veritas as its case study. Veritas is a right-wing flak mill that, using media, has set out to professionally damage people and organizations across almost a decade. The investigation telescopes in on two Veritas stunts that provoked reviews by the justice systems of California and Texas. In these cases, the California Attorney General and Texas special prosecutors delivered astringent criticisms of Veritas' covertly-recorded "sting" videos, while largely or wholly exonerating their flak targets (Association of Community Organizations for Reform Now *[ACORN], Battleground Texas). Along with conceptualizing and critiquing flak, the investigation concludes with a call for news that extends beyond fact-checking and the limited, complacent techniques of objectivity in favor of more ambitious pursuit of truth.*

Introduction: Are Ineptitude and Ideological Ax-Grinding the New Truth?

> *Magna est veritas, et praevalebit* [Translated from Latin: "Truth is great and will prevail"]

> *You can play the media, you can defeat the media and you can get the media to react…*
> Project Veritas founder James O'Keefe III (2016, 6)

"Fake news" is a phrase that has come into wide circulation recently, largely due to right-wing activists who alternately benefit from tsunamis of specious discourse *and* also use the term to dismiss reporting that does not align with their political project. By contrast, media scholars have long argued that the news is strongly conditioned by elite institutions and agendas—even if news is not simply invented. Scholars who have made their arguments at book length, and who decidedly lean politically left, include Bagdikian (1992), Bennett (2001), Davies (2009), Franklin (2004), Gans (2004), Goss (2013), Herman and Chomsky (1988), and Said (1997). In this vein, W. Lance Bennett (2001) posits that news that covers a train wreck may not be fake—but it does present a whiff of systematic distortion when that same news is agnostic to the class-valenced issue of the everyday performance of public transit.

In other words, there was much understood to be wrong within the realm of news prior to the "fake news" meme. However, even as the status quo antebellum is not satisfactory, some of the worst aspects of news performance are now evident in heightened forms.

More specifically, flak is becoming a more prominent feature of news discourses. In responding to this still consolidating news environment, the purpose of this investigation is to, first, initiate a more elaborate understanding of flak. It is a concept that has, to my knowledge, never been covered at book length and other literature explicitly dedicated to flak is scant (one example: Goss 2009). Thus, an important stake of this investigation is to commence critical, sustained attention to flak. The second purpose of this investigation advances the first by illustrating flak discourse as it plays out in practice. In particular, I will elaborate a case study of Project Veritas, a flak mill that has come to prominence in the past decade.

In making a first pass at concisely defining flak, I characterize it as "political harassment." Along with regular indifference toward or active defiance of truth, flak is corrosive to community bonds. While flak is certainly disruptive to the entity to which it is targeted—for example, a public figure or an NGO—it can simultaneously mobilize supporters of the flak message on exaggerated or false pretexts; the result is intensified confrontation, or even intractable social division. While complex (post-)industrial societies have never lent themselves to easy consensus, intensification of flak strongly works against the effort toward a community of shared interests. In Latin, *com* signifies "with" and, as such, is embedded in many Latinate words that express deep ties of togetherness (communicate, commune, commiserate). It follows that community signifies commitment to shared group life, with its myriad concomitants in political expression and social life more broadly. Flak is, by contrast with the cultivation of community, conducive to heightened cynicism and distrust.

In this investigation, flak is the center of gravity, while the work of the right-wing flak mill Project Veritas furnishes the extended case study. Why examine Project Veritas? On one hand, it is an organization whose founder, James O'Keefe III (born 1984, New Jersey) has been prosecuted over his flak stunts (Media Matters 2016, 8, 13–14). Veritas' targets of flak also present a roster of the bêtes noires of the contemporary right: alleged election mischief (Project Veritas 2015b), border/immigration control (Project Veritas 2014a), gay marriage (Project Veritas 2008), higher education (Project Veritas 2015a) and news media (Project Veritas 2011). At each of these sites, the political right pressures marginal segments of society and their sources of support; or, in the case of universities and media, the right trolls' institutions that are embedded within prevailing power relations, but deemed insufficiently zealous in support of them. The restoration of raw, pyramidal hierarchy is the alpha and omega of the right-wing project, as political theorist Corey Robin argues (2011)—and tactics of flak can be readily mobilized to serve this strategic end.

Introducing Veritas

Jane Meyer's 2016 feature on Veritas opens with the embarrassing episode of O'Keefe's attempt to penetrate George Soros' Open Society Foundation via telephone—and then failing to hang up the phone correctly. As a result, O'Keefe left what amounted to a seven-minute memorandum on how he planned to take down Soros on Open Society's message machine, as he regaled visitors to his office about guerilla tactics.

Regular bouts of ineptitude do not, however, make an organization innocuous. Veritas has torpedoed organizations, sullied reputations (besides its own), and compromised careers. Examples include Veritas' 2011 video on National Public Radio (NPR) fundraising executive Ron Schiller that was secretly recorded over lunch. Veritas imposters approached NPR with the apparent intent of seeking to bring political Islam to the airwaves. The resultant 11-minute Veritas video tossed and teased the original two-hour recording to specifications that prompted Schiller's immediate resignation. Schiller was also terminated from another position that he was about to assume. In short order, NPR fired Betsy Liley who was present at the lunch and CEO Vivian Schiller (no relation) who was not (Folkenflik 2011).

In a right-leaning publication, *The Blaze*, Scott Baker (2011) avers that Schiller exhibited moments of poor judgement in the unedited recording. Baker also characterizes the edited Veritas video as misleading. To wit, Schiller's apparently bemused response to sharia law supposedly on the march was spliced-in from an unrelated moment of the discourse—a blatant deception through editing. Schiller's criticisms of the Republican Party were also amped up. In the full video, Schiller was not exclusively flagging his personal views; rather, he was channelling criticisms that were widely held and that Schiller's establishment Republican friends had endorsed. Schiller acknowledged sharing many of the criticisms, while also praising conservatives (for supposed fiscal discipline). Veritas' videotape suppresses an impression of Schiller as a thoughtful professional, reconciling conflicting ideas, in favor of conjuring a damaging caricature. Al Tompkins, a journalist and ethics instructor at the Poynter Institute, makes similar observations on comparing the full tape with Veritas' edited-for-distribution version: "'The message that he [Schiller] said most often—I counted six times: He told these two people that he had never met before that you cannot buy coverage. … He says it over and over and over again'." Tompkins concludes that, "'there are two ways to lie": "One is to tell me something that didn't happen, and the other is not to tell me something that did happen. I think they [Veritas] employed both techniques'" (quoted in Folkenflik 2011). In this and other instances, Veritas prejudges the conduct of its flak targets—and then mobilizes editing and framing commentaries toward unconditional, pre-fabricated conclusions.

"The Truest Form of Journalism"

In contrast with mainstream news workers whom he derides as "such corrupt scum," O'Keefe characterizes his work at Veritas in martyred terms: An arduous decade of "civil lawsuits, jail, defamation, lies, slander" (2016, 2). O'Keefe also asserts that he steers "twelve full-time journalists *risking their lives*" (emphasis added, 2016, 6). In other words, Veritas positions as an amalgamation of James Bond, Jason Bourne and Ethan Hunt, with shades of Nelson Mandela thrown in. Nonetheless, in the same speech, O'Keefe namechecks supporters that include the late Andrew Breitbart (his "mentor"), NewsCorp/Murdochian ideologue Sean Hannity, multi-billionaire (and, by then, "president-elect") Donald J. Trump. Despite the baldly elitist company, O'Keefe insists that, "We need people in this country who are going to fight for something greater than themselves, but the politicians are never going to do it. It has to be the citizens. It has to be ordinary people who do extraordinary things" (2016, 6). Notwithstanding O'Keefe's dense right-wing jive, one can consult Veritas' resume of flak projects that document its ideological patrol missions against the margins and on behalf of privilege.

"What I do," O'Keefe contends, "is the truest form of journalism there is. We hit the record button and show people what we found" (quoted in Mayer 2016, 11). It is, he says, the cause of "an investigative journalist" committed to "a more ethical and transparent society"—although, as Jane Mayer observes, O'Keefe "refused to be transparent about who is funding him" when she asked (2016, 10). What is known is that Donors Trust, a vehicle designed to fund right-wing causes with discretion for the donor, has funneled monies to Veritas (Mayer 2016). The Trump Organization is also known to be a contributor to Veritas and candidate Trump invited O'Keefe to be a guest to one of the autumn 2016 debates (Smith 2016). Moreover, along with the impulse to "hit the record button," Veritas has displayed facility with the pause and delete buttons in the editing suite, in order to enhance their videos' impact. Veritas includes framing material (title cards, voice overs) around the covertly-recorded video that have, in turn, invited misleading conclusions.

Despite seething antipathy toward journalism, Veritas assays to coopt the prestige of the profession and to penetrate its mainstream discourses (as flagged in the epigram). While the status of professional journalism has absorbed blows in recent decades, it retains the greatest reach for news discourse. In this view, Veritas seeks the prize of the mainstream's approval and its vestigial prestige that O'Keefe otherwise dismisses. Hence, "Project Veritas journalist" title cards in its videos tendentiously assert Veritas personnel's qualifications to mainstream specifications. Despite its bids for professional authority, Veritas manifestly defies the letter and the spirit of journalism ethics.

However flawed journalism may be in practice, the Society of Professional Journalists' "Code of Ethics" gives specific shape to the profession's vision of being "accurate, fair and thorough" (2014, 1). The current version of the code presents the following guidelines: "Avoid undercover or other surreptitious methods of gathering information unless traditional, open methods will not yield information vital to the public" (2014, 2). As Greg Marx observes (2010), undercover journalism had a checkered record and reputation, even prior to Veritas' stunts. Moreover, Veritas actively eschews this ethical directive and reaches for surreptitious methods in the first instance and not as a last resort. In a related vein, the code warns about "undue intrusiveness" (2014, 2), in contrast with Veritas' "go-to" method of clandestine recording. Another pillar of the "Code of Ethics" maintains that journalists should "Never deliberately distort facts or context, including visual information"—and that journalists should, "Clearly label illustrations and re-enactments" (2014, 2). As will be demonstrated later, Veritas has baldly violated these guidelines.

Veritas similarly disregards directives to be sensitive to private citizens who lack the institutional power to countermand news discourses. In this vein, ethical news workers are further urged to, "Consider the long-term implications of the extended reach and permanence of publication. Provide updated and more complete information as appropriate" (2014, 3). By contrast, during Veritas' attempts to stage election fraud in Colorado, O'Keefe's motive to act as judge/jury/executioner and cause harm was on display on his Twitter fed: "this time, people may lose their jobs" (quoted in Kroll 2014). Although Veritas has been fact-checked by external observers, it also eschews the Society for Professional Journalists' charge for self-correction.

While other investigators have assayed a more exhaustive catalogue of Project Veritas' stunts (Media Matters 2016), I will telescope in on Veritas' videos that have prompted investigations convened by the justice systems of California and Texas. Before I consider the case studies of Veritas' videos on the Association of Community Organizations for Reform Now (ACORN) and Battleground Texas, I will assay a brisk but thorough account of flak.

Introducing Flak

While rolling out the Propaganda Model in 1988, Edward S. Herman and Noam Chomsky telegraphically characterize flak as "negative responses to a media statement or program." At the time, flak could be expressed through myriad channels: "letters, telegrams, phone calls, petitions, lawsuits, speeches and bills before Congress, and other modes of complaint, threat, and punitive action" (1988, 16). "If flak is produced on a large scale, or by individuals or groups with substantial resources," they observe, "it can be both uncomfortable and costly"—with all of the professional and personal implications that follow.

As noted, since flak has not yet been subject to book-length discussion, I seek to flesh out Herman and Chomsky's brief discussion—and to stimulate further examination that explicitly brings flak into the analysis of media campaigns. A foundational assumption in elaborating flak is that the current, media-saturated environment is laden with organizations designed to produce it in copious quantities. These "flak mills" often operate under the veneer of being "think tanks" or NGOs (Goss 2013, 141–166). Flak may also be construed as intensifying due to the proliferation of media platforms and rise of 24-hour news cycles. In contrast with daily papers in the past, the news hole now requires perpetual replenishment—all day, every day—generating demand for even dubious content to which PR mongers as well as flak merchants can answer (Davies 2009).

Herman and Chomsky's propaganda model posits deeply embedded structures that are permeated with elite social and economic power and, in turn, shape the discourses of news performance. The filters that Herman and Chomsky interpret as conditioning the news—ownership patterns, commercial imperatives, news workers' professional routines, dichotomized ("us" versus "them") narratives—constitute a powerful set of constraints. Nevertheless, these constraints are not iron-clad, nor are they normally coercive, and there is appreciable autonomy in news work. The constraints presented by the concerted influence of the filters are, however, palpable and have long turned the US' news narratives toward elite imperatives. In this vein, I have furnished a recent, filter-by-filter account of the structural constraints on news that are finally manifested in its discourses (Goss 2013). Moreover, one very important pattern endures despite the convulsions in politics and media since the introduction of the propaganda model in 1988. To wit, the enactment flak is steeped in (often, very raw) power relations.

Flak: Beyond Scandal

Writing early in the internet era, John B. Thompson stresses that scandal has become a more prominent part of the political landscape (2000, 5). Thompson's straightforward model of scandal proposes a first phase of wrongdoing that he calls "transgression and concealment," followed by "public disclosure and public allegations." In turn, these discourses prompt "public disapprobrobation" as the scandal begins to gain traction (2000, 24). Once the hub-bub begins to consolidate into a scandal, reputations may be tarnished or torched; and, in a milieu of competitive (commercial and political) brands, reputation is an all-important currency. While political actors may push back against the allegations, the effort to thwart a scandal narrative readily gives it further oxygen (2000, 13–14).

As a scandal plays out, "it becomes a narrative with multiple plots and subplots, many of which fizzle out but some of which may evolve into minor scandals of their own ('subscandals') or even into 'offshoot' scandals" (2000, 25). Moreover, as occurs in reading "a good novel," an audience following the scandal will be rewarded with new strains of suspicion and revelations as morality play plotlines unfold (2000, 73). Thompson also argues that, "Disclosure through the media, and commentary in the media, are not secondary or incidental features of these forms of scandal; they are partly constitutive of them" (2000, 61). In being shaped into media events, scandals acquire the warps and distortions that reflect the demands of media work; for example, demands for concision (two-minute news item) or the writ of formal objectivity, even when it is absurd to pretend that "both sides" of the story have equal merit.

Flak dynamics resemble those that Thompson ascribes to scandal. However, I posit several important differences between flak and scandal. Whereas scandal begins with transgression, there is no demand for a flak campaign of harassment to have any grounding in a plausible transgression. Think about what this means: Flak may proceed straight to "disclosure" and subsequent allegation—which is, of course, denied by the accused if no transgression occurred (while denial is itself suspicious, within a flak framework!). If the objective is to put heat on political opponents, any pretext will do—including no pretext at all. There is no upper limit to how contrived flak can be, as demonstrated by the moronic "birther" charade against Barack Obama.

In Thompson's view, along with carnivalesque trappings, scandal narratives affirm or negate the truth-value of claims through their narrative resolution. Thus, Thompson emphasizes that scandal is not merely a trivialization of political discourse; scandal can, indeed, advance the objective of closer vetting of political actors and better governance. By contrast, as a form of political harassment, the purpose of flak is to keep the heat on political opponents, regardless of whether any claims are true and irrespective of whether better governance is a likely outcome. Moreover, if a flak narrative is never resolved, suspicion continues in perpetuity. Political harassment becomes open-ended and part of the ongoing "mood music" of current events; and, by flak logics, that lingering mood music may indeed present a better outcome than scandals that are resolved by either punishment or exoneration. Flak can, of course, mutate into a mature scandal if stepped-up scrutiny and investigation eventually uncovers evidence. However, the mere fact of flak-driven suspicion *in-and-of itself* exerts pressure on political opponents, regardless of whether the contrived conjuring of smoke leads back to fire. Indeed, the lack of a transgression committed by the target of a flak campaign can itself *be perceived as a crime*, if audiences to the flak become convinced of the target's guilt; in this scenario, the flak target is regarded as the beneficiary of a golden parachute by the convinced flak audience!

Thompson (2000) is, in this view, effectively agnostic toward flak. He implicitly "normalizes" what I am calling flak tactics by collapsing all controversy into scandal and its quest to establish truth. In a signature example of missing a distinction between flak and scandal, Thompson posits that, "the Clinton–Lewinsky scandal emerged out of a quite separate investigation relating to the Paula Jones sexual harassment case and to a failed real estate deal [Whitewater] in Arkansas" (2000, 25). However, by bringing flak into the analysis, we can posit the contrived Jones and Whitewater episodes as instances of flak that were designed to open or continue investigatory lines. Indeed, Clinton lost money on the Whitewater deal to a fraudulent and mentally ill former friend/investment partner (Conason and Lyons 2000). Nevertheless, special prosecutors continued to pore over the president's affairs, enacting a form of open-ended flak with its "drip-drip-drip" of mediated insinuation of wrongdoing; and whether it finally yielded an actual scandal or an ongoing infinite regress of suspicion, flak was an effective tactic. Notice that, the Clinton discourses of the 1990s were also illustrative of the nascent impact of what were then "primitive" new media platforms (for example, *Drudge Report*) in conjuring steady streams of flak. New media as well as flak have only scaled up since then.

Power matters when flak is employed as a political tactic. Whether enacted against people who wield authority (such as Clinton) or against people who demonstrably do not, a defining feature of flak is that it is an instrument at the disposal of agents who hold power. By contrast, activism is an (oftentimes guerilla-style) tactic of weaker parties against stronger ones to leverage whatever advantage they are able to muster through, for example, pickets, boycotts and improvised media. As such, activism can be characterized as "white hat," underdog activity. In turn, campaigns on behalf of elite interests may appropriate the veneer of activism through subterfuge. In "AstroTurf" campaigns, powerful industries recruit front groups as the public faces of their self-interested complaints (Stauber and Rampton 2001). When the automobile industry sponsored citizens' opposition to pollution regulations (Greider 1992, 37–38), the astroturfed campaign to pressure legislators concealed the corporate fingerprints. As flak is wound up with power, it may also necessitate the concealment of that power.

Flak's Impact on Community

A flak paradox: Scrupulous organizations may be more vulnerable to flak stunts. That is, the more scrupulous an organization is, the more likely it will be to perform due diligence and investigate even dubious claims of wrongdoing within its ranks. A hit squad is not, by contrast, concerned about its "good name." Moreover, as an instrument of power, a flak campaign almost invariably weakens its target. Costs include time, effort and money for defense—and even successfully deflected flak engenders reputational costs (transient or otherwise). Flak can be construed as akin to *anti*-public relations campaigns that contrast with PR designed to place clients in the best possible light via puffery and relentless positive vibes.

Vicarious supporters of a flak campaign may also gain inspiration and reinforcement from seeing flak that they favor in motion. It is given that complex societies are composed of competing and at times irreconcilable interests. However, flak heightens these conflicts in the effort to demoralize one group, while at the same time enticing another group to rally to its perceived interests without compromise (and even if the flak discourses are specious). As a result, flak strongly undermines efforts to perform the delicate work of forging consensus out of disparate interests. The elites who may directly or indirectly cultivate flak campaigns stand as the main beneficiaries when flak provokes divisive battles among the people down below, while elite interests hover unscathed above the scene.

With backstory on Veritas and conceptualization of flak in place, I will pivot to the organization's campaigns on behalf of the right-wing project of starkly-drawn sociopolitical hierarchies. In particular, I examine Veritas' campaigns against urban advocacy (ACORN) and voter participation (Battleground Texas).

Origins: ACORN Agonistes

ACORN's project was to advocate for low income citizens on, for example, the minimum wage, housing issues, and predatory lending practices. The organization also engaged in voter registration drives. For harboring progressive goals of curbing untrammeled class privilege, ACORN fit the profile that the political right lividly contests. In Republican Congressman Darrel Issa's assessment, ACORN is a "left-leaning syndicate of labour unions and political agitators" (2009, 1). Moreover, part of the animus toward ACORN in 2009 stemmed from newly installed President Obama's previous work for the group.

Prior to Veritas' interventions, ACORN had already been subject to Issa's polemically titled report, *Is ACORN Intentionally Structured as a Criminal Enterprise?* However, Veritas' more media-friendly flak effectively finished off the organization with a fast-track to wide circulation—even as Veritas' recordings were not as they seemed. In particular, Hannah Giles and ÓKeefe impersonated a prostitute and her boyfriend as they covertly taped interactions with low-level employees of ACORN. After entering offices on a contrived premise, the pair posed leading questions and covertly record the encounters. Veritas then cut the clandestine recordings and pasted in further sensationalized material to misleading effect —and finally fed the videos into media channels, where the resultant spectacle "went viral."

Veritas' versions of their visits to ACORN premiered on the Andrew Breitbart-founded *Big Government* webpage on 10 September 2009. Further Veritas "scoops" continued over the course of a week. In short order, the US House and Senate voted to exclude ACORN from receiving federal funds (about 10 percent of the organization's US$25 million budget), while private funds also quickly dried up due to negative publicity around the videos (Office of the Attorney General 2010, 4–6).

Following Veritas' hair-raising reports about ACORN, Governor Arnold Schwarzenegger ordered an investigation of the group's activities in California. Seven months later, California Attorney General Edmund "Jerry" Brown's report faulted ACORN for extortion by the founder's brother that had been long covered up at the national level. Where California was specifically concerned, the Attorney General found carelessness with documents, a tangled bureaucracy that lacked transparency, substandard training, and failure to submit a tax return in 2007. Brown also notes voter registration infractions, while emphasizing that, "The difference between individual voter fraud and voter registration fraud is important" (Office of the Attorney General 2010, 19).[1] Despite flagging serious problems with ACORN, Brown's report may be taken as more acerbic in what it says about Veritas. In introducing the findings in a press release, Brown states: "The evidence illustrates … that things are not always as partisan zealots portray them through highly selective editing of reality. Sometimes a fuller truth is found on the cutting room floor" (State of California Department of Justice 2010, 2).

Alongside its criticism of ACORN, Brown's office found no recognizable crimes to pursue, even as the flak storm convened by Veritas ruined ACORN. When instructed to investigate by the US House in December 2009, the Congressional Research Service similarly reported no violations of law by ACORN salient to Veritas' videos, nor did states beyond California that scrutinized ACORN (Media Matters 2016, 14). While committing no crime is not a lofty standard to meet, the outcomes of these state-sponsored investigations contrast with the wild flak accusations directed at ACORN. (Moreover, when they are investigated, blue chip corporations often fail to meet the standard of no crimes committed.)

Although tasked with examining ACORN, Brown found it necessary dwell on Veritas' conduct. The Attorney General writes:

> O'Keefe and Giles agreed to produce the full recordings if the Attorney General agreed not to prosecute them for violations of California's privacy laws. This Office determined that the fastest and most efficient means to comply with the Governor's request was to agree not to prosecute. (Office of the Attorney General 2010, 17)

Following an overview of pertinent statues and precedents, Brown concludes that had immunity not been granted in advance, the Veritas flaksters would almost surely have faced prosecution: "An application of these principles to the facts presented here strongly suggests that O'Keefe and Giles's violated state privacy laws and provides fair warning to them and others that this type of activity can be prosecuted in California" (Office of the Attorney General 2010, 17).

While O'Keefe and Giles were immunized from prosecution by the State of California, they were not sheltered from civil action by the victims of their flak stunt. ACORN fired Juan Carlos Vera on the day that Veritas' edited version of an encounter with him was published. Vera was subsequently compensated to the tune of $150,000 in a civil action against O'Keefe and Giles over striking misrepresentations in the published version of the tape (Media Matters 2016, 13). On viewing the complete tapes of the encounter, Brown's report states that Vera tried to steer the discourse with O'Keefe and Giles toward programs for mortgages for first time home buyers. Upon hearing O'Keefe and Giles' ruse about transporting underage Salvadoran prostitutes into California, Vera continued the discourse to gather details. He then signaled that he would call the couple in a few days as a means of dismissing them from the premises. Brown confirms that Vera immediately called the San Diego Police Department with the information he had gleaned. To reiterate, the only crime besides Veritas' covert recording resided in the flak-fevered imaginations of O'Keefe and Giles—and their hidden camera was of no use in capturing the "veritas" of Vera's thoughts during a stunt that pivoted on deception.

The unedited tapes also reveal that the ACORN staff with whom Veritas interacted were low-level employees (e.g., receptionist) and even friends of employees who were not identified as such. ACORN receptionist Tresa Kaelke seemed to be humoring O'Keefe and Giles over their sex work yarns, as she answered with her own outlandish tall-tale of having killed her husband (Office of the Attorney General 2010, 11–13). Like Vera, she was fired from her position as a result of contact with Veritas' flak stunt.

O'Keefe also employed image and voice-over to speciously frame encounters with ACORN as having occurred while he was costumed as an (over-the-top) 1970s-style pimp. The ghastly costume still features on Veritas' landing page as of August 2017. Nevertheless, O'Keefe actually wore a suit and tie to the ACORN offices and claimed to be a law student. The deception is worth noting for more than "academic" reasons or for its transgression against journalist ethics around accurate accounts of the context of reportage. Although Veritas self-nominates as "transcendent truth," even on the matter of what O'Keefe wore, subterfuge and manipulation were in play—with the further, implication for credulous viewers of the edited video that urbanites in 2009 would not be surprised to see someone in a caricatured Blaxploitation costume.

After trolling a modestly funded organization that served low income people, O'Keefe posited on the *Big Government* webpage that he had confronted a behemoth:

> ACORN has ascended. *They elect our politicians and receive billions* in tax money. Their world is a revolutionary, socialistic, atheistic world, where all means are justifiable. And

they create chaos, again, for it's [*sic*] own sake. (emphasis added, quoted in Office of the Attorney General 2010, 6)

Putting aside the other livid right-wing obsessions that O'Keefe channels—and the fact that ACORN offices O'Keefe visited manifestly did not resemble omnipotent command centers —ACORN's national operations received US$2.5 million from the federal government in the year prior to its dissolution (Office of the Attorney General 2010, 4). By straightforward arithmetic, 400 years of such funding would be necessary to reach first of the "billions" in funding asserted by O'Keefe.

Whatever "veritas" was conveyed in the ACORN stunt was almost inadvertent, but there are some truths it may be taken to reveal. In Brown's assessment, ACORN was not rigorous or well-trained—and many US citizens can certainly use more support than such an organization can muster. The contrast with the legal assistance that a wealthy client could commandeer for his or her problems is striking. Veritas' flak was directed at an organization that, however well-intentioned, had little chance of rebooting the situation of "have-nots," aside from the occasional triumph against the odds. In this view, Veritas' flak stunt was steeped in right-wing reaction; to harass the mere existence of even spotty efforts at empowerment for disadvantaged socioeconomic classes. Moreover, investigators with an authentic interest in staggering government waste could have examined the roughly contemporaneous frauds enacted in post-2003 Iraq invasion sub-contracting in which billions of dollars vanished (Chatterjee 2004; Taibbi 2007).

To this day, Issa's slurs against ACORN as "offering advice about the illegal smuggling of underage Salvadoran prostitutes" endures on his ".gov" web page (2009, 1); the same slurs for which O'Keefe and Giles settled with Vera out of court. Moreover, ACORN endures in the right-wing imagination as (*somehow*) supernaturally omnipotent from beyond its grave. For years after ACORN's demise, Republican legislators have insisted on including language about blocking funds to it in bills. Moreover, "Public Policy Polling found that nearly half of Republicans believed President Obama only won re-election because of ACORN's interference—although ACORN didn't exist at the time" of the 2012 election (Benen 2014, 1). Down to its postscripts, the campaign against ACORN presents a textbook case of flak.

Ballot Battleground

Following the contemporary right-wing obsession with (empirically negligible) "voter fraud," Veritas has taken up the issue. Results have been dire. In the appraisal of professor of election law Richard L. Hasen, "It seems like most of the fraud O'Keefe uncovers he commits himself"—and thus may illuminate no one's conduct but his own (quoted in Mayer 2016, 7). The boomerang stunts are due to Veritas' aggressive attempts to stage-manage "reality," while reality often resists the script forced upon it.

ACORN: The Reboot

Following earlier success in undermining ACORN, by 2014, Veritas pursued Battleground Texas, a group it dubbed "the new ACORN" (Project Veritas 2014b). Veritas' video asserted Battleground Texas employed an "illegal data collect" around its voter registration efforts. Along with trolling Battleground Texas, Veritas' video places Democrat Wendy

Davis' campaign for Texas governor within the frame of alleged electoral mischief. At the video's conclusion, O'Keefe ambles through what looks a simulation of a Manpower office, vowing to "get results." He also makes an appeal for funds, perhaps in an effort to suggest grassroots *bona fides* for the Westchester County, New York-based organization.

After Veritas published the seven-minute video on Battleground Texas, Republican officials cried foul. Texas Attorney General Greg Abbott recused himself from investigating since he was concurrently Davis' opponent for the Texas governor. The case was eventually placed in the hands of Special Prosecutors Christine Del Prado and John M. Economidy. In other words, despite crude production values (and an unlistenable, portentous quasi-rap beat in the opening minute), Veritas' video prompted serious judicial scrutiny. In turn, the peremptory conclusion of Del Prado and Economidy's review is that "the complaint [against Battleground Texas] be dismissed for insufficient evidence and failure to state an offense" (2014, 18).

While unpacking the content of the video, Del Prado and Economidy note Veritas' claims that Texas Election code forbids recording phone numbers off voter registration forms. The video also features footage of a Battleground Texas deputy registrar who explains that she copies down registrants' phone numbers in order to remind people whom she registered to vote on polling day. "The next scene," Del Prado and Economidy deadpan, "is unusual": "It purports to show a person from Battleground Texas calling a voter on behalf of (Texas gubernatorial candidate) Wendy Davis, whose photo is then displayed" for added emphasis. However, mismatches between Veritas' visuals and audio evoke (if unwittingly) surrealist stylistics that Luis Buñuel might admire: "while this caller is on screen, the screen also has a banner that suggests the caller is a 'PV [Project Veritas] investigator'. While the female depicted has a voice over indicating that she is making a call, the filmed caller's lips never move" (2014, 3). Veritas appears to be deliberately coy about staging the scene for the camera, *contra* journalistic ethics ("Clearly label illustrations and re-enactments" [Society of Professional Journalists 2014, 1]). In turn, Veritas' pastiche of visuals and audio may slide hazily into viewers' impressions as unstaged events.

Elsewhere in their review, Del Prado and Economidy suggest that footage passed off as on-site recording was actually staged. To wit, a presumptive voter registration form on a clipboard around which ostensible Texans congregate is obviously not the correct size. The special prosecutors also flag Veritas' voice-over claim that Davis' campaign is using embargoed voter data—"maybe even health data," a chilling assertion about invasive campaigning that the special prosecutors forcefully dismiss in their conclusion (2014, 4).

Following 16 pages of measured and meticulous prose, Del Prado and Economidy's conclusion is blistering:

> The Veritas video was little more than a canard and political disinformation. The video was particularly unprofessional when it suggested that the actions of Battleground Texas were advocated by a Texas gubernatorial candidate and that the actions of a single volunteer deputy registrar may even involve health data, which is not involved in the voter registration process.

That is, voter registration cards *do* include registrants' phone numbers. Moreover, specially deputized, voluntary election registrars (i.e., the woman featured in the video) are permitted to copy phone numbers, as it is not classified as confidential information within Texas election law, as its codes have been interpreted by state attorneys general on other occasions. By contrast, the official county registrar is *not* permitted to copy phone numbers for his or her purposes. Along with ignoring the clearly codified distinction between a deputy registrar and the county registrar, Veritas' wild contention that Davis' campaign (*somehow*) vacuumed up health data vibrates with black propaganda (Simpson 1994, 12–13) against the Democratic Party candidate.

Even as Veritas' claims were slapped down, the complaints against Battleground Texas were deemed serious enough that the Texas justice system empaneled special prosecutors. Indeed, Battleground Texas was "on trial" in the Del Prado and Economidy review, even as the special prosecutors' criticisms finally focused on the probity of Veritas. Sensational accusations with the apparent authenticity of videotape may, nevertheless, blast through the busy news agora to capture attention, or cascade into hype in internet echo chambers. By contrast, rigorous (and long-after-the-breaking-news) analysis of the claims does not readily lend itself to the same impact, since thoroughness is not as nimble as a matter of definition. Then again, the purpose of this cheap-shot grade of flak is not necessarily to secure prosecutions. Bruised reputations in the electoral arena will suffice, while cuing the political optics that suggest prosecutions are *always already* in motion against the center-left party.

It does not follow from Veritas' efforts to discover, contrive or entrap US election malfeasance that the health of the nation's electoral system is robust (Hasen 2012). As Rutgers University, political scientist Lorraine C. Minnite (n.d.) observes, "the use of baseless voter fraud allegations for partisan advantage has become the exclusive domain of Republican party activists," for whom a wider and more diverse electorate is disadvantageous (Minnite n.d., 17). In this vein, the Brennen Center for Justice at the New York University School of Law claims that, "fraud by voters at the polls is vanishingly rare" (2017, 1). The Center cites about two dozen rigorous investigations by government, academic and investigative journalist researchers in support of its claims. Typical findings: Justin Levitt (2014) identifies 31 credible (but not legally proven) instances of voter impersonation fraud in the United States from 2000 to 2014—or, about one case of impersonation *fraud for every 33 million votes cast*, across more than one billion ballots during the period of study. Despite the immense investment in locating voter fraud and the paucity of cases, the majority of US states have introduced voter identifications laws of varying strengths to deal with the phantom crime-wave (Hasen 2012, 41–73); a success in cultivating flak against voters less likely to have identification (students, elderly, poor people) in which Veritas has done its part.

Conclusion: What is to be Done?

As noted at the outset, an important stake in this investigation is to stimulate a critical literature on, as well as to present conceptualizations of, flak. Regardless of who sponsors or creates it, flak is junk discourse to be resisted. By contrast with ideologically-driven flak that "confirms" what is always already assumed about (for example) urban empowerment or voter registration, investigative journalism is for the people—and a discomfort (not a funded adjunct) to the writ of elite authority. And real investigation is skilled, difficult work—not an occasion for crude ax-grinding, or a peep-show melodrama contrived in the editing suite.

Along with confronting flak, the way forward toward better news to serve the community is decidedly not a return to journalism's status quo antebellum. That status quo featured news that, in Bennett's astute appraisal, was relatively strong on facts, but weak on truth (2001). Reinforcement of a complacent objectivity doctrine, and its valorization of "he said/she said" formal balance that skims across the surface of events, is inadequate in troubled times. Reinvigorated fact-checking of news, while desirable for obvious reasons, is not ambitious enough to turn the battleship around. To mint a homely analogy: cross-examining bad faith political discourses solely by fact-checking them is akin to pursuing financial fraudsters for parking tickets, even as the fraudsters hold the economy hostage. Moreover, a public informed by even well-intentioned news media with bullet-pointed concision is insufficient to the rigors of modern life that demand being educated and fluent on issues that reverberate at once locally and globally. In a milieu increasingly beholden to flak, the contemporary moment demands enthronement of news methods that unabashedly seek truth and fair-minded investigation of the myriad forms of power that condition our everyday lives. To confront the many laminae that constitute the truth is the goal—and not valorization of the rituals and techniques of objectivity for its own sake.

Media scholar James Curran (2007) provides a modest but constructive map toward how to better proceed. For Curran, mass media that is professional and structured as independent from state and commercial power, on one hand, constitutes the basic infrastructure for a commonly-held agenda to recruit well-briefed, deliberative citizens. At the same time, niche media can fill in the vital streams of formal and informal politics as they intersect with distinct interest groups (that may operate along generational, class, ethnic, regional, or gendered lines). In all cases, educating for empowerment is the objective—and not more merely "informing" audiences by flagging prominent events denuded of deep context. Flak campaigns may not become extinct in a media-saturated age, but they can be marginalized by thoughtful (and emotionally-literate) programming that answers to audience members' desire to grasp the implications of the world as it stands. In this view, more thoughtful programming that empowers citizens can stimulate demand for more—the "mere exposure effect" that social psychologist Robert B. Zajonc seminally investigated, in which what is familiar comes to be liked more (1965). In this view, the ratings crack of sensation is often preferred by audiences because that is what is regularly on offer.

While that may seem a simple approach to the formation of stronger political communities dedicated to common solutions, it presents a stark contrast with the current milieu of truncated news agendas, mediated echo chambers, and pervasive flak—up to and including glib or preemptive dismissal of ideologically incompatible reportage as "fake news." As Pedro-Carañana and Fenton (2016) remind us, a media-centric paradigm is not the alpha and omega of a program for pro-social interventions. Nevertheless, a substantial component of pro-social change implicates media—as a shaper of consciousness, as an elaborately illustrated textbook on how to be a sociopolitical subject, as a place where *what is imagined can start to be.*

ACKNOWLEDGEMENTS

A shout-out of thanks to Dale Fuchs for providing insight and additional sources. *Gracias mil* to John Nerone, Delia Dumitrica, Anne Dewey, Jack Bratich and Murphy Barney for furnishing generous comments and trenchant guidance.

DISCLOSURE STATEMENT

No potential conflict of interest was reported by the author.

NOTE

1. Minnite (n.d., p.6) explains that, "The Justice Department defines election fraud as 'conduct that corrupts the process by which ballots are obtained, marked, or tabulated; the process by which election results are canvassed and certified; or the process by which voters are registered'." By contrast, "Voter fraud is a subcategory of election fraud, or the intentional corruption of the electoral process by voters" that mainly implicates casting a ballot when not eligible to do so. Later, I will focus on the almost non-existent level of voter fraud, but the evidence shows that all forms of electoral fraud are exceedingly rare in the United States.

REFERENCES

Bagdikian, Ben H. 1992. *The Media Monopoly*. 4th ed. Boston: Beacon Press.

Baker, Scott. 2011. "Does Raw Video of NPR Expose Reveal Questionable Editing and Tactics?" *The Blaze*, March 10. http://www.theblaze.com/news/2011/03/10/does-raw-video-of-npr-expose-reveal-questionable-editing-tactics/.

Benen, Steve. 2014. "Congress Finally Declares Victory over ACORN". *MSNBC*, August 8. http://www.msnbc.com/rachel-maddow-show/congress-finally-declares-victory-over-acorn.

Bennett, W. Lance. 2001. *New: The Politics of Illusion*. 4th ed. New York: Addison Wesley Longman.

Brennen Center for Justice. 2017. "Debunking the Voter Fraud Myth", January 31. http://www.brennancenter.org/analysis/debunking-voter-fraud-myth.

Chatterjee, Pratap. 2004. *Iraq, Inc*. New York: Seven Stories Press.

Conason, Joe, and Gene Lyons. 2000. *The Hunting of the President*. New York: Saint Martin's Press.

Curran, James. 2007. "Rethinking Media and Democracy." In *The Political Communication Reader*, edited by Ralph Negrine and James Stanyer, 27–31. London: Routledge.

Davies, Nick. 2009. *Flat Earth News*. London: Vintage.

Del Prado, Christine, and John M. Economidy. 2014. Review of Compliant on Using Voter Registration Information, No.2014-W-0128, Bexar County, Texas. http://www.scribd.com/document/216868925/Special-prosecutors-review-of-complaints-in-Texas-v-Battleground-Texas#fullscreen&from_embed.

Folkenflik, David. 2011. "Elements of NPR Gotcha Video Taken Out of Context". *National Public Radio*, March 14. http://www.npr.org/2011/03/14/134525412/Segments-Of-NPR-Gotcha-Video-Taken-Out-Of-Context.

Franklin, Bob. 2004. *Packaging Politics*. London: Hodder Arnold.

Gans, Herbert J. 2004. *Deciding What's News*. Evanston: Northwestern University Press. First published 1979.

Goss, Brian Michael. 2009. "'The Left-Media's Stranglehold': Flak and Accuracy in Media Reports 2007-08)." *Journalism Studies* 10 (4): 455–473.

Goss, Brian Michael. 2013. *Rebooting the Herman and Chomsky Propaganda Model in the Twenty First Century*. New York: Peter Lang.

Greider, William. 1992. *Who Will Tell the People*. New York: Simon & Schuster.

Hasen, Richard L. 2012. *The Voting Wars*. New Haven: Yale University Press.

Herman, Edward S, and Noam Chomsky. 1988. *Manufacturing Consent*. New York: Pantheon.

Issa, Darrel. 2009. "Acorn, Lies and Videotape." Darrell Issa Congressman: In the News. September 25. https://issa.house.gov/op-eds/2009/09/25/acorn-lies-and-videotape.

Kroll, Andy. 2014. "Colorado Dems: We Caught James O'Keefe and His Friends Trying to Bait Us into Approving Voter Fraud". *Mother Jones*, October 20. http://www.motherjones.com/politics/2014/10/colorado-dems-james-okeefe.

Levitt, Justin. 2014. "A Comprehensive Investigation of Voter Impersonation Finds 31 Credible Incidents out of one Billion Ballots Cast". *Washington Post*, August 6. http://www.washingtonpost.com/news/wonk/wp/2014/08/06/a-comprehensive-investigation-of-voter-impersonation-finds-31-credible-incidents-out-of-one-billion-ballots-cast/?utm_term=.5c5969ee3629.

Marx, Greg. 2010. "The Ethics of Undercover Journalism". *Columbia Journalism Review*, February 4. Accessed August 24: http://sites.dlib.nyu.edu/undercover/sites/dlib.nyu.edu.undercover/files/documents/uploads/editors/The%20Ethics%20of%20Undercover%20Journalism%20_%20Columbia%20Journalism%20Review.pdf.

Mayer, Jane. 2016. "James O'Keefe Accidently Stings Himself". *New Yorker*, May 30. http://www.newyorker.com/magazine/2016/05/30/james-okeefe-accidentally-stings-himself.

Media Matters. 2016. "James O'Keefe's October Surprise Shows He's Still a Hack, Not a Journalist". October 12. http://www.mediamatters.org/research/2016/10/12/james-okeefes-anti-clinton-october-surprise-shows-hes-still-hack-not-journalist/213783.

Minnite, Lorraine C. n.d. *The Politics of Voter Fraud*. Washington, DC: Project Vote.

Office of the Attorney General. 2010. *Report of the Attorney General on the Activities of ACORN in California*. Sacramento: California Department of Justice.

O'keefe, James. 2016. "The Mainstream Media Is Dead: We Won". *FrontPage Mag*, December 6. http://www.frontpagemag.com/fpm/265043/james-okeefe-mainstream-media-dead-we-won-frontpagemagcom.

Pedro-Carañana, Joan, and Natalie Fenton. 2016. "A Conversation with Natalie Fenton." In *Talking Back to Globalization: Texts & Performances*, edited by Brian Michael Goss, Mary Rachel Gould and Joan Pedro-Carañana, 5–20. New York: Peter Lang.

Project Veritas. 2008. "Non-Gay Men with Girlfriends get Married to Each Other". *YouTube*, November 16. http://www.youtube.com/watch?v=Ruh3TZvdkQ0.

Project Veritas. 2011. "To Catch a Journalist: *New York Times*, Clay Shirky, Jay Rosen". *YouTube*, October 31. http://www.youtube.com/watch?v=qBFOmUXR080.

Project Veritas. 2014a. "James O'Keefe as Osama bin Laden crosses border from Mexico to US". *YouTube*, August 11. http://www.youtube.com/watch?v=fB37TCDcZBg.

Project Veritas. 2014b. "Battleground Texas Illegally Copying Voter Data" *YouTube*, February 19. http://www.youtube.com/watch?v=gXKwQI_0kDI.

Project Veritas. 2015a. "Hidden Camera Captures Officials Shredding Constitution at Vassar College as it 'Triggers' Students". *YouTube*, November 3. http://www.youtube.com/watch?v=3PZAzLTQIX8.

Project Veritas. 2015b. "Hidden Cam: Hillary's National Marketing Director Illegally Accepting Foreign Contribution". *YouTube*, September 1. http://www.youtube.com/watch?v=-qxF7Z2N7Y4.

Robin, Corey. 2011. *The Reactionary Mind*. New York: Oxford University Press.

Said, Edward. 1997. *Covering Islam*. 2nd ed. New York: Vintage Books.

Simpson, Christopher. 1994. *The Science of Coercion*. New York: Oxford University Press.

Smith, Allan. 2016. "Experts: Actions of Democratic Operatives in Latest Undercover James O'Keefe Video Likely Not Violation of Law". *Business Insider*, 25 October. http://nordic.businessinsider.com/james-okeefe-project-veritas-hillary-clinton-donald-duck-2016-10/.

Society of Professional Journalists. 2014. "SPJ Code of Ethics". http://www.spj.org/ethicscode.asp.

State of California Department of Justice. 2010. "Brown Releases Report Detailing a Litany of Problems with ACORN, But No Criminality", April 1. https://oag.ca.gov/news/press-releases/brown-releases-report-detailing-litany-problems-acorn-no-criminality.

Stauber, John, and Sheldon Rampton. 2001. *Trust Us, We're Experts!*. New York: Penguin Putnam, Inc.

Taibbi, Matt. 2007. "The Great Iraq Swindle". *CorpWatch*, August 23. http://www.corpwatch.org/article.php?id=14686.

Thompson, John B. 2000. *Political Scandal*. Cambridge, UK: Polity Press.

Zajonc, Robert B. 1965. *The Attitudinal Effects of Mere Exposure*. Ann Arbor: Institute for Social Research / University of Michigan.

RE-THINKING TRUST IN THE NEWS

A material approach through "Objects of Journalism"

Nikki Usher

This article argues that trust in journalism is a critical mechanism in social cohesion. However, trust research in journalism has a critical flaw, since trust is measured as news consumption, while journalists' roles are considered via questions of authority. However, scholars have thought about trust in limited ways that have failed to address the relational nature of trust that includes journalists, audiences, sources, and other social actors such "objects of journalism." The material turn in journalism is invoked as a way to move beyond this dichotomy. Via hard and soft objects of journalism, discussed here as news buildings, "raw materials" of journalism, and digital news products like software inspire new ways of thinking about trust.

Introduction

"Trust" in the news media is under assault. In the US context, troubles have been brewing since the 1970s and accelerated in the 1990s, but the election of President Trump revealed the alarming consequences of the problem. A 2016 Gallup poll conducted before the US election showed that under a third of Americans (32 percent) had a "great deal" or "fair amount" of trust in the media, while only 14 percent of Republicans said they trusted the media—which Gallup notes is "easily the lowest confidence among Republicans in 20 years" (Swift 2016).

Trust in all institutions is at an all-time low for many structural reasons (Malone 2016), but the situation facing mainstream journalism is especially concerning. Trust is a problem elsewhere in many Western democracies that have had stable press institutions, as seen in a 36-countrywide survey from the Reuters Institute for the Study of Journalism (2017). In the United States, the situation is particularly critical, especially given recent attacks on the news media by the President of the United States and other Republicans, the "fake news" moral panic, and deep political polarization. While "make people trust journalism again" is as falsely nostalgic as "make America great again," wherever the equilibrium point between healthy skepticism and blind faith may be, trust in news still matters. If less than a third of Americans trust the news, we are in a crisis of journalism, notwithstanding any talk of economic issues facing the news industry.

This article argues that the current state of scholarship around trust in journalism is also broken. To improve our inquiry into trust, the article posits a different way for studying trust in journalism through research into the "objects of journalism." Through the lens of materiality, scholars, journalists, and news consumers alike can broaden the discussion about trust in journalism beyond just the content of the news and questions about medium preference. Through the "form, durability and matters of concern" of objects of journalism (De Maeyer 2016, 472), we can consider materiality may or may not inspire trust in news. As a starting point for inquiry, I suggest three types of objects of journalism: news buildings, the "raw materials" of news, and news products. This article most specifically considers objects of journalism with newspapers in mind, in part because questions of journalistic authority are often taken up with newspapers as the "idealized" form of news (Carlson 2017, 81; Meltzer 2009), and in part because local metropolitan newspapers are under the most severe pressure to survive.

While rooted in an American-centric context, the lines of inquiry posed nonetheless have cross-media and cross-cultural relevance and are inspired by global research. First, I establish why trust matters in journalism. I note existing problems with trust in journalism studies; trust, often thought of as media credibility, is an "audience" issue, while journalistic authority (related to trust but not the same) is a news production issue. I then make the case for using the "material turn" in journalism (Anderson and De Maeyer 2015; Boczkowski 2015) as an alternative direction for analysis of trust in journalism.

Why Trust in Journalism Matters

Blind faith in journalism as truth is not a desirable outcome for a democratic society and has been the aspiration of autocrats throughout modern history. Nonetheless, trust in news is still important for overall social cohesion; issues of political economy and hegemony aside, a sharply divided, sharply polarized United States has made for a toxic environment for civil discourse that coincides with and contributes to a lack of trust in mainstream news. The fragmentation and blurring of journalism's boundaries may be partially to blame (Carlson and Lewis 2015), as well as the impact of the economic challenges and the pressures on journalists in a 24/7 news environment (Usher 2014a).

If news consumers don't trust professional journalism, journalists can't properly act as watchdogs or as conveners of shared experiences (Carey 1992; Schudson 2000). Trust in journalism is a critical element of social cohesion: trust enables news media to set the public agenda (Wanta and Hu 1994), influences media effects (Tsfati 2003), and is ultimately the factor that links journalists and audiences together (Ganziano 1988). As Tsfati and Cappella (2003) note, "trust plays a part in almost every human interaction" (505). The outcomes of lack in trust in journalism are concerning: greater media cynicism and media skepticism have been shown to lead consumption of non-mainstream sources and to undermine journalists' efforts at public service (Cappella and Jamieson 1997; Tsfati and Cappella 2003;), and has been linked to the partisan divides reflected in opinion polling. But trust is risky: to trust someone or something is an inherently unequal relationship, and one must make a bet that someone else or something can be relied upon (Rotter 1967). Trust relies on the journalist having something (e.g. information) other people don't, and on news consumers depending on these journalists to help them in some way through this exchange.

Authority, however, at least as it is imagined in the context of journalism studies, is a claim to "legitimate authority," whereby "compliance is voluntary and based on a belief in the right of the authority to demand compliance" (Turner 2007). The difference between trust and authority is important: trust is at its core about belief, while authority is ultimately about the power to compel belief (Cook 2007; Fukuyama 1995). Scholars operationalize the instability of professional journalism as "journalistic authority," or the "right to be listened to" Carlson (2017). The role of trust in journalistic authority, though, has been dismissed as overly simplistic. As Carlson writes, "authority seems to have an intuitive meaning as some form of trust or credibility to be possessed, coveted or lost," and argues while this may be a familiar way people thinking about journalistic authority, equating trust and authority "doesn't explain much about journalism" (3). However, authority is not trust; the "right to be listened to" is a claim to the ability to have one's voice heard; trust does not necessarily follow from being heard.

Without getting too deep into political sociology or even philosophy, this difference between trust and authority does matter. Both are relational, in fact, trust is often described in these terms. As Cook (2007) explains:

> ... trustor A trusts actor B with respect to some particular matter(s) x, y ... z when A believes that her interests are included in B's utility function, so that B values what A desires primarily because B wants to maintain a good relationship with A ...

though it is also operationalized more generally as "the belief that the trustee will not take advantage of a truster's vulnerability." Trust is a process, it is relational, but it is also limited. In an excellent literature review on trust as it relates to journalism, Blöbaum (2014) writes:

> Whenever there exists a potential lack of information in a certain situation someone has to take a risk. As no one has total information and everything could be contingent there is frequently a need for trust. In this respect, the importance of trust in journalism becomes obvious. (14)

Trust is not just centered in people, of course, and must be considered on a structural level —across institutions, organizations, and even modes of knowledge production.

Trust and authority are very difficult concepts to differentiate and have merited rich consideration from journalism studies. Both put professional journalists in the position of power. But audience trust—perhaps best operationalized as a second-order belief that journalists are acting in their best interests—is different from journalists claiming legitimate social knowledge. A key difficulty with trying to reconcile this literature is that the idea of "audience" is now fragmented. As one way to close this gap, I suggest uniting producers and consumers of news through a dimension of trust that has not so far been considered: the materiality of journalism as instantiated through objects of journalism.

Trust and Authority Research in Journalism

Two big moments seem to have generated most of the research on trust: the rise of broadcast and the rise of news consumption on the Web. The research on "media credibility," as it is often operationalized, begins with post-war consumption research. Hovland, Lumsdaine, and Sheffield (1949) were interested in what might impact source credibility, and considered the impact of trustworthiness (defined as impartiality) and perceptions of expertise across individuals, groups, or organizations (see also Kiousis 2001). Research on "medium credibility" (the channel which delivers the content) can be traced to 1959, when Burns W. Roper, on behalf of the "Television Information Office," began asking about the relative credibility of radio, TV, and newspapers (Roper Organization 1989). Other research comparing all three mediums or broadcast and newspapers followed (see for example: Abel and Wirth 1977; Jacobson 1969; Lee 1978; Liebeskind 1997; Meyer

1974; Newhagen and Nass 1989). General findings suggested that over time, "seeing is believing," with audiences more often than not finding television more credible than newspapers (Gaziano and McGrath 1986). There is one consistent flaw across existing research on credibility: the failure to distinguish between local and national media, meaning we have little sense about how what happens in national media and national politics implicates relationships on the local level.

More recent work has focused on whether the Web is a credible source of information, though some findings seem out of step with today's highly partisan and social media-infused information environment. For example, Flanagin and Metzger (2000), Metzger et al. (2003), and Johnson and Kaye (1998, 2004) looked at whether the pre-Web 2.0 internet or traditional media sources were more credible; Johnson and Kaye (1998) found that across all groups, campaign literature was the least credible source of information. Today, some polling indicates that the public may trust Trump more than mainstream news media.[1] Similarly, their 2004 study suggested that news consumers viewed "weblogs" as less fair but more comprehensive, whereas many Republican Party (GOP) partisans today ignore mainstream sources in favor of highly partisan internet ones. These articles appear especially dated with titles and introductions that wonder about the power of "this new information age" and "weblogs" (see also Kiousis 2001). Nonetheless, this credibility work hints at the role the materiality of news might play in negotiating trust.

All too often the research has not been particularly clear on what's being assessed. There's significant debate in the research stretching back to the 1960s about what factors should account for measuring media credibility (Westley and Severin 1964)—not just as general concepts but as elements of a scale. Shaw's (1973) "Media Credibility: Taking a Measure of a Measure" or West's (1994) "Validating a Scale for the Measurement of Media Credibility: A Covariance Structure Modeling Approach" reflect this tone of preoccupation with measurement. As scales got validated, invalidated, and revalidated, understanding media credibility itself was obscured. Meyer (1988) offers some indicators that appear across most of these scales: credibility as trust, evaluation of the fairness of a story, completeness, accuracy, and bias and defines them by their own definitions (accurate "is accurate," 161). Findings likely don't reflect the contemporary news environment: for example, one study suggested those in urban areas trusted newspapers more but those of higher educational achievement were less trusting (Newhagen and Nass 1989), while another suggested that despite demographic and political differences, the public could be treated as a single group (Ganziano 1988).

An important development has been to use the word "trust" instead of credibility, more appropriate given the framing of the questions asked by polling organizations and the crisis at hand. Trust reflects a second-order concept as opposed to the narrower "media credibility" and establishes trust in journalism as a critical element of social order (Kohring and Matthes 2007; Tsfati and Cappella 2003, 2005). Such work has focused on public perceptions of media fairness (Bennett et al. 2001), the influence of trust in the news media and its ability to affect agenda setting (Kiousis 2001), the rise of media cynicism (Capella and Jamieson 1997), and the impact of media skepticism (Tsfati and Cappella 2003, 2005). Definitional issues nonetheless emerge: Kohring and Matthes (2007) break their categories into "trust in the selectivity of facts," "trust in the accuracy of depictions," "trust in the selectivity of topics," and "trust in journalistic assessment," though these categories seem to overlap and there have not been sufficient tests of these measures' replicability.

The relationship between fragmented publics and trust is a critical direction for future research, with Ladd's (2011) seminal work setting an agenda for future research. As a whole, trust research is focused on consumer preferences, remains for the most part a relic of the broadcast and early web era, and has definitional issues.

On the other hand, production-focused studies on journalistic authority tell us about problems with journalistic role performance rather than audience issues with trust. Research on journalistic authority examines the decentering of professional journalists from their singular role as claiming to be truth tellers, watchdogs, and the voice of the public. Trust is assumed to be an ancillary byproduct. Carlson (2017) argues journalists' power to "create legitimate discursive knowledge about events in the world for others" (13) comes from a "contingent relationship" (13) among a variety of actors, from sources to audiences to critics to journalists themselves. Journalistic authority emerges out of practice and habit and it is deeply contextual, depending on cultural, social, political, economic, and technological conditions.

What gives journalists a claim that what they do is special springs from the idea that professions possess autonomy and authority because they have a particular jurisdiction over knowledge (Abbott 1988/2014). Journalism is a specific form of knowledge production that has as its endpoint a "truthful account" of the world (Schudson and Anderson 2009, 89). Journalists assert dominance over other potential providers of this truthful accounting—other institutions, like political and religious institutions, individual sources, and audiences, to name a few. Moreover, journalists act as brokers between experts and the public, making expert knowledge knowable for their audiences while not necessarily having those expertise themselves—what Reich (2012) calls "bipolar interactional expertise."

There is ample empirical research on the contested nature of journalistic authority via social media (Belair-Gagnon 2015); the rise of citizen journalism (Örnebring 2013), on time pressure and journalism (Usher 2017); via new business models (Konieczna and Robinson 2014), economic pressures (Sjøvaag 2014), and beyond. But journalists' claim to provide trustworthy accounting of events in the world better than anyone else also has to be considered from the perspective of whether anyone actually trusts them. Understanding news consumer trust has focused too much on content or distribution platforms. The objects of news have not been taken into account: whether the newspaper reaches the door step, whether there's a physical place to go to complain, whether a mobile app works or not, whether interview transcripts or documents are made available to news consumers—the "hard" and "soft" things of news.

Materialism and Trust

Materialism is a way to think about objects as co-produced and indeterminate; the objects themselves have agency, as do people that incorporate these objects into their lives. Objects of journalism (Anderson and De Maeyer 2015) are sites of contest where what can and should be trusted is negotiated by consumers, journalists, and others. Looking to these objects of journalism, in turn, can "provide us with a nuanced understanding of power as it manifests in society," as Anderson and De Maeyer (4) suggest. Operationalizing objects of journalism as objects of trust makes sense. For news consumers, trust requires believing in these objects of news. The relational nature of objects refracts the relational nature of trust. If these objects of journalism are problematic, then Tsfati and Cappella's (2005) argument follows: the side being trusted (the journalists) has violated the side that has placed trust in them (the audiences) and acted contrary to the expectations of the others. What news consumers think about the objects of news compared to how journalists think about them matters; these objects have a social history and context (Boczkowski 2015). If these objects of journalism can be trusted, they should do something news consumers could not do on their own, such as providing them with orientation to their social environment and negotiating expectations for other social actors (Kohring and Matthes 2007).

The three types of objects I propose here as sites of contestation over trust represent what Schudson (2015) calls "hard things" and "soft things": news buildings, the "raw materials" of news, and digital news products. Some of these objects have indeed been studied before, often through the science and technology studies (STS) approach to materialism (see for example Annany and Crawford 2015; Lewis and Usher 2016), but my intention is to show through these specific cases how materialism enables scholars to overcome thinking about trust in isolation, allowing them to think about trust as relational, uniting journalists, news consumers, and other actors through a single starting point. News buildings are objects in the real world—something that can be felt, touched, seen, and visibly destroyed. The "raw materials of news" may exist physically or digitally, but they are often rendered in digital forms to reach audiences. News software is "built" and often thought of as a "tool," (Usher 2016), its materiality rendered through "traces of association" (Plesner 2009) formed by digital bits.

STS's application to journalism through a material turn forces scholars away from techno-determinism by acknowledging that objects have their own agency and contested associations. This focus on materialism makes sense for understanding journalism in transition regardless of whether an STS approach is used or not. Latour (1990) suggests that "whenever we discover a stable social relation, it is the introduction of non-humans that accounts for this relative durability" (111), but also notes that when objects stop being taken for granted, then it's time to start paying attention to them. As historical research suggests (Keith 2015; Le Cam 2015), the objects for journalism have rarely been taken for granted, and they reflect the unstable social relations between journalists, news consumers and other actors. Though Boczkowski (2015) hopes that this "material turn" will help orient journalism studies away from the newsroom, so far, much of the focus has been on journalists' co-production of technology inside newsrooms. A focus on objects of journalism and their role in producing audiences' trust (as well as trust in other social actors) may provide another way out of the newsroom.

Hard Things: Buildings as Physical Manifestations of Trust

The intangibles of trust may have little to do with the perceived quality of news itself and rather may be arguments of the "things" of news themselves—how the materiality of news manifests in people's lives as they go about the world. Thus, scholars and journalists would do well to consider how the "stuff" or "things" or "places" that journalists inhabit or make (or don't) also have communicative properties that can enhance or dismantle perceptions of trust. Wallace's (2005, 2012) historical work underscores this point, showing how the architecture of news buildings was an argument about why newspapers should be trusted. The raw materials chosen to build them, their heights, their location, their design, and their technologies communicated a publisher's vision of his newspapers' role in a city to his readers. News buildings were part of the rituals of people's lives and brought people together for shared experiences—places for viewing New Years' Eve fireworks, watching news tickers during major events, and following distant baseball games through box scores on the buildings.

Whether communities know it or not, many newspapers buildings have (or had) nicknames that speak to their sense of how their architecture was intended to communicate a particular message to communities. *The Dallas Morning News'* building is nicknamed "The Rock of Truth." *The Philadelphia Inquirer's* old building was called the "Tower of Truth." Both *The New York Daily News'* old building and *The Des Moines Register*'s were called "The Daily Planet," a reference that recalls Superman as journalist. Where these newsrooms were located mattered too—often within blocks of major civic institutions like city hall, courts, police headquarters, and arts and entertainment destinations such as theaters or stadiums. The rationale for proximity had more to do with than just newswork; the centrality and visibility of these newsrooms were signs that newspapers were institutions that mattered (Usher 2015). They were often built with the intention of making a mark on a city's skyline—and even today, while newspapers often have tenants filling many of the floors of their building, their names can be seen from vantage points around the city. *The Fort Worth Star Telegram's* news operation occupies only four floors of its new building, but its banner is on the building and it has chosen to remain downtown so as to be visible to the city—a point emphasized by its editor (Usher 2014b).

Today, these buildings are no longer taken for granted and in fact, their instability may also undermine the stability of social relations among audiences, journalists, sources, and other social actors. Across the United States, United Kingdom, Scandinavia, and elsewhere, newspaper offices are shutting down and/or relocating. The disappearance of these buildings are contemporary signs of newspapers' disintegration in the lives of the communities they cover (Usher 2014, 2015). On YouTube, one can find multiple videos of newspaper buildings like *The Wichita Eagle* being destroyed by wrecking balls. The destruction of *The Miami Herald's* news building got Hollywood treatment; it was blown up on TV's Burn Notice. As newspapers move into transit centers above restaurants (*The Plain Dealer*-Cleveland) or non-descript skyways, as their old buildings become condos (such as in Des Moines, Philadelphia, and Los Angeles), and as some abandon their downtowns (as in Miami and Denver), news buildings become less visible from public life. How newsrooms moving to new newsrooms undermines trust in news institutions may matter in ways that are simply not being captured by current assessments of audience trust in news or journalists' role in building trust.

These news buildings are material manifestations of the role that journalists play in a community—aspects of newswork and journalistic cultural identity that move beyond content. Newspaper buildings are ways that journalists have historically made an argument to be trusted and established the right to be listened to. These arguments have been substantially weakened as these material reminders have disappeared. When newspapers disappear from sight or abandon their downtowns, it's a powerful argument that suggests the institutions are significantly weakened and are even removed from the cities that they cover. "Have you visited your local newspaper?" "Do you know where your local newspaper/TV station/etc., is located?" are not often questions asked (and perhaps have never been asked) in any academic studies or other surveys on media credibility, though research on audience engagement has considered the importance of thinking about some of these factors.

Buildings and other physical dimensions of news deserve further consideration as a way to get at the relational nature of trust. Other signs of material presence and absence in communities, like newspaper boxes, newspapers' presence at community events, branding at baseball stadiums, sponsorships on T-shirts for local athletic teams, ads in programs for charity events, and even the existence of print newspapers have not yet been quantified by existing discussions of trust and authority. Even the physical presence or absence of actual journalists in a town or a community, where people no longer "know" journalists or see them as community members, has been hypothesized to be undermining trust in news (Benton 2017). The physical infrastructure that limits or enhances news distribution deserves attention—the absence or presence of broadband technology, mobile satellites, and media hubs for digital provide other entry points for inquiry (Braun 2015a; Hemmingway 2008). An objects of journalism approach to trust that takes into account the places of news and the physical presence/absence of news as "hard thing" experienced by a network of actors beyond journalists.

Soft Things: "Raw Materials" of News

The call for transparency in journalism recognizes that journalism is indeed a "thing" created via social practices. Journalism is constructed knowledge (Schudson 2003), made through decisions about what to include and exclude from the raw materials of news. Revealing what these raw materials of journalism are—interviews, b-roll, documents, data, even code—reflects what Gitelman (2014) calls "knowing-showing." Gitleman makes the argument that what documents people get to see and what documents are created "can never be disentangled from power, or, more properly, control" (5). Making "known" the objects used to create news, or more simply put, when journalists show their work and how they do it, people have a better sense of why the news work has been constructed in a certain way.

As Schudson (2015) notes, an interview may be thought of as "thingy," noting, "it is a social thing—with certain practices and conventions a reporter employs when doing an interview with a public official or a bystander at a fire or a wounded victim at a crime scene" but it is also a "news format." Though perhaps less "thingy than others," thinking about news as objects means understanding how these interviews, documents, data, photos, b-roll, code, and beyond are indeed socially-produced "things" of news, co-created by journalists and sources but also things that exist on their own terms.

In fact, these raw materials of news have a certain elemental structure. "Structured journalism," a close relative of data journalism, reflects the extent to which news has fundamental ordering that may be thought of as "meta data" of news. Quotes, ledes, headlines, actors in stories, tweets and other images and texts integrated into a story are some aspects of the "metadata" of journalism that may be reshaped and even excerpted from their original form. Graves (2015) shows the endpoint of thinking about the raw materials of journalism, whereby annotative journalism builds on existing news articles and published documents to reach conclusions that may be contrary to what has been taken as established fact.

Some scholars have suggested that making these "raw materials" and the "metadata" of journalism available to audiences is one way to make journalism knowable. Academics have advocated bringing the best of open source values to journalism, noting that open source provides a level of "showing work" that might give audiences a better sense of how journalists do their jobs (Lewis and Usher 2013; Usher 2016). A variety of news startups have thought about journalism as "metadata," such as Circa and Buzzfeed, but so far, this approach remains visible only on the back-end via content management systems. The rise of programing in journalism has led some to conclude that providing raw data and other source material gives people the capacities to create narratives that are personalized and meaningful (or "see it yourself journalism") (Usher 2016). Crowdsourced reporting offers ability to involve audiences in processing this "raw material" and turning it into stories. Post-election, some industry thinkers renewed the call that journalists could do well to make a case for their trust by doing a better job of showing the raw elements of their reporting, such as sharing interview transcripts or reporting methods (Rosenstiel 2016).

However, more access to the "meta data" of journalism might be harmful. Being able to understand how news is made might well reveal something that journalists don't like to acknowledge or provide further ammunition to those who already distrust news. In particular, revealing how the sausage is made—what gets left in and what gets left out—may in fact underscore how the "relational" dance of authority does not treat all members of a news ecosystem with equal weight. Nonetheless, a look inside at these raw materials offers the potential to think about trust in a different way.

Objects of Journalism: The "Products" of News

Other "soft things" include digital news products as objects of journalism are also sites where power is negotiated among the actors that use them, the actors that make them, and by the objects themselves, and in turn, invoke different claims about trust. As Domingo (2015) notes, the decisions about how news technologies are designed and then adopted reflect "the contingent nature of news practices and journalism as an institution" (72). News products can be front-end (an iPad app, interactives, news alerts, websites, chatbots, fact-checks, or even examples of automated journalism), back-end (such as content management systems or internal databases, among others, that facilitate news production before audiences ever see the content), or both. They are sometimes designed by journalists, but in other cases are platforms that host news. Facebook, of course, blurs the definitions of journalist and audience, muddies the distribution channel for news and information, and thanks to "viral fake news," is perhaps emblematic of the way that battles over trust in journalism that can occur through and on software.

The materiality ascribed to these software products reflects how they still bear a fundamental physicality. The programmer journalists who make some of these news products talk about their work as "building" and sometimes describe what they do as "making tools" (Usher 2016). Moreover, these products are meant to be used—clicked on, scrolled on, chatted with, read, watched or otherwise consumed by audiences. Their materiality may be a "string of bits" (Buckland 1997) or "traces of association" (Plesner 2009). As De Maeyer (2016) notes, "far from being seamless and immaterial, digital 'stuff' seems to make a difference in newsmaking" (461). However, the focus is still inside the newsroom, not how those tools are experienced by news consumers. Consider *The Wall Street Journal's* "Blue Feed: Red Feed" interactive, which had a fantastic trust-building opportunity that showed users the tension between Facebook's algorithm and their choices about news. However, metajournalistic discourse about the tool focused on what the goals of the producers were behind the app, not how users experienced it (Bilton 2016).

From a production perspective, news products might be the best-researched aspect of digital materialism in journalism. There is scholarship on content management systems (Anderson and Kreiss 2013; Braun 2015b; Rodgers 2015); apps (Ananny and Crawford 2015); wiki-creation and hyperlinks (Ford 2015), and on thinking about news production and innovation as networked processes (Schmitz Weiss and Domingo 2010). This is a valuable step forward, but the point of inquiry still privileges the relationship between journalist (or journalist/technologist) and object, ignoring the relationship between objects and other social actors. From Google AMP and Facebook Instant Articles to the display of news on wearables, new objects of journalism present themselves to be trusted. These products are created with specific designs that make an argument about why journalism should be trusted; they enhance and limit the ability of journalists to do their work and also impact the ways that audiences and other actors access and engage with news.

Conclusion: Where Next?

A material turn in journalism studies provides a different way to think about trust. In fact, Domingo (2015) argues that this material turn may actually fulfill researchers' moral commitments to make the world a better place. Through showing journalists how they are responsible for their work, Domingo argues scholars enable journalists "to fight for a change in whatever they do not feel comfortable with" and to collaborate with researchers to "explore the alternatives" (72). Materiality is another way to understand why journalists do what they do and to a lesser extent, how the news industry is changing (Neff 2015), but materiality has so far been not been connected to thinking about trust. Despite aspirations to de-center the place of the newsroom and journalists in scholarship, research on materiality in news still has little to do with audiences, sources, or other institutions. Because trust is relational and conditional, materialism becomes a useful way to illuminate the differential power of objects of news, journalists, audiences, and these other actors who trust and who are trusted.

Thus far, I have argued that three types of objects of journalism merit additional consideration as objects that can communicate trust and be trusted: the "hard thinginess" of actual objects in the real world—like news buildings— and the "soft thinginess" of the raw materials of journalism and digital news products. A material approach to questions about trust in news suggests that the places where news is made, the ways that news is made, and the products and infrastructures of journalism matter to how trust is negotiated by journalists, audiences, sources, and other social actors.

The way that journalism's thinginess implicates questions of trust also helps move concerns about trust beyond thinking about journalism as knowledge construction and information provision. Perhaps we need to start thinking about how objects of journalism may also be a form of ritual communication that Carey (1992) argued was so critical to understanding technology. The objects of journalism can contribute to the ordering of time and space and the construction of shared meaning, which is at the core of ritual communication, but to do so depends on a constellation of trust among social actors. A more fruitful relationship between trustee and trustor may be established via the objects of journalism and might well facilitate the continuity and cultural cohesion that is so very needed at the current moment. "Make people trust journalism again" may well be nostalgia for a time that never was, but locating objects of journalism as arguments for trust and sites of relational negotiation about trust reminds us that journalism is a thing that is constructed and contingent.

DISCLOSURE STATEMENT

No potential conflict of interest was reported by the author.

NOTE

1. http://nypost.com/2017/04/28/more-voters-trust-trump-than-the-political-media-poll/

REFERENCES

Abbott, Andew. [1988] 2014. *The System of Professions: An Essay on the Division of Expert Labor*. Chicago: University of Chicago Press.

Abel, John D., and Michael O. Wirth. 1977. "Newspaper vs. TV Credibility for Local News." *Journalism Quarterly* 54: 371–375.

Ananny, Mike, and Kate Crawford. 2015. "A Liminal Press: Situating News App Designers Within A Field of Networked News Production." *Digital Journalism* 3 (2): 192–208.

Anderson, C. W., and Daniel Kreiss. 2013. "Black Boxes as Capacities for and Constraints on Action: Electoral Politics, Journalism, and Devices of Representation." *Qualitative Sociology* 36 (4): 365–382.

Anderson, C. W., and Juliette De Maeyer. 2015. "Objects of Journalism and The News." *Journalism: Theory, Practice & Criticism* 16 (1): 3–9.

Belair-Gagnon, Valerie. 2015. *Social Media at BBC News: The Re-Making of Crisis Reporting*. London: Routledge.

Bennett, Stephen E., Staci Rhine, L. Flickinger, and S. Richard. 2001. "Assessing American's Opinions About the News Media's Fairness in 1996 and 1998." *Political Communication* 18: 163–182.

Benton, Josh. 2017. "From the Unbanked to the Unnewsed." *Nieman Journalism Lab*, March 29. http://www.niemanlab.org/2017/03/from-the-unbanked-to-the-unnewsed-just-doing-good-journalism-wont-be-enough-to-bring-back-reader-trust/

Bilton, Ricardo. 2016. "The Wall Street Journal's New Tool Gives a Side-by-Side Look at the Facebook Political News Filter Bubble." *Nieman Journalism Lab*, May 18. http://www.niemanlab.org/2016/05/the-wall-street-journals-new-tool-gives-a-side-by-side-look-at-the-facebook-political-news-filter-bubble/

Blöbaum, Bernd. 2014. *Trust and Journalism in a Digital Environment*. Oxford: Reuters Institute for the Study of Journalism.

Boczkowski, Pablo J. 2015. "'The Material Turn' in the Study of Journalism: Some Hopeful and Cautionary Remarks From an Early Explorer." *Journalism: Theory, Practice & Criticism* 16 (1): 65–8.

Braun, Joshua A. 2015a. "News Programs: Designing MSNBC.Com's Online Interfaces." *Journalism: Theory, Practice & Criticism* 16 (1): 27–43.

Braun, Joshua A. 2015b. *This Program Is Brought to You By ... : Distributing Television News Online*. New Haven: Yale University Press.

Buckland, Michael K. 1997. "What is a 'Document'?" *Journal of the American Society for Information Science* 48: 804–809.

Capella, Joe and Jamieson, Kathleen Hall. 1997. *Spiral of Cynicism: The Press and the Public Good*. New York: Oxford University Press.

Carey, James W. 1992. *Communication as Culture* (Revised Edition: Essays on Media and Society.) London: Routledge.

Carlson, Matt. 2017. *Journalistic Authority: Legitimating News in the Digital Era*. New York: Columbia University Press.

Carlson, Matt, and Seth C. Lewis, eds. 2015. *Boundaries of Journalism: Professionalism, Practices and Participation*. London: Routledge.

Cook, Karen S. 2007. "Trust." In *Blackwell Encyclopedia of Sociology*, edited by George Ritzer. London: Blackwell Publishing, Blackwell Reference Online http://www.sociologyencyclopedia.com/subscriber/tocnode.html?id=g9781405124331_chunk_g978140512433126_ss1-52

De Maeyer, Juliette. 2016. "Adopting a 'Material Sensibility' in Journalism Studies." In *The SAGE Handbook of Digital Journalism*, edited by Tamara Witschge, C. W. Anderson, David Domingo and Alfred Hermida, 460–461. Thousand Oaks, CA: Sage.

Domingo, David. 2015. "Research That Empowers Responsibility: Reconciling Human Agency with Materiality." *Journalism: Theory, Practice & Criticism* 16 (1): 69–73.

Flanagin, Andrew J., and Miriam J. Metzger. 2000. "Perceptions of Internet Information Credibility." *Journalism and Mass Communication Quarterly* 77: 515–540.

Ford, Heather. 2015. "Infoboxes and Cleanup Tags: Artifacts of Wikipedia Newsmaking." *Journalism: Theory, Practice & Criticism* 16 (1): 79–98.

Fukuyama, Francis. 1995. *Trust: The Social Virtues and the Creation of Prosperity*. New York: Free Press.

Gaziano, Cecile, and Kristin McGrath. 1986. "Measuring the Concept of Credibility." *Journalism Quarterly* 63: 451–462.

Gaziano, Carol. 1988. "How Credible is the Credibility Crisis?" *Journalism Quarterly* 65 (2): 267–278.

Gitelman, Lisa. 2014. *Paper Knowledge: Toward a Media History of Documents*. Durham, NC: Duke University Press.

Graves, Lucas. 2015. "Blogging Back Then: Annotative Journalism in IF Stone's Weekly and Talking Points Memo." *Journalism: Theory, Practice & Criticism* 16 (1): 99–118.

Hemmingway, Emma. 2008. *Into the Newsroom: Exploring the Digital Production of Regional Television News*. London: Routledge.

Hovland, Carl I., Arthur A. Lumsdaine, and Fred D Sheffield. 1949. *Experiments on Mass Communication: Studies in Social Psychology in World War II*. New Haven, CT: Yale University Press.

Jacobson, Harvey K. 1969. "Mass Media Believability: A Study of Receiver Judgments." *Journalism Quarterly* 46 (1): 20–28.

Johnson, Thomas J., and Barbara K Kaye. 1998. "Cruising is Believing?: Comparing Internet and Traditional Sources on Media Credibility Measures." *Journalism and Mass Communication Quarterly* 75: 325–340.

Johnson, Thomas J., and Barbara K Kaye. 2004. "Wag the Blog: How Reliance on Traditional Media and the Internet Influence Credibility Perceptions of Weblogs Among Blog Users." *Journalism and Mass Communication Quarterly* 81 (3): 622–642.

Keith, Susan. 2015. "Horseshoes, Stylebooks, Wheels, Poles, and Dummies: Objects of Editing Power in 20th-Century Newsrooms." *Journalism: Theory, Practice & Criticism* 16 (1): 44–60.

Kiousis, S. 2001. "Public Trust or Mistrust? Perceptions of Media Credibility in the Information Age." *Mass Communication and Society* 4: 381–403.

Kohring, Mattias, and Jorge Matthes. 2007. "Trust in News Media: Development and Validation of a Multidimensional Scale." *Communication Research* 34 (2): 231–252.

Konieczna, Magda, and Sue Robinson. 2014. "Emerging News non-Profits: A Case Study for Rebuilding Community Trust?" *Journalism: Theory, Practice & Criticism* 15 (8): 968–986.

Ladd, Jonathan M. 2011. *Why Americans Hate the Media and How it Matters*. Princeton, NJ: Princeton University Press.

Latour, Bruno. 1990. "Technology is Society Made Durable." *The Sociological Review* 38 (S1): 103–131.

Le Cam, Florence. 2015. "Photographs of Newsrooms: From the Printing House to Open Space Offices. Analyzing the Transformation of Workspaces and Information Production." *Journalism: Theory, Practice & Criticism* 16 (1): 134–152.

Lee, R. S. 1978. "Credibility of Newspaper and TV News." *Journalism Quarterly* 55 (2): 282–287.

Lewis, Seth C., and Nikki Usher. 2016. "Trading Zones, Boundary Objects, and the Pursuit of News Innovation: A Case Study of Journalists and Programmers." *Convergence: The International Journal of Research Into New Media Technologies* 22 (5): 543–560.

Lewis, Seth C., and Nikki Usher. 2013. "Open Source and Journalism: Toward new Frameworks for Imagining News Innovation." *Media, Culture and Society* 35 (5): 602–619.

Liebeskind, Ken. 1997. "Credibility Problems Plague All Media." *Editor and Publisher* 130 (50): 23.

Malone, Claire. 2016. "Americans Don't Trust Their Institutions Anymore." *Fivethirtyeight*, November 16. https://fivethirtyeight.com/features/americans-dont-trust-their-institutions-anymore/

Meltzer, Kimberly. 2009. "The Hierarchy of Journalistic Cultural Authority: Journalists' Perspectives According to News Medium." *Journalism Practice* 3 (1): 59–74.

Metzger, Miriam J., Andrew J. Flanagin, Keren Eyal, Daisy R. Lemus, and Robert M. McCann. 2003. "Credibility for the 21st Century: Integrating Perspectives on Source, Message, and Media Credibility in the Contemporary Media Environment." *Annals of the International Communication Association* 27 (1): 293–335.

Meyer, Timothy. 1974. "Media Credibility: The State of the Research." *Public Telecommunications Review* 2 (4): 48–52.

Meyer, Philip. 1988. "Defining and Measuring Credibility of Newspapers: Developing an Index." *Journalism and Mass Communication Quarterly* 77: 515–540.

Neff, Gina. 2015. "Learning From Documents: Applying New Theories of Materiality to Journalism." *Journalism: Theory, Practice & Criticism* 16 (1): 74–78.

Newhagen, John, and Clifford Nass. 1989. "Differential Criteria for Evaluating Credibility of Newspapers and TV News." *Journalism Quarterly* 66: 277–284.

Örnebring, Henrik. 2013. "Anything you can do, I can do Better? Professional Journalists on Citizen Journalism in six European Countries." *International Communication Gazette* 75 (1): 35–53.

Plesner, Ursula. 2009. "An Actor-Network Perspective on Changing Work Practices." *Journalism: Theory, Practice & Criticism* 10 (5): 604–26.

Reich, Zvi. 2012. "Journalism as Bipolar Interactional Expertise." *Communication Theory* 22 (4): 339–358.

Reuters Institute for the Study of Journalism. 2017. "Digital News Report." Oxford: Oxford University. http://www.digitalnewsreport.org/

Rodgers, Scott. 2015. "Foreign Objects? Web Content Management Systems, Journalistic Cultures and the Ontology of Software." *Journalism: Theory, Practice & Criticism* 16 (1): 10–26.

Roper Organization. 1989. *America's Watching: 30th Anniversary 1959–1989*. New York: Television Information Office.

Rosenstiel, Tom. 2016, December 20. *What the Post-Trump Debate over Journalism gets Wrong*. Washington, DC: Brookings Institution. Retrieved from: https://www.brookings.edu/research/what-the-debate-over-journalism-post-trump-gets-wrong/

Rotter, Julian B. 1967. "A New Scale for the Measurement of Interpersonal Trust." *Journal of Personality* 35: 651–665.

Schmitz Weiss, Amy, and David Domingo. 2010. "Innovation Processes in Online Newsrooms as Actor-Networks and Communities of Practice." *New Media and Society* 12 (7): 1156–1171.

Schudson, Michael. 2000. *The Good Citizen: A History of American Civic Life*. New York: Free Press.

Schudson, Michael. 2003. *The Sociology of News*. New York: Norton.

Schudson, Michael. 2015. "What Sorts of Things are Thingy? And What Sorts of Thinginess Are There? Notes on Stuff and Social Construction." *Journalism: Theory, Practice & Criticism* 16 (1): 61–64.

Schudson, Michael, and C. W. Anderson. 2009. "Objectivity, Professionalism, and Truth Seeking in Journalism." In *The Handbook of Journalism Studies*, edited by Karen Wahl-Jorgensen and Thomas Hanitzsch, 88–102. New York, NY: Routledge.

Shaw, Eugene F. 1973. "Media Credibility: Taking the Measure of a Measure." *Journalism Quarterly* 50: 306–311.

Sjøvaag, Helle. 2014. "Homogenisation or Differentiation? The Effects of Consolidation in the Regional Newspaper Market." *Journalism Studies* 15 (5): 511–521.

Swift, Art. 2016. "Americans' Trust in News Media Sinks to New Low." *Gallup*, September 14. http://www.gallup.com/poll/195542/americans-trust-mass-media-sinks-new-low.aspx

Tsfati, Yariv. 2003. "Does Audience Skepticism of the Media Matter in Agenda Setting?" *Journal of Broadcasting and Electronic Media* 47: 157–176.

Tsfati, Yariv, and Joseph N Cappella. 2003. "Do People Watch What They Do Not Trust? Exploring the Association Between News Media Skepticism and Exposure." *Communication Research* 30: 504–529.

Tsfati, Yariv, and Joseph N Cappella. 2005. "Why do People Watch News They do not Trust: Need for Cognition as a Moderator in the Association Between News media Skepticism and Exposure." *Media Psychology*, 7: 251–272.

Turner, Stephen. 2007. "Authority and Legitimacy." In *Blackwell Encyclopedia of Sociology*, edited by George Ritzer. London: Blackwell Publishing. Blackwell Reference Online http://www.sociologyencyclopedia.com/subscriber/tocnode.html?id=g9781405124331_chunk_g97814051243317_ss1-81

Usher, Nikki. 2014a. *Making News at The New York Times*. Ann Arbor, MI: University of Michigan Press.

Usher, Nikki. 2014b. *Moving the Newsroom: Post-Industrial News Spaces and Places*. New York: Columbia Journalism School: Tow Center for Digital Journalism.

Usher, Nikki. 2015. "Newsroom Moves and the Newspaper Crisis Evaluated: Space, Place, and Cultural Meaning." *Media, Culture and Society* 37 (7): 1005–1021.

Usher, Nikki. 2016. *Interactive Journalism: Hackers, Data, and Code*. Chicago: University of Illinois Press.

Usher, Nikki. 2017. "Breaking News Production Processes in US Metropolitan Newspapers: Immediacy and Journalistic Authority." *Journalism*, 1464884916689151.

Wallace, Aurora. 2005. *Newspapers and the Making of Modern America: A History*. Westport, CT: Greenwood Publishing Group.

Wallace, Aurora. 2012. *Media Capital: Architecture and Communications in New York City*. Chicago: University of Illinois Press.

Wanta, Wayne, and Yu Wei Hu. 1994. "The Effects of Credibility, Reliance, and Exposure on Media Agenda-Setting: A Path Analysis Model." *Journalism Quarterly* 71: 90–98.

West, Mark D. 1994. "Validating a Scale for the Measurement of Credibility: A Covariance Structure Modeling Approach." *Journalism Quarterly* 71: 159–168.

Westley, Bruce, and Werner Severin. 1964. "Some Correlates of Media Credibility." *Journalism Quarterly* 41: 325–335.

COMMUNITY REPAIR THROUGH TRUCE AND CONTESTATION
Danish legacy print media and the Copenhagen shootings

Henrik Bødker and **Teke Ngomba**

On 15 February 2015, a gunman attacked a public event on art and freedom of expression in Copenhagen, leaving one person dead. Later, trying to force his way into a bat mitzvah celebration, the gunman killed a Jewish guard. These incidents produced public discourses at the intersection of security, social control, rights and tolerance and, with that, questions related to religious, secular and national communities and identities. At the political level, this was an attempt to repair a national community divided in relation to questions of security, integration and the curbing of immigration. Mainstream print journalism faced a similar challenge in its attempt to reassert its national relevance while remaining loyal to its audience communities within a market increasingly separated by taste and platforms. Politicians and news media thus shared an interest in both repairing and contesting a Danish community. This article analyses how discourses of community repair, cohesion and exclusivity permeated the appropriation of this disruptive event into the public realm. Progressing from an intersection of cultural approaches to journalism studies and political communication, the analysis will, in addition to other concepts, aim to combine insights from research on "disruptive media events" with studies of "belonging".

Introduction

The institutions, practices and texts of journalism are linked to community formations on a number of levels: "interpretive communities" (Zelizer 1993) and/or "communities of practices" (Meltzer and Martik 2017) among journalists; institutional efforts of audience segmentation and community management and, linked to that, processes of news consumption through which users may situate themselves as part of various collectivities. Such processes of communion are increasingly moving online, which has caused some to argue that "[Benedict] Anderson's sense of an authoritative national view and imagined community has largely receded" (Sheller 2015, 15).

National media, however, retain their significance and this is especially so when what Figenschou and Thorbjørnsrud (2016, 1) call a "disruptive media event threatens the establishment and hence force democratic societies to mobilize, reinforce and [perhaps] rethink core values". In the "aftermath of terror", they continue, "the [mainstream] media play a key role as meaning makers, guardians of appropriate discourse and facilitators of critical debates" (1). Figenschou and Thorbjørnsrud focus on editorial considerations about the inclusion of alternative voices and on how editors negotiated national consensus and dissent in the Norwegian media following the Breivik attacks in 2011. This article applies a similar perspective to the mediation of the 2015 Copenhagen shootings. On Saturday 14 February 2015—about five weeks after the attack on *Charlie Hebdo* in Paris—a lone gunman attacked a public event on the theme "Art, Blasphemy and Freedom of Expression" held at a small culture centre called "Krudttønden". The Swedish cartoonist, Lars Vilks, who once had drawn the Prophet Muhammad, participated and so did the French ambassador to Denmark. The gunman did not make it into the venue but killed filmmaker Finn Nørgaard outside and wounded three police officers. Later that night the gunman tried to get into a bat mitzvah celebration at Copenhagen's main synagogue. Here he killed a Jewish guard (Dan Uzan) and wounded two police officers. Early Sunday morning the police tracked down the assumed attacker, which resulted in a shootout, leading to the death of the suspect, who was identified as Omar Abdel Hamid El-Hussein, 22, born and raised in Denmark by his Palestinian parents.

This event was rapidly framed in public discourse as Denmark's initiation into terrorism; and as terror is often seen as "a drama that calls for commitment and resolute action" (Laustsen and Ugilt 2015, 366, authors' translation), we ask: How did Danish national media, public officials and other opinion leaders react to the shooting? And how were notions of community and belonging textually constructed within these reactions?

The analyses show how two Danish national legacy news media (*Jyllands-Posten* and *Politiken*), with and against politicians, negotiated a transition from truce (i.e. a consensual public reaction to terror) to contestation (i.e. different, oppositional reactions and measures relating to the aftermath of the event) and how these reactions positioned different communities in relation to each other.

The two newspapers thus created a stage on which different actors, including the news media themselves, positioned this terror event within the trajectory of the national community of Denmark. The unfolding coverage developed (broadly) from commitments to an overall vague and non-divisive unity (truce) to more specific avenues of action and responsibility that brought forth ideological and cultural tensions (contestation). The findings show how the terror event brought forth a sense of loss and subsequent articulations and enactments of different measures to *repair* or *restore* what had been lost. The coverage thus contains both very explicit invocations of a national community as an affront to perceived threats as well as more indirect ones related to more specific measures of repair as well as community formations. Before analysing these issues in more detail, we will outline the relevant background, the analytical framework and methodology.

Relevant Background

As the shooter belonged to the Muslim community and as one of the venues targeted was a synagogue, the following three issues need mentioning. Firstly, Jews in Denmark have a specific history: while efforts to save Danish Jews during the German occupation (1940–1945) have been venerated, there have also been indications that the Danish government was actually collaborating with the Nazi regime and thus responsible for the deaths of several Danish Jews (see Kisch 1998; Lichtenstein 2004). Secondly, immigration and integration-related issues have been central topics in the media and political debates in Denmark for a number of years—largely because of the increase in the number of non-Western immigrants in Denmark, especially Muslims (see Statistics Denmark 2017); and an anti-Muslim rhetoric has characterised these debates (see Hervik

2012; Mouritsen and Olsen 2013), a rhetoric that, at some levels, is linked to the fallout from the cartoon affair in 2005.[1] Thirdly, while the Muslim and Jewish communities in Denmark have been experiencing similar incidents of discrimination/hate attacks, they are also written into broader structures of mutual suspicion and at times violence (see Kisch 1998, 228; European Union Agency for Fundamental Rights 2016; Porat and the Kantor Center Team 2016). These elements make up the context in which the shootings in Copenhagen occurred and it is also in this context that the reactions and interpretations of the shootings should be understood.

Analytical Frame and Methodology

How the political elites and mainstream media react to the "chaos and fear" bred by a terrorist attack (Thorbjørnsrud and Figenschou 2016, 3) can offer insights into national values, social cohesion and logics of inclusivity. In some ways, previous scholarship has shown that there are central patterns in the ways national communities and mainstream media react. Based on 9/11, Collins (2004) has argued that reactions to disruptive events proceed in four major phases from shock, through solidarity and consensus, to a return to dissensus. A key point within this trajectory is the "revival of partisanship" on the heels of displays of solidarity. As he puts it, "the period of intense national solidarity temporarily suppresses or supplants normal partisan conflicts" (truce) but with the passage of time, this "phase of consensus" returns to "normal dissensus" (contestation) (73).

In relation to news media, Matthews (2016) has, based on the work of Philip Elliot (1980) and after studying the British media coverage of the London terror attacks in 2005, argued that the immediate reactions of "traditionally differentiated newspapers" involve an abandonment of normal routines and the adoption of a "generic reporting template", which features a "collective response". This response is characteristically "marked by representations of condemnation, solidarity and law enforcement, brought together within human-interest story treatments" (Matthews 2016, 173). Broadly speaking, this pattern has been found in studies from places as varied as the United States (Allan and Zelizer [2002] 2011), Israel (Zandberg and Neiger 2005), the United Kingdom (Matthews 2016; Iqbal 2017), Norway (Figenschou and Beyer 2014) and Denmark (Jørndrup 2016).

Mainstream media's reaction to terror attacks can be seen as a "ritual type of journalism that fosters adherence to shared values and support for national authorities" (Thorbjørnsrud and Figenschou 2016, 1). From this perspective, journalism plays a central role for the "maintenance of society through time, [by] representing shared beliefs, understandings and emotions" (Riegert and Olsson 2007, 144). In the reporting about traumatic events, this societal maintenance role becomes central as a way to move "whole populations from trauma to recovery through questions of identity" (Allan and Zelizer [2002] 2011, 2). In her examination of how mainstream news magazines covered 9/11, Kitch (2003, 213) showed how news media created a "forum for national mourning" where stories of "vulnerability and fear were replaced by heroism and patriotic pride".

Such mediatised rituals (Cottle 2006) are, as Allan and Zelizer ([2002] 2011) note, aligned with "questions of identity" as they invariably end up touching on communal boundaries. In a post-9/11 world where the "global fight against terrorism" has taken ethno-religious undertones, terrorist attacks, especially those committed in the West by Muslims, in many ways trigger contested discourses "over defining the nation and who belongs to it" (Pratsinakis 2017, 3).

At the heart of the scholarly debate about immediate reactions to terror attacks is not that journalists do not engage in critical reporting but rather when and how they start engaging in critical reporting (see Zandberg and Neiger 2005; Nossek 2008; Jørndrup 2016; Thorbjørnsrud and Figenschou 2016). In relation to this, we argue that professional restraint should not be seen as an abdication of responsibilities but rather as a tactical negotiation between journalists and politicians as each group attempts to decipher the right time to break the thaw in a manner that will reflect cognizance of the scale and broader impact of the attack while not upsetting the sensibilities of the core communities they address.

Methodology

This article is based on articles from two national Danish dailies, *Politiken* and *Jyllands-Posten*, from 14 February (the day of the first shooting) to 13 March (one month later). The early stages of disruptive events like terrorist attacks are vital in relation to understanding a community's reaction. These early stages often feature the "establishment of frames" about the event and this increases the defining role of mainstream media when the public's need for information "is at its highest level" (Falkheimer and Olsson 2015, 77).

This explains in large part why several studies have analysed the immediate reactions to terrorist attacks from the first 8 days (Matthews 2016) to 11 days (Zandberg and Neiger 2005) and two weeks (Nossek 2008; Falkheimer and Olsson 2015). Apart from enabling us to capture these immediate reactions, the one-month period selected also allows us to trace how notions of community embedded within the mainstream media's coverage of the attacks were constructed over time.

While acknowledging that social media play an increasingly important role for the contemporary construction of publics, we focus in this study only on newspapers because they arguably remain central as definers of reality. In an argument worth quoting at length, Cushion et al. recently pointed out in the case of the United Kingdom, that on the one hand, current debates about newspapers highlight their "limited lifespan with dramatic headlines about declining levels of circulation" but on the other hand that

> [n]ewspapers or print journalists remain a frequent reference point for rival news media, and a routine source for understanding how an event or issue is interpreted. Many broadcast news programmes, including heavyweight political shows, not only review the day's papers but ask journalists themselves to interpret the significance of particular stories or to comment upon "the mood" of the press in the wake of the latest political drama or breaking news story. Far from the power of newspapers being diminished, from this perspective, it appears newspapers continue to play an important agenda-setting role in raising debate about the stories they select and editorially frame. (Cushion et al. 2016, 1–2)

The two titles studied here were chosen for their different ideological positions on the market for mainstream print media. *Politiken* is largely positioned to the left of the centre while *Jyllands-Posten* is to the right; and while both carry a lot of content on national and international politics, the former has a core focus on issues of culture and urban life-styles while the latter is more centred around traditional and family-centred lifestyles. It is also important to point out that *Jyllands-Posten* was the newspaper that in 2005 published the Muhammad cartoons and in the aftermath of that event *Politiken* positioned itself in opposition to the reasoning behind publishing the cartoons (for a broader discussion, see, for instance, Hjarvard 2007).

The articles were obtained from the database MediaWatch, which contains full articles from a range of Danish print media. The database does not contain photographs so our analysis only draws on texts. The search string used was "Krudttønden [the name of the place of the first attack] AND angreb [attack] OR Uzan [the surname of the guard killed at the synagogue]". This resulted in 126 articles of differing length including news articles, opinion pieces as well as letters to the editor. The unit of analysis was the individual texts. In choosing to analyse this entire spectrum of texts, our aim is to capture the published reactions from a range of actors: journalists, experts, politicians and opinion leaders.

The 126 published pieces were subjected to a qualitative thematic analysis, which, basically, is "a method for identifying, analysing and reporting patterns (themes) within data" (Braun and Clarke 2006, 79). As Gutsche and Salkin (2016, 459–460) point out, qualitative thematic analysis is an important approach for identifying how cultural themes and meanings are "embedded in news texts" and, as such, the approach is deemed appropriate for the analytical aims of this study.

Specifically, the selected articles were analysed following the step-by-step guide indicated by Braun and Clarke (2006) on how to do qualitative thematic analysis. This involves reading the different articles closely and several times to look for central themes in the data in light of the main research questions and analytical aims, collating different units of the data into potential themes, reviewing, defining and naming these themes through a "recursive process" of back and forth movement with the data and discussions between the authors (see Braun and Clarke 2006, 87).

The key aim was to identify broad patterns in the ways different actors reacted to and interpreted the shootings, how these patterns changed over the first month and the how this was related to community constructions, repair, cohesion and contestation. The analysis below is structured in two overall sections that to some extent mirror the evolvement of the coverage from truce and/or unity as a measure of repair to contestation related to more divisive measures.

Truce as Measures of Community Repair

The Loss of the Denmark That We Knew

While the coverage in the immediate aftermath of the shootings were focused on detailed descriptions of the attack on "us" and the necessity of standing firm on the values of democracy and freedom, there was simultaneously a strong sense of a major national change: "the Denmark that awoke on Sunday morning was no longer the Denmark that we knew" said a front-page article entitled "The Denmark That We Didn't Know" (*Politiken*, February 16, 2015).[2] What seemingly had been lost was a sense of security linked to deeper feelings of trust, cohesion, equality and ease. While a small drawing of a smiling Muhammad placed together with flowers at Krudttønden could be interpreted as a sign of stupidity, it is here seen as "a drawing of something else": "A little defiant and quirky Danish answer, not too rash and not too loud but with a slight distance. The Denmark we know" (*Politiken*, February 16). What has been lost is thus also the ability (or right) to not take things too seriously. While the cartoon crisis in 2005 raised similar issues, the Copenhagen shootings in a more direct way threatened a presumed innocence. At this early period of mourning, the presumed loss of innocence was not linked to an activist Danish foreign policy or anything else. What was invoked was rather an implicit and for a majority largely recognisable quality of what it means to be Danish.

Normalcy and the Everyday

The most immediate mode of repair consists of the very tactile elements of an everyday as "we" know it. The Monday after the attacks *Jyllands-Posten* (February 16) interviewed a mom at the playground with her four-year-old girl in the park close to the site of the first shooting: "I probably would not have come", she says, "if I knew that there were so much police here". Another regular visitor, the man owning the coffee stall, is more defiant:

> It was really important for me to come back to the park today and signal to people in the neighbourhood that they can count on us, who come here daily. If we stay away because we are afraid the killer will get it his way.

Such quotidian defiance and its emphasis on continuity appear as both descriptions of actual practices and proclamations in much of the early coverage: "Nothing is stronger in the face of extremism than the everyday, which we are all part of", said the leading article of *Politiken* the day after the attack (February 16); and when the party leaders met at the Prime Ministry the day after the attack, the shadow Prime Minister (Lars Løkke Rasmussen)—according to *Jyllands-Posten* (February 16)—"deliberately walked from his home in Nyhavn ... without protection to emphasise that life must go on and terror must not change the lives of Danes".

While the quotidian in one sense implies a commonality that is beyond division, i.e. simply going about one's ordinary business in undisturbed ways, the "normalcy" is simultaneously exaggerated—does the shadow Prime Minister normally walk to work? Such an exaggeration comes out clearly in the way *Jyllands-Posten* (February 17) describes a commemoration event two days after the attacks: "Even though Copenhagen normally is a town of cyclists, they seemed—despite a severely cold and biting wind—almost to define the cityscape on Monday night"; and, at the event

> the bikes arrived at a silent community, lit by torches, and the many ordinary citizens mingled with Crown Prince Frederik, leading people from government with Prime Minister Helle Thorning-Schmidt in front, the other party leaders as well as a range of society's other notables.

While Collins (2004, 65) describes how people may fake or exaggerate "gestures of solidarity", it here rather seems as if the journalistic rendering in itself exaggerates a recognisably Danish everyday—walking, biking and mingling across status barriers—that here becomes an embodiment of the nation and its values, and this apparent tangibility is underlined in the description of how "people kept closely together and made long chains by holdings hands" while "mobile phones remained inside the winter coats in this quiet moment". It is at this "unmediated" moment, what Collins (2004, 61) identifies as "peak experiences of solidarity", that the Prime Minister is described as taking the stage and uttering: "Our answer is a strong community".

The everyday as a measure of repair is thus intricately linked to unity and cohesion, which—as the quote by the Prime Minister makes clear—is also seen as a measure in its own right. Yet, on its own this measure is also relatively fragile. There is a limit, after all, to what an exaggeration of normalcy can do. What this does, however, is to invoke a deeper sense of unity and cohesion.

Unity and Cohesion

The most salient responses in the immediate aftermath of the terror event are attempts to restore what is perceived as a pre-existing unity of the nation. After the first shooting (February 15), the leading article in *Politiken* is headlined "We Remain Firm on Freedom" and ends with "We must remain firm on democracy. And we are strongest". The day after, *Jyllands-Posten* (February 16)—in an article aptly entitled "Party Leaders: The Time is Not for Divisions and Politics"—cites Prime Minister Helle Thorning-Schmidt as saying: "as a joint and united nation we must show who we are. It is time for unity". The same article cites a number of party leaders backing the Prime Minister in her calls for unity and the same day *Politiken* cites her saying that "Denmark will grow with this tragedy. We must stand together as a people instead of splitting up into fractions eyeing each other with suspicion". There is, however, seeds of division as the Prime Minister is cited further down for saying that "this is not a religious war and that they [Muslims] should not be vilified. Without saying it directly she is asking", the journalists inserts, "the rest of us to behave".

Later articles praise or cite people praising Helle Thorning-Schmidt for her words in the period after the attacks. Indeed, in a news analysis in *Politiken* (February 18) it is underlined that even the "right-leaning press has praised" the ways she had been conducting herself. The leading and main articles and the politicians' reactions in the days after the attack thus appear as a cleansing of ideological, political, cultural and ethnic tensions from the national community in order to restore something akin to what Anderson ([1983] 1991, 7) calls a "deep, horizontal comradeship".

This broadly constructed unity is linked to situations of truce within specific relations, i.e. between politicians, between journalists and politicians, as well as between normally competing news outlets. This is, thus, not only a question of the news "media … spreading the master narrative" as Thorbjørnsrud and Figenschou (2016, 4) argue, but rather a collective process where journalists and politicians share an interest in sustaining "the idea that there is a social centre and that media are privileged access-points to that centre" (Couldry 2003, 5). Yet within this, and almost right from the beginning, there is also a shared sense that this is temporary and this partly comes out in the instances where there are references to the comments on social media. On February 16, a sociologist is quoted in *Jyllands-Posten* for saying that "social media is boiling over with people who had the need to get rid of their frustrations in the form of angry status updates". While acknowledging frustration and division, the two studied newspapers initially position themselves above this fray in the sense that they, as legacy media, seemingly take on the responsibility together with "political authorities to maintain and re-establish control" (Figenschou and Thorbjørnsrud 2016, 1).

This was, however, a situation in which both politicians and journalists (independently and in relation to each other) were searching for an opportunity to use the event without coming across as opportunistic. This seemed, somehow, almost a scripted performance in which "underneath the surface of the truce everybody is ceaselessly watching each other while simultaneously concentrating on not stumbling in the difficult political balancing act", as it says in *Jyllands-Posten* on February 16 where the journalist is also speculating about how long "the truce will last". This is related to an issue that lingered almost from the beginning with regard to whether the level of security was raised after the Paris attacks, as claimed by the Prime Minister (which will be discussed in more detail below) and, as it said in *Jyllands-Posten* on February 17, "journalists [had been] hungry at the many press conferences held by the police and politicians" in the immediate aftermath of the attacks. Although many questions were asked, there was somehow also an understanding that the politicians did not want to open the political debate just yet. In one sense, then, it seemed that the newspapers, just as the politicians, were treading a thin line between a focus on cohesion and mourning and deliberately using this as a way to position themselves within a competitive media landscape. When such positioning began, it was mainly in relation to two contested measures of repair, namely security and immigration/integration.

Contestation as Measures of Community Formation

Controversies and Debates About Pre- and Post-attack Security

The breakdown of the truce between the news media and politicians on security revolved around two major issues: how to protect society in general and how to stop future attacks and the level of security for the Jewish community. On the first point, contentious issues were the number of armed security officials in the streets, more surveillance cameras, more security forces and provision of security equipment to the police, and more monitoring of vulnerable people straddling the line of gang membership and radicalisation given that the attacker was a gang member.

The discussions relating to the level of security of the Jewish community had a range of explicit and implicit connections to community constructions. The first of these centres on whether the synagogue had organised appropriate security, an issue that was the most contentious in the discussions among the central actors in the analysed reports. Importantly, the debate also served as one of the first attempts to effectively puncture the constructed unity and verbal cease-fire, especially within the political establishment.

At the heart of the contestation was the claim that the synagogue was not properly secured and that the government had not increased the security of the Jewish community following the attacks in France (see, for instance, *Jyllands-Posten*, February 17). Such critical reporting, coming barely three days after the attack, demonstrates a relatively quick transition away from consensus and solidarity and also underscores the fact that in the period following such disruptive events, journalists, unlike what scholars such as Zandberg and Neiger (2005) and Nossek (2008) suggest, can and do ask critical questions in line with the professional logics of watchdog journalism.

While the security of the Jewish community prior to the attack was contentious, there was less contestation from both the media and political leaders in relation to security measures in the future. An example is the declaration that

> the Jews are threatened and need protection … [and our] society needs to move on that by both actually protecting the Jews better and by assuring them that we appreciate them as citizens and will do everything to keep them. (*Politiken*, February 16)

In a move that signalled this resolve, the police announced an improvement of security measures aimed at the Jewish community shortly after the attack. An issue noticeable by its absence was a clear, unapologetic demonstration of concern about protecting the

Muslim community whose members, for instance, clearly expressed fears of backlash following these attacks. There is also no major articulation of the potentially important roles Muslim leaders could play in furthering security and fighting radicalisation.

This contrasts sharply with how Prime Minister Thorning-Schmidt, who was described in one report as someone who has "all the time been a politician with a warm heart for the state of Israel and the Jewish community" (*Politiken*, February 21), clearly declared to the Jewish community that "you are an important part of Danish society and you are not standing alone" (*Politiken*, February 17). These clear, unapologetic articulations of the imperative to secure the Jewish community can be seen, on the one hand, as an invocation of the broader cultural memory of "us" having saved the Danish Jews during the German occupation and, on the other, as echoes of a national "making right overtures" by the Danish authorities towards the Jewish community in light of the unspoken memories of the controversial role of the Danish state in the protection of Jews during World War II.

Taken together, the coverage signals clear discrepancies in the attention given to the Muslim community, which is discursively annihilated while the Jewish community is hailed as a "worthy" minority. This discrepancy fits the pattern identified by Skey (2014, 326), who noted that current debates in the West around issues relating to immigration and migrant communities are "informed by hierarchies of belonging with some groups seen to belong more and therefore deserve more, than others."

Iqbal (2017) has also shown that mediated reactions to the 2005 London terrorist attacks signalled to the British Muslim community that they were not part of the broader British community. Such signals, both in their subtle and more overt formats, are important markers of belonging, especially given the increasingly "communicative nature of communities" (Delanty 2003, 187).

Debating the Inevitable: Immigration and Integration Discourses

Given the shooter's background, debates about the incident delved into immigration and integration issues with a resultant termination of the hitherto tactical truce between politicians. A good example of this was the indication that "with an eye on the voters, and despite the truce, there is an on-going speculation about whether and if so how the terror attack will affect the polls, which everybody is studying with extra attention in an election year" (*Jyllands-Posten*, February 16). Politicians are here presented as strategic, skilled and scheming individuals with clear ambitions to grab political opportunities triggered by tragedy without appearing opportunistic. This political posturing was oriented in two major directions as far as the debate on immigration and integration was concerned. The first concerns the arguments put forth by some politicians and journalists that an underlying cause of the shootings is the perceived shortcomings of the immigration/integration policies in Denmark.

In an editorial piece widely panned by *Politiken* and others, *Jyllands-Posten* (February 17) wrote that the shootings indicated that Denmark was involved in a "new kind of war" and that

> [d]espite European citizenship and even though they are born and raised in Denmark they have never culturally and in terms of values arrived in Europe. It therefore ought to be uncontroversial to establish that a grim result of the immigration from the Middle East

is the attacks in recent years ... [and] many of today's politicians need to face up to the fact ... that they bear the responsibility for opening up for this mass immigration.

Such claims, characteristically un-nuanced, are symptomatic of the longstanding value struggle in Danish media and politics in which "Danish values", however defined, are presented as being "threatened by, should be defined in contrast to, or had to be defended against an increasingly essentialized Islamic other" (Meer et al. 2015, 719). This specific identification of immigrants with Muslim background as constituting a problem contrasts sharply with the heralding of the Jewish community as having been central players in helping Muslim minorities to integrate in Denmark (*Politiken*, February 17). This reference to the Jewish community as a "model worth copying" is a long-established feature of the ways in which mainstream Danish media and political elites as well as ordinary Danes comparatively talk about different minority communities in Denmark (Hervik 2012).

The questioning of belonging was positively echoed in the media and by the political establishment following the exhortation by Benjamin Netanyahu, Israel's Prime Minister, for Jews in Denmark to relocate to Israel following the attack. Dan Rosenberg, head of the Jewish community in Denmark, declared that: "we are thankful for the concern that has been expressed for us but I wish to underline that we are Danish citizens. We live in Denmark and we wish to continue to live in Denmark" (*Jyllands-Posten*, February 16). Mette Bentow, another member of the Jewish community, also declared that: "no thanks, we are not going home to Israel, we are already at home" (*Jyllands-Posten*, February 18).

Such declarations of belonging are also present among ordinary Muslims. In reacting to the potential backlash Muslims face after such attacks, a young Muslim said: "It is a completely insane act. We are also Danish ... if we hear of something similar about to happen we stand together as Danes" (*Politiken*, February 18). In many ways, these assertions of belonging by members of these minority communities are similar and echo the "emotional attachment about feeling 'at home'" which is characteristic of discourses of belonging (Yuval-Davis 2006, 197). There is, however, a major difference in both the tone of these assertions and the ways they are received or echoed by the mainstream media and political elites. While the Prime Minister Thorning-Schmidt, for instance, can be said to have positively echoed the assertions of the Jews quoted above by her declarations mentioned earlier that "you are an important part of Danish society and you do not stand alone", a comparable signal to the Muslim community is absent.

In asserting their belonging to the broader Danish community, the Muslims might therefore be said to be engaged in a process of challenging their "contested civic status" (Meer and Mouritsen 2009, 336). Such contestations are central to the politics of belonging, which revolves around contestations of the valuation of identities and attachments as these relate to "participatory dimensions of citizenship as well as in relation to issues of the status and entitlements such membership entails" (Yuval-Davis 2006, 205).

Overall, the immigration/integration and security-related dimensions of reactions to and interpretations of the shooting incident underscore the tensions within and between different strata of the broader Danish community; and this demonstrates the ways and extent to which a sense of belonging in the broader Danish community was articulated by members of minority communities and reciprocated by politicians, the media and state officials, and the ways in which the politics of belonging inadvertently permeates different actors' discourses on the disruptive events in Copenhagen.

Concluding Discussion

This article set out to examine constructions of community and belonging in the reports about the February 2015 shooting incident in Copenhagen. Based on a thematic analysis of the first one month of coverage in *Politiken* and *Jyllands-Posten*, we conclude by pointing to the following central tendencies. Firstly, similar to existing research, the broader processes of community repair moved through phases of condemnation, demonstrations of unity, resilience and resolve, and instances of contestations/dissensus. A key consideration in this is, as Jørndrup (2016) also noted in an analysis of how the Danish public broadcaster covered the shootings, that there was no significant articulation of shock—perhaps because there was widespread expectation that a terrorist attack in Denmark was imminent. In addition, a noticeable pattern in the examined reports as it connects to these phases of reactions is the relatively quick way in which the phases marked by solidarity, unity and criticism/conflict succeeded each other compared to what other scholars have found, for instance in the United States (Collins 2004) or Norway (Figenschou and Thorbjørnsrud 2016). What accounts for this is not too clear. Nevertheless, one reason may be the relatively limited scale of the attack, which was historical but arguably not significantly devastating in terms of casualties. At best, the national trauma was "tamed". Another reason could be that the underlying tensions that marked reactions to the incident had been "rehearsed" during the 2005 Muhammad cartoons controversy—especially between the two newspapers in focus here. In this sense, there was no need for a lengthy period of détente. In any case, what these observations point to is that the phases and temporalities of journalism in the wake of disruptive events need to be understood in relation to specific political and media-related contexts as well as the context and scale of the disruptive events.

Secondly, and related to the above, this study shows that during moments of disruptive events like domestic terrorist attacks, journalists and politicians engage in a discursive tug-of-war in which both camps act out the theatrics of unity and solidarity while demonstrating calculative impatience to move beyond such limited, "scripted" role enactments. These patterns, at times overtly asserted and at other times merely implied, are enacted by politicians and journalists with a very conscious awareness of the sensibilities of their respective target "audiences" (constructed as readers for the journalists and voters for politicians). The length of the truce period during moments of community repair, we argue, is a function of the nature of the balance reached by these two central sets of definers of reality in their tactical, discursive tug-of-war.

Thirdly, as concerns issues of community and its contestation and what these relate to as far as values and ideologies are concerned, journalists, politicians and opinion leaders engaged in the construction of "hierarchies of belonging". Broadly speaking, three layers of referential points of belonging emerge from the analysed reports: the broader *ethnic* Danish community as the core, followed by the Jewish minority community and lastly the Muslim minority community. This logic of perceptible "hierarchies of belonging" underlies the different ways in which these two minority communities are perceived by central actors in the examined reports: the broader *ethnic* Danish community and Jewish minority community as the victimised, attacked, threatened communities in need of protection, and the Muslim minority community as the threatening community warranting "handling".

In concluding this article, we would like to identify three possible areas of further research on this topic—two of which relate, in some ways, to shortcomings of this study. The first concerns the focus on national legacy media. While they are obviously central in shaping dominant understandings of events like domestic terrorist attacks, domestic regional and local media—especially those far away from the epicentre of specific domestic attacks—may operate under different temporalities and have different discourses pertaining to community repair. Research on media coverage of disruptive events from Norway (Thorbjørnsrud and Figenschou 2016, 9) and the United States (Gutsche and Salkin 2016, 457), for instance, seem to indicate that this is the case. Following this, it would be worthwhile examining how local media across Denmark covered this attack.

Secondly, as Denmark can be characterised as having a "hybrid media system" (Chadwick 2013), social media are playing an increasingly central role as avenues of public commentary during disruptive events (see, for instance, Al Nashmi 2017). The patterns of unity and solidarity seen in the pages of mainstream national newspapers thus constitute only one layer of "public" reactions to disruptive events. For instance, while there was virtually no anti-Semitic discourse from journalists, politicians, other opinion leaders and ordinary citizens in the examined reports, reference was made in some reports to the fact that social media was full of both anti-Semitic and Islamophobic discourses following the shootings (e.g. *Politiken*, February 28). Research from Norway indicates that editors monitored and "censored" social media commentaries as they crafted their narratives of the Breivik attack (Thorbjørnsrud and Figenschou 2016, 9). Journalists from the public service media in Denmark also monitored social media closely as the shootings in Copenhagen unfolded (Jørndrup 2016, 90–92). Analysing social media reactions (e.g. the #copenhagenshooting tweets), as well as how journalists both monitored and gate-kept content from social media in their reporting of this disruptive event, will significantly expand our understanding of the mediated constructions of community repair and discourses of belonging in contemporary hybrid media environments.

Lastly, while Zandberg (2010, 7) and others argue that journalists act as "collective memory agents", the connections between the present and past were largely left implicit and *untraceable* in the texts/discourses studied, although a *sense of its presence* was arguably perceptible. Were journalists consciously thinking of the experiences of Danish Jews during the World War II era when writing about the obligations of protecting Jews following the February 2015 shootings? If so, why are there no explicit connections in their texts to these? A study interviewing journalists who covered this incident about these issues will go a long way to supplementing our understanding of the ways in which mainstream journalists, as special public communicators, help shape public discourses and thus communities in the wake of disruptive events.

ACKNOWLEDGEMENTS

The authors wish to thank the two reviewers for their comments and suggestions.

DISCLOSURE STATEMENT

No potential conflict of interest was reported by the authors.

NOTES

1. For detailed discussions of this cartoon affair from multiple perspectives, see, for instance, the collection of essays in Volume 44, Issue 5 of the journal *International Migration* and Volume 9, Issue 3 of *Ethnicities*.

2. All newspaper articles have been translated by the authors; and, since all the referenced newspaper articles are from 2015, subsequent references will only have the date.

REFERENCES

Allan, Stuart, and Barbie Zelizer. [2002] 2011. "INTRODUCTION. When Trauma Shapes the News." In *Journalism After September 11*, edited by Stuart Allan, and Barbie Zelizer, 1–31. London: Routledge.

Al Nashmi, Eisa. 2017. "From Selfies to Media Events: How Instagram Users Interrupted Their Routines After the Charlie Hebdo Shootings." *Digital Journalism*. doi:10.1080/21670811.2017.1306787.

Anderson, Benedict. [1983] 1991. *Imagined Communities*. London: Verso.

Braun, Virginia, and Victoria Clarke. 2006. "Using Thematic Analysis in Psychology." *Qualitative Research in Psychology* 3 (2): 77–101.

Chadwick, Andrew. 2013. *The Hybrid Media System: Politics and Power*. Oxford: Oxford University Press.

Collins, Randall. 2004. "Rituals of Solidarity and Security in the Wake of Terrorist Attack." *Sociological Theory* 22 (1): 53–87.

Cottle, Simon. 2006. "Mediatized Rituals: Beyond Manufacturing Consent." *Media, Culture & Society* 28 (3): 411–432.

Couldry, Nick. 2003. "Television and the Myth of the Mediated Centre: Time for a Paradigm Shift in Television Studies." May 2003. Accessed April 2014. http://cmsw.mit.edu/mit3/papers/couldry.pdf.

Cushion, Stephen, Allaina Kilby, Richard Thomas, Marina Morani, and Richard Sambrook. 2016. "Newspapers, Impartiality and Television News: Intermedia Agenda-setting during the 2015 UK General Election Campaign." *Journalism Studies*. doi:10.1080/1461670X.2016.1171163.

Delanty, Gerard. 2003. *Community*. London: Routledge.

Elliott, Philip. 1980. "Press Performance as Political Ritual." In *The Sociology of Journalism and the Press* (Sociological Review Monograph, No. 29), edited by Harry Christian, 141–177. Keele: University of Keele.

European Union Agency for Fundamental Rights. 2016. *Discrimination and Hate Crime Against Jews in EU Member States: Experiences and Perceptions of Antisemitism*. Luxembourg: European Union Agency for Fundamental Rights.

Falkheimer, Jesper, and Eva-Karin Olsson. 2015. "Depoliticizing Terror: The News Framing of the Terrorist Attacks in Norway, 22 July 2011." *Media, War & Conflict* 8 (1): 70–85.

Figenschou, Tine Ustad, and Audun Beyer. 2014. "The Limits of the Debate: How the Oslo Terror Shook the Norwegian Immigration Debate." *The International Journal of Press/Politics* 19 (4): 430–452.

Figenschou, Tine Ustad, and Kjersti Thorbjørnsrud. 2016. "Disruptive Media Events: Managing Mediated Dissent in the Aftermath of Terror." *Journalism Practice*. doi:10.1080/17512786.2016.1220258.

Gutsche Jr., Robert E., and Erica Salkin. 2016. "Who Lost What? An Analysis of Myth, Loss, and Proximity in News Coverage of the Steubenville Rape." *Journalism* 17 (4): 456–473.

Hervik, Peter. 2012. "Ending Tolerance as a Solution to Incompatibility: The Danish 'Crisis of Multiculturalism'." *European Journal of Cultural Studies* 15 (2): 211–225.

Hjarvard, Stig. 2007. "Den Politiske Presse: En Analyse af Danske Avisers Politiske Orientering." *Journalistica* 5: 27–53.

Iqbal, Muhammad Zubair. 2017. "Terrorism in the Backyard: Coverage of London Attacks, 2005 by the British TV News Channels." *Journal of Broadcasting & Electronic Media* 61 (2): 449–466.

Jørndrup, Hanne. 2016. "News Framing in a Time of Terror. A Study of the Media Coverage of the Copenhagen Shootings." *Nordicom Review* 37: 85–99.

Kisch, Conrad. 1998. "The Jewish Community in Denmark: History and Present Status." *Judaism* 47 (2): 214–231.

Kitch, Carolyn. 2003. "Mourning in America: Ritual, Redemption and Recovery in News Narrative After September 11." *Journalism Studies* 4 (2): 213–224.

Laustsen, Carsten Bagge, and Rasmus Ugilt. 2015. "Kampen om terrorbegrebet." *Politica* 3: 366–385.

Lichtenstein, Tatjana. 2004. "Jews in Denmark." In *Encyclopedia of Diasporas: Immigrant and Refugee Cultures Around the World*, edited by Melvin Ember, Carol Ember, and Ian Skoggard, 934–943. New York: Springer Science & Business Media.

Matthews, Julian. 2016. "Media Performance in the Aftermath of Terror: Reporting Templates, Political Ritual and the UK Press Coverage of the London Bombings, 2005." *Journalism: Theory, Practice & Criticism* 17 (2): 173–189.

Meer, Nasar, and Per Mouritsen. 2009. "Political Cultures Compared: The Muhammad Cartoons in the Danish and British Press." *Ethnicities* 9 (3): 334–360.

Meer, Nasar, Per Mouritsen, Daniel Faas, and Nynke de Witte. 2015. "Examining 'Postmulticultural' and Civic Turns in the Netherlands, Britain, Germany and Denmark." *American Behavioral Scientist* 59 (6): 702–726.

Meltzer, Kimberly, and Emily Martik. 2017. "Journalists as Communities of Practice: Advancing a Theoretical Framework for Understanding Journalism." *Journal of Communication Inquiry* 41 (3): 207–226.

Mouritsen, Per, and Tore Vincents Olsen. 2013. "Denmark between Liberalism and Nationalism." *Ethnic and Racial Studies* 36 (4): 691–710.

Nossek, Hillel. 2008. "'News Media'-Media Events: Terrorist Acts as Media Events." *Communications* 33 (3): 313–330.

Porat, Dina, and the Kantor Center Team. 2016. "Antisemitism Worldwide 2016: General Analysis." Accessed June 6, 2017. http://kantorcenter.tau.ac.il/sites/default/files/Doch_full_2016_040517.pdf.

Pratsinakis, Manolis. 2017. "Established and Outsider Nationals: Immigrant-Native Relations and the Everyday Politics of National Belonging." *Ethnicities*. doi:10.1177/1468796817692838.

Riegert, Kristina, and Eva-Karin Olsson. 2007. "The Importance of Ritual in Crisis Journalism." *Journalism Practice* 1 (2): 143–158.

Sheller, Mimi. 2015. "News Now." *Journalism Studies* 16 (1): 12–26.

Skey, Michael. 2014. "'How Do You Think I Feel? It's My Country': Belonging, Entitlement and the Politics of Immigration." *The Political Quarterly* 85 (3): 326–332.

Statistics Denmark. 2017. *Denmark in Figures 2017*. London: Statistics Denmark.

Thorbjørnsrud, Kjersti, and Tine Ustad Figenschou. 2016. "Consensus and Dissent After Terror: Editorial Policies in Times of Crisis." *Journalism*. doi:10.1177/1464884916657519.

Yuval-Davis, Nira. 2006. "Belonging and the Politics of Belonging." *Patterns of Prejudice* 40 (3): 197–214.

Zandberg, Eyal. 2010. "The Right to Tell the (Right) Story: Journalism, Authority and Memory." *Media, Culture & Society* 32 (1): 5–24.

Zandberg, Eyal, and Motti Neiger. 2005. "Between the Nation and the Profession: Journalists as Members of Contradicting Communities." *Media, Culture & Society* 27 (1): 131–141.

Zelizer, Barbie. 1993. "Journalists as Interpretive Communities." *Critical Studies in Mass Communication* 10 (3): 219–237.

DIVERGING PROJECTIONS OF REALITY
Amplified frame competition via distinct modes of journalistic production

Curd Benjamin Knüpfer

A shared communicative space has generally been assumed to provide a basis for democratic deliberation processes wherein problems are defined, while competing political actors advocate for their preferred policies. In a mass media environment, grounds for politically motivated frame competition therefore arose primarily over limited opportunities for public attention. With ongoing processes of media fragmentation, modes of frame competition have increasingly shifted to the sites of journalistic production: media attain the means of projecting realities in tune with their audiences' preferences, leading to a segmented perception of reality. Routinely, such processes are conceptualized as hermetically sealed echo chambers or filter bubbles. But such concepts do not provide us with a coherent analytical framework, nor do they account for overlap or feedback between competing projections of reality. This paper introduces a model through which frame competition via different modes of journalistic production might be systematically observed. It consists of four distinct levels by which (1) sets of information emerge within a sphere of accessible discourse, (2) distinct selection processes of particular frames occur, (3) potentially overlapping projections of reality are formed and (4) feed back into the spectrum of available discourse.

Introduction: Media Fragmentation and Diverging Projections of Reality

"Reality is, above all, a scarce resource," James Carey (2008, 66) first wrote in 1989, and "like any scarce resource it is there to be struggled over." In the era of broadcast news, mass media provided the primary site of such struggles, causing Carey to conclude: "reality is scarce because of access: so few command the machinery for its determination" (67). This premise of a fairly monolithic media environment, in which political actors compete to define *the* news agenda in order to address and persuade *the* public, still supplies the foundation of our current understanding of political communication. In fact, two of journalism's key functions have traditionally been to provide the site of struggle *over* reality and to ultimately ensure that such struggles retain some form of connection *to* reality (Schudson 2009, 2017). But how do these dynamics play out in an increasingly inclusive and abundant information environment, in which publics are afforded a choice over which "sites" they observe? Does reality become less scarce? Can multiple versions of reality co-exist within the same media system? What would this entail?

As the "information commons" (Bennett and Iyengar 2008, 717) provided by mass media increasingly become more dispersed and fragmented (Mancini 2013), one key concern for scholars has been the potential of selective news exposure to "undermine the democratic culture of debate between differing points of view" (Dahlgren 2015, 27). As one overview of the burgeoning literature on media fragmentation has suggested, these dynamics have given rise to an information environment, in which "governments, political institutions and news media have lost their exclusive status of reality construction" (Van Aelst et al. 2017, 16).

Yet even against the backdrop of massive shifts in communication environments marked by increasingly high levels of political polarization, a systematic analysis of the literature from 1997 to 2007 found that "there has been little research on the effects of multiple frame conditions, where the same subjects get alternative frames of an issue" (Borah 2011, 251). Others have noted that much of the diverse literature on framing often fails to take differences in organizational processes along with "structural divisions and power constellations" into account when explaining frames as "part of a collective struggle over meaning" (Vliegenthart and van Zoonen 2011, 112); and where approaches towards such effects have been offered, the resulting models of frame competition tend to rest on the premise that political actors will compete within a mutual space (Entman 2004; Entman, Matthes, and Pellicano 2009) in order to strategically promote particularly effective frames to garner a broad audience's attention (Chong and Druckman 2007; Hänggli and Kriesi 2012). Other studies have looked at how agenda setting and frame competition might play out over various media platforms (Neuman et al. 2014; Guggenheim et al. 2015). These have focused on the differences these environments afford to specific forms of communication and how these may be generally advantageous to specific actors, issues or frames.

In order to amend this literature by connecting processes of media fragmentation with a possible analysis of ongoing struggles over reality, this article argues that a fragmented news media environment affords political actors and institutions significantly more leeway in how and where they promote a favored narrativization of events. The proposed concept of *amplified frame competition* will therefore not only involve individual actors or frames vying for authority within a given mass medium, but may simultaneously take place via specific modes of journalistic production, as well as subsections of the public whose cultural stocks and knowledge networks may be selectively engaged and who might further alter and disseminate a particular set of information. Fueled by competing ideological or material interests and beliefs, such distinct framing cycles may come to compete on various levels involved in projecting and perceiving a specific version of mediated reality. Within a fragmented news media environment, in other words, observing, tracing, and comparing such processes will need to incorporate various stages at which frame competition might occur, while considering the possibility that diverging feedback loops between sources and audiences may become increasingly isolated.

Indeed, the effects of such diverging perceptions are no longer difficult to make out. This holds especially true for the United States, where fragmentation processes and political polarization have been two coinciding trends (Pew Research Center 2014). In analyzing public concerns about terrorism, Nacos, Bloch-Elkon, and Shapiro (2011, 46) reported significant partisan differences among American news consumers in terms of their "perceptions of reality." Others have found similar connections between selective news consumption and public attitudes towards environmental issues (McCright and Dunlap 2011), justifications for military intervention (Lewandowsky et al. 2005), as well as such seemingly nonpolitical issues as vaccination programs (Baum 2011).

Results like these are not necessarily indicative of knowledge gaps, but rather of diverging (and often factually incorrect) stocks of information (Nyhan and Reifler 2010). This suggests that perceptions of the same issues would differ depending both on the form of mediation and the audience in question. Unsurprisingly, such observations have been made particularly in regard to topics from which the average citizen is usually far removed—either spatially or through a lack of expertise—and is therefore highly dependent on media representation. Such findings support Bennett and Iyengar's (2008, 722) premonition "that the interaction between increasingly individualized reality construction and proliferating personal media platforms" was likely to accelerate. It was the same observation of an increasingly cyclical relationship between media exposure and belief systems that caused Farhad Manjoo (2008, 21, emphasis in original) to point towards a "post-fact society," in which political controversies have increasingly come to be seen as "a fight over two competing *versions of reality.*"

Recognition of these dynamics has not been confined to academic debates. In regard to what became known as the "climategate" scandal in 2009, right-wing talk radio host Rush Limbaugh proclaimed: "We live in two universes." While one of these is governed by "lies" and ideological interests, "the other universe is where we are, and that's where reality reigns supreme and we deal with it" (Limbaugh 2009). Unintended irony aside, Limbaugh might be on to something in singling out a distinctly conservative information universe: coverage of the Trump Administration's first months in office by right-wing news sites provides a recent example. In light of the staggering divergence from mainstream media narratives of missteps and potential scandals, one analysis concluded: "We're experiencing different realities of the same event—and that reality is solidified every time these alternate storylines are repeated" (Chang 2017). Another study places the website *Breitbart.com* at the heart of a flourishing informational ecosystem, aimed at insulating and reinforcing its audience's world views in its coverage of the 2016 US presidential election. The authors conclude that this created "an environment in which the President can tell supporters about events in Sweden that never happened, or a presidential advisor can reference a non-existent 'Bowling Green massacre'" (Benkler et al. 2017).

Such dynamics are not limited to the American media system. Studies of Europe's recent sprout of populist parties have demonstrated how crucial the availability of social media has been in connecting the leadership and political supporters (Ernst et al. 2017). Meanwhile, links between various right-wing movements throughout Europe are not just heavily connected to one another through social media, but also tap into many of the same transnationally available sources of information, which deliberately position themselves as alternatives to more established forms of journalism. This, as Maan et al. (2017) note, has come to constitute a robust international network, built on specific information channels, which foster a shared sense of truth and moral purpose among its members.

Apart from somewhat paradoxical assertions of parallel "realities" or "universes," the notions of "echo chambers" (Hall Jamieson and Cappella 2008) and individualized "filter bubbles" (Pariser 2011) have been used to encapsulate such dynamics. Yet, while metaphors like these have become part of the vernacular on media fragmentation, political communication scholarship still lacks a cohesive framework with which to address them (Van Aelst et al. 2017, 20). Meanwhile, two central questions for research on the effects of media fragmentation are to what degree specific modes of journalistic production might produce divergence in their output, and under what conditions such divergence is to be expected. This article therefore provides a basic and generalizable model aimed at tracing processes of amplified frame competition in a fragmented media environment, through which sites of journalistic production offer platforms for distinct problem definitions and can differ significantly in the output they produce, i.e. the realities they come to project.

A Four-level Model of Amplified Frame Competition

As argued above, one of the main challenges for conceptualizing the dynamics of media fragmentation is that they amplify processes of frame competition, while at the same time calling into question the very existence of a unified information environment in which such struggles are perceived to take place. Rather than focus on one specific locality, any systematic approach will therefore need to incorporate the various stages of how a given projection of reality might emerge. Furthermore, many of the emergent concepts by which news consumers supposedly form epistemic communities within hermetically sealed information environments seem to overstate the actual degrees of separation between various news audiences (Van Aelst et al. 2017, 14). In doing so, they do not account for overlap between competing projections of reality. A more useful conceptual model would retain foundational elements of previous scholarship, while incorporating a way to gauge the potential impact of novel dynamics.

Previous research on media "echo chambers," for example, has been able to demonstrate the potentially isolating effects of strong levels of cohesion between specific media outlets and individual actors. Part of this research has focused on the circulation of specific sets of information by partisan modes of journalistic production and on how this can foster stark divergence in the output of various media spheres (Hall Jamieson and Cappella 2008). In other cases, the term has been used to assess the conditions under which social media might come to foster (political) homophily (Barberá 2015).

As important as these lines of inquiry have been, the concept of a "chamber" might come with certain limitations, as it is likely to evoke a rather rigid locality in which information reverberates, instead of fluidly transitioning from one communicative level to the next. In this regard, the model presented below can provide more conceptual clarity, while incorporating previous research findings into a procedural framework of how information circulates within a larger media environment. Doing so will also help to expand the scope of such research agendas by broadening the possible scope of explanatory factors which drive such dynamics. These processes may involve political interests, potential overlap and degrees of separation between competing framing cycles. Including these factors may thus help us better understand under which circumstances "echo chamber" effects may emerge, and to better pin down what we mean by the phenomenon.

To do so, the approach presented here offers four levels at which such analytical distinction could be made: (1) in the localities from which various types of information are selected; (2) in the mechanisms of news production; (3) in the output (i.e. projections of reality) that these media produce; and (4) in the circulation of frames between institutions or elites, the media, and the public.

Ultimately, this is meant to offer scholars a basic and easily amendable guideline for how to approach instances of amplified frame competition in fragmented news media environments. The various levels incorporated draw from and can add to different research programs within political communication and journalism studies scholarship while comparative approaches can employ different analytical tools to observe the impact of diverging modes of news production. Table 1 presents an overview of the underlying theoretical assumptions and possible methodological approaches likely to generate research designs through which the four analytical levels could be further fleshed out. In doing so, the table introduces suggestions for how scholarly research might engage with each of these stages or synthesize various research findings into a coherent account of amplified frame competition.

The proposed conceptual levels are further outlined in two subsequent steps: first, the basic mechanisms by which reality projection can be understood to occur are explained, by synthesizing existing observations about the processes of mediated political communication. Building on this, a second step will lay out how such processes are potentially altered by the dynamics of media fragmentation. The following sections maintain this two-step structure in addressing (1) a general process of how mediated information can sequentially form a specific projection of reality and (2) how political contestation and processes accompanying the phenomenon of media fragmentation may affect these processes.

Figures 1 and 2 illustrate this distinction. Figure 1 synthesizes the basic process through which political communication would typically understand a given projection of reality via news media to occur. It serves as an illustration of four distinct levels by which (1) sets of information emerge and are drawn from within the confines of what we can conceptualize as a sphere of accessible discourse. (2) A given mode of journalistic production selects from the array of informational building blocks, assembles and reframes them, in order to (3) maintain a projection of reality, which (4) feeds back into the sphere of discourse. The mode by which information circulates within this process can be conceptualized as an ongoing framing cycle. Each of these conceptual levels is explained in more detail below.

Meanwhile, Figure 2 illustrates how media fragmentation could be expected to affect this process. The four stages are maintained, yet slightly altered by the emergence of two distinct framing cycles enabled through different modes of journalistic production. These create what might be understood as diverging projections of reality that feed back into the sphere of accessible discourse, while expanding the spectrum of emerging sets of information. Over time, this would foster an increasing disconnect between members of the public who tap into different framing processes and come to hold different beliefs over what is occurring outside their immediate realm of experience. Media consumers might be increasingly primed to respond to the same set of events or information in different

TABLE 1
Amplified frame completion—underlying frameworks and approaches

Level of analysis	Theoretical approaches	Methodological approaches
1. Emergence of information	Discourse theory; public sphere theory; critical theory	Discourse analysis; critical analysis/deconstruction
2. News production	Institutionalism; field theory	Sociological observation; network analysis; interviews
3. Projections of reality	Frame theory; comparative case studies	Qualitative or quantitative content analysis
4. Frame circulation and feedback loops	Media effects theory; priming	Surveys; experiments

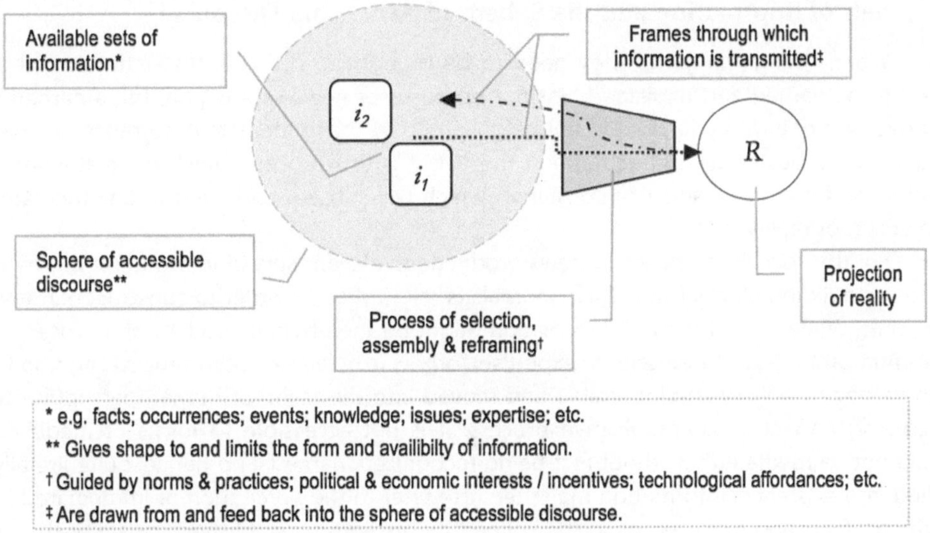

FIGURE 1
Conceptual levels of reality projection

ways, as their beliefs about the nature of reality rooted in memory and historical contexts via previous news consumption can differ significantly.

Furthermore, while there is room for distinction here, divergent framing cycles are still assumed to be part of the same media system. They can thus be expected to generate some degree of overlap, while feeding back into a shared discursive realm. Nevertheless, the model depicted here would assume the largest possible degree of distinction within such an environment. It is entirely feasible to assume that overlap might occur in terms of sourcing or frames being employed. In addition to testing whether two projections are ultimately in fact distinct from one another, the model therefore aims to provide a basis for comparative approaches through which to gauge potential similarities. Each of these conceptual stages is discussed in more detail below.

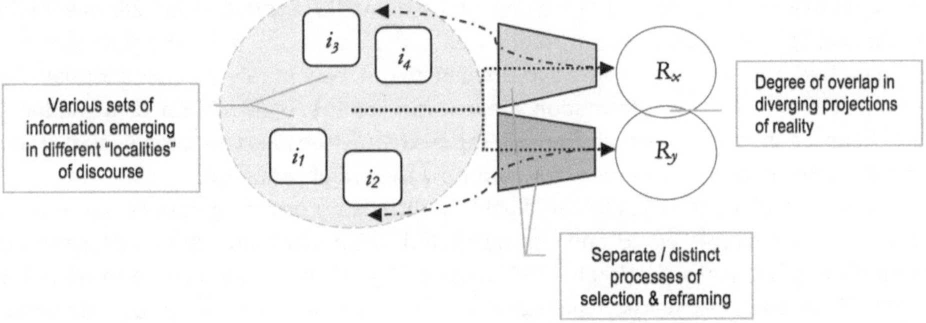

FIGURE 2
Amplified frame competition via distinct modes of journalistic production

Sets of Information and the Sphere of Accessible Discourse

When "things happen," they need to be brought to our collective attention, they need to be named and explained. For the purposes of news production, the emergence of novel sets of information would not be governed by the immediate occurrence of a particular event, but rather by recognition thereof. It is this process which generates information, and it is these sets of information which will subsequently inform any mediated projection of reality.

For the specific purposes of news production, relevant sets of information therefore form the building blocks from which journalists might draw in order to construct narrative accounts. While some forms of information might be the obvious product of a process of communication (e.g. statements or expertise), others (e.g. facts or occurrences) can also be understood as only becoming visible and moved into the realm of human perception by becoming part of a communicative process: it is not accessible to forms of media—it could not be mediated—without first being recognized, named, and hence, quite literally, called into existence. Information may therefore refer to the perception of immediate and verifiable facts and occurrences, or be shaped by previously established social constructs, expertise or interpretative processes. As they become relevant to news production, either of these forms might emerge through journalistic inquiry, eyewitness accounts, live coverage, etc., or be provided by institutions, policy elites or experts within a specific field.

Additionally, various implicit demarcation lines may limit the breadth and scope of information perceived to be available, and which can be associated with a specific social, political or cultural context. Building on critical theory, Daniel Hallin (1994, 32) observed that there exist limits beyond which "the basic structure of human communication cannot be stretched." For the specific purposes of news production, the scope of accessible discourse might therefore also be described as the general information environment, or "the aggregate supply of news or political information that is 'out there'" (Van Aelst et al. 2017, 5). Therefore, information can only be derived from the sphere of accessible discourse which represents both the totality of what might become available to news media as part of the observable world, society, and culture within which they function, as well as the permeable boundaries limiting the scope of obtainable and communicable information. All potential sets of information can be understood as emerging and being drawn from within this conceptual sphere.

The vast majority of occurrences on which our collective sense of reality is based is, of course, never explicitly recognized as such. This is especially true for the particular sets of information that might be relevant for a given form of media report: if a tree falls over in the metaphorical sphere of discourse, it might well make a sound. But for the purposes of a news narrative, the information thus produced might be entirely inconsequential. The question of which sets of information are relevant to the construction of a mediated reality therefore involves a certain form of imposed structures and hierarchies that determine relevance, as well as where, when, and how they might emerge.

Such hierarchies of visibility can illustrate underlying power dynamics that govern access to the observable world and can be rooted in language and the constellation of communicative networks (Edelman 1985; Castells 2009). They may also be regarded as a series of overlapping fields, which impose an amalgamation of various dynamics onto a given situation (Bourdieu 2005), or be tied to specific actors, who might enjoy more leeway in generating information that will ultimately garner public attention

(Bennett 1990). According to such observations, democratic media systems have typically navigated the disorderly sphere of discourse by relying heavily on the hierarchies provided by political and institutional power. Likewise, certain social conventions and norms might lead particular subsidiary spheres to be regarded as consensus worthy and legitimate, while others are generally deemed deviant, causing information that emanates from here to largely be ignored. As Hallin's (1986, 177) model of concentric spheres has shown, these boundaries are far from static and can change over time, meaning that the spheres of consensus and legitimate controversy can expand, and come to include ideas previously considered off limits.

Media fragmentation alters these dynamics by imposing new hierarchies and thus substantially widening the scope of information that becomes available to various forms of news production. This is not necessarily a feature of the information environment itself. Events occur, knowledge is produced, experiences are made in much the same way and perhaps to the same degree as before. However, through a more abundant media environment, public focus becomes scattered and may selectively shift towards or away from particular types of discourse. Particular forms of knowledge production, for example through scientific methods or government institutions, might lose significance, while other discourses may attain more recognition (Van Aelst et al. 2017, 16). Increasingly, specific types of media deliberately draw from what might otherwise be considered the sphere of deviance, in order to mark their status as alternative information sources and cater to a niche audience (Stroud 2011).

It is therefore not the productive capacity of various discourses that would be directly affected by processes of media fragmentation, but rather the hierarchies and structures imposed upon them by journalists and media outlets. It might be somewhat misleading, in other words, to assume that the dynamics of media fragmentation *create* more information. Instead, they lead to additional *emergence* of information by expanding the possibilities through which it would be recognized as such.

Mechanisms of Journalistic Production

A basic function of news media is to determine which sets of information are to be transformed into mediated projections of reality. Any such process will involve a mechanism by which media outlets produce news (Gans 1980). As pointed towards above, various preferences might emerge in regard to which (or whose) sets of information are habitually selected by any given mode of news production. Journalism scholarship has also defined various aspects of news values (Harcup and O'Neill 2017), which refer not just to the particularities of specific sets of information, but define these in terms of how well they meet specific preferences and requirements of journalists and media outlets.

Furthermore, analytical frameworks like those of "cascading frame activation" (Entman 2004) or "market equilibrium" (Baum and Groeling 2010) have outlined the hierarchical dynamics by which information circulates between policy elites, news media, and the public. While media projections are therefore somewhat dependent on the emergence of sets of information from which to sample and select, the act of mediation will inevitably involve a more or less deliberate process of reframing by journalists, who ultimately do not "provide a copy of reality, but reality in a frame, reality enhanced, reality reconfigured" (Schudson 2017). This affords various types of news production a certain degree of autonomy in regard to how they select, but also how they reframe sets of information.

Vliegenthart and van Zoonen (2011, 111) note that "the knowledge, attitudes and behaviours of individual producers are the product of professional and organizational processes in the newsroom, rather than traits or decisions of autonomous individuals." As comparative approaches to news production within various media systems have established, it is primarily political, commercial constraints, as well as culturally embedded norms and practices that, to varying degrees, "directly shape news content and form" (Benson 2010, 616). Distinction might therefore be the result of a variety of different constellations: particular business models (Hamilton 2004) or specific ideological preferences (Hall Jamieson and Cappella 2008) might give rise to modes of news production which seek to establish themselves precisely based on their similarities or dissimilarities to other forms of journalism: a diverse spectrum of regional news might emulate the dominant norms of the legacy press and come to select information based on many of the same criteria that will be at work in other professionalized newsrooms, while niche media might define themselves in direct opposition to these traits (Stroud 2011).

Such systematic preferences by which particular biases arise need not be limited to ideological and economic factors or to specific sets of norms and practices. Rather than being based on conscious decisions, they might also be the result of the limits or affordances inherent to a particular medium: therefore, social media news feeds based on artificial intelligence-driven algorithms may exhibit unintended biases in what sets of information they may deem newsworthy (Diakopolous 2012). Even generally non-ideological news aggregators, which do not directly produce their own media content, can therefore cater to the expected preferences of their individual users (Pariser 2011).

These different factors tell us nothing about size or reach. Various combinations of such mechanisms might well underlie the majority of what might be referred to as "mainstream" news production. They might also be traced back to single institutions or even individuals who deliberately choose different approaches to how they assemble sets of information and frame events. However, in order to remain sustainable over time, it is more likely than not that socio-politically relevant forms of reality projection will be established by institutions that are powerful and autonomous enough to do so. Instead of individual media outlets, it is therefore likely that diverging projections of reality will emerge from what has been described as distinct media ecosystems (Benkler et al. 2017).

The question of distinction is crucial here and can be addressed through systemic differences: are there mechanisms and incentives in place which will consistently lead to different modes of assembling information and therefore create a distinct output? These might rest on a blend of ideological preferences, economic incentives, institutional interests and practices, professional norms, ethic guidelines or codes of conduct. Hence, even if news outlets are market competitors, this fact alone might not make them distinct from other modes of news production and the output they produce, i.e. the realities they project will overlap to the point of being essentially the same.

Within a fragmented news environment, these factors may have serious implications for the dynamics of frame competition and the superimposed hierarchies by which information is made available to a larger public. Hence, there is an important distinction to be made between the act of selection by specific actors and the theoretical availability of a wide array of discourses providing possible sets of information. Both impose limitations on the perception of reality via news media projection. Yet while the first level might be understood as a mutually shared sphere from which information is derived, it is by diverging mechanisms of selection and reframing that these perceptions would become increasingly isolated from one another. News media thus attain more leeway in how they assemble information. Yet even so, such modes of production would not enjoy complete autonomy over how they could frame events and construct projections of reality. They are not only still dependent on sources of information, but also part of a media environment in which they compete for attention and trust. A third level of analysis, focused on journalistic output, can therefore help to establish common constraints and further establish where distinction might occur.

Projections of Reality

In addressing possible divergence in news media output, a central question here would be the relationship of what might be conceptualized as a *projection of* reality to that which a mediated projection is meant to signify—i.e. what we might deem *actual* or *physical* reality. Within the model presented here, the impact of "the real world" can be explained via the continuous emergence and availability of specific sets of information. In this sense, reality would hold the potential to factor into any particular projection of reality through the incessant emergence of particular sets of information. Reality, in other words, constantly creates occurrences, spawns observations, fosters opposing points of view, and hence, continuously generates information on a given topic. It is thus highly likely that it will play an important, if not the primary factor in delimiting and hence shaping the range of possible projections of the external reference points provided.

As scholars of journalism studies and political communication, we would do well to note that this likelihood is not a guarantee that actual reality would be a primary force in giving shape to projections of itself. In referring to their concept of the "elasticity of reality," Baum and Groeling (2010, 10) argue that while policy elites and media outlets enjoy a certain leeway in agenda setting, framing, and depicting events, over time this "elasticity" is diminished, while "reality asserts itself." In the mid- to long term, in other words, it becomes more likely that reality will impact media reports and hence the ability to spin a story or engage in strategic framing is gradually diminished. However, casting reality as an acting subject might be somewhat misleading. In the sense that it is understood here, reality does not "assert itself," but must rather *be* asserted. In democratic societies, liberal institutions like academia or independent journalism are typically in the business of providing this service to the public. Yet at the same time, the mere existence of such institutions is in no way an automatic guarantee that truth and accuracy will prevail in the long run (Schudson 2009). Inaccurate or even demonstrably false projections of reality can thus be sustained over long periods of time, especially in places in which their projection would have relatively little impact on the immediate recipient of the information. This might be the case with views on foreign events or complex phenomena such as climate change—in which the large mass of individual news recipients have no immediate personal stake in ensuring the veracity of the information they receive and few possibilities of gauging the trustworthiness of the sources they prefer.

Another important conceptual distinction lies between a sustained projection of reality and the framing of a singular news item or event. The model presented here is meant to be understood as a continuous flow of information, and not merely as the depiction of an individual occurrence. We can understand a projection of reality to be consistent with a specific set of underlying logics and moral evaluations, which may consist of previously established narratives and beliefs. A singular news item, topic or frame would therefore have to feed into such a projection, which could consequently be altered but would generally find ways of incorporating this occurrence into a previously existing and generally stable framework.

Even within a single, internally diverse media outlet, one might habitually encounter various framing processes based on the same sets of information. Yet in such cases it is still assumed that the process of frame competition or deliberation over the interpretation of events would lead to a shared and mutually accepted understanding of what is and is not viewed as being real. In some cases, journalists might simply get it wrong, or pass along false information. At other times, news coverage of an issue or event might entail the realization that different views on a specific matter can co-exist. Ultimately, such pluralistic tendencies are still able to shape a common understanding of the same projection of what is real and considered to be true. Contradiction and controversy might exist, in other words, but over time these would still need to be incorporated into the same understanding of how the world works (Schudson 2017).

Diverging projections of reality are not a necessary outcome of media fragmentation. It is entirely plausible to assume that even within a highly segmented and fragmenting news environment the same projection of reality is ultimately constructed and maintained. This would imply that the outputs of various modes of journalistic production would not differ to such a degree as to make them significantly distinct from one another. Yet in other cases, such difference can be starker and ultimately incompatible within the same mechanism of projection. The clearest examples for this would be shaped by a binary divergence in which the existence of one thing would exclude the possibility of another (Van Aelst et al. 2017, 14). Affirmation or negation of the existence of a particular set of information would be one example: while various interpretations of a particular occurrence might be found within the same projection of reality, it would be unsustainable to assume that the same occurrence could be projected both as having taken place and not having taken place, for example.

Since the conceptual model presented here rests on a singular, albeit fragmented media system, the question of overlap between two potentially distinct projections of reality becomes additionally relevant. As has been explained, the model would assume that two (or more) separate modes of journalistic production would draw from and feed into the same, mutually shared sphere of discourse. At times this might mean that they would select the same sets of information, but frame these in diverging ways. Other times, entirely different sets of information might be drawn from initially, yet over time their salience would increase and may gradually play a role within separate framing processes. This may occur, for example, when the consequences of or the very existence of an alternative projection of reality are acknowledged by a diverging or competing mode of news production (cf. Benkler et al. 2017).

One projection of reality might therefore be seen as distinct from another, if the degree of overlap between two forms of mediated reality is smaller than the degree to which they differ from one another. The conceptual challenge here is obvious: what would the unit of analysis be, on which such measurements and comparison might be based? In various projections of reality, up will be up and the sky will be blue. Yet they may differ significantly in regard to the most basic premises of what constitutes a political problem.

It (therefore) becomes clear that for the purposes of the claims that might be tested via this model, distinction in the projection of realities must always occur in regard to a specific set of information. In observing an ongoing transition into "the fourth age of political communication," Jay Blumler (2013) has pointed towards a possibly increasing "tendency to talk about the same issues and events but more often interpreting them differently." He too suggests that the perhaps most useful and conceptually fleshed out unit of analysis in this regard is that of framing.

As Entman's classic definition will tell us, distinction (and contestation) can occur on various levels including problem definition and causal analysis, as well as moral evaluation and remedy promotion (Entman 2004, 5). While divergence in projections of reality can be expected to occur on all of the levels, it would be observable primarily through the foundational act of problem definition along with the secondary question of causal analysis. In other words, the factual basis implied by the affirmation or negation of the very existence of a particular problem would be the most obvious unit of analysis to focus on, when gauging degrees of difference or overlap in terms of a particular projection of reality. These would-be struggles form the foundation of frame competition, which increasingly shifts from the various discursive spheres out of which journalists would draw their information and well into the process of journalistic production itself.

Within a fragmented news media environment, the consensual basis of factuality may thus be undermined through the various mechanisms that might otherwise provide a platform for frame competition. The initial act of problem definition, on which such competition would be based, is moved into the realm of journalistic production itself. This reduces the aspect of frame competition to the very basis of factual deliberation and thus amplifies the process by which such struggles may occur.

Feedback Loops and the Circulation of Frames

As suggested, there is a distinction to be made between a specific framing process and the projection(s) of reality such frames tie into. Framing may begin with the emergence of a particular set of information, be altered via specific modes of selection, mediation and reframing, first by sources, then by journalists and media institutions, and feed into a particular form of media representation. In this sense, frames can be regarded as the unit by which information is transmitted and by which it circulates within the model outlined here.

The four levels therefore do not necessarily constitute a process by which the emergence of information successively leads to the projection of reality. They are rather part of an ongoing cycle, by which an already-established projection of reality can co-determine which sets of information might emerge within the realm of observable discourse. The narratives, beliefs, and schemata that sustain such a projection require certain frames, which in turn would lead the mechanisms of news production to select and assemble (frame) information that might otherwise be left unreported. In this way, the supposed succession from level one to level four is effectively reversed.

Such feedback may also emerge through the well-established effects of agenda setting and priming, by which news coverage begets more news coverage: as an occurrence is brought into public focus and a specific form of reality is projected, more interest in this spectrum of available information is created. This causes novel sets of information to emerge while sparking new incentives for forms of frame competition. Accordingly, various diverging projections of reality might, over time, lead to distinctly different sets of information, which are in turn linked to a specific mode of news production further incentivized by cumulative audience demand: various modes of journalistic production will therefore aim to "provide the kind of content that their target groups demand in order to remain competitive" (Van Aelst et al. 2017, 5).

It is in this sense that mediated projections of reality can "create" reality in that they provide beliefs about the world, which in turn serve as the basis for further debate, decisions, and political action. Such circulation is typically understood to involve three sets of actors: political elites or institutions, the news media, and an assumed audience. In order to glean what the public's preferences and opinions might be, political elites therefore become part of a process in which they "relentlessly contend to influence the very news frames that influence them" (Entman 2004, 123).

Divergences in news production by various forms of media production expand and exacerbate this aspect of frame competition: rather than competing over dominance within a mutually shared environment, political actors and institutions may now become part of distinct feedback loops competing for public attention. Political elites thus gain incentives to communicate selectively, in order to ensure that their frames are in tune with the perception of reality of the addressed audience. In other words, political actors are likely to increasingly seek out and tap into those projections of reality and framing cycles, which are strategically advantageous. This, in turn, is likely to lead to less immediate dialogue between political opponents via a mutually shared media venue, as well as an increase in the emergence of information catered to specific needs of diverging modes of journalistic production (Baum and Groeling 2010, 292–296).

In terms of the well-established dynamics of *indexing* (Bennett 1990, 2017), this would suggest that political actors can increasingly communicate selectively and actively fuel alternative framing cycles by lending their professional standing to promoting a particular set of information. Hence, novel incentives arise, which would lead political figures to advocate for policies based on problems that are only defined and perceived within increasingly isolated framing cycles. Furthermore, a fragmented news media environment may lead to modes of news production, in which the hierarchical structures described by indexing or cascading frame activation (Entman 2004) may be circumvented while new dynamics come to determine why and how some frames tend to find an audience, while others do not.

In such cases, the needs of alternative media outlets for novel sources who might lend their name to a given news story may well still resemble previous modes of news production. But this resemblance might be superficial. In US politics, recent examples of novel indexing dynamics included prominent figures with little to no institutional standing. One might name Sarah Palin's influence on the "deathpanel debate" (Nyhan 2010) or the role played by a pre-presidential Donald Trump in advocating the racist "birtherism" narrative (Bennett 2017). In such cases, previously held beliefs about reality among partisan members of the public may well have driven niche media outlets to focus on these sources, all the while catering to their audience's perceived demands and subsequently causing the emergence of resilient framing cycles. Doing so meant to seek out personas on the fringes of political discourse, which were both eager and incentivized to provide novel sets of information in order to further drive a particular narrative. In such cases, the levels of analysis proposed here might well be turned on their head: media fragmentation may force us to consider how selective perception gives rise to modes of journalistic production, which in turn incentivizes the genesis and promotion of particular sets of information in what has been termed "the proliferation of citizen-drive spectacle" (Mihailidis and Viotty 2017). The widespread circulation of "fake news" during the 2016 US presidential election serves as a salient example, wherein partisan beliefs incentivized the emergence and rapid dissemination of misinformation deemed too good to be untrue.

Elsewhere, similar mechanisms along with the information providers that fuel them have been referred to as "disinformation orders" (Bennett and Livingston, forthcoming). As this terminology suggests, there may well be ideological interests and disruptive intent driving the initial stages of such mechanisms: whether through the provision of specific sets of information or by facilitating the mechanisms that drive the production of alternative narratives. In such cases, amplified frame competition and the projection of an alternative reality might not necessarily aim at ensuring hegemony for a preferred mode of interpretation or a gradual synthesis of diverging viewpoints, but rather mark a deliberate attempt at subverting and negating what might otherwise become a widely accepted projection of reality. While such attempts to intentionally subvert and hinder public deliberation processes are certainly not new to democratic societies (Oreskes and Conway 2012), media fragmentation affords such interests novel opportunities of disruption and provides an array of entry points on all four levels outlined here, to engage in amplified frame competition and shape or mobilize partisan beliefs.

In broader terms, such developments might mean that diverging feedback loops collectively expand the scope of available information within the sphere of available discourse, while at the same time being more narrowly focused on a specific projection of reality. The larger the degree to which two or more projections of reality diverge within the same media system, the stronger these effects are likely to be—and vice versa. Hence, within a fragmented media environment, spiral effects may emerge over time, by which divergence is likely to increase up to the point at which institutional structures and the boundaries of mutually shared discursive spheres halt and possibly reverse these developments.

Another, more troubling end result of such processes would be the eventual paralysis of democratic institutions, whose claim to normative legitimation tends to rest on pluralistic deliberation, eventual compromise, and a potential for consensus-building. In modern democratic systems, these elements might well depend on a media environment capable of fostering a shared perception of reality among the public and policy elites. At its worst, it is therefore not difficult to foresee how prolonged and highly polarized instances of amplified frame competition might contribute to the dissolution of the social fabric underlying liberal societies.

Conclusion

Scholars seeking to explain processes of political communication and democratic deliberation are increasingly likely to encounter stark differences in public perception and knowledge stocks. Accordingly, comparative approaches based on various modes of journalistic production within the same media environments are likely to become progressively important. The model presented here could offer a baseline from which to measure and gauge degrees of overlap and difference in terms of mediated output. This, in turn, can provide new classifications of various forms of news media. Thus, even if the notion of separate and distinct projections of reality is challenged by empirical findings, varying degrees of overlap on an idealized scale might still serve a useful conceptual function.

Pointing towards commonalities in the way various forms of news production project reality, I certainly do not mean to imply that any such mechanism is as good as any other. Yet only by acknowledging the fundamental similarities between various types of news production will it be possible to highlight the actual degree to which they may differ in their output. Any form of distinction between two or more formats must therefore rest on differences that scholars can accurately name in order to locate them. While the underlying theoretical implications of the analytical levels presented here may differ strongly, it would still be possible to combine this analysis for comparative purposes in a unified approach within a single study. Such holistic approaches might examine media fragmentation as one aspect pertaining to a larger crisis of liberal institutions marked by their potential loss of hegemony in deliberative practices and collective truth-finding:

1. A first level of analysis addresses *sourcing of information*: which agenda items can be found, which topics, facts or events are mentioned, and where/how did they originate?
2. A second level of analysis focuses on *mechanisms of news production* and categorizes media outlets based on these criteria. Indicators here might be self-identification with particular ideology, business or ownership models, technological affordances, or particular practices.
3. A third level of analysis compares *news media content*. Text- or multimedia-based data can be evaluated via quantitative or qualitative analysis focused on framing or agenda setting, for example.
4. A fourth level of analysis might focus on *media effects*, in order to address possible links in media consumption habits of specific segments of the public and factors such as partisanship, political behavior, or beliefs on a given topic. In order to study the impact of feedback loops and frame circulation, we might hypothesize that continuous divergence in news consumption will lead to increases in polarization along these indicators over time.

Finally, the model presents a workable approach in answer to concerns about an ongoing shift towards "post truth" politics within democratic communication environments (Manjoo 2008; Mihailidis and Viotty 2017). These dynamics have been marked by postulations of alternative facts, the rise of fake news, or perceptions of the world resting on misinformation and debunked claims. A systematic approach to diverging projections of reality can help us approach these similar yet separate phenomena. For example, postulations of alternative facts can be incorporated into a level-one analysis focused on the emergence of particular sets of information from particular sites of the discursive sphere. Where do such sets of information originate and by which discursive logics are they distributed? The emergence of fake news primarily presents a challenge for analysis on the second level: here, research might address the question of how technological affordances, coupled with economic or political incentives, might foster the mechanisms driving this particular form of reality projection. Meanwhile, pronouncements by which information might be deemed both "fake but accurate" (*Washington Post*, May 15, 2017) could be approached on the third and fourth levels of analysis, by which projections of reality and feedback loops in framing cycles gradually come to foster forms of selective perception and self-sustaining worldviews.

ACKNOWLEDGEMENTS

I am indebted to Mathias Großklaus and Katharina Metz (Freie Universität Berlin), W. Lance Bennett (University of Washington), as well as the two anonymous reviewers for their immensely helpful feedback and comments.

DISCLOSURE STATEMENT

No potential conflict of interest was reported by the author.

REFERENCES

Barberá, Pablo. 2015. "Birds of the Same Feather Tweet Together: Bayesian Ideal Point Estimation Using Twitter Data." *Political Analysis* 23 (1): 76–91.

Baum, Matthew A. 2011. "Red State, Blue State, Flu State: Media Self-selection and Partisan Gaps in Swine Flu Vaccinations." *Journal of Health Politics, Policy and Law* 36 (6): 1021–1059.

Baum, Matthew A., and Tim J. Groeling. 2010. *War Stories: The Causes and Consequences of Public Views of War*. Princeton: Princeton University Press.

Benkler, Yochai, Robert Faris, Hal Roberts, and Ethan Zuckerman. 2017. "Breitbart-led Right-wing Media Ecosystem Altered Broader Media Agenda." *Columbia Journalism Review*. http://www.cjr.org/analysis/breitbart-media-trump-harvard-study.php

Bennett, W. Lance. 1990. "Toward a Theory of Press-State Relations in the United States." *Journal of Communication* 40 (2): 103–127.

Bennett, W. Lance. 2017. "Press–Government Relations in a Changing Media Environment." *The Oxford Handbook of Political Communication*, edited by Kate Kenski and Kathleen Hall Jamieson, Vol. 1, 249–262. The Oxford Handbook of Political Communication.

Bennett, W. Lance, and Shanto Iyengar. 2008. "A New Era of Minimal Effects? The Changing Foundations of Political Communication." *Journal of Communication* 58: 707–731.

Bennett, W. Lance, and Steven Livingston. Forthcoming 2018. "The Disinformation Order: Disruptive Communication and the Decline of Democratic Institutions." *European Journal of Communication*.

Benson, Rodney. 2010. "Comparative News Media Systems: New Directions in Research." In *The Routledge Companion to News and Journalism*, edited by Stuart Allan, 614–626. London: Routledge.

Blumler, Jay G. 2013. "The Fourth Age of Political Communication." Keynote lecture presented at the DFG Forschergruppe 1381, September 17. http://www.fgpk.de/2013/gastbeitrag-von-jay-g-blumler-the-fourth-age-of-political-communication-2/

Borah, Porismita. 2011. "Conceptual Issues in Framing Theory: A Systematic Examination of a Decade's Literature." *Journal of Communication* 61 (2). Blackwell Publishing Ltd: 246–263.

Bourdieu, Pierre. 2005. "The Political Field, the Social Science Field and the Journalistic Field." In *Bourdieu and the Journalistic Field*, edited by Rodney Benson and Erik Neveu, 29–47. Cambridge and Maiden, MA: Polity Press.

Carey, James W. 2008. *Communication as Culture: Essays on Media and Society*. Revised ed. New York: Routledge.

Castells, Manuel. 2009. *Communication Power*. Oxford and New York: Oxford University Press.

Chang, Alvin. 2017. "We Tracked the Trump Scandals on Right-wing News Sites. Here's How They Covered It." *Vox*, May 18. https://www.vox.com/policy-and-politics/2017/5/18/15646098/right-wing-media-collective-memories.

Chong, Dennis, and James N. Druckman. 2007. "A Theory of Framing and Opinion Formation in Competitive Elite Environments." *Journal of Communication* 57 (1). Blackwell Publishing Inc: 99–118.

Dahlgren, Peter. 2015. "The Internet as a Civic Space." In *Handbook of Digital Politics*, edited by Stephen Coleman and Deen Freelon, 17–34. Cheltenham: Edward Elgar Publishing.

Diakopolous, Nick. 2012. "Understanding Bias in Computational News Media." *Nieman Journalism Lab*, December 10. http://www.niemanlab.org/2012/12/nick-diakopoulos-understanding-bias-in-computational-news-media

Edelman, Murray. 1985. "Political Language and Political Reality." *American Political Science Association Ps* 18 (1): 10–19.

Entman, Robert M. 2004. *Projections of Power: Framing News, Public Opinion, and U.S. Foreign Policy*. Chicago: University of Chicago Press.

Entman, Robert M., Jörg Matthes, and Lynn Pellicano. 2009. "Nature, Sources, and Effects of News Framing." In *The Handbook of Journalism Studies*, edited by Karin Wahl-Jorgensen and Thomas Hanitzsch, 175–190. New York: Routledge.

Ernst, Nicole, Sven Engesser, Florin Büchel, Sina Blassnig, and Frank Esser. 2017. "Extreme Parties and Populism: An Analysis of Facebook and Twitter across Six Countries." *Information, Communication & Society* 20 (9):1347–1364.

Gans, Herbert J. 1980. *Deciding What's News: A Study of "CBS Evening News", "NBC Nightly News", "Newsweek", and "Time"*. New York: Vintage Books.

Guggenheim, Lauren, Mo Jang, Soo Young Bae, and W. Russell Neuman. 2015. "The Dynamics of Issue Frame Competition in Traditional and Social Media." *The ANNALS of the American Academy of Political and Social Science*, edited by Dhavan V. Shah, Joseph N. Cappella, and W. Russell Neuman. London: SAGE Publishing. 659 (1): 207–224.

Hall Jamieson, Kathleen, and Joseph N. Cappella. 2008. *Echo Chamber. Rush Limbaugh and the Conservative Media Establishment*. New York: Oxford University Press.

Hallin, Daniel C. 1986. *The "Uncensored War" – The Media and Vietnam*. New York: Oxford University Press.

Hallin, Daniel C. 1994. *We Keep America on Top of the World. Television Journalism and the Public Sphere*. London: Routledge.

Hamilton, James T. 2004. *All the News That's Fit to Sell: How the Market Transforms Information into News*. Princeton: Princeton University Press.

Hänggli, Regula, and Hanspeter Kriesi. 2012. "Frame Construction and Frame Promotion (Strategic Framing Choices)." *American Behavioral Scientist* 56 (3): 260–278.

Harcup, Tony, and Deirdre O'Neill. 2017. "What Is News?" *Journalism Studies* 23 (1). Routledge: 1–19.

Lewandowsky, Stephan, Werner G. K. Stritzke, Klaus Oberauer, and Michael Morales. 2005. "Memory for Fact, Fiction, and Misinformation." *Psychological Science* 16 (3): 190–195.

Limbaugh, Rush. 2009. "ClimateGate Hoax: The Universe of Lies Versus the Universe of Reality." *The Rush Limbaugh Show*, November 24. Transcript. http://www.rushlimbaugh.com/daily/2009/11/24/climategate_hoax_the_universe_of_lies_versus_the_universe_of_reality

Maan, Noura, Fabian Schmid, Markus Hametner, and Josef Šlerka. 2017. "Le Pen schenkt HC ein Like: Wie sich Europas Rechte vernetzen." *DerStandard.at*, May 24. http://derstandard.at/2000058082824/Le-Pen-schenkt-HC-ein-Like-Wie-sich-Europas-Rechte

Mancini, Paolo. 2013. "Media Fragmentation, Party System, and Democracy." *The International Journal of Press/Politics* 18 (1): 43–60.

Manjoo, Farhad. 2008. *True Enough. Learning to Live in a Post-fact Society*. Hoboken: Wiley.

McCright, Aaron M., and Riley E. Dunlap. 2011. "The Politicization of Climate Change and Polarization in the American Public's Views of Global Warming, 2001–2010." *Sociological Quarterly* 52 (2): 155–194.

Mihailidis, Paul, and Samantha Viotty. 2017. "Spreadable Spectacle in Digital Culture: Civic Expression, Fake News, and the Role of Media Literacies in 'Post-Fact' Society." *American Behavioral Scientist* 61 (4). SAGE PublicationsSage CA: Los Angeles, CA: 441–454.

Nacos, Brigitte L., Yaeli Bloch-Elkon, and Robert Y Shapiro. 2011. *Selling Fear: Counterterrorism, the Media, and Public Opinion*. Chicago: University of Chicago Press.

Neuman, W. Russell, Lauren Guggenheim, S. Mo Jang, and Soo Young Bae. 2014. "The Dynamics of Public Attention: Agenda-Setting Theory Meets Big Data." *Journal of Communication* 64 (2). Wiley Subscription Services, Inc.: 193–214.

Nyhan, Brendan. 2010. "Why the Death Panel Myth Wouldn't Die: Misinformation in the Health Care Reform Debate." *The Forum* 8 (1): 1–24.

Nyhan, Brendan, and Jason Reifler. 2010. "When Corrections Fail: The Persistence of Political Misperceptions." *Political Behavior* 32 (2): 303–330.

Oreskes, Naomi, and Erik M. Conway. 2012. *Merchants of Doubt: How a Handful of Scientists Obscured the Truth on Issues from Tobacco Smoke to Global Warming*. London: Bloomsbury.

Pariser, Eli. 2011. *The Filter Bubble: What the Internet is Hiding from You*. New York: Penguin Press.

Pew Research Center. 2014. "Political Polarization and Media Habits." October 21. http://www.journalism.org/files/2014/10/Political-Polarization-and-Media-Habits-FINAL-REPORT-10-21-2014.pdf

Schudson, Michael. 2009. "Factual Knowledge in an Age of Truthiness." In *The Changing Faces of Journalism: Tabloidization, Technology and Truthiness*, edited by Barbie Zelizer, 104–114. London, New York: Routledge.

Schudson, Michael. 2017. "Here's What Non-fake News Looks like." *Columbia Journalism Review*, February 23. http://www.cjr.org/analysis/fake-news-real-news-list.php

Stroud, Natalie J. 2011. *Niche News: The Politics of News Choice*. New York, NY: Oxford University Press.

Van Aelst, Peter, Jesper Strömbäck, Toril Aalberg, Frank Esser, Claes de Vreese, Jörg Matthes, David Hopmann, et al. 2017. "Political Communication in a High-choice Media Environment: A Challenge for Democracy?" *Annals of the International Communication Association* 41 (1): 3–27.

Vliegenthart, Rens, and Liesbet van Zoonen. 2011. "Power to the Frame: Bringing Sociology Back to Frame Analysis." *European Journal of Communication* 26 (2): 101–115.

USING THE ELABORATION LIKELIHOOD MODEL TO EXPLAIN TO WHOM "#BLACK LIVES MATTER" … AND TO WHOM IT DOES NOT

Lanier Frush Holt

Officer-involved shootings have become an unfortunate regular part of news coverage. After such events, the media often select expert sources to explain the news to the public. Social media has changed this media–source dynamic. Today, laypeople—often African Americans—can go online and provide information that counters the media's narrative. This analysis examines the effect people's perception of sources has on their opinion of the Black Lives Matter Movement (#BLM). It also tests what other factors shape audiences' beliefs about this issue. It finds that people who oppose #BLM have a strong orientation toward social dominance, are less likely to view America as the land of opportunity, and have ideas akin to those of modern racists, in that they oppose Affirmative Action and other race-based programs. This analysis also proposes a change to the Elaboration Likelihood Model, which serves as its theoretical basis. On racially charged issues, the personal relevance of an issue does not appear to matter; people will evaluate such topics via central processing.

Introduction

Officer-involved shootings, and the inevitable media coverage that follows, have become an increasingly recurring part of both traditional news and online media discussion groups in recent years (McLaughlin 2015). Traditionally marginalized groups, often lacking in money, power, and influence, have long used the mass media to bring their grievances to the forefront of the public's consciousness, with hopes of garnering support and allies for their causes (Edwards and Gillham 2013). Perhaps most notably, many scholars have argued that images of Blacks being bitten by dogs, mowed down by fire hoses, and the horrific scenes of church bombings, were highly instrumental in changing Whites' attitudes about race, integration, and drumming up support for the Civil Rights Movement (Burstein 1979; Lee 2002; Morris 1986).

Today, a central issue surrounding civil rights is police shootings. The *Washington Post* reports that since 2015, more than 950 people a year have been killed by police nationwide, with African Americans comprising a disproportionate number of those victims (Washingtonpost.com 2015, 2016). While some in the mainstream media have questioned if the frequency of police shootings has increased in recent years, owners of African American media outlets say they have been covering this issue for more than a century, and what the non-minority public is seeing now is not an increase in police shootings, but an increase in White media outlets reporting it (McLaughlin 2015).

Social media is not as reliant on media conglomerates for the dispersal of information. The Black Lives Matter Movement (#BLM) emerged on social media in August 2014, after the police shooting of unarmed teenager Michael Brown by Police Officer Darren Wilson, and in response to the violent police reaction to protesters in Ferguson, Missouri (Freelon, McIlwain, and Clark 2016). Social media also has arguably forever changed the journalist–source dynamic. Unlike in years past, when journalists alone dictated who served as an official source, social media allows anyone to become a voice on an issue with an audience that is limited only by that person's number of social media followers. Recent movements like Occupy Wall Street and the Arab Spring, and now #BLM, have all turned to social media to generate support for their causes (Eltantawy and Wiest 2011). Social media also enables social movements to grow quickly. An analysis of social media found that between June 1, 2014, and May 31, 2015, the hashtag #BlackLivesMatter was used 40.8 million times on Twitter alone (Freelon, McIlwain, and Clark 2016).

Today, media, though more plentiful in number and venues (e.g., CNN, MSNBC, blogs, etc.), are still controlled by a small minority of, predominantly, White male owners who determine almost all of what people, see, hear, and know about the world from the media (Bagdikian 2004). Also, although the team of reporters who provide the news is becoming more diverse, the editors in newsrooms, who ultimately decide what becomes news, is still dominated by Whites (Abbady 2017). Perhaps not just coincidentally, researchers find that despite the political and social gains made by African Americans over the past decades, negative messages about African Americans have remained consistent into the new millennium (Entman and Rojecki 2000). The image most often cultivated by the media is that of the dangerous African American male: ominous, dangerous, and pre-emptively perceived as guilty, especially in cases involving violent crime (Dixon and Linz 2000; Peffley, Shields, and Williams 1996).

As it is on many issues, opinions on police actions are splintered along racial lines (Chaney and Robertson 2013; Levin and Thomas 1997). A Pew Research Center study found that 71 percent of Whites strongly support the police, and believe they treat both African Americans and Whites equally, whereas only 36 percent of African Americans share that view (Pew Research Center 2015). Despite these divergent views, little—if any—research has examined what factors lead people to supporting—or denigrating—#BLM. This analysis aims to fill that gap in knowledge.

The Role of Media and Sources on Perception

Ever since Lippmann (1922) first likened media coverage to a searchlight bringing one obscure element from darkness into light, then another, scholars have known that the way the media depict reality is distorted. However, scholars also have long known that the media help shape the perception of large swaths of the population by how they portray events and groups, especially racial minorities (Entman and Rojecki 2000; Gerbner et al. 2002). The sources whom the media choose to tell their stories also influences what topics people talk about and how they talk about them (Cohen 1963; McCombs 2004). In relation to race, the media's conflation of criminality with blackness has been shown to cause some Whites to believe criminality is an inherent trait in African Americans (Gilliam and Iyengar 2000). Hence, media messages are far from neutral; they have an influence, and the source the media use to convey that message could have an appreciable influence on people's perceptions as well.

Journalistic practices wed reporters to specific beats, and tie them to specific sources who are often perceived as experts; these experts, in turn, determine how a story is told and framed for the audience (Holt and Major 2010). Media, however, cannot be at all places at all times. Consequently, for on-the-spot news, they are increasingly becoming reliant on regular citizens to give first-person accounts of what happened at the scene of a crime (Allan 2013). Police shootings often fall into this category. In addition to hearing about such incidents from police officers and spokespersons, laypeople—who are often African Americans—can now go online and give their account of events, which often counters the narrative given by the media's official sources (Freelon, McIlwain, and Clark 2016).

How people perceive the news might be influenced by the news source. Research on sources has long shown that when given information, people automatically assess their level of similarity to the news source (Hovland and Weis 1951). When audience members perceive the source as being similar to themselves, they also assume that the source also shares other beliefs with them as well (Feick and Higie 1992). However, when members of marginalized groups speak out to the majority group on perceived racial discrimination, they are more likely than not to be viewed as complainers and be highly criticized for their beliefs (Petty, Fleming, and White 1999). Kaiser and Miller (2001), for example, found that when African Americans claimed they were discriminated against, they often were received more negatively than were Whites when they spoke up on African Americans' behalf (Schultz and Maddox 2013). Additional research has found that even on the subconscious level, when prejudiced Whites hear racial information about which they disagree, they dismiss it out of hand, and do not even cognitively process the information to assess the validity of the claim (Holt, Ellithorpe, and Ralston 2016).

The role of the media in shaping people's perceptions cannot be understated. Today, very little of what people know about the world comes from their own actual experience. Increasingly, what fills the gap in what people know from first-hand experience, and what they come to believe about the world, are media messages (Gorham 1999). Media are ubiquitous. Nielsen (2016), which provides viewership numbers for television programs, places the number of televisions in America today at roughly 120 million. Although, some researchers find that Whites have no racial bias in terms of their news preferences (Appiah 2003; Appiah, Knobloch-Westerwick, and Alter 2013), far more evidence finds that Whites show considerable racial prejudice against African Americans both in news preferences and socially (Capehart 2016; Dixon and Linz 2000; Holt, Ellithorpe, and Ralston 2016; Schultz and Maddox 2013). Some Whites perceive racism as a zero-sum game in which gains for minority groups are perceived as losses for Whites (Norton and Sommers 2011). To wit, despite the lack of evidence showing #BLM is not directly, or indirectly, tied to hostility or ill-feeling toward Whites in general, or police officers in particular, some Whites believe #BLM to mean "anti-White," with some going so far as to consider #BLM to be a hate group (Capehart 2016; Lim 2016).

Research done 20 years ago found that as many as one in two Whites have negative beliefs about African Americans (Peffley, Hurwitz, and Sniderman 1997). The potential democratization of social media does not appear to have done anything to change these racially balkanized beliefs. A 2014 study found that out of 100 friends on Facebook, 75 percent of White people have zero non-White friends in their self-selected social network (Ingraham 2014). Although the numbers are higher for African Americans, who have eight White Facebook friends out of 100 (Ingraham 2014), the numbers are still pretty dismal given that Whites are more than three-quarters of the US population (United States Census Bureau 2016). Given the paucity of interracial interactions in the real world, it is likely that the only place in which discussions about race occurs is in the media. Thus, is it imperative that we learn more about the role media, and media sources, have on people's perceptions of racial issues. In order to measure these perceptions, this analysis uses the Elaboration Likelihood Model (ELM), which has long been used to examine the effect of different types of persuasive messages, as its theoretical basis.

Explaining the ELM

The ELM model of persuasion is a dual-processing theory, developed in the field of psychology by Petty and Cacioppo (1986), to explain the ways in which different people process and make sense of the vast amounts of persuasive information regularly presented to them. It is premised on the notion that people cannot process all of the information they receive. Consequently, they process information either centrally or peripherally based on their personal motivations, need for cognition, and their ability to process this new information. If a person has the motivation (i.e., they are free from distraction and have the cognitive ability to understand the message), new information is processed centrally. This means a person will expend considerable mental effort on the message and then will decide if they will believe it or not, based largely on whether they find it to be of high or low quality (Petty and Cacioppo 1986). Another key factor in determining motivation is whether the person finds the message to be personally relevant or not. In the context of #BLM, this means that audience members who find the issue to be personally relevant, and of high quality, will be more likely to use central processing, and be persuaded by the message if they find its content to be of high quality.

If a person lacks the motivation, or is unable to process the information (i.e., the person is distracted or lacks sufficient knowledge about the topic), then their attitude about the message will be more influenced by peripheral cues, such as the credibility of the speaker. These people, in turn, will be *less* likely to mentally elaborate on the message itself and base their decision on whether they buy into the claims of the message largely on their perception of the messenger or other exogenous variables (Petty and Cacioppo 1986). In the case of #BLM, this suggests that for audience members for whom police shootings are a less salient part of their reality, information about #BLM will be processed peripherally, with their judgment of it being based on factors beyond just the quality of the message itself.

The ELM, however, has rarely, if ever, been tested on racial issues, which might present a unique test for the model. Race is an especially powerful issue in the United States. Economic disparities based on race (Herring and Henderson 2016) still exist in the United States, as do the 917 hate groups that still roam the country (SPLC.org 2017), along with the Alt-Right, which has proposed a program of *peaceful ethnic cleansing*, in which racial minorities will be given the *opportunity* to voluntarily leave the country (Welch and Ganim 2016). In short, race is not like the innocuous topics that are usually tested by the ELM, on which people can opt in or opt out. It is an endurable, seemingly indefatigable concept that, like #BLM, has real-world consequences. In applying it to this issue, the question is will the ELM still apply in the same way as it does on less racially sensitive hot-button issues.

Racially Fractured Perceptions of #BLM

Ample evidence suggests there is a racial divide in terms of how African Americans and Whites feel about the police. For example, in a June 2017 Associated Press story about the jury selection for the trial of Ray Tensing, the White University of Cincinnati police officer who faced charges for the killing of unarmed African American motorist Sam DuBose, an African American man was excused from serving on the jury because he said he believes the police unfairly target African Americans. However, in that same jury pool, a White man was also turned away, but in his case, it was after he said that he believed Tensing deserved a medal for killing DuBose (Sewell 2017). These racially bifurcated beliefs are long-standing. In 1969, a Gallup poll found that while Whites had an overall favorable view of police officers, 40 percent of Blacks thought that the police were more harmful than helpful to civil rights (Roper Center for Public Opinion Research 2017). In 1991, a CBS/*New York Times* poll found that about 60 percent of African Americans believe police brutality happens in their neighborhood, compared to just 37 percent of Whites feeling the same way (Roper Center for Public Opinion Research 2017). These numbers are similar to those reported by the Ferguson Commission in 2014, which found that almost 70 percent of Whites believe police officers do either an excellent or good job compared to only 38 percent of African Americans feeling the same way (Roper Center for Public Opinion Research 2017). Given these racial disparities in attitudes about police behavior it is predicted here that:

> **H1:** African Americans will have a more favorable view of #BLM than will Whites.

Understanding the Role Personal Experience Has on Beliefs About #BLM

One reason for the racial difference in attitudes about the police could be that African Americans' experiences with police officers are quantitatively and qualitatively different from such experiences for Whites (Miller et al. 2017). In 2016, 233 African Americans were killed by police officers (Washingtonpost.com 2017). Although almost 50 percent more Whites (465) were killed by police that year, Whites are six times more plentiful in number (77 percent of the population) in the US population than are African Americans (13 percent) (United States Census Bureau 2016). African Americans are also far more likely than Whites to encounter police officers, even when those encounters are non-fatal (Miller et al. 2017).

The ELM predicts that when people are given information about a topic that is highly relevant, they will encode this information via central processing. This means the source of the message will matter less to these people than will its quality, which they will use as the primary means to determine if the message is believed (Herold, Tarkianinen, and Sundqvist 2016; Petty and Cacioppo 1979). However, when presented with information that is not personally relevant, the ELM predicts that people are more likely to evaluate it based on peripheral cues, like the credibility of the speaker, more so than the quality of the message itself (Herold, Tarkianinen, and Sundqvist 2016; Petty and Cacioppo 1979). Hence, in relation to #BLM, it is hypothesized that:

> **H2a:** Since police brutality is so relevant to them, the source of information (e.g., expert or novice) will not matter to African Americans, who will have a high opinion of #BLM regardless.

H2b: However, as a more peripheral issue, the source of the message will matter to Whites who will be more amenable to #BLM when the media use an expert as a source of information about the issue.

If there is a difference in how African Americans and Whites view #BLM, beyond just journalistic sources, further analysis examining what other factors lead to this dichotomy is also warranted. Since this is more exploratory, the following research question is also being asked:

RQ1: Which traits in audience members might also explain their opinions about #BLM?

Method

Participants

This study used an adult sample of 541 participants who were at least 21 years of age or older. Participants were collected via Qualtrics, a data collection agency that has often been used by researchers to collect data from participants across the United States. Individual ages were not calculated. Participants were asked into what age range (e.g., under 21, 35–44, 45–64, 65+) did their age fall. The percentage of participants in each category matched the percentage of people in each category in the general population in order to increase the generalizability of these findings.

This study included an almost equal number of male ($N = 271$, 50 percent) and female participants ($N = 270$, 50 percent). Approximately half of the participants were African Americans ($N = 271$) and half were Whites ($N = 270$). African Americans were oversampled compared to their actual percentage of the general population in order to make equitable comparisons between their group and the White sample. Approximately 25 percent of the sample were African American women ($N = 135$), 25 percent were African American men ($N = 136$), 25 percent were White women ($N = 135$), and 25 percent were White men ($N = 135$).

Stimulus Materials

A former newspaper reporter wrote all of the articles used this analysis, which were two op-ed columns which study participants were told were written by either an African American or White college professor, or an African American or White high school senior, all of whom support #BLM. The articles did not mention a specific source (e.g., Fox News, MSNBC, *New York Times*, etc.) from which the column was taken in order to decrease the possibility of participants being biased based on their previous beliefs about a particular news source. Each of the stories included a photo of the supposed author. Each photo was pre-tested on graduate students at a large Midwestern university to ensure that they were equal in terms of attractiveness, friendliness, and the degree to which they believed the person listed as the source could have written the article. No one used in the pre-test participated in the actual analysis.

Both stories written by the professors were identical except for the race of the author. The stories ostensibly written by the high school seniors were also identical except for the author's race as well. All authors were men in order to limit the variables participants used to evaluate the articles to just the race of the source and the source's perceived expertise on the topic. Arguments for the op-ed columns were collected from several media accounts including the #BLM website, the *New York Times*, and several magazines including *Time* and *Newsweek*. Some information was also collected from the opposing viewpoint, the Blue Lives Matter website, in order for the purported authors to have responses to study participants' possible counter-claims about #BLM.

The questionnaires used in this analysis were a well-established social dominance orientation scale (Pratto et al. 1994), which asks participants their opinions about equal opportunity programs and racial policies like affirmative action. This scale was included because previous research has found that social dominance is inversely correlated with people's attitude toward programs favoring African Americans (Pettigrew 2017). An equal opportunity questionnaire (Pratto et al. 1994), which asks if people believe America is still the land of opportunity, and if they believe minorities receiving lower wages reflects their having less skill and education, was also included in this analysis. The final questionnaire, racial policies (Pratto et al. 1994), asked participants the degree to which they believed the government should help minorities get a better education and better housing. The latter two questionnaires were added because they ask more probing questions about respondents' thoughts on racial matters, which might be correlated with their beliefs about #BLM.

A modified version of the ELM, that asked people's opinion about #BLM was also used in this analysis. Questions included, "My personal attitude about the Black Lives Matter Movement is … " and "In terms of the Black Lives Matter Movement, I think what the protesters are doing is … " All responses were measured on a 1–7 scale with lower scores indicating a very negative reaction to the question and higher scores indicting more positive agreement. Some questions were reverse-coded in order for all lower scores to indicate a less positive response and higher scores to indicate a more positive one.

A series of filler questions were also added to each questionnaire in order to mask the actual intent of the study. Studies have long shown that when asked their opinions about racial issues, participants will hide their true beliefs or give socially desirable answers in order to appear more racially egalitarian than they are in reality (Fazio et al. 1995; Lowery, Hardin, and Sinclair 2001; Olson and Fazio 2004).

Procedures

Each participant first answered demographic questions to determine if they were eligible for the study. Each of the participants received a pre-determined amount that was pre-arranged by an agreement with Qualtrics and the university of the study's principal investigator. Participants then read one of the columns supporting #BLM. Participants took a little more than 14 minutes to complete the study (mean = 14.6).

Although both the equal opportunity (Pratto et al. 1994) and racial policy scales (Pratto et al. 1994), have been validated in previous studies, reliability analyses were conducted on both scales. The principal component analysis with orthogonal rotation (varimax) showed acceptable levels of reliability ($\alpha = 0.798$) for this scale. The Kaiser–Meyer–Olkin (KMO) measure verified the use of these items (0.80). Their reliability was also acceptable ($\alpha = 0.759$). The KMO measure also verified the use of these items (0.76).

The dependent variables were African Americans' and Whites' attitudes about #BLM, and the degree to which the source (expert or novice) influenced their opinions on the issue.

To measure African Americans' and Whites' beliefs about #BLM (H1), the six questions used from the ELM were combined into a single item to make it a more robust measure. A reliability check was then conducted on this new scale as well as a principal component analysis with orthogonal rotation (varimax). The KMO measure verified the use of these items, KMO = 0.95 ("superb" according to Field 2009), and all the KMO values were >0.83, which far exceeds the acceptable limit of 0.5 (Field 2009). Bartlett's test of sphericity $\chi^2(15) = 4439.2$, $p < 0.001$, indicated that the correlation items were sufficiently large for principal component analysis. An initial test run to calculate the Eigenvalues showed the six items in the scale loaded on a single factor, with four items accounting for more than 96 percent of the variance. Given the large sample size used in this study, the remaining two variables were retained for the final analysis (as suggested by Field 2009). The new scale was found to be highly reliable ($\alpha = 0.973$).

To test H2a and H2b, which examined the influence expert versus novice sources have on people's opinions about #BLM, answers from respondents who read stories from both college professors were combined to create one independent variable that was labeled "Expert." Responses from the teenagers were also combined together to create the "Novice" independent variable. Collapsing these data allowed for two 2 × 2 two-way ANOVAs: [2 (Expert source/Non-Expert source) × 2 (African American study participant/White study participant)] and [2 (African American source/White source) × 2 (African American study participant/White study participant)] to be conducted comparing the main effect of the race of the study participant and the competence of the news source, and to examine if there is an interaction between the race of the source and perceptions of the source's credibility.

In an effort to explore what other factors influence people's attitudes about #BLM, beyond just the media's influence, linear regression was used to answer RQ1. Demographic variables such as participants' age and race were also fed into the regression model.

Results

This analysis first sought to establish if racial attitudes toward #BLM were fractured along racial lines (H1). The ELM postulates that as a more obtrusive issue for African Americans than it is for Whites, Black participants will have greater motivation to support #BLM than will Whites. An independent samples *t*-test showed support for H1 indicating that, on average, African Americans had more positive attitudes toward #BLM (mean = 5.53, SE = 0.99) than Whites (mean = 3.91, SE = 1.21). This difference was significant, $t(519) = 10.418$, $p < 0.0001$, with a medium-sized effect, $r = 0.42$.

In accordance with the ELM, it was predicted that the source of the media's message would not affect African Americans' attitude about #BLM (H2a). However, peripheral cues, like the credibility of the source, will matter to Whites for whom #BLM is a less obtrusive issue (H2b).

The ANOVA revealed a main effect for participant race on attitudes about #BLM, $F(1, 533) = 106.193$, $p < 0.0001$, $\eta_p^2 = 0.166$. African Americans had a more positive view of #BLM than did Whites. The ANOVA also revealed an interaction between the race of the media source and the perceived credibility of the source, $F(1, 533) = 4.956$, $p = 0.026$, $\eta_p^2 = 0.009$ (see Figure 1). The interaction was due to credibility being higher for the teen than the professor when the source of the information was an African American (4.92 versus 4.64; a difference of 0.28), versus the credibility being higher for the professor than the teen

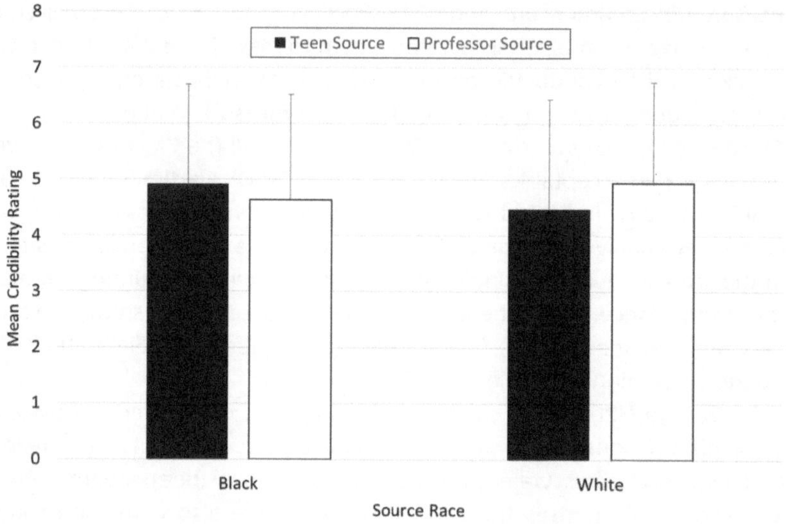

FIGURE 1
Mean perceived credibility rating (+ 1 SD) for each source (Black and White) as a function of the source's perceived level of expertise. The professor was coded as the expert source and the teen as the novice source

when the source was White (4.95 versus 4.48; difference of 0.47). In other words, participants viewed White professors as more credible than White teenagers, whereas they viewed Black teenagers as slightly more credible than Black professors on issues regarding #BLM (Table 1). Although the differences were small, they were nearly twice as large when the source was White than when the source was Black.

Whereas participant race was a significant main effect, it did not interact with source credibility or source race; therefore, H2a was supported. Neither the race (African American or White) nor expertise (expert or novice) influences African Americans' attitudes about #BLM. Inconsistent with H2b, however, this also was true for Whites' view of #BLM.

In answering RQ1, the regression analysis showed that three factors significantly influenced the variability in people's attitudes toward #BLM: their attitude about racial policies, their beliefs about equal opportunity, and the race of the study participant. People with a positive attitude toward racial policies, like Affirmative Action and racial quotas, which have long been viewed as ways to improve African Americans' progress, were also more likely to support #BLM ($\beta = 0.557$, SE = 0.054, $p < 0.0001$). In contrast, people who had negative beliefs about equal opportunity, which included beliefs that lower wages for women and ethnic minorities reflects their having lesser education and fewer skills, were also less likely to support #BLM ($\beta = -0.080$, SE = 0.095, $p = 0.025$). Also, people

TABLE 1
Analysis of variance results for attitudes toward #BLM

Significant main effects and interactions	F	p	η_p^2
Participant race	$F(1, 533) = 106.193$	<0.0001	0.166
Media source race × Media source credibility	$F(1, 533) = 4.956$	0.026	0.009

harboring negative beliefs about #BLM were also more likely to be White ($\beta = -0.228$, SE = 0.134, $p < 0.0001$) (Table 2). No other variables reached significance.

General Discussion

This analysis finds that Whites have a more negative view of #BLM than African Americans. As predicted by the ELM, this is not surprising given that the police shoot a disproportionately higher number of African Americans than Whites (Miller et al. 2017), which makes the issue more pertinent and critical to African Americans than it is to Whites.

However, what is surprising, is how much *more* important #BLM is to African Americans than it is to Whites. Out of the 271 African American participants in the study, 197 (72 percent) supported #BLM, compared to only 104 (39 percent) of Whites. The dichotomy is also seen in how many Whites were not neutral, but openly disliked #BLM (105 Whites; 39 percent) compared to African Americans (only 30 Blacks, or 11 percent of all the African American sample). There were almost as many Whites who disliked #BLM *a lot* (28) than the total number of African Americans who said they had *any* measurable level of dislike for #BLM. Perhaps since most police officers involved in high-profile shootings are White and the victims are often African Americans, Whites' reactions could reflect some sort of preference for their own racial group. It could also be that #BLM triggers a defense mechanism in some Whites who simply cannot believe that anyone could be shot for doing seemingly nothing, as claimed by #BLM supporters. Perhaps admitting to this would jeopardize how safe these Whites feel about the world and the people therein, because it would mean that the police who are in charge of protecting them and their families are actually killers themselves, and they often kill innocent people. Moreover, if they admit that #BLM is right, they would also have to concomitantly acknowledge that the world is a more racist place than they had previously believed it to be, which is something they simply might not *want* to believe is possible today. Future research should explore this possibility.

This analysis also finds that the source the media use to convey information can influence Whites' attitudes on racial issues. Media can have an inordinate influence on people's perception of others and on topics with which people are not familiar (Fujioka 1999). This analysis found a surprising interaction between the race of the news source and that source's perceived credibility. It was predicted that the #BLM message would matter more that peripheral cues to African Americans, for whom the topic is more personally relevant. Findings here refute this tenet of the ELM. It is suggested here that maybe the ability of the ELM to explain how people process information is different when applied to racial issues on which people have strong pre-existing attitudes. It is further suggested that on these often emotionally charged topics, pre-existing opinions could be so calcified on the polar extremes of the issue, personal relevance does not matter; people will encode

TABLE 2
Regression analysis results on factors that influence people's positive attitudes toward #BLM

Significant factors	β	SE	*p*
Positive attitude toward racial policies	0.557	0.054	<0.0001
Negative beliefs about equal opportunity	−0.080	0.095	0.025
More likely to be White	−0.228	0.134	<0.0001

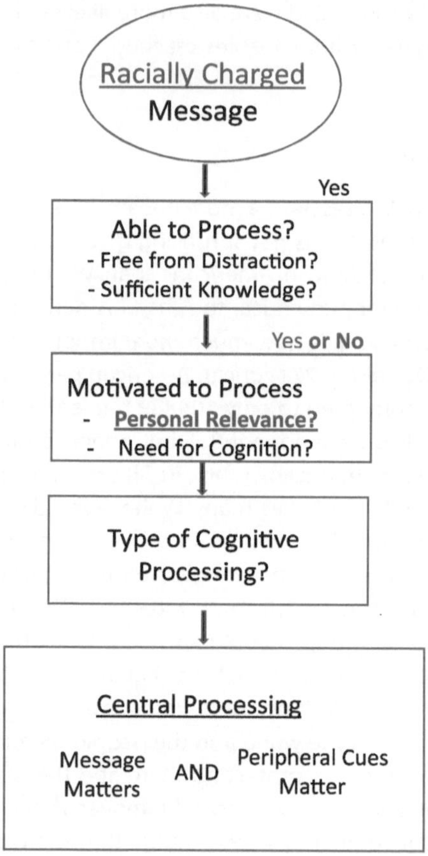

FIGURE 2
Proposed modification to the current ELM for when central processing occurs. This change is designed to show the difference racially charged messages have on perception and how such messages might diminish the role of personal relevance in determining if a message is encoded via central or peripheral processing

information via central processing in that both the message *and* peripheral cues will be used to evaluate the message. More research should be done to examine this possibility. If this is proven, this finding reaffirms recent research showing that on racially charged news stories, people's pre-existing beliefs supersede other factors in influencing how they perceive such messages (Holt, Ellithorpe, and Ralston 2016). In response to this possibility, this analysis proposes a slight modification to the traditional ELM to explain how it operates differently when applied to racial issues (see Figure 2). Additional research, using the ELM to examine attitudes on other critical race topics, like Affirmative Action and immigration, should be done to determine if this change is warranted.

This analysis also looked to find what other factors influence people's attitudes toward #BLM. It found that people who support racial policies aimed at providing benefits to African Americans were also in favor of #BLM. People who opposed #BLM were more likely to be White, and less likely to believe in equal opportunity, Affirmative Action, and racial quotas. Attitudes of people in this group are akin to those whom scholars call "Modern Racists" (Entman 1992; Sears 1988). Such people are highly unlikely to say that they are racist because they would be looked upon unfavorably by others. Instead, they are more likely to show their racism via an overall anti-Black effect, opposing programs like Affirmative Action and African American politicians, and say that African Americans are moving too far and too fast. These beliefs are often more pernicious and damaging than outright bigotry because they are subtler and couched in more acceptable beliefs like egalitarianism rather than racism (Entman 1992; Sears 1988). Qualitative research, or more open-ended questions in quantitative studies, should be done to provide deeper information about the reasoning behind people hating #BLM and other race-based initiatives.

Although this research provided insight about attitudes regarding #BLM, it is not without its limitations. For example, only the attitudes of African Americans and Whites were measured in this analysis. Given the increasing diversity within the United States, other racial groups should be included in future analyses to provide a broader understanding of more groups' thoughts about #BLM. Another limitation is that there were no open-ended questions in this dataset. Allowing participants to explain why they thought something, as well as what they thought, could provide richer insight. Future analyses should also discern if the differences found here are endemic of a specific gender. For example, whether White women feel differently about this issue than White men would be a good follow-up to this analysis. Despite these limitations, this analysis does add to the literature on ELM and media effects. Specifically, it proposes modification to the traditional ELM, suggesting that it be modified to incorporate the role of race and the potential role of pre-existing beliefs about race on cognitive processing.

Racial issues are particularly unique and problematic in the United States. They have arguably become the proverbial "third rail" of interpersonal communication; a topic no one dare touch due to the harm that doing so could cause. However, the role of race has been interwoven in the fabric of both US and global society, perhaps since time immemorial. This analysis finds that given the lack of actual in-person interracial contact in society today, media have the opportunity—perhaps the responsibility—to be an agent of change by reporting on issues like #BLM so the White majority knows about issues plaguing people who are different from those in their self-selected social networks. Further, journalists no longer have to be at the forefront of providing information from official sources. For African Americans, the source of the message does not matter; what matters is that the information is reported in a high-quality manner. White academicians also have a responsibility to discuss issues of race. Whites are more likely to believe other Whites than they are people of color on racial issues. Ironically, and sadly, although young African Americans are the ones who are disproportionately getting shot by police, Whites are still more likely to view White professors as the "experts," this study finds. Nonetheless, this still could present a unique opportunity for both the media and academic community. Perhaps, if the predominantly White media and White academicians start regularly addressing racial issues, and having quality discussions about this topic, then Whites in the general population will also start discussing such issues amongst themselves. Perhaps then, research on racially sensitive issues like #BLM will do more than show models like the ELM might need to be changed in order to incorporate the role of race in America, but society also needs to change to account for the difference race makes as well.

ACKNOWLEDGEMENTS

The author would like to thank Professors Brad Bushman and Richard Petty at The Ohio State University for their help, advice, and guidance on this project.

DISCLOSURE STATEMENT

No potential conflict of interest was reported by the author.

REFERENCES

Abbady, Tal. 2017. "The Modern Newsroom is Stuck Behind the Gender and Color Line. NPR, May 1. http://www.npr.org/sections/codeswitch/2017/05/01/492982066/the-modern-newsroom-is-stuck-behind-the-gender-and-color-line.

Allan, Stuart. 2013. *Citizen Witnessing: Revisioning Journalism in Times of Crisis*. Polity Press, MA: Malden.

Appiah, Osei. 2003. "Americans Online: Differences in Surfing and Evaluating Race-Targeted Web Sites by Black and White Users." *Journal of Broadcasting & Electronic Media* 47 (4): 537–555. doi:10.1207/s15506878jobem4704_4.

Appiah, Osei, Sylvia Knobloch-Westerwick, and Scott Alter. 2013. "Ingroup Favoritism and Out-group Derogation: Effects of News Valence, Character Race, and Recipient Race on Selective News Reading." *Journal of Communication* 63 (3): 517–534. doi:/10.1111/jcom.12032.

Bagdikian, Ben. 2004. *The New Media Monopoly: A Completely Revised and Updated Edition with Seven New Chapters*. 20th ed. Boston: Beacon Press.

Burstein, Paul. 1979. *"Public Opinion, Demonstrations, and the Passage of Antidiscrimination Legislation." Public Opinion Quarterly* 43 (2): 157–172. doi:10.1086/268508.

Capehart, Jonathan. 2016. "No, "Black Lives Matter" is not "Inherently Racist"." *Washingtonpost.-com.*, July 13. https://www-washingtonpostcom.proxy.lib.umich.edu/blogs/postpartisan/wp/2016/07/13/no-black-lives-matter-is-not-inherently-racist/.

United States Census Bureau. 2016. "Quick Facts: United States." https://www.census.gov/quickfacts/fact/table/US/PST045216.

Chaney, Cassandra, and Ray V. Robertson. 2013. "Racism and Police Brutality in America." *Journal of African American Studies,* 17: 480–505.

Cohen, Bernard C. 1963. *The Press, the Public and Foreign Policy*. Princeton, NJ: Princeton University.

Dixon, Travis L., and Daniel Linz. 2000. "Race and the Misrepresentation of Victimization on Local Television News." *Communication Research,* 27 (5): 547–573.

Edwards, Bob, and Patrick F. Gillham. 2013. *"Resource Mobilization Theory."* In *The Wiley-Blackwell Encyclopedia of Social and Political Movements*, 1–6. Hoboken, NJ: Blackwell. doi:10.1002/9781405198431.wbespm447.

Eltantawy, Nahed, and Julie B. Wiest. 2011. "Social Media in the Egyptian Revolution: Reconsidering Resource Mobilization Theory." *International Journal of Communication* 5: 12017–11224. doi:10.1386/jammr.4.2-3.273_1.

Entman, Robert M. 1992. "Blacks in the News Television, Modern Racism and Cultural Change." *Journalism Quarterly* 69 (2): 341–361. doi:10.1177/107769909206900209.

Entman, Robert M., and Andrew Rojecki. 2000. *The Black Image in the White Mind: Media and Race in America*. Chicago: University of Chicago Press.

Fazio, Russell H., Joni R. Jackson, Bridget C. Dunton, and Carol J. Williams. 1995. "Variability in Automatic Activation as an Unobtrusive Measure of Racial Attitudes: A Bona Fide Pipeline?" *Journal of Personality and Social Psychology* 69 (6): 1013–1027.

Feick, Lawrence, and Robin A. Higie. 1992. "The Effect of Preference Heterogeneity and Source Characteristics on Ad Processing About Endorsers." *Journal of Advertising* 21 (2): 9–24. doi:10.1080/00913367.1992.10673364.

Field, Andy. 2009. *Discovering Statistics Using SPSS*. 3rd ed. Thousand Oaks, CA: Sage.

Freelon, Deen, Charlton D. McIlwain, and Meredith D. Clark. 2016. "Beyond the Hashtags." *Center for Media & Social Impact*: 1–92.

Fujioka, Yuki. 1999. "Television Portrayals of African-American Stereotypes: Examination of Television Effects When Direct Contact is Lacking." *Journalism and Mass Communication Quarterly* 76 (1): 52–75. doi:10.1177/107769909907600105.

Gerbner, George, Larry Gross, Michael Morgan, Nancy Signorelli, and James Shanahan. 2002. "Growing Up with Television: Cultivation Processes." In *Media Effects: Advances in Theory and Research*, 2nd ed., edited by James Bryant and Dolf Zillmann, 43–68. Mahwah, NJ: Lawrence Erlbaum Associates.

Gilliam, Franklin Jr., and Shanto Iyengar. 2000. "Prime Suspects: The Influence of Local Television News on the Viewing Public." *American Journal of Political Science* 44 (3): 560–573.

Gorham, Bradley W. 1999. "Stereotypes in Media: So What?" *Howard Journal of Communications*, 10: 229–247.

Herold, Kristiina, Anssi Tarkianinen, and Sanna Sundqvist. 2016. "How The Source of Word-of-Mouth Influences Information Processing in The Formation of Brand Attitudes." *Journal of Marketing for Higher Education* 26 (1): 64–85. doi:10.1080/08841241.2016.1146387.

Herring, Cedric, and Loren Henderson. 2016. "Wealth Inequality in Black and White: Cultural and Structural Sources of the Racial Wealth Gap." *Race and Social Problems* 8 (1): 4–17. doi:10.1007/s12552-016-9159-8.

Holt, Lanier F., Morgan Ellithorpe, and Rachel Ralston. 2016. "So why do you Think that Way?: Examining the Role Implicit Attitudes and Motivation Play in Audience's Perception of a Racially-Charged Issue." *Media Psychology* 25 (4): 1–23.

Holt, Lanier F., and Lesa Hatley Major. 2010. "Frame and Blame: An Analysis of How National and Local Newspapers Framed the Jena Six Controversy." *Journalism & Mass Communication Quarterly* 87 (3/4): 582–597.

Hovland, Carl, and Walter Weis. 1951. "The Influence of Source Credibility on Communication Effectiveness." *Public Opinion Quarterly* 15: 635–660. doi:10.1086/266350.

Ingraham, Christopher. 2014. "Three-Quarters of Whites Don't Have any Non-White Friends." *Washington Post*, August 25. https://www.washingtonpost.com/news/wonk/wp/2014/08/25/three-quarters-of-whites-dont-have-any-non-white-friends/?utm_term=.2fc37a5acdf1.

Kaiser, Cheryl R., and Carol T. Miller. 2001. "Stop Complaining! The Social Costs of Making Attributions to Discrimination." *Personality and Social Psychology Bulletin* 27 (2): 254–263. doi:10.1177/0146167201272010.

Lee, Taeku. 2002. *Mobilizing Public Opinion: Black Insurgency and Racial Attitudes in the Civil Rights Era*. Chicago: University of Chicago Press.

Levin, Jack, and Alexander R. Thomas. 1997. "Experimentally Manipulating Race: Perceptions of Police Brutality in an Arrest: A Research Note." *Justice Quarterly* 14 (3): 577–586.

Lim, Naomi. 2016. "Rudy Giuliani: Black Lives Matter "Inherently Racist."" *CNN.com.*, July 11. http://www.cnn.com/2016/07/11/politics/rudy-giuliani-black-lives-matter-inherently-racist/index.html.

Lippmann, Walter. 1922. *Public Opinion*. New York: Harcourt, Brace.

Lowery, Brian S., Curtis D. Hardin, and Stacey Sinclair. 2001. "Social Influence Effects on Automatic Racial Prejudice." *Journal of Personality and Social Psychology* 81 (5): 842–855.

McCombs, Maxwell. 2004. *Setting the Agenda: The Mass Media and Public Opinion*. Malden, MA: Blackwell.

McLaughlin, Elliott C. 2015. "We're Not Seeing More Police Shootings, Just More News Coverage." *CNN.com.*, April 21. http://www.cnn.com/2015/04/20/us/police-brutality-video-social-media-attitudes/index.html.

Miller, Ted R., Bruce A. Lawrence, Nancy N. Carlson, Delia Hendrie, Sean Randall, Ian R.H. Rockett, and Rebecca S. Spicer. 2017. *Perils of Police Action: A Cautionary Tale from US Data Sets*. Calverton, MD: Pacific Institute for Research and Evaluation.

Morris, Aldon D. 1986. *The Origins of the Civil Rights Movement*. New York, NY: Simon and Schuster.

Nielsen 2016. "Nielsen Estimates 118.4 Million TV Homes in the U.S. for the 2016–17 TV Season. http://www.nielsen.com/us/en/insights/news/2016/nielsen-estimates-118-4-million-tv-homes-in-the-us–for-the-2016-17-season.html.

Norton Michael I., and Samuel R. Sommers. 2011. "Whites See Racism as a Zero-Sum Game That They Are Now Losing." *Perspectives on Psychological Science* 6 (3): 215–218.

Olson, Michael A., and Russell H. Fazio. 2004. "Trait Inferences as a Function of Automatically Activated Racial Attitudes and Motivation to Control Prejudiced Reactions." *Basic and Applied Social Psychology,* 26 (1): 1–11.

Peffley, Mark, Jon Hurwitz, and Paul M. Sniderman. 1997. "Racial Stereotypes and Whites' Political Views of Blacks in the Context of Welfare and Crime." *American Journal of Political Science,* 41 (1): 30–60.

Peffley, Mark, Todd Shields, and Bruce Williams. 1996. "The Intersection of Race and Crime in Television News Stories: An Experimental Study." *Political Communication,* 13 (3): 309–327.

Pettigrew, Thomas F. 2017. "Social Psychological Perspectives on Trump Supporters." *Journal of Social and Political Psychology* 5 (1): 107–116. doi:10.5964/jspp.v5i1.750.

Petty, Richard E., and John T. Cacioppo. 1979. "Issue Involvement Can Increase or Decrease Persuasion by Enhancing Message-Relevant Cognitive Responses." *Journal of Personality and Social Psychology* 37 (10): 1915–1926.

Petty, Richard E., and John T. Cacioppo. 1986. *Communication and Persuasion: Central Peripheral Routes to Attitude Change*. New York: Springer-Verlag.

Petty, Richard E., Monique A. Fleming, and Paul H. White. 1999. "Stigmatized Sources and Persuasion: Prejudice as a Determinant of Argument Scrutiny." *Journal of Personality and Social Psychology* 76 (1): 19–34. doi:10.1037/0022-3514.76.1.19.

Pew Research Center. 2015. "Divide Between Blacks and Whites on Police Runs Deep." *Pewresearchcenter.org*. Accessed March 21. http://www.pewresearch.org/fact-tank/2015/04/28/blacks-whites-police/.

Pratto, Felicia, Jim Sidanius, Lisa M. Stallworth, and Bertram F. Malle. 1994. "Social Dominance Orientation: A Personality Variable Predicting Social and Political Attitudes." *Journal of Personality and Social Psychology* 67 (4): 741–763.

Schultz, Jennifer R., and Keith Maddox. 2013. "Shooting the Messenger to Spite the Message? Exploring Reactions to Claims of Racial Bias." *Personality and Social Psychology Bulletin* 39 (3): 346–358. doi:10.1177/0146167212475223.

Sears, David O. 1988. "*Symbolic Racism.*" In *Eliminating Racism*, edited by Phyllis Katz and Dalmas Taylor, 53–84. New York: Plenum Press.

Sewell, Dan. 2017. "Potential Jurors Asked Opinions in Ohio Cop's Murder Retrial." *Associated Press*, June 5. https://apnews.com/09db516e864148b1bc31890c989e067a.

SPLC.org. 2017. "917 Hate Groups are Currently in the U.S. Track Them Below with our Hate Map." https://www.splcenter.org/hate-map.

Roper Center for Public Opinion Research. 2017. "Black, White and Blue: Americans' Attitudes on Race and Police." July 28. https://ropercenter.cornell.edu/black-white-blue-americans-attitudes-race-police/.

Washingtonpost.com. 2015. "991 People Shot Dead by Police in 2015." https://www.washingtonpost.com/graphics/national/police-shootings/.

Washingtonpost.com. 2016. "Fatal Force." Accessed 8 January. https://www.washingtonpost.com/graphics/national/police-shootings-2016/.

Washingtonpost.com. 2017. "Fatal Force." https://www.washingtonpost.com/graphics/national/police-shootings-2017/.

Welch, Chris, and Sara Ganim. 2016. "White Supremacist Richard Spencer: "We Reached Tens of Millions of People" with Video." *CNN.com.*, December 6. http://www.cnn.com/2016/12/06/politics/richard-spencer-interview-texas-am-speech/.

COVERAGE OF THE SURGICAL STRIKE ON TELEVISION NEWS IN INDIA

Nationalism, journalistic discourse and India–Pakistan conflict

Sushmita Pandit and **Saayan Chattopadhyay**

On 29 September 2016, the Indian army conducted a surgical strike along the India–Pakistan border. The mainstream news media in India followed the event with assertive nationalistic rhetoric. What was supposed to be a covert military operation against terrorism became morphed into political rhetoric aggravated by the unwarranted jingoism of television news channels and social media. The coverage of the strike on television news is typically characterized by a confluence of militant nationalist discourses, and the ideologically imbued labelling of specific communities. Within this context, drawing from the close reading of the coverage, this article analyses how Indian television news sustains the construction of a fictive "we", conflated with the government policies and military strategies, and speaks for a supposedly homogeneous national consensus that also consciously obscures the dissent through minority voices. The article emphasizes the relationship between communities, formal politics, and the supposedly non-political spaces and practices of news media in India.

Introduction

During periods of national conflict, critical discourse theorists suggest that the news media are typically involved in circulating the ideological beliefs and values endorsed by the ruling political regime (Van Dijk 2006, 356). The communicative action during the time of a national crisis usually involves an intensified focus on divisions between "us" and "them" (Mihelj, Bajt, and Pankov 2009). The television news coverage of the surgical strike at the India–Pakistan border is similarly characterized by an aggressive nationalist discourse that purposefully obscures the dissent expressed by marginalized voices.

The television news industry in India is among the fastest growing in the world. From the early 1990s, following neoliberal reforms, the long-standing monopoly of the government over broadcast media gradually weakened and a wide range of private media companies entered the political and public cultural arena. Within neoliberal imperatives, the number of Indian households with access to television increased exponentially. According to government data, the television universe is presently more than 50 per cent of the Indian population, and the medium reaches approximately 475 million people each day (Sharma 2016). With 869 registered private satellite television channels, the television industry in India stands at an estimated size of INR 588 billions in 2016 and is expected to grow as both advertising and subscription revenues are projected to exhibit strong growth (KPMG 2017, 58).

The transformation of Indian television news over the past two decades has been particularly noteworthy. Since 2016, there have been 397 registered "news and current affairs" channels in India (TRAI 2016). However, studies on the changing practices of television news media in India, and how these transformations have a formative influence on political and social issues and practices in the world's largest democracy, remains somewhat inadequate (Jeffrey 2000; Ninan 2007; Kohli-Khandekar 2013). While print media in India have received ample scholarly attention, television news has received limited critical attention excluding a few important studies (Mankekar 1999; Rajagopal 2001; Rai and Cottle 2007; Mehta 2008). Nonetheless, it is important to explore the role of television news in facilitating multi-party democracy in a developing non-western nation and to understand, how journalistic practices manage to negotiate conflicting ideologies and transform forms of identity and imaginings within particular national contexts.

The introductory section of this article offers a brief overview of the historical and political context of the surgical strike, locating it within the larger political context. The next section discusses, how media in general and television in particular become an essential conduit of nationalism, especially in the time of national conflict; and in what way television offers a different formal and narrative space for articulation of specific national imaginings. The article then describes the methodological framework and presents the thematic blocks, tied to the specific ways of constructing national imaginings. The third section, drawing from the close reading of the coverage of the surgical strike, analyses how Indian news television sustains the construction of a fictive "we" that is conflated with the government policies, military strategies and speaks for a supposedly homogeneous national consensus. The next section outlines in what way the mainstream news channels persistently follow the militant "patriotic" line of reporting and consciously obscure the disagreement through minority voices. The following section argues that both English- and Hindi-language television news channels operate in the same registers of aggressive nationalistic identity politics, connecting the divide between the "split public", which was operational in the early 1990s. The concluding section offers an overview of the key arguments, emphasizing the relationship between formal politics and the supposedly non-political spaces and practices of news media in India.

The Fraught Politics of the Surgical Strike

Before moving into the analysis, it is necessary to describe the historical and political context of the surgical strike. Territorial conflict between India and Pakistan over Muslim-majority Kashmir has been continuing for decades. However, hostilities escalated in 2016 after a militant attack on an Indian army base in Uri town of Kashmir left 18 Indian soldiers dead.[1] Nearly 10 days after the Uri attack, on 29 September, Indian army commandos claimed to carry out a surgical strike in Pakistan-occupied Kashmir (PoK), inflicting heavy casualties on terrorists and the Pakistani army. This also indicated a change of policy, abandoning the policy of strategic restraint in favour of a militarily assertive behaviour.[2] However, the Pakistani officials denied any such surgical strike, and stated that only two of their soldiers were killed, in the usual cross-border firing that took place during the night.

It is important to note, following the Uri attack and the Pathankot attack, the prime minister's cult persona of being "a strong decisive, no-nonsense leader" was severely spoiled and the Bharatiya Janata Party (BJP) assumed that this could unfavourably affect the forthcoming high-stake assembly polls in different states. The surgical strikes, according to party officials, transformed all of that, and the BJP then changed the framework of the entire electoral campaign; instead of only "development" and "governance", a third important element, "national security", was also included (Singh 2016).

Interestingly, within weeks, the BJP's election posters and banners in Uttar Pradesh prominently displayed military images in the background, with an armed soldier and a reference to the "surgical strikes". In the foreground, it depicted Narendra Modi, with his clenched fist upraised, threatening Pakistan. Another poster portrayed Narendra Modi as Lord Rama, Prime Minister of Pakistan, Nawaz Sharif as Ravana and Chief Minister of Delhi, Arvind Kejriwal as Meghanad (son of Ravana). The former poster contained the controversial and provocative sentence: "We will kill you and kill you for sure with our gun, our bullet, at our time of convenience but at your place" (*The Hindu* 2016). Although opposition leaders criticized such depictions, neither the army chief nor the Indian army headquarters officially objected (Shukla 2016). Nonetheless, a rising assertive nationalistic mood helped Narendra Modi and it practically swayed the 2017 assembly elections in Uttar Pradesh and Uttrakhand, which witnessed a historic landslide verdict in favour of the BJP and its allies.

Discursive Construction of Nationalism and Television News in India

The shifting political regimes in the country continue to periodically modify and appropriate the popular assertion of nationalism in India. Studies on nationalism often point out that nationalism itself can be defined as a kind of a "metanarrative or discourse" which is not formed through specific narratives of particular nations. Instead, it manifests through a blend of spatial, temporal, symbolic and everyday dimensions (Özkirimli 2005, 178). In other words, national identity can be conceptualized as structures of meaning, which can only be located within representation; "that is a story we tell about the self in order to know who we are" (Hall 1996, 346), or as a discursive construct constituted by particular nation-identity narratives (De Cillia, Reisigl, and Wodak 1999, 154).

It is important to mention, while conceptualizing nation and nationalism, Anderson (1983) underlines the difference between bound seriality and unbound seriality, which broadly corresponds to the distinction between nationalism and the politics of ethnicity. Chatterjee (1999, 131), however, considers such classification of serialities and the separation between them as "utopian": "people can only 'imagine' themselves in empty homogeneous time; they do not live in it" (131). To put it more simply, Chatterjee points out that Anderson's idea of classical nationalism imagines nationalism without modern governmentality, while modern governmentality is supposed to be an essential element that allows individuals to construct or even "imagine" the nation. Hence, an individual's admittance to govenmentality, at least hypothetically, confirms one's contribution into nationhood (132).

In a multi-ethnic, multilingual, developing neoliberal country like India, contradictory discourses about the nature of Indian national identity and the porousness of its cultures that draws from conventional and ideologically modulated views of its history shape the perceptions of common individuals. Media in general and television in particular become an important discursive conduit of nationalism, especially in the time of national conflict.

An emphasis on the discursive construction of journalistic content engages directly with the circuit of culture paradigm. It also underlines its political aim of positioning the forms of texts, the process of production of texts and the process of reading, parallel to the structures of power (Hall 1997; Kress 1990). A focus on the discursive trajectory of news television inherently links it with study of frames in media texts. Although discourse analysis in media research has become a conventional approach in contrast to the classical approach of content analysis, the number of studies exploring the discursive practices of mass media content is still limited. It needs to be mentioned that there are a significant number of ways discourse analysis in media research has been used. While earlier studies focused on stylistic studies of linguistic orientation (Crystal and Davy 1969; Leech 1966), later the focus shifted towards more critical linguistics approaches (Fowler 1991) and studies on social semiotics (Kress and Hodge 1979). These studies are the product of differing philosophical viewpoints with different approaches towards the analysis of data. In other words, some studies centred on the rigidly empirical interpretation of speech events (Hutchby and Wooffitt 1998), others accommodated critical theoretical discussion of wider socio-cultural effects (Fairclough 1995). While, there remains an evident theoretical and ideological multiplicity of these approaches, there is an increasing assimilation of linguistic, semiotic and discourse-analytical approaches (Hartley 1982). However, the pioneering work of the Glasgow University Media Group (1982) on television news in a series of studies and the cultural studies approach of the Centre for Contemporary Cultural Studies (Hall et al. 1980) emphasized the ideological and political dimensions of discourse.

Television, to be specific, offers a different formal and narrative space for articulation of particular national imaginings. In his influential book-length studies on television, John Ellis (1992) pointed out that a segmented narrative form distinguishes all television programmes, both fictional and non-fictional genres. The news stories will usually lack rudiments of narrative structure, typical of fictional genres (Fulton et al. 2005). Such frameworks remain the ideal, if not the dominant ways of presenting the news on television. However, this emphasis on the absence of narrative consistency in news bulletins can be contrasted with studies that underscore the fact that the television news narrative is much more integrated and unified than newspaper news narratives (Weaver 1975, 85). The mainstream Indian television news channels often purposefully construct an intensely dramatic narrative, particularly in the time of national conflict or crisis, that has a positive relation with audience approval, reflected through consistently high rating points of this coverage (BMIB 2016). Nonetheless, in the context of India, news discourse, particularly television news discourse, has received little academic attention.

In light of these circumstances, this article moves beyond a narrow focus on narrative structures of news media texts, and considers their links with the socio-political context as well as with particular ideological attitudes towards reporting events. This project seeks to answer a few related questions. How does television news in India explicitly define the fictive "we" as a national we? In the time of national crisis, in what way do mainstream Indian news anchors adopt a militant, nationalist stance and shape their narratives by focusing on the conflict between "us" and "them", between "our nation" and its enemies? Drawing examples from popular news programmes broadcast on Indian television, this paper aims to question whether such popular reporting practices primarily provide the site for the formation of particular identity categories rather than rational public debate. By engaging with these issues, the article emphasizes the need to pay attention not only to the ideological formation of specific ethno-religious communities but also to the relationship between formal politics and the supposedly non-political spaces and practices of news media in India.

Methodology

The key idea behind this kind of study is that discourse invests in the constitution of community identities, social situations, and the relationships between the nation-state and individuals (Fairclough 1985, 745). National imaginings are, thus, naturally perceptible in the discursive field (Van Dijk 2006). Considered from a discourse-analytic standpoint, television news represents a form of institutional communication which is, nevertheless, highly conversational. Even in usual newscasts, conversation with the anchor and the reporter in the field or in-studio interviews during the newscast are not conversations as such, but conversational features are exploited which connects with the element of performativity. The use of fictive "we" also has a performative use as its utterance reifies and offers materiality to a specific community. At times, the signifier may simply refer to the journalists, or to the media institution, they represent (Hallin and Mancini 1984); in other contexts, it operates as a direct reference to an aggressive nationalistic discourse (Allan 1999; Billig 1995).

For the purpose of this study, we distributed our sample into thematic blocks, tied to the specific ways of constructing national imaginings linked with the mutually constitutive relations of the nation-state, politics, religion and language in India.[3] We take a closer look at each of these sample sections, focusing on the manner in which news anchors or the interviewees themselves discursively construct their identities, noting how the process of that interpretation affects the nature of the coverage. Our sample includes all primetime television news bulletins broadcast in the period from 29 September to 5 October 2016, the period during and immediately after the surgical strike. The contents are drawn from two television stations, Times Now, the most watched English-language news channel and Aaj Tak, the leading Hindi-language news channel during 2016 (BARC 2016).[4] The sample of news reports from Times Now and Aaj Tak contains 97 primetime news items concerned with the surgical strike. The present study includes the standard news bulletins during the primetime slot as well as the special reports, special bulletins and panel discussions. Often the news items are titled "exclusive report" or "special report". These reports include a mix of recorded report of the event followed by studio discussions amongst panellists and, at times, telephonic conversations with audience and other experts. During the period of an event of national interest, the Hindi news channels name the programme dramatically, often with reference to popular Hindi films. Majority of these primetime news items contain panel discussions or debates packaged with particular news reports addressing specific aspects of the surgical strike and India–Pakistan conflict.

Analysis and Discussion

In order to better map this complex discursive field interconnecting television news, militant nationalist ideologies and the rising religious fundamentalism in India, we take a closer look at the coverage of the surgical strike in Times Now and Aaj Tak, and investigate the ways in which the journalistic discourse becomes intertwined with nationalist discourse. As mentioned earlier, this section of analysis is divided into three thematic blocks, each tied to one of the key ways of constructing national imaginings linked with the mutually constitutive relations of the nation-state, politics, religion and language in India.

The Fictive "We" and the National Consensus: Journalists Represent the Voice of the Nation

A news bulletin can be considered as a narrative about events that involves a specific imagined community on a particular day, or which are believed to be significant enough for all members of that community to know. Moreover, the conventional dialogic mode of address on a television news bulletin acts as a conduit of the imagined connection that links the news bulletin to its anticipated audience. Indian news television often employs such a mode of address, as if speaking to each individual viewer, utilizing dialogical, personalized forms of address to engage the audience. Naturally, an imagined bond is established between the institutional voice of the television news and the imagined viewer, which supports the construction of a fictive "we" ("*Hum*" in Hindi) comprising of the newsreader and the viewers (Allan 1999). This fictive "we" does not only refer to the imagined community of a nation, but also functions as a typical reminder of national belonging (Billig 1995).

Here, it is instructive to examine in detail how the two leading television news channels covered the India–Pakistan conflict, and in what way the reporters negotiated their position and incorporated themselves into a supposedly national narrative, in such a way that the journalists themselves seem to represent the voice of the nation.

Aaj Tak mostly presented the coverage of the surgical strike as an emotion-driven, aggressive, nationalistic frame rather than as balanced, impartial reporting of conflicts between two nations. Such an interpretation was evidently visible in the very first primetime coverage of the event, titled "Modi-ka Masterstroke" ("The Masterstroke of Modi"):

> India has finally answered to Pakistan, for which the entire nation was waiting. India has replied severely with a surgical strike. Entering PoK, transgressing the LoC [Line of Control], destroying seven terrorist camps and killing 38 terrorists. Whenever terrorists die, Pakistan becomes apprehensive. Now Pakistan has again become frantic, saying that we did not conduct any such surgical strike. Nevertheless, the Indian military may produce proof of the surgical strike. Let us now reveal what can be produced as truth … We are now in the *war-room.* (Anchor, Aaj Tak, September 29, 2016)[5]

The anchor, Anjana Om Kashyap, in forceful language and with aggressive gestures blurts out a list of death tolls and injuries. The studio with a three-dimensional map and computer graphics is turned into a "war-room". The anchor holding an actual drone in her hands starts speculating on the proof of the surgical strike that can be presented to the viewers. She repeatedly mentioned "us, the Indians" and "our war with Pakistan" and used expressions such as "the entire nation is congratulating", "entire nation is saluting" and "all of us were waiting for this" in a way that made clear, she was referring to a homogeneous national community of Indians, who collectively and irrefutably despise Pakistan.

The "Foxification" of Indian news channels is not new as it delivers news with a known slant, commentary or viewpoint. However, what is noteworthy is the extent to which this opinionated, blatant denunciation of a particular nation was evident during the coverage of the surgical strike on Indian news channels. In all the primetime news bulletins, the newsreaders used explicit deictic references to an imagined Indian national community. Such use of deixis was not limited primarily to the voices of the panellists and experts. Following the opening of a news report titled "Modika Badlapur" ("The Revenge of Modi") broadcast on Aaj Tak in the primetime slot can provide a useful illustration:

> Thirty-eight terrorists were blown away in one surgical strike by *us*. But the issue is whether Pakistan will realize that *we* have replied harshly? (Anchor, Aaj Tak, September 29, 2016, emphasis added)

Again, the "*hum*" (the Hindi word for "we") is conflated with the government policies, military strategies and speaks for a supposedly homogeneous national consensus. The deixis does not establish a division between "us", the reporter, and "you", the audience, instead the anchor is speaking on behalf of an imagined national community, through the communicative platform of news television. Hence, the deictic mode of address does not disengage the news anchor from the events she is reporting. News media explicitly forgrounds such positioning in the time of national conflict and instead of professional, analytical, non-partisan reporting of events, the coverage was infused with deictic expressions, which were unambiguously tied to India.

The following excerpt of a primetime news bulletin in Times Now, broadcast a day after the surgical strike, provides a characteristic example. The anchor, Arnab Goswami, known for "shouting, screaming and browbeating people into submission" (Daily Bite 2017), while conducting a panel discussion on the surgical strike, says to Abid Rao, former Air Vice-Marshal of Pakistan: "Wake up! Smell the coffee and learn to behave yourself in the future, because we will have to do it again if required, Abid Rao! This is a surgical strike!" (Times Now, October 1, 2016). In another programme, *Newshour*, Goswami, while conducting a panel discussion on whether the Indian military should deliver proof of the surgical strike against Pakistan, irately shouts to an interviewee: "you should be silent tonight; you should only be hearing the nation's voice" (Times Now, October 2 2016)

By forcefully emphasizing "the nation's voice", the anchor clearly posits himself and his audience within the same imagined community and ascribes him the position of the voice of the nation. In another instance, while interviewing Mahmood Khan Achakzai, a member of the National Assembly of Pakistan, the explicit endorsement of military might and violence displaces the conventional journalistic dialogue:

> **Anchor:** Achakzai, you realize you are dealing with the Indian army. This is not your cottage industry army. This is a sophisticated force.
>
> **Achakzai:** Your countrymen have been killed on our border today …
>
> **Anchor:** Not one, not one, not one! But if you check Mr Achakzai, you will find out the number of casualties of the Pakistani army personnel and the number of casualties of Pakistani terrorists. There are more bodies than you can put in those trucks tonight. Mr Achakzai! (Times Now, September 30, 2016)

Although there are numerous such examples from the coverage of the surgical strike on Indian news television, the very first news report on Times Now needs to be mentioned:

> Good evening and welcome to this special edition of the *Newshour*. The entire nation is celebrating as news was given out by *our* army in a press conference this morning, that *we* have carried out surgical strikes and crossed the Line of Control in Pakistan-occupied Kashmir. (Anchor, Times Now, September 29, 2016, emphasis added)

Not only the anchor discursively situates himself and his audience into the same national community, but at the same time he also begins reporting the events of the day from that location, that is, from the perspective of a nationalistic "us" or a homogeneous nation. It is important to note that the framing of the coverage presumes that every individual among "us" is assenting with the attitude towards India's military might and towards the triumphant response of the news channel. Times Now even unswervingly claims to build a consensus, which may be able to overwhelm any voice of dissent.

The above excerpt can also serve as an example of how the national "we" provided the explicit basis for internal focalization in news narratives. The other key actor in the same narrative is identified as Pakistan as a homogeneous nation-state and is quite explicitly cast into the role of an offender, who can jeopardize "our" victory. Thus, it may be possible to identify an analogous pattern of representing the "voice of the nation" through journalistic discourse in both the leading television news channels reporting India–Pakistan conflict. Evidently, both news channels identified themselves and their audiences largely as part of a homogeneous national community entwined by "a deep, horizontal comradeship" (Anderson 1983, 7) which endures beyond any discrete politics, ideological positions or individual dissent.

Hindu Nationalism and the Mainstream Television News Discourse

It is important to locate the coverage of the surgical strike within the growing hindutva movement in India.[6] In the 2014 general election (national parliamentary election) the BJP, that allegedly advocates a conservative religious ideology of Hindu nationalism, secured a landslide victory. Narendra Modi, the provocative Chief Minister of the Indian state of Gujarat, became the Prime Minister and that marked a pivotal moment of change in the public perception of Indian secularism and the contested relationship between religious nationalism and electoral democracy in a multi-ethnic-religious-lingual nation like India. Interestingly, the coverage of India–Pakistan conflict also reflected such aggressive nationalist discourse. The news channels often defined "patriots" and "traitors" in terms of their religious affiliations.

In the opening of a special news report on Aaj Tak channel, the anchor, in reference to former cricketer and Pakistani political leader, Imran Khan's comment on the conflict, says, "From cricketer to politician, Pakistan's Imran Khan today proved that there is some flaw in the DNA of Pakistan" (Aaj Tak, October 1, 2016). Conflating Pakistan and Islamic terrorism, the news reports often situate the surgical strike within ethno-religious identity politics. Impugning the genetic characteristic of an entire nation, the anchor frames the report in a highly problematic manner. In the same way, in the exclusive report titled "Operation Surgical Strike" on Aaj Tak, the reporter personifies the nation as the figure of the terrorist:

> India took revenge for the death of those 24 martyrs, who died in the Uri conflict. India paid Pakistan back in the same coin. Pakistan could not imagine that India will strike this way, by entering their territory. Pakistan was surely stunned. (Reporter, Aaj Tak, September 30, 2016)

The masculinist assumptions underpinning the dominant nationalist discourse effortlessly blends with the popular news discourse in India and shapes such troubled journalistic practices, which underline the belief that the nation is constituted by one homogeneous, organic popular community, where the Muslim other becomes an object of intense hatred. In Times Now, with accompanying visuals, the reporter in a jubilant tone says, "After the surgical strike by the army the entire nation is celebrating Diwali" (Times Now, September 29, 2016). It is important to remember that the reference to Diwali, which is a

Hindu religious celebration, once again accentuates the belief that "Hindus, therefore, are the natural constituents and authentic citizens of the Indian nation state" (Bannerji 2006, 374).

In addition, through the comments of interviewees, religious identities become the ground for political subjectivities. Moreover, parallel to the coverage and follow-up of the surgical strike, Times Now also broadcast news reports on the status of Muslims in India or debates on the need for prohibiting Pakistani artists from working and performing in India. All such articulations are clearly positioned within discourses that brings with it ideological, moral and religious proscriptions, therefore, subordinating other ethnic religious communities.

It is also important to remember that later, in early 2017, as mentioned earlier, election banners showed references and images of the surgical strike, particularly with allusion to the Hindu epic *Ramayana*. Posters depicted Narendra Modi as Lord Rama fighting with the Prime Minister of Pakistan, Nawaz Sharif, portrayed as the 10-headed demon king, Ravan. Moreover, the Indian Defense Minister in his statement compared the Indian army to that of Lord Hanuman, loyal to Lord Rama in the epic *Ramayana*. "In establishing this epic as a literal and historical narrative and source material for a Hindu nation, Indian history was made into hindu history, thus laying claim to antiquity and origin for legitimation of a political project" (Bannerji 2006, 382).

Identity Politics Versus Rational Public Debate

According to Schudson's (2003) categorization of news reporting, the professional standards of news reporting are concomitant with the Habermasian idea of the audience as a rational public, instead of the idea of an imagined community. Therefore, news stories are supposed to provoke rational public debate, and are not for shaping ideologically imbued subjectivity and agency. However, a closer look at the reporting of the surgical strike in both the leading Indian news channels points to a different direction.

The anchor of the primetime news on the Times Now channel begins the programme with these opening lines:

> Welcome to this part of the debate on the need to end the kid gloves treatment to Pakistan … You know, this group that consistently says talk, talk, talk; engage with the enemy nations. I hope that group is beginning to introspect. (Anchor, Times Now, September 30, 2016)

Rational public debate includes everyone concerned with creating a platform on which all pertinent contributions are heard and it ensures that the better argument wins the day. However, with the aforementioned introductory statement, the dialogic mode of journalism crumples down and the public debate becomes inconsequential. In the same episode the anchor, after introducing the panellists, starts asking questions to a senior journalist, Saba Naqvi, regarding the India–Pakistan bilateral talk effort in the aftermath of the surgical strike. In a familiar patronizing tone, the anchor continuously interrupts the panellist's responses and poses rhetorical questions, foregrounding the news organization's pro-military, pro-government stance:

> **Anchor:** Saba come on, you do not expect anyone to talk today after this, do you? Do you want talks to happen even now?

Saba: Are you going to allow me to speak Arnab? Otherwise, I can also keep quiet if you do not want to hear what I have to say.

Anchor: No, I am going to stop you if I feel what you are going to say is unfair. You do not try to generalize the blame. We are clear. We are united and we support the army. (Times Now, September 29, 2016)

Similarly, in another programme, Saeed Akhtar Mirza, veteran Hindi filmmaker, who made an effort to speak against the aggressive militant nationalism, was continuously interrupted by the anchor until he angrily replied, "Ultra-patriots disgust me! Adolf Hitler was a damn ultra-patriot! They do not allow a damn debate to occur … which has to be rational, compassionate" (Times Now, October 1, 2016).[7]

Deliberative democracy entails public deliberation not only for producing public reasoning leaning towards the common good and collective decision-making within formal and semi-formal settings, but also as a means of producing public reasoning and building mutual understanding within the more informal communicative spaces of the public sphere, like primetime news and panel discussions. However, the mainstream news channels in India, at least during the period of national conflict, hardly seem to accommodate public deliberation. In a special news report titled, "Modi Ka Mutod Jawab" ("The Ruthless Reply of Modi"), the anchor in forceful gestures begins her report:

> We may triumph over the terrorist but we have been defeated by our own. Today we are going to discuss about the greatest misfortune of India. Today, India was defeated not by the terrorists but by the politicians … Questions are being raised about the Indian army's action! The politics surrounding the deadliest attack against Pakistan-supported terrorism is making every citizen sad. (Anchor, Aaj Tak, October 5, 2016)

In the same way, Times Now broadcast a *Newshour* debate on primetime, titled "Army's Word Not Proof Enough?", which once again underlined the unquestionable status of the military action and the nation-state's policy regarding India–Pakistan conflict.

Furthermore, the anchors or the representatives of the news organization in both the leading news channels repeatedly intervened, in various ways, to confuse the possibility of multiplicity of voices and politics of identities to be conveyed to the audience. In steadfastly clinging on to the militant "patriotic", nationalistic reportage, the reporter or anchor obscures the dissent among minority voices and creates an imagined monolithic solidarity. By deliberately not allowing the act of questioning the state or the military, popular news television in India creates a constricted communicative space that may be counterproductive for the world's largest democracy.

The Collapse of the Split Public

Considering the coverage of the surgical strike by these two leading news channels, we argue that the cultural division between the English-language and vernacular news media, which was functional during the early 1990s, has collapsed. English-language and Hindi-language news media, especially television news channels, operate in the same registers of aggressive nationalistic identity politics, bridging the rift between the "split public" that Arvind Rajagopal (2001) talked about in his study on politics after television in India.

In the context of the Ram Janmabhumi Movement, Rajagopal argued that the Hindu nationalists utilized the cultural fault lines between the English-language and vernacular press to gain publicity. While the English-language press offered criticism, the Hindi-language press were more sympathetic. However, the fear generated by the English-language press indirectly reinforced the sympathy offered by the vernacular-language press. The English-language press thus unintentionally offered the hostility essential for the growth of the Hindu nationalist movement.

In the early 1990s, there were substantial differences in the understandings of news, contingent on dissimilar arrangements of institutional practices in the English- and Hindi-language news media. English-language news, according to Rajagopal, focused on the truth-value of news, as information catering to a critical-rational public, consciously avoiding the story-telling attribute to be objective and neutral. In contrast, Hindi news media experienced a more challenging relation to power, and could not undertake an impartial, neutral approach to the news. The dramatized, narrative aspect of news was much more evident in Hindi-language news and objectivity was one of a range of potential values in the news. The Hindu nationalists were successful in using this deep cultural faultline. They developed sympathy for their cause through an accommodating Hindi-language press and permitted resistance through the English-language press owing to their confrontational stance (Rajagopal 2001, 152).

However, in the contemporary scenario, particularly in Indian news television, in the context of rising militant nationalistic fervour, the split between English-language and Hindi-language news media is no more evident. Both the English and vernacular news organizations consciously employ the trope of "patriotism" and "nationalism", especially in the time of national conflict that centres on the fraught identity politics in the lines of ethno-religious subject formation. Thus, both news channels broadly speak in favour of a militant aggressive nationalism, which is called for often in the name of defence and security of the nation-state. The ratings for the Aaj Tak channel during the surgical strike coverage grew by almost 64 per cent compared to previous weeks, while the viewership of Times Now almost doubled. Aaj Tak set a record of 160 million viewers during the coverage of the surgical strikes (Latief 2016). Both these channels continued to enjoy the number one position during the coverage and the viewership of English news channels doubled compared to a regular week. These facts point to a growing consensus regarding the creation of a national community and animosity towards the enemy "others", who are "located in an univocal monopolistic interpretation of religion, culture, tradition and community, and are articulated to the morality and identity of a constructed unified and collective subject" (Bannerji 2006, 364).

Conclusion

Three key conclusions can be drawn based on our study. First, our analysis confirms that journalistic reporting in India, during the time of national conflict, is characterized by a confluence of aggressive nationalist and communal discourse, where the journalists themselves seem to articulate the voice of the nation. Utilizing deictic expressions, personalized forms of address to engage the audience, Indian news television often establishes an imagined bond between the institutional voice of the television news and the imagined viewer, which supports the construction of a fictive "we" or "*Hum*" in Hindi, comprising the newsreader and the viewers. This "we" is conflated with the government policies and military strategies, and speaks for a supposedly homogeneous national consensus. Second, the news channels, in the context of national conflict, persistently adhere to the militant "patriotic" nationalistic line of reporting and consciously obscure the disagreement through minority voices. By deliberately making it difficult to question the nation-state or the military, popular news television in India constructs a restricted communicative space that may be deleterious for the world's largest democracy. Third, bearing in mind the coverage of the surgical strike by these two leading news channels, we argue that English-language and Hindi-language news media, especially television news channels, operate in the same registers of aggressive nationalistic identity politics connecting the divide between the "split public" which was effective in the early 1990s. Now, both English and Hindi news channels largely speak in favour of a militant aggressive nationalism, within the background of defence and security of the nation-state.

However, the study remains limited since it was conducted with a small sample base and with a narrow focus on the coverage of only one event. It would be interesting to investigate whether differences in perceptions can be observed in the way the surgical strike was covered in Pakistani news channels. Moreover, a longitudinal study of the vernacular news channels could be more appropriate to understand the nuances of the split public. Similarly, a detailed analysis of the visuals accompanying the news programmes may also offer a more critical understanding of the reporting practices. Nonetheless, the relevance of this study remains in its aims to fill the gap in examinations of nationalist discourse in journalistic genres, particularly in non-western, developing nations like India. These arguments are posited within the idea that ideology is an essential device for producing ways of thinking, conceptual categories that produce constriction, dehistoricization and depoliticization in our understanding of the social (Bannerji 2006). It is important to consider the coverage of the India–Pakistan conflict in popular news television since cultural politics is as important as the supposed "real" politics, and the separation between the political and the cultural or the social is precarious.

DISCLOSURE STATEMENT

No potential conflict of interest was reported by the authors.

NOTES

1. On 18 September, four militants attacked an Indian Army brigade headquarters in Uri town, near the Line of Control, in the Indian-administered state of Jammu and Kashmir. Within a week, Prime Minister Narendra Modi claimed that those behind the terror attack in Uri "will not go unpunished", which triggered considerable speculation, including the option of a surgical strike that India could exercise in Pakistan-occupied Kashmir.
2. It might be useful to consider the origin of the term "surgical strike" here. The first use of the phrase recorded in *The Second Barnhart Dictionary of New English* is from an article in *Harper*'s magazine of November 1971, which referred to it as "the 'surgical strike' for chasing and mowing down peasants from the air by spraying them with 8,000 bullets a minute" (Safire 1986). However, earlier but unverified references position the origin of surgical strike in the early 1960s. A decade later, H. R. Haldeman, Chief of Staff to President Richard Nixon, used the term in the context of the Soviet Union's likely attack against Chinese nuclear plants. While strike refers to tactics, and gives a humane touch to military operations, surgical underlines the accurate, swift and penetrating nature of the attack.

3. Due to the limited scope of this paper, we were not able to include a detailed consideration of visual footage.
4. Aaj Tak, launched in December 2000, is a 24-hour Hindi news channel, owned by India Today Group. Within six months of its launch, Aaj Tak emerged as India's number one news channel. It continued to hold on to its leading position for decades, in both urban and rural markets. Times Now, launched in 2006, is a 24-hour English news channel in India. As the flagship channel of Times Network, the broadcast arm of Bennett Coleman & Co, Times Now has consistently been the most watched English news channel over the last nine years and continues to dominate the market. It commands 43 per cent market share in the English News category and 58 per cent overall market share during primetime English News, according to the Broadcast Audience Research Council (BARC) India.
5. All translations from Hindi to English are by the authors, unless mentioned otherwise.
6. Hindutva refers to a reformational work to create an essentialized version of Hinduism. In other words, hindutva or hinduness aims to invent or construct an authentically "hindu" culture and identity. The term was popularized by Vinayak Damodar Savarkar in 1923, and continues to be the predominant form of Hindu nationalism in India.
7. In response to Mirza's comment, Times Now broadcast a special *Newshour* debate on 5 October 2016 between Saeed Akhtar Mirza and veteran actor Anupam Kher on the issue of "ultra-patriotism".

REFERENCES

Allan, Stuart. 1999. *News Culture*. Buckingham: Open University Press.

Anderson, Benedict. 1983. *Imagined Communities: Reflections on the Origins and Spread of Nationalism*. London: Verso.

Bannerji, Himani. 2006. "Making India Hindu and Male: Cultural Nationalism and the Emergence of the Ethnic Citizen in Contemporary India." *Ethnicities* 6 (3): 362–390.

BARC. 2016. "Weekly Data." *Broadcast Audience Research Council*, 30 November. http://www.barcindia.co.in/statistic.aspx.

Billig, Michael. 1995. *Banal Nationalism*. London: Sage.

BMIB. 2016. "News Channels Strike Highest Ever Viewership Post Surgical Strike Week." *Best Media Info*, 14 October. http://bestmediainfo.com/2016/10/news-channels-strikehighest-ever-viewership-post-surgical-strike-week-2/.

Chatterjee, Partha. 1999. "Anderson's Utopia." *Diacritics* 29 (4): 128–134.

Crystal, David, and Derek Davy. 1969. *Investigating English Style*. London: Longman.

Daily Bite. 2017. "Nation Confused. Arnab Goswami Attacking His Own Kind of Journalism." *Daily O*, 10 January. http://www.dailyo.in/variety/arnab-goswami-republic-newchannel-lutyens-media-journalism/story/1/15018.html.

De Cillia, Rudolf, Martin Reisigl, and Ruth Wodak. 1999. "The Discursive Construction of National Identities." *Discourse & Society* 10 (2): 149–173. doi:10.1177/0957926599010002002.

Ellis, John. 1992. *Visible Fictions*. London: Routledge.

Fairclough, Norman. 1985. "Critical and Descriptive Goals in Discourse Analysis." *Journal of Pragmatics* 9 (6): 739–763. doi:10.1016/0378-2166(85)90002-5.

Fairclough, Norman. 1995. *Critical Discourse Analysis*. Harlow: Longman.

Fowler, Roger. 1991. *Language in the News: Discourse and Ideology in the Press*. London: Routledge.

Fulton, Helen, Julian Murphet, Rosemary Huisman, and Anne Dunn. 2005. *Narrative and Media*. Cambridge: Cambridge University Press.

Glasgow University Media Group. 1982. *Really Bad News*. Durrington: Littlehampton Book Services.

Hall, Stuart. 1996. "Ethnicity: Identity and Difference." In *Becoming National: A Reader*, edited by Ronald Grigor Suny, and Geoff Eley, 339–351. Oxford: Oxford University Press.

Hall, Stuart. 1997. *Representation: Cultural Representations and Signifying Practices*. London: Sage.

Hall, Stuart, Doothy Hobson, Andrew Lowe, and Paul Willis, eds. 1980. *Culture, Media, Language*. London: Hutchinson.

Hallin, Daniel C, and Paolo Mancini. 1984. "Speaking of the President: Political Structure and Representational Form in U.S. and Italian Television News." *Theory and Society* 13 (6): 829–850.

Hartley, John. 1982. *Understanding News*. London: Methuen.

Hutchby, Ian, and Robin Wooffitt. 1998. *Conversation Analysis: Principles, Practices and Applications*. Cambridge: Polity Press.

Jeffrey, Robin. 2000. *India's Newspaper Revolution*. Delhi: Oxford University Press.

Kohli-Khandekar, Vanita. 2013. *The Indian Media Business*. New Delhi: Sage.

KPMG. 2017. "Media for the Masses: The Promise Unfolds." *KPMG India-FICCI Indian Media and Entertainment Industry Report*. https://assets.kpmg.com/content/dam/kpmg/in/pdf/2017/04/FICCI-Frames-2017.pdf.

Kress, Gunther. 1990. "Critical Discourse Analysis." *Annual Review of Applied Linguistics* 11: 84–99.

Kress, Gunther, and Robert Hodge. 1979. *Language as Ideology*. London: Routledge & Kogan Paul.

Latief, Samiya. 2016. "Aaj Tak Sets Record of 160 Million Viewers for Second Week." *India Today*, 14 October. http://indiatoday.intoday.in/story/aaj-tak-record-viewerssecond-week/1/787278.html.

Leech, Geoffrey N. 1966. *English in Advertising*. London: Longman.

Mankekar, Purnima. 1999. *Screening Culture, Viewing Politics*. Durham, NC: Duke University Press.

Mehta, Nalin. 2008. *India on Television*. New Delhi: Sage.

Mihelj, Sabina, Veronika Bajt, and Miloš Pankov. 2009. "Television News, Narrative Conventions and National Imagination." *Discourse & Communication* 3 (1): 57–78. doi:10.1177/1750481308098764.

Ninan, Sevanti. 2007. *Headlines From the Heartland*. New Delhi: Sage.

Özkirimli, Umut. 2005. *Contemporary Debates on Nationalism: A Critical Engagement*. Basingstoke: Palgrave Macmillan.

Rai, Mugdha, and Simon Cottle. 2007. "On the Changing Ecology of Television News." *Global Media and Communication* 3 (1): 51–78.

Rajagopal, Arvind. 2001. *Politics After Television*. Cambridge: Cambridge University Press.

Safire, William. 1986. "On Language; On Surgical Strike." *New York Times*. May 4. http://www.nytimes.com/1986/05/04/magazine/on-language-on-surgical-strike.html.

Schudson, Michael. 2003. *The Sociology of News*. New York: W.W. Norton.

Sharma, Meghna. 2016. "Broadcasters and the Big Data Bonanza." *Financial Express*, August 16. http://www.financialexpress.com/industry/broadcasters-and-the-big-databonanza/348222/.

Shukla, Ajai. 2016. "Army Mute as BJP Election Posters Feature Soldier, Surgical Strikes." *The Wire*, 9 October. https://thewire.in/71973/army-silent-surgical-strikes-bjp-electionposters/.

Singh, Sanjay. 2016. "Surgical Strike: Is Kejriwal, Chidambaram's Demand for Proof a Mere Coincidence?" *First Post*, 4 October. http://www.firstpost.com/politics/surgicalstrikes-is-kejriwal-chidambarams-simultaneous-demand-for-proof-a-coincidence-3034696.html.

The Hindu. 2016. "BJP Banners Across U.P. Laud 'Surgical Strikes'." *The Hindu*, 5 October. http://www.thehindu.com/news/national/other-states/BJP-banners-across-U.P.-laud-'surgical-strikes'/article15425612.ece.

TRAI. 2016. "Indian Telecom Services Performance Indicator Report" for the Quarter ending March, 2016." [Press Release]. *Telecom Regulatory Authority of India*. http://www.trai.gov.in/sites/default/files/Indicator_Report_05_August_2016.pdf.

Van Dijk, Teun A. 2006. "Discourse and Manipulation." *Discourse & Society* 17 (3): 356–383.

Weaver, Paul. 1975. "Newspaper News and Television News." In *Television as a Social Force: New Approaches to TV Criticism*, edited by Douglass Cater, 81–94. London: Praeger.

http://orcid.org/0000-0002-8267-1451
http://orcid.org/0000-0002-9321-9516

PLEASE FOLLOW US
Media roles in Twitter discussions in the United States, Germany, France, and Russia

Svetlana S. Bodrunova, **Anna A. Litvinenko**, and **Ivan S. Blekanov**

The media are normatively expected to play significant roles in conflictual discussions within national and international communities. As previous research shows, digital platforms make scholars rethink these roles based on media behavior in online communicative environments as well as on the structural limitations of the platforms. At the same time, traditional dichotomies between information dissemination and opinion formation roles, although seemingly universal, also vary across cultures. We look at four recent conflicts of comparable nature in the United States, Germany, France, and Russia to assess the roles that legacy media have performed in the respective ad hoc *discussions on Twitter. Our approach differs from previous studies, as we combine content analysis of tweets by the media and journalists with the resulting positions of the media in the discussion graphs. Our findings show that, despite the overall trend of the "elite" and regional media sticking to information dissemination, online-only media and individual journalists vary greatly in their normative strategies, and this is true across countries. We also show that combining performance in content and social network analysis may allow for reconceptualization of media roles in a more flexible way.*

Introduction

The evolution of online journalism in the past decades has triggered the transformation of traditional journalism conceptions, challenging some core principles of journalism, such as the gatekeeper role and objectivity (Schudson and Anderson 2009) and blurring the boundaries of the profession (Franklin 2014). A rich body of research has explored the shift in journalism role perceptions (Schudson and Anderson 2009; Hermida 2012; Waisbord 2013; Weaver and Willnat 2016) as well as in journalism practices and performance (Pavlik 2000; Lasorsa, Lewis, and Holton 2012; Vis 2013). There is an understanding that technologies shape journalism practices (Pavlik 2000; Mellado 2015); however, it contests whether the use of digital platforms has led to a change in the core values of journalism. Some scholars have assumed that the major norms of journalism and journalistic roles still endure (Fenton 2010; Waisbord 2013; al-Rawi 2017), while others have concluded that old norms are being transformed by new practices (Gillmor 2010; Reese 2010; Lindner, Connell, and Meyer 2015).

Cross-national comparisons provide evidence that these processes may differ in various socio-political contexts (Hallin and Mancini 2012). However, most of the studies explore Western contexts (Engesser and Humprecht 2015; Larsson, Kalsnes, and Christensen 2016). There are several that have recently gone beyond Euroatlantics (Akoh and Ahiabenu 2012; al-Rawi 2017; Saldaña et al. 2017), but they still selected the countries based on their regional proximity. By contrast, our study looks at the role performance of different types of legacy media on Twitter, both in and beyond the Western world.

Our approach combines the assessment of role performance as based on the content of tweets by the media and journalists with an estimation of the positions of media/journalist accounts in the discussion network. Thus, we argue, we are able to link the role-based practices of the media/journalists to their resulting positions within online discussions.

To answer our research questions, we look at recent inter-ethnic conflicts in the United States, Europe, and Russia; these conflicts were all triggered by violence, provoked social polarization and massive public discussions, heavily involved authorities and local communities, and had policy implications. Despite different scales of global reach, they all made it into the national trending Twitter topics and today remain the reference points for public discussions on inter-ethnic relations in the respective countries. For such conflicts, it is crucial to know whether media fulfill the roles of bridging the discussion echo chambers, providing information, and organizing discussion zones within Twitter.

The remainder of the paper is organized as follows. First, we review the literature on journalism roles in the digital age, with special attention given to media performance on Twitter and to the technical ways of defining key users in the discussion. Then, we present the hypotheses and methods of our research, followed by findings and discussion. Drawing on the results of our analysis, we propose our typology of media roles in Twitter discussions.

Research Premises

Journalistic Roles in the Digital Age

The classification of journalistic role models began in the 1960s, with the dichotomist typology introduced first by Cohen (1963) and then by Johnstone, Slawski, and Bowman (1972), wherein reporters were described as neutral observers or participants. A similar approach was also used by Weaver and Wilhoit (1986, 1996) in their survey of US journalists. They added one more role type to the earlier classification, labeling the roles as "disseminator," "interpreter," and "adversarial."

In the twenty-first century, McNair proposed three role models according to the roles of journalists in the democratic process: watchdog/fourth estate, mediator/representative, participant/advocate (McNair 2009). Hanitzsch (2007) explored the cultural backgrounds of journalists to develop his typology of role models, which he applied to the cross-country study of journalism cultures (Hanitzsch et al. 2011). Mellado (2015) developed her typology based on factors such as the relationship of journalism with elites, the level of subjectivity in the content, and journalist–audience relations, defining disseminator–interventionist, loyal, watchdog, civic, service, and infotainment role models (see also Mellado and Lagos 2014).

Obviously, not all of these typologies can be operationalized to compare journalism roles across democratic and non-democratic contexts. Also, most of them are aimed at studying the role concepts as articulated by journalists, whereas our study aims to analyze the role performance based on content analysis and on the resulting positions of media and journalists in the discussion structure. Therefore, in our study of journalism role performance on Twitter, we have set sail from the earlier typology based on how journalists construct their content: (1) disseminators (convey facts) and (2) interpreters (convey not only facts but also opinions). Then, we have combined this knowledge with the positions of the media in the discussion web graphs and user top lists. The resulting roles that we have formulated trace this "performance-position" axis. We have left out the role perception aspect, as this lies beyond our scope.

Cross-national comparisons of professional journalism have shown the prevalence of some role models in certain countries (Donsbach 2008; Hanitzsch et al. 2011; Waisbord 2013) and journalistic role perception being influenced by the type of media system (Willnat, Weaver, and Choi 2013). Thus, advocacy journalism has been historically more popular in Western Europe compared to the United States (Waisbord 2013) and in Eastern Europe compared to Western Europe. A survey of political journalists in Denmark, Germany, the United Kingdom, and Spain (van Dalen, de Vreese, and Albæk 2012) revealed that Spanish journalists were more partisan in delivering news than their colleagues in other countries. The comparison of the perception of journalism functions in Germany and Russia has also shown crucial differences: in Russia, journalists often perceive themselves as "educators" of the audience, and opinionated journalism is more popular compared to Germany (Litvinenko 2013). Comparison of professional journalistic cultures in Poland, Russia, and Sweden (Nygren and Dobek-Ostrowska 2015) supports the view of Russia as a country with more blurred boundaries between impartial journalism and media advocacy practices.

Drawing on these studies, we would assume that, in our sample, the Western media would look more like information disseminators compared to the Russian media. Among the Western cases, the US legacy media should, in theory, be more restrained from expressing opinions than French and German media outlets.

Apart from the macro-level factors such as socio-political context, media scholars have also focused on exploring organizational factors that shape role performance. The same technologies are being adopted in different ways depending on organizational factors within newsrooms (Boczkowski 2004; Domingo 2008; Paulussen and Ugille 2008), "routine influences and organizational location [being] stronger and more consistent predictors of role enactments" than the role conceptions articulated by journalists (Tandoc, Hellmueller, and Vos 2013, 550).

Lasorsa, Lewis, and Holton (2012), in their study of journalists' performance on Twitter, have found that the "elite" media stick more to their role of "neutral observers" compared to other outlets. Another difference in role performance may arise from the institutional status of the Twitter accounts—that is, media accounts would differ from those of individual journalists, and the latter also have different degrees of openness in sharing their opinions, depending on their personal branding strategies (Lasorsa, Lewis, and Holton 2012). In our study, we have explored whether these patterns also work across national contexts.

Journalistic Roles on Twitter: Platform Dependence or New Flexibility?

Since the launch of Twitter in 2006, a large body of academic research has emerged studying different aspects of its impact on journalism, with two major research strands exploring (1) how media and journalists use the affordances of the platform in their work (Broersma and Graham 2013; Mellado and van Dalen 2014; Paulussen and Harder

2014; Hedman 2015; Weaver and Willnat 2016; Tandoc and Vos 2016) and (2) how the use of Twitter transforms the core norms of journalism (Bruns and Highfield 2012; Hayes, Singer, and Ceppos 2007; Hermida 2012; Skogerbø and Krumsvik 2015).

It seems that the Twitter strategies of media accounts so far have formed a smaller research field than the Twitter practices of individual journalists. For institutionalized media accounts, previous research shows that, in their online behavior, the media tend to preserve the pre-Twitter communicative hierarchies, where they played the role of key nodes in information flows and participated in top-down information dissemination (for a review, see Bodrunova, Litvinenko, and Blekanov 2016). Thus, the media are usually retweeted by more users than on average and gain authority, but are still "far and away the most followed" and are the least active in retweeting or commenting on other users—except for their fellow journalists (Lotan et al. 2011; Groshek and Tandoc 2017). Some works have also demonstrated that the importance of media accounts in shaping the discussion structure and dynamics is exaggerated, as "only a small portion of tweets received by ordinary users come from media outlets" (Bastos, Raimundo, and Travitzki 2013, 269). However, the media still remain highly relevant for Twitter users in times of crises or natural disasters (Vis 2013; Bruns 2014); thus, we expect them to be among the high-ranking users.

As for journalists, studies of their role models on Twitter usually show the tendency of journalists to "normalize" their practices, so that they fit into the existing traditional role models (Lasorsa, Lewis, and Holton 2012; Tandoc and Vos 2016). Early research on the political blogosphere (Singer 2005) has shown that journalists prefer to perform their traditional roles as gatekeepers while working with Web 2.0 platforms. Comparison of Arabic and English news organizations on Twitter revealed that the editors followed the same news values as on other media channels (al-Rawi 2017). However, most studies also show that the affordances of Twitter force journalists to adjust their existing norms and "re-invent" journalistic identity to a certain degree (Olausson 2017), as journalists "frequently experience confusion between their roles as reporters, editors, critics, or independent individuals" and, as a consequence, "use Twitter in a way that supplements their traditional role as information disseminators" (Papacharissi and de Fatima Oliveira 2012, 267). Lasorsa, Lewis, and Holton (2012) built their study on the research by Singer (2005), exploring how the platform challenges the existing norms of journalists, making them, *inter alia*, deviate from their role as nonpartisan information providers by expressing personal opinions, which contests the journalistic norm of objectivity (Lasorsa, Lewis, and Holton 2012). The authors also spotted different strategies of conduct of journalists on Twitter, depending on the status of their media outlets: the local editors were more willing to share their personal opinion than journalists from the nationwide elite media (Lasorsa, Lewis, and Holton 2012). Our study scrutinizes this aspect of deviation from the traditional norms (a tendency of more opinionated journalistic content on Web 2.0) suggested by Singer and explored on Twitter by Lasorsa and colleagues, and expands the analysis to a cross-national level.

Journalists as Influencers: Technical Ways to Assess User Roles in Online Discussions

As stated above, assessment of the discursive performance of the media/journalists has been predominantly based on a normative understanding of journalistic roles in society and content analysis that corresponds with this understanding to varying extents. However, previously, scholars have rarely been able to link role performance to the actual place of media within open discussions.

Today, social network analysis (SNA) allows for the structural representation of the roles of users within discussions on social media platforms. With understandable limitations that come from the fact that the dynamics of the discussion is presented statically, SNA-based research on social media provides ways to link the user position within the network, or the so-called *influencer* status (Patterson et al. 2007), to other user-related factors, such as the nature of the account, user behavior, content of tweets, or his/her offline status. For this paper, we have tried to link a content-based assessment of media roles to the positions of the media within the discussion networks, which would allow for assessment of not only the normative performance but also the resulting position—and, later, tracing whether observer or interpreter roles lead to greater influence within a discussion. So far, such research has been scarce (see Enli and Simonsen 2017).

As we have shown elsewhere (Bodrunova, Litvinenko, and Blekanov 2016, 2017), two approaches for measuring user influencer status may be seen in today's literature; the difference has been conceptualized as "activity metrics versus connectivity metrics." Thus, the first approach relies on user activity metrics expressed in absolute figures, such as the number of tweets, likes, retweets, and comments, as well as on the number of followers. Among these metrics, the latter is less relevant for *ad hoc* discussions due to their short-term nature. Regarding other metrics, retweets are considered, in the vast majority of literature, to be the most adequate metric for detecting influencers (Freberg et al. 2011; Bruns and Burgess 2015; Sajuria et al. 2015; see also earlier works by boyd, Golder, and Lotan 2010; Cha et al. 2010). Nonetheless, there are also works that demonstrate the importance of comments and measures combining likes, retweets, and comments (Vis 2013); thus, we have used them all and checked whether media enter the top user lists by these metrics.

Another line of research relies on SNA-based metrics such as various types of graph centralities (Cha et al. 2010; Dubois and Gaffney 2014), as well as their combinations (González-Bailón, Borge-Holthoefer, and Moreno 2013) and author-specific derivatives (Maireder et al. 2017). This approach differs from the first due to the fact that some SNA metrics are network-dependent—that is, the position of a given user in the user ranking by this metric is relative and depends on the overall shape of the network. Thus, these metrics tend to be more discussion-specific, while the authority measured by absolute metrics (such as the number of followers) may be inherited by the users from the pre-discussion period.

For this research, we have assessed positions of the media/journalists in top user lists by several SNA metrics. These metrics would be indegree, outdegree, degree, betweenness, and pagerank centralities. The first three assess the number of individual users who have interacted with a given account (indegree), with whom the given account has interacted (outdegree), and their sum (degree), which shows the level of user involvement in the discussion. These metrics are not identical to the number of likes, retweets, or comments, as one user may "like" or comment on tweets by another user many times, but the connection will still count as 1. Betweenness centrality, in its essence, shows the capacity of a user to be a shortcut between other users and user groups. Pagerank centrality shows how authoritative a given user is among other authoritative users. In our view, these metrics allow for assessment of the structural position of a user with enough precision.

However, it may happen that a user is ranked high by several metrics, so this needed to be assessed separately. For this, we have used reconstructed web graphs that show top users for whom the network metrics were combined.

Research Questions and Hypotheses

Having in mind everything stated above, we have formulated the following research questions:

> **RQ1:** How do the roles of the media/journalists in the conflict discussions on Twitter differ based on the institutional status of the tweeter (the media/journalist), the online/offline nature of the media, and the media format and reach?
>
> **RQ2:** Do these differences repeat across countries? Or, do they differ the way the respective media systems do?
>
> **RQ3:** Do the media play important roles in the discussion structure across cultures? How can we re-conceptualize the media/journalist roles based on their place in the discussion?

To answer RQ1 and RQ2, we have stated the following hypotheses:

> **H1:** In all four cases, due to the nature of Twitter as a platform, the media will tend to perform the roles of information disseminators more than those of interpreters/opinion propagators.
>
> **H2:** Of all the media, large-scale quality media (that is, national news and public affairs outlets) will adhere to the information disseminator role, unlike other types of media and individual journalists.
>
> **H3:** However, in Russia, legacy media will have more opinionated content compared to Western countries, and, in France and in Germany, more than that in the United States.

For RQ3, we suggest the role descriptions based on the assessment of the content of tweets, the aforementioned user metrics for top users, and the visual positions of influential media and journalists in the discussion graphs. We have evaluated the graphs qualitatively to see whether media of the same type tend to be in similar graph positions.

Methodology, the Research Process, and the Cases Under Scrutiny

The Cases Under Scrutiny

The cases selected for comparative analysis had six features in common, as they all: (1) had a violent trigger; (2) caused outstanding public discussions (reaching national and sometimes global Twitter trending topics) and significant social polarization; (3) were related to inter-ethnic/inter-race tensions; (4) caused street action; (5) demanded intense involvement of local and national authorities; (6) had policy consequences in terms of public security and/or migration. These features allow us to say that these cases, despite their differing scales of international coverage, are comparable within national contexts. Thus, the cases included:

- Clashes between local dwellers and immigrants from Central Asia in the Moscow district of Biryulevo, Russia, September 2013. After an alleged killing of Muscovite Egor Scherbakov by Uzbek immigrant Orkhan Zeinalov, the population of the Biryulevo district has ruined the local warehouse where hundreds of immigrants dwelled and traded (many of them illegally). Several peaceful "people's gatherings" followed.
- Anti-police riots in Ferguson, Missouri, United States, August 2014. After white police officer Darren Wilson killed an unarmed African American teenager named Mike Brown, the town of Ferguson, as well as other places across America, exploded with street protests and peaceful support actions.
- An attack on *Charlie Hebdo* in Paris, France, January 2015. Attackers killed 10 journalists and cartoonists from the French magazine and more people in Paris and beyond. Massive peaceful support actions followed in France and around the world; the public split under the hashtags #JeSuisCharlie and #JeNeSuisPasCharlie.
- Mass public harassment of females on New Year's Eve in Cologne, Germany, January 2016. During the celebrations, over 1000 (self-reportedly) were harassed, mostly by men of North African and Middle Eastern origin. Protest actions followed, as well as intense discussions on social media, while national legacy media remained silent for several days.

Research Methodology and the Research Process

Overall, our methodology is comprised of vocabulary-based Web crawling within Twitter ("Twitter crawling"), discussion graph reconstruction, formation of top user lists based on the aforementioned user metrics, manual selection of media and journalists' accounts from top user lists, automated sampling of their tweets from the corpora of the tweets uploaded, manual coding of content from the tweet datasets, assessment of the saliency of opinionated content, and qualitative clustering of the media/journalists based on the saliency of opinionated content as well as on the media's type and reach.

Our pre-tests included comparison of our uploads to standard application programming interface- (API) based ones, as well as dealing with the *ad hoc* nature of the discussions. Previous literature raised the problem of the non-comparability and low predictability of *ad hoc* discussions formed by "affective" and unstable "issue publics" (Bruns and Burgess 2015; Papacharissi 2015); we argue that the discussions are more comparable in their structural nature than was thought before, though the results have not yet been fully reported.

Then, the research steps were the following:

1. For each case, hashtags and keywords were selected on trendinalia.com; for Russia and Germany, "snowballing" reading of over 1000 tweets helped to define additional keywords.
2. We conducted Twitter crawling based on the selected keywords. For this, we used a specially developed Web crawler with adaptable modules (Blekanov, Sergeev, and Martynenko 2012). Our crawler uses a collection technique similar to manual collection, and thus minimizes the well-known API limitations, such as limits on GET-requests, the impossibility of defining the IDs of commenters and retweeters, limitations on historical data, and distortions due the changing "tweet popularity" algorithm. The crawling procedure included two steps: (1) collecting all the publicly available tweets with the pre-defined keywords and (2) collecting likes, comments,

and retweets for these tweets, for us to be able to reconstruct the discussion graph. No exclusions were made within the automated procedure; irrelevant tweets were eliminated from tweet collections later on (see Step 7).

3. Then, we reconstructed the discussion graphs and analyzed the user metrics, both absolute and relative. The resulting directed graphs had users as nodes and their interactions (likes, comments, and retweets) as edges. *N* tweets posted affected the size of the node; *N* interactions affected the visual closeness of users to each other. The visual representations of the graphs, however, were non-directed, for the sake of clarity; despite the fact that this has made the representation of directions of the communication flows in the graphs impossible, we have preferred to focus on the discussion structure and key users.
4. We formed lists of the top 100 users via nine metrics (*N* tweets, likes, retweets, and comments; indegree, outdegree, degree, betweenness, and pagerank centralities); thus, we received lists containing altogether 3600 mentions of Twitter accounts. The real number of the accounts for each case was, of course, lower, as some of the accounts were found in more than one top list. We established the threshold of the top 100 users per metric not only because of its feasibility, but also in accordance with our previous research (Bodrunova, Litvinenko, and Blekanov 2016, 2017), where we have seen that, within 100 users, there are quite a lot of those who are in the top lists by many parameters; below 100 top users, the divergence of the lists grew.
5. We manually checked the 3600 account mentions to find the media and journalists. All the media accounts, as well as those of journalists, were double-checked outside Twitter. Only journalists from established media outlets (licensed newspapers and registered audiovisual and online-only media) were taken into account; no freelance commentators, bloggers, or individual Web portal creators were included; media-like Twitter accounts were also outside our scope. We also drew the line between foreign and domestic media, which was not always easy. Thus, local media in languages other than the "title" language of the case (like *The Moscow News*), as well as state-supported "overseas broadcasting" companies (Deutsche Welle, RT (Russia Today)), were considered foreign and were not included in the samples for coding, while franchise outlets in local languages (like *LeHuffPost* or *Forbes Russia*) were included in the samples. We included (mostly from the United States) several accounts of online-only media that had grown out of user-generated content (like *The Huffington Post*, *Mediaite*, or *Mashable*), as they had gained a significant position in the respective media markets, and excluding them would have distorted the real picture of the discussions.
6. We extracted all tweets by media and journalists from the uploaded tweet collections and formed four datasets for manual coding.
7. We coded all the media tweets with the help of experienced coders. The coding followed a simple scheme: 0—information tweet or full quote; 1—opinionated tweet (opinion, rhetoric question, emotional claim, call for action, commented quote); 99—irrelevant tweet (spam, tweets in other languages/of irrelevant topics/containing hashtags only, and same-day full replicas—that is, tweets that fully replicated other tweets posted by the same user the same day, which is one of the indications of bot activity). Two coders for each country (one media expert and one native speaker) performed the coding; their interrater reliability was checked in pre-code tests and was over 0.68 (Cohen's kappa) in each case. The main coder

was the media expert; native speakers were involved for random double-checks and coding of controversial cases.

8. We clustered the accounts according to: (1) their type (hybrid/online-only/journalist), reach (national/other for hybrid media) and format (quality/other for hybrid media), and (2) the percentage of opinionated tweets in their content. We understand those under hybrid media to have both online and offline versions (Chadwick 2013) and to have started offline. To distinguish quality media from tabloid and entertainment media, we used the definition by Norris (2000, 71) as based on physical format, style of writing, subject matter of the content (including what is considered news for a given media outlet), and orientation with potential political impact (or its absence).
9. We have visualized the discussion graph in two forms: (1) the full graphs and (2) the users from the top lists, to see where media of various types and reaches stood within the discussions. We highlighted local media, journalists, and foreign media among top users and qualitatively assessed their place in the discussion graphs.
10. We described the roles of the media/journalists based on the saliency of opinionated content and the place of the media/journalists in the top lists and the graphs.

Sampling and its Limitations

Due to differing scales of coverage of the cases in both legacy and social media, we had to be flexible with our sampling strategy. Moreover, the apparatus limitations came into play when we encountered the volume of uploads for the US and French cases. The third consideration was that the cases were different in their pace, and thus the upload periods would differ as well.

Therefore, we uploaded the content from two weeks of the discussion for Russia and Germany, one week for the United States, and only three days for France. The biggest limitations that we experienced were with Ferguson; in 2014, we were still unable to upload the first week of the discussion due to its volume, and we focused on the second week, with Mike Brown's funeral as the central event. As later research revealed, we were right in our selection, as Week 2 showed only a slight decline in the presence of both hybrid and online-only media entities in the discussion of Ferguson (Groshek and Tandoc 2017). The three-day limitation for France is explained by the necessity of making the datasets comparable and feasible for coding. Thus, our initial sampling resulted in 901 tweets for Russia, 1010 tweets for the United States, 1692 tweets for Germany, and as many as 4739 tweets for France.

Another point of discussion for sampling was the media and journalists included in the samples. Our strategy was to include only the media that openly claimed to be such, including legacy media and online-only media that focused on current affairs and public agendas; niche media (sports, music, etc.) were excluded, as well as activist media sites, blogs, Twitter-only news streams, bots, and news aggregators. Also, in each case, we excluded international media and national media working in other languages; thus, RT in Russian was included for Russia, but RT in English was excluded for Russia, the United States, and France. Regarding journalists, we excluded foreign journalists, as well as bloggers, freelance journalists with no stated affiliation, and journalists with undetectable work affiliation. Thus, we formed the datasets of national legacy (offline and online-only) media and their journalists.

Then, after formation of the full lists of media, we excluded from the analysis the media that had posted fewer than four tweets, as calculating percentages for their tweets would create large distortions in the overall picture. Thus, the results that we are presenting only include the media and journalists who posted four tweets or more. After eliminating low-activity accounts and tweets coded 99, the datasets included the number of users and tweets shown in Table 1.

Results

Testing the Research Hypotheses

H1. To assess the saliency of opinionated content in various types of media, we have conducted content analysis of the tweet datasets from Table 1. The resulting distributions of media/journalists' accounts by type and reach are shown in Table 2.

From Table 2, we see that, indeed, the majority of the media in our samples gravitate towards information dissemination rather than towards opinion formation: in Russia, 26 out of 29 (89.6 percent), in Germany, 28 out of 32 (87.5 percent), in France, 29 out of 37 (78.4 percent), and in the United States, 8 out of 11 (72.7 percent) papers, online media, television channels, or individual television programs had less than 50 percent of opinion content. Our coding also shows that there is a clear similarity between France and Germany, where quality media was distributed along the "disseminator–interpreter" role axis, with television being close to 50/50. In these countries, as well as in the United States, there seems to be a "normal rate" of opinionated tweets, somewhere between 15 and 30 percent, while this is not true for Russia, where more media had less than 10 percent of tweets opinionated. Thus, H1 is true in all cases, and the "center of gravity" may be designated between 15 and 30 percent.

H2. However, at the same time, we see differences in the saliency of opinion tweets for media of various types and reaches. Thus, as expected, national hybrid quality media had mostly focused on informing the audience in all the cases, while entertainment media in Germany and France were coded as highly opinionated. Interestingly, tabloids in Russia and Germany tended to use highly informational strategies on Twitter. Other cross-country similarities are that (1) all the regional media were below 50 percent in opinionated tweets; (2) online-only media tended to be diverse in their strategies, but, in the Western countries, unlike in Russia, they all were below 50 percent in opinion content; and (3) journalists in all four countries tended to "polarize": The majority demonstrate either "0 comment" or highly opinionated strategies, with only some exceptions. Thus, H2 has been

TABLE 1
The final datasets

	Russia	United States	Germany	France
Total users	29	14	48	47
Media	26	11	32	37
Journalists	3	3	16	10
Total tweets	805	558	1512	3277
Tweets by media	785	408	1149	2808
Tweets by journalists	20	150	363	469

TABLE 2
Saliency of opinionated content in media accounts

	Hybrid				
Percentage of opinion tweets	**National quality/public service**	**National other**	**Regional**	**Online-only**	**Journalists**
Russia					
Under 10	*Kommersant*	*Lifenews*	*The Moscow News*	*Foxtime.ru*	A. Poltoranin
	Silver Rain radio	*Izvestia*	Federal Press	*Okno v Rossiyu*	
	Voice of Russia	*Krugozor*		*Pravde v glaza*	
	RT Russian	Mir24			
	Public Service TV	NTV			
		Sovershenno Sekretno			
11–30	RBC	*Metro*		National News Service	
	TV Rain	*Komsomolskaya Pravda*			
		REN TV			
		REN TV News			
31–50	*Novaya gazeta*			*Grani.ru*	V. Zlobin
51 and over				*Pravda.ru*	A. Kotz
United States					
Under 10	Fox 2 News St. Louis				R. Reilly
					L. Brown
11–30	MSNBC		STL Public Radio	*Mashable*	
	The Washington Times			*Mediaite*	
31–50			St. Louis on the air	*HuffPost Politics*	
51 and over	*Newsweek*	*Politico*			
The Nation			M.Caccioppoli		
Germany					
Under 10	*Der Tagesspiegel*	*Bild*	MDR Aktuell		D. v. Osten
	DLF Nachrichten		*Rheinishe Post*		J. v. Altenbockum
	Frankfurter Rundschau		WDR		M. v. Mauschwitz
	Die Welt		ZDF Studio NRW		M. Küpper
	ZDF *Heute*				T. Dorfer

(*Continued*)

TABLE 2
(Continued)

	Hybrid				
Percentage of opinion tweets	**National quality/public service**	**National other**	**Regional**	**Online-only**	**Journalists**
11–30	Deutschlandfunk *Frankfurter Allgemeine Zeitung* Puls (Bayerische Rundfunk) *Spiegel Online* *Die Tageszeitung* *Zeit Online*	*Stern*	Berlin direct *Berliner Zeitung* BR24 *Kölner Stadt-Anzeiger* WDR Aktuelle Stunde	Heckmeck.TV	J. Diehl N. Martin R. Dullinge
31–50	Das Erste *Tagesschau* ZDF *Heute Plus*	Neues Deutschland			H. Voigts M. Meisner
51 and over	Maischberger *Süddeutsche Zeitung*	*Der Freitag* *EMMA*			D. Majic D. Alphonso F. Krautkrämer T. Lokoschat S. Brandenburg H. Mueller-Vogg
France					
Under 10	i24NEWS Français *Liberation*		*La Voix du Nord*	*LesNews*	C. Politi
11–30	AFP *Le Journal du Dimanche* *Le Monde* *Le Monde Live* *Le Soir* *Les Décodeurs* *Les Echos* TF1 News	*20 Minutes* France Bleu	*7 à Poitiers* France Bleu Paris *La Provence* *Le Parisien* *Sud-Ouest*	*Dreuz.info*	

31–50	BFM TV FRANCE 24 FranceInfo *Le Figaro* *Le Point*	*Atlantico* *L'OBS*	*Ouest-France*	*Le HuffPost*	A. Delpérier R. Fiorucci
51 and over	Europe 1 CNews (iTELE)	C8 TV Canal+ FranceInter *Le Grand Journal* Radio VL RMC Radio RTL France			A. Francois G. Klein J.-P. Duthion S. Lefebvre L. de Montalem M. Mompontet D. Rieu

proven in terms of preferences for informational tweeting by quality media (even if there are notable exceptions) and in terms of differences between public affairs and entertainment media. It also supports earlier findings by Lasorsa, Lewis, and Holton (2012), who discussed the individualization of journalists' strategies; we state evidence of the polarization of their strategies. However, H2 was not supported in terms of differences between regional and national media, or between quality and tabloid outlets, which all tend to be informational on Twitter.

H3. We expected that, in general, Russian media would be more opinionated than Western media, which proved to be wrong. Russian media show the highest number of media under 50 percent and even under 10 percent opinion content; in all the media types, information dissemination dominates. For journalists' accounts, Russia followed the general pattern of the polarization of individual strategies on Twitter. However, one more observation needs to be made about Russia: unexpectedly, the liberal-oppositional media (RBC, *Novaya gazeta*, Grani.ru, and, to a lesser extent, TV Rain) tend to be more opinionated than the state-funded media (Voice of Russia, RT Russian, and Public Service TV). Evidently, such a strategy came from them trying to challenge both the actions of the authorities (e.g., by asking rhetorical questions) and the "neutral" discourse of state-affiliated media. This strategy may make them more vulnerable to criticism, while the state media would gain dominant positions in information dissemination. This, perhaps, deserves further research in post-Communist contexts. Thus, H3 must be rejected for Russia, but the configuration of information and opinion in Russian media accounts in social networks merits further investigation.

As to US media versus continental European media, we see that, in the United States and France, the layer of strictly informational media was thin, while, in Germany, a significant number of media outlets chose the informational strategy of Twitter presence. At the same time, the overall distribution of the media along the information/opinion clusters in Germany and France is quite similar; this is especially true for the evident opposition between public affairs media and entertainment media, while, in the United States, the same opposition shows up between the news media and political outlets. Thus, the logic of the three divergent media systems (Hallin and Mancini 2004) is applicable here, but Germany and France show more similarities despite belonging to different media models.

Suggestions for the Role Typology

To define the resulting roles of media and journalists, we have combined our knowledge on the saliency of opinionated content in media/journalist accounts with their positions within the discussions (in user top lists and visualized graphs).

First, we needed to decide which metrics would affect our decision-making. Among our cases, in Germany and the United States, top media by absolute metrics mirror top media by SNA metrics; in Russia and France, other media outlets enter SNA metrics. This supports our earlier claim (Bodrunova, Litvinenko, and Blekanov 2016, 2017) that the number of retweets does not always help users to become influential within *ad hoc* discussions. We have used network-based metrics to define the media roles within online discussions; the suggested roles are displayed in Table 3.

In Table 3, indegree is associated with content dissemination, degree with discussion potential, betweenness with the potential of linking users and user groups, pagerank with

TABLE 3
Suggested journalistic roles within online discussions

	Percentage of opinion in content	
Metric of top list	**Under 50**	**50 or more**
Indegree only	Information disseminator	Opinion propagator
Degree only	Discussant informer	Discussant interpreter
Betweenness only	Information bridge	Opinion bridge
Pagerank only	Informer of the elite	Elite interpreter
Combination of metrics	Authoritative informer	Authoritative interpreter

authority among other influential users (the "elite"), and the combination of metrics (two or more) with the overall authority of a given account. Outdegree was excluded from the analysis: the media were (understandably) virtually absent from all the four top lists by this metric, as they rarely commented or retweeted other users. Based on this, we have defined 10 possible roles: (1) informing-oriented: information disseminator, discussant informer, information bridge, informer of the elite, authoritative informer; and (2) opinion-oriented: opinion propagator, discussant interpreter, opinion bridge, elite interpreter, authoritative interpreter.

Then, we distributed the media and journalists found in top lists by network metrics into the role clusters (see Table 4).

Table 4 shows that, cross-culturally, over two-thirds of all media (67 percent in the United States, 71 percent in France, 73 percent in Germany, and, notably, 90 percent in Russia) are "authoritative informers." That is, they reach the top by several metrics and thus have capacities to perform multiple discussion roles. The next group, "authoritative interpreters," though uniting only several media outlets in each country, also shows up repeatedly. Also, the notable absence of "bridging" roles (except for *Liberation* in France) is explained by the fact that this role goes along with other roles. Cross-cultural differences, however, are also present. Thus, US and Russian media are all multi-role, while, in both France and Germany, the roles are more diversely distributed, and several media outlets are single-role in the graph—for instance, several of them belong to the list of high-pagerank users, but do not show the capacity for bridging the discussion clusters, and graph visualizations support this view (see below).

Unlike the media, individual journalists show much more divergent role models, with single roles being just as possible as multi-role positions for German and French correspondents and anchors. Thus, we see that, for journalists, both informing-oriented and opinion-oriented strategies can gain them a place within the "discussion core." In Russia and the United States, the number of journalists who made it through to the network-metric top lists is too low to draw conclusions.

Analysis of the Discussion Graphs

To supplement our (more or less arbitrary) division between information- and opinion-oriented roles, we have also examined the graph visualizations. Figures 1–4 (for Russia, the United States, Germany, and France, respectively) show the general discussion graphs (graph a) and visualizations of the top users (graph b). We have marked the national media green, national journalists blue, foreign media/journalists lilac, and other users gray/

TABLE 4
Clusters of media according to their role performance

	Under 50 percent	**50 percent or more**	
In Russia			
Information disseminator			Opinion propagator
Discussant informer			Discussant interpreter
Information bridge			Opinion bridge
Informer of the elite			Elite interpreter
Authoritative informer	*Lifenews* RT Russian *Izvestia* RBC *Forbes Russia* Grani.ru *Metro* *Komsomolskaya Pravda* TV Rain Voice of Russia *Kommersant* Krugozor NTV *Sovershenno Sekretno* REN TV *The Moscow News* National News Service	*Novaya gazeta* Pravda.ru A. Kotz	Authoritative interpreter
In the United States			
Information disseminator			Opinion propagator
Discussant informer			Discussant interpreter
Information bridge			Opinion bridge
Informer of the elite			Elite interpreter
Authoritative informer	MSNBC *The Washington Times* STL Public Radio *Mashable* *Mediaite* *HuffPost Politics* R. Reilly L. Brown	*Newsweek* *Politico* *The Nation* M. Caccioppoli	Authoritative interpreter
In Germany			
Information disseminator	*Rheinishe Post* H. Voigts	*Der Freitag*	Opinion propagator
Discussant informer			Discussant interpreter
Information bridge			Opinion bridge

(*Continued*)

TABLE 4
(*Continued*)

	Under 50 percent	**50 percent or more**	
Informer of the elite	Berlin direct Puls (Bayerische Rundfunk) Heckmeck.TV M. v. Mauschwitz M. Küpper J. Diehl R. Dullinge	T. Lokoschat S. Brandenburg	Elite interpreter
Authoritative informer	*Der Tagesspiegel* DFL Nachrichten *Frankfurter Rundschau* *Die Welt* ZDF *Heute* Deutschlandfunk *Frankfurter Allgemeine Zeitung* *Spiegel Online* *Die Tageszeitung* *Zeit Online* Das Erste *Tagesschau* *Bild* *Stern* WDR ZDF Studio NRW BR24 *Kölner Stadt-Anzeiger* WDR *Aktuelle Stunde* D. v. Osten J. v. Altenbockum M. Meisner	*Süddeutsche Zeitung* *EMMA* D. Alphonso F. Krautkrämer	Authoritative interpreter
In France			
Information disseminator			Opinion propagator
Discussant informer	*Atlantico*		Discussant interpreter
Information bridge	*Liberation*		Opinion bridge
Informer of the elite	*7 à Poitiers* France Bleu France Bleu Paris C. Politi R. Fiorucci	S. Lefebvre	Elite interpreter

(*Continued*)

TABLE 4
(Continued)

	Under 50 percent	**50 percent or more**	
Authoritative informer	AFP	CNews (iTELE)	Authoritative interpreter
	Atlantico	Europe 1	
	BFM TV	FranceInter	
	FRANCE 24	RMC Radio	
	FranceInfo	A. Francois	
	FranceInter	G. Klein	
	La Provence	M. Mompontet	
	Le Figaro	L. Montalem	
	Le HuffPost		
	Le Journal du Dimanche		
	Le Monde		
	Le Monde Live		
	Le Point		
	Le Parisien		
	Le Soir		
	LesNews		
	Les Echos		
	L'OBS		
	Ouest-France		
	RTL France		
	Sud-Ouest		
	TF1 News		
	A. Delpérier		

black for each case; top users by absolute metrics, by one network metric only, and by combination of metrics differ in intensity of color. Thus, one can correlate Table 3 with the graphs (b) to see the "authoritative" media and journalists intensely highlighted.

The graphs add to our understanding of the media roles, as we can see how and where the media and journalists are grouped.

What we see in Figures 1–4 adds to the pictures. As for Russia and the United States, we can see political polarization within the top-100 user graphs, especially in terms of the media. In Russia, there is a pro-state cluster (RT Russian, Voice of Russia, and two more outlets) and a liberal-oppositional cluster (including Radio Liberty in Russian and *Novaya gazeta)*. We also see that the pro-state *Lifenews* news holding and the more liberal *Forbes Russia* were important foci of discussion outside these clusters. In the case of Ferguson, polarization shows up in a different way, as the more left-leaning media, such as MSNBC, *HuffPost Politics*, *The Nation*, and *Mediaite*, stand closer to the discussion center and are multi-role, while Fox News and its programs are more peripheral and single-role; the St. Louis media sit close to each other. In Russia, only a few media are positioned in the discussion center; in the United States and Germany, they sit around it, and, in the latter case, one may see a television news bulletin cluster, a neutral/left-leaning cluster (from *Zeit* to *Aktuelle Stunde*), a tabloid cluster (*Bild* and *Stern*), and a more conservative cluster (with *Frankfurter Allgemeine Zeitung* and *Die Welt*). The French case, in its turn, shows a huge presence of global media that form a sort of field quite separated from the French-speaking discussion core where some French media find their place, but most of them form a distinct cluster beside the main discussion nebula. Thus, we see that the capacity of normative role performance for media which are ranked high by

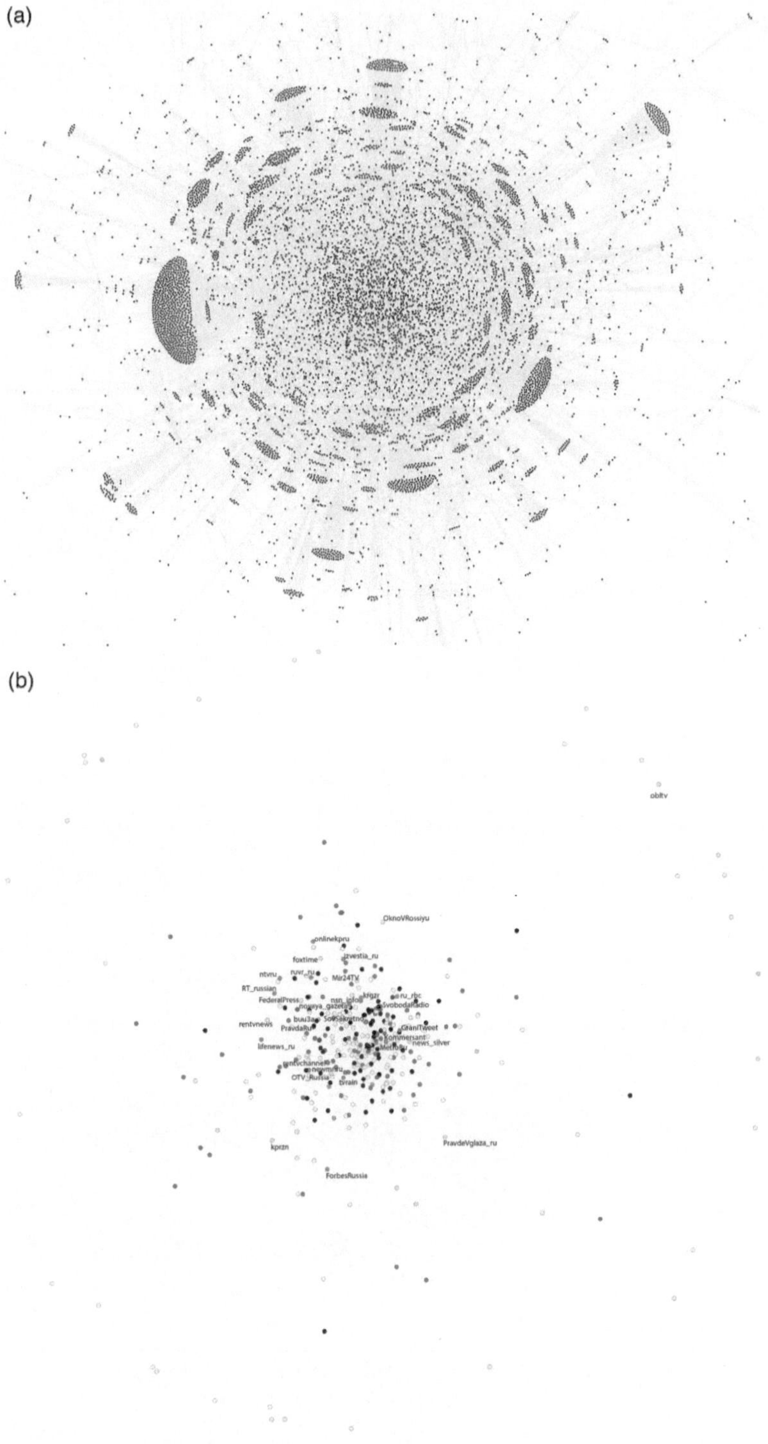

FIGURE 1
Web graphs and influencers in the discussions on inter-ethnic conflicts in Russia: (a) the discussion graph; (b) the representation of top users by nine metrics

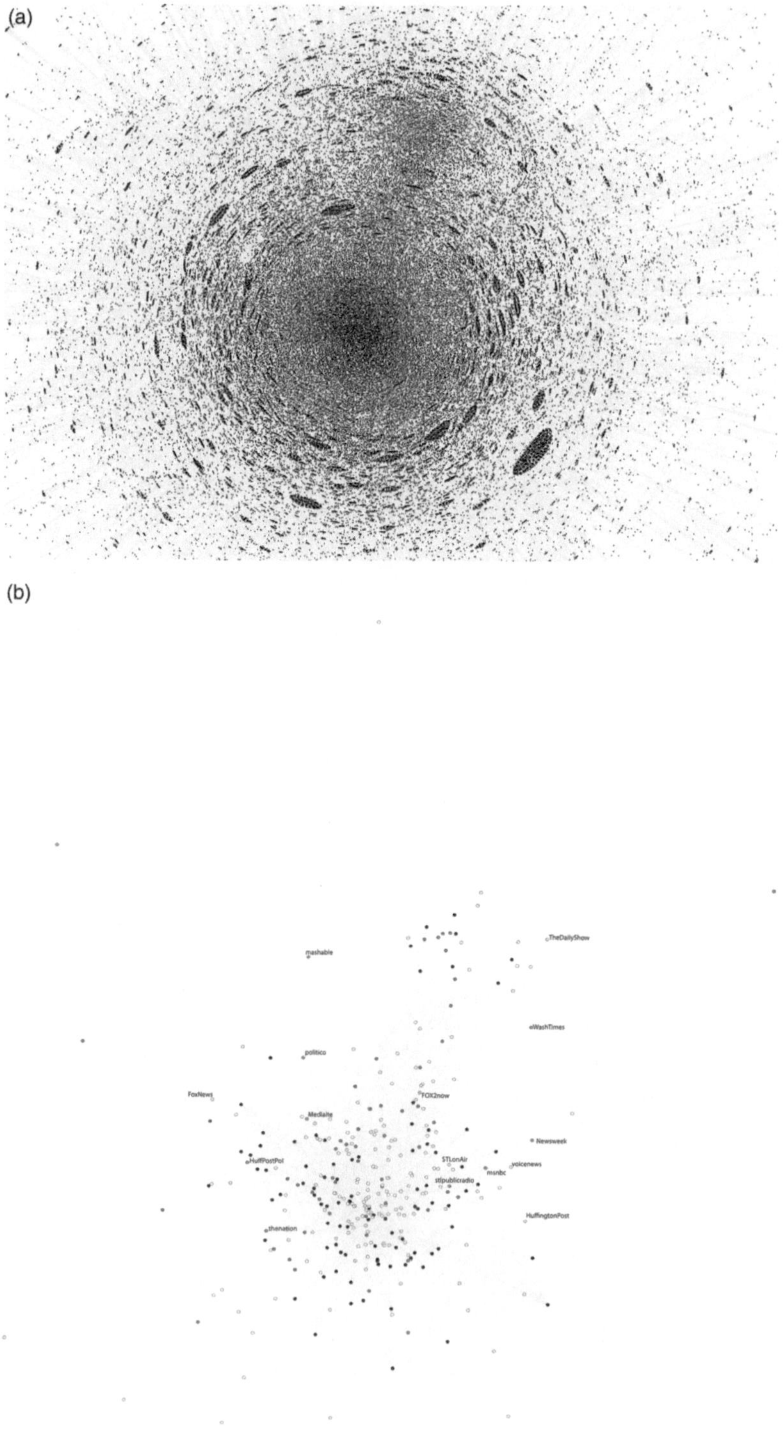

FIGURE 2
Web graphs and influencers in the discussions on inter-ethnic conflicts in the United States: (a) the discussion graph; (b) the representation of top users by nine metrics

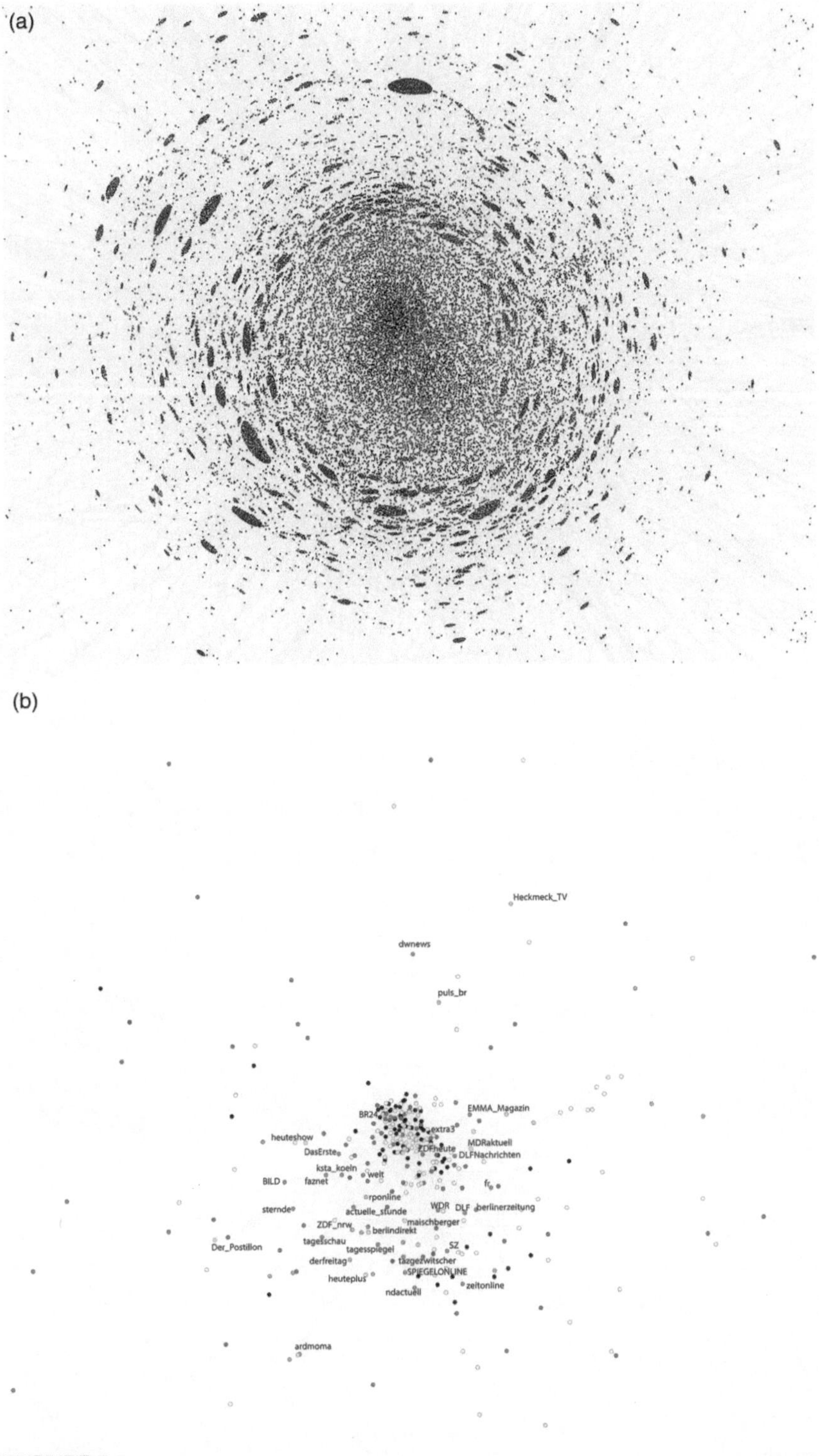

FIGURE 3
Web graphs and influencers in the discussions on inter-ethnic conflicts in Germany: (a) the discussion graph; (b) the representation of top users by nine metrics

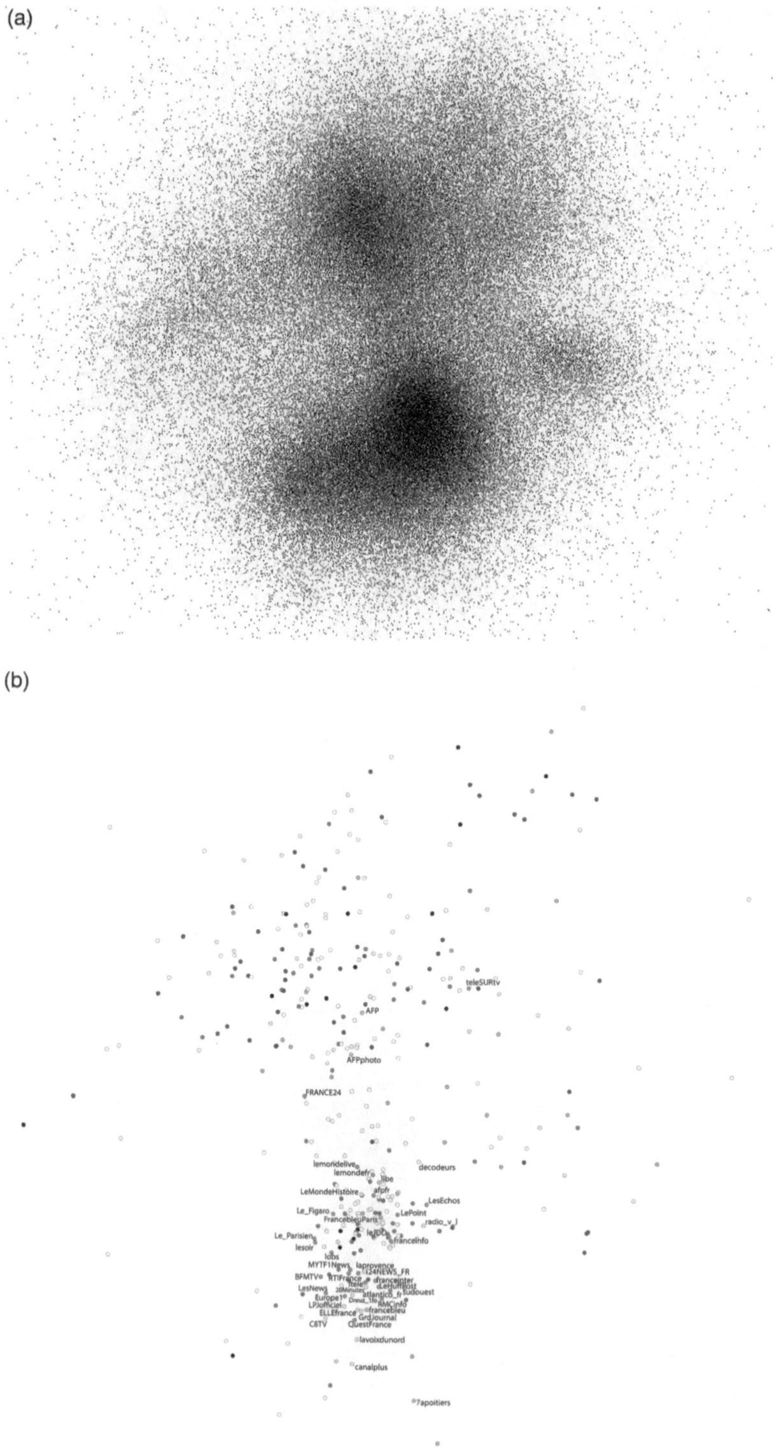

FIGURE 4
Web graphs and influencers in the discussions on inter-ethnic conflicts in France: (a) the discussion graph; (b) the representation of top users by nine metrics

centrality metrics may still be limited—the media, indeed, are important nodes in the discussion, but they tend to result in grouping according to format and bias, which means they speak mostly to mini-audiences that prefer these biases and formats.

One more observation is worth noting. In the United States, Germany, and France, and, to a lesser extent, in Russia, the media sit either alone or in mini-clusters around the discussion core, forming a "second layer" around it. Thus, the assessment of graphs (a) and (b) suggests that we can talk about the roles of all media on the whole: all together, they link the discussion core to the periphery and provide the graph center with input for discussion. Moreover, most single-role media and those with low centrality rankings (even if high numbers of posts, likes, or shares) are situated farther from the discussion core than multi-role media. Thus, the relations between user centrality and role strategy on social networks deserve more investigation for both the media and journalists.

Discussion

The findings of the four case studies can obviously be generalized only to a certain extent. However, they show that combining network analysis and content analysis may help to better define today's roles of the media and journalists online.

We have suggested defining media roles in online discussions by combining the percentage of opinionated content and the position of a given account by SNA metrics. The volume of opinionated content may be used as a hint for role performance—information disseminators publish less than 30 percent of it, balanced interpreters up to 50 percent, and opinion propagators over 50 percent. We see this formal approach as suitable for assessing the strategies of individual media/journalist accounts, but it is also useful to look at the discussion graphs to see whether users gaining top ranking positions work as real opinion bridges or, vice versa, echo chamber centers.

We have seen that significant similarities exist in media strategies across Western and non-Western contexts, including Russia. Most legacy media tend to perform informing-oriented roles and are posting informational tweets. Often, the latter are announcements of news pieces designed for inviting Twitter users to follow them. However, more diverse strategies also exist, and European media tend to be similar in how they distribute between informing and opinion propagation.

At least two-thirds of the media in each country appear to reach the position of "authoritative informers" with multi-role performance. At the same time, in all the cases, there are media clusters divided due to format and bias, which is an obvious obstacle for performing the discursive roles efficiently. In all these respects, Russian media do not differ much from those of other countries.

We have also seen cross-cultural patterns of role performance based on format differences, but, unexpectedly, tabloid and regional media chose the same informing-oriented strategies as the quality media, while the entertainment media were more opinionated across the cases. Thus, the audience niche plays a less important role in defining media roles on Twitter than topicality and overall format (public affairs versus entertainment).

Journalists, unlike the media, have shown not only divergent but "polarized" strategies of role self-assignment, and this pattern is clearly present across countries and supports earlier findings by Lasorsa, Lewis, and Holton (2012) on the rise of journalists' branding strategies.

Thus, our case studies have shown that Twitter has been "normalized" enough to show universal trends in media behavior within discussions on crises, but, in several aspects, national media markets and media traditions still prevail over the universality of Twitter. As we have found cross-national differences for *ad hoc* discussions, it may be important to apply the same research questions to "calm" periods in Twitter discussions.

Individual countries have also provided input for further research. Thus, the French case has demonstrated how the global media are entangled with the local media within a discussion; in Russia, the political alignment of the media influenced the role performance significantly; in the United States, the relative scarcity of media presence after just one week of the conflict was unexpected. These smaller findings may provide further grounds for comparative research, as well as research of the notion of the roles of the media community within online discussions.

DISCLOSURE STATEMENT

No potential conflict of interest was reported by the authors.

FUNDING

This research has been supported in full by the Russian Science Foundation [grant number 16-18-10125 (2016)].

REFERENCES

Akoh, Ben, and Kwami Ahiabenu. 2012. "A Journey Through 10 Countries." *Journalism Practice* 6 (3): 349–365.

al-Rawi, Ahmed. 2017. "News Organizations 2.0: A Comparative Study of Twitter News." *Journalism Practice* 11 (6): 705–720.

Bastos, Marco Toledo, Rafael Luis Galdini Raimundo, and Rodrigo Travitzki. 2013. "Gatekeeping Twitter: Message Diffusion in Political Hashtags." *Media, Culture & Society* 35 (2): 260–270.

Blekanov, Ivan, Sergey Sergeev, and Irina Martynenko. 2012. "Construction of Subject-Oriented Web Crawlers Using a Generalized Kernel." *Scientific and Technical Bulletins of St. Petersburg State Polytechnic University* 157: 9–15.

Boczkowski, Pablo J. 2004. "The Processes of Adopting Multimedia and Interactivity in Three Online Newsrooms." *Journal of Communication*, 54 (2): 197–213.

Bodrunova, Svetlana, Anna Litvinenko, and Ivan Blekanov. 2016. "Influencers on the Russian Twitter: Institutions vs. People in the Discussion on Migrants." Proceedings of ACM conference "electronic governance and open society: challenges in eurasia", St.Petersburg, Russia, 212–222.

Bodrunova, Svetlana, Ivan Blekanov, and Alexey Maksimov. 2017. "Measuring Influencers in Twitter Ad-Hoc Discussions: Active Users vs. Internal Networks in the Discourse on Biryuliovo Bashings in 2013." Proceedings of the AINL FRUCT 2016 conference, St.Petersburg, Russia, item #7891853.

boyd, danah, Scott Golder, and Gilad Lotan. 2010. "Tweet, Tweet, Retweet: Conversational Aspects of Retweeting on Twitter." Proceedings of 43rd hawaii international conference on system sciences (HICSS), 1–10.

Broersma, Marcel, and Todd Graham. 2013. "Twitter as a News Source." *Journalism Practice* 7 (4): 446–464.

Bruns, Axel. 2014. "Social Media and Journalism During Times of Crisis." In *The Social Media Handbook*, edited by Jeremy Hunsinger, and Theresa Senft, 159–176. London: Routledge.

Bruns, Axel, and Jean Burgess. 2015. "Twitter Hashtags From Ad Hoc to Calculated Publics." In *Hashtag Publics: The Power and Politics of Discursive Networks*, edited by Nathan Rambukkana, 13–28. Bern: Peter Lang Publishing.

Bruns, Axel, and Tim Highfield. 2012. "Blogs, Twitter, and Breaking News: The Produsage of Citizen Journalism." In *Producing Theory in a Digital World: The Intersection of Audiences and Production in Contemporary Theory*, edited by Rebecca Ann Lind, 15–32. Bern: Peter Lang Publishing.

Cha, Meeyoung, Hamed Haddadi, Fabricio Benevenuto, and Krishna P. Gummadi. 2010. "Measuring User Influence on Twitter: The Million Follower Fallacy." Proceedings of the 4th international AAAI conference on weblogs and social Media, Washington, DC, 10–17.

Chadwick, Andrew. 2013. *The Hybrid Media System: Politics and Power*. Oxford: Oxford University Press.

Cohen, Bernard C. 1963. *The Press and Foreign Policy*. Princeton, NJ: Princeton University Press.

Domingo, David. 2008. "Interactivity in the Daily Routines of Online Newsrooms: Dealing with an Uncomfortable Myth." *Journal of Computer-Mediated Communication* 13 (3): 680–704.

Donsbach, Wolfgang. 2008. "Journalists' Role Perceptions." In *The International Encyclopedia of Communication*, edited by Wolfgang Donsbach, Vol. VI, 2605–2610. Malden: Wiley-Blackwell.

Dubois, Elizabeth, and Devin Gaffney. 2014. "The Multiple Facets of Influence: Identifying Political Influentials and Opinion Leaders on Twitter." *American Behavioral Scientist* 58 (10): 1260–1277.

Engesser, Sven, and Edda Humprecht. 2015. "Frequency or Skillfulness." *Journalism Studies* 16 (4): 513–529.

Enli, Gunn, and Chris-Adrian Simonsen. 2017. "'Social Media Logic' Meets Professional Norms: Twitter Hashtags Usage by Journalists and Politicians." *Information, Communication & Society* 44 (2): 1–16.

Fenton, Natalie, ed. 2010. *New Media, Old News: Journalism and Democracy in the Digital Age*. Los Angeles: Sage.

Franklin, Bob. 2014. "The Future of Journalism." *Journalism Practice* 8 (5): 469–487.

Freberg, Karen, Kristin Graham, Karen McGaughey, and Laura A. Freberg. 2011. "Who Are the Social Media Influencers? A Study of Public Perceptions of Personality." *Public Relations Review* 37: 90–92.

Gillmor, Dan. 2010. *Mediactive*. San Francisco, CA: Dan Gillmor.

González-Bailón, Sandra, Javier Borge-Holthoefer, and Yamir Moreno. 2013. "Broadcasters and Hidden Influentials in Online Protest Diffusion." *American Behavioral Scientist* 57 (7): 943–965.

Groshek, Jacob, and Edson Tandoc. 2017. "The Affordance Effect: Gatekeeping and (Non) Reciprocal Journalism on Twitter." *Computers in Human Behavior* 66: 201–210.

Hallin, Daniel C., and Paolo Mancini. 2004. *Comparing Media Systems: Three Models of Media and Politics*. Cambridge: Cambridge University Press.

Hallin, Daniel C., and Paolo Mancini, eds. 2012. *Comparing Media Systems Beyond the Western World*. Cambridge: Cambridge University Press.

Hanitzsch, Thomas. 2007. "Deconstructing Journalism Culture: Toward a Universal Theory." *Communication Theory* 17 (4): 367–385.

Hanitzsch, Thomas, Folker Hanusch, Claudia Mellado, Maria Anikina, Rosa Berganza, Incilay Cangoz, Mihai Coman, et al. 2011. "Mapping Journalism Cultures Across Nations." *Journalism Studies* 12 (3): 273–293.

Hayes, Arthur S., Jane B. Singer, and Jerry Ceppos. 2007. "Shifting Roles, Enduring Values: The Credible Journalist in a Digital Age." *Journal of Mass Media Ethics* 22 (4): 262–279.

Hedman, Ulrika. 2015. "J-Tweeters." *Digital Journalism* 3 (2): 279–297.

Hermida, Alfred. 2012. "Tweets and Truth." *Journalism Practice* 6 (5-6): 659–668.

Johnstone, John W. C., Edward J. Slawski, and William W. Bowman. 1972. "The Professional Values of American Newsmen." *Public Opinion Quarterly* 36 (4): 522–540.

Larsson, Anders O., Bente Kalsnes, and Christian Christensen. 2016. "Elite Interaction." *Journalism Practice* 44 (2): 1–21.

Lasorsa, Dominic L., Seth C. Lewis, and Avery E. Holton. 2012. "Normalizing Twitter." *Journalism Studies* 13 (1): 19–36.

Lindner, Andrew M., Emma Connell, and Erin Meyer. 2015. "Professional Journalists in 'Citizen' Journalism." *Information, Communication & Society* 18 (5): 553–568.

Litvinenko, Anna. 2013. A New Definition of Journalism Functions in the Framework of Hybrid Media Systems: German and Russian Academic Perspectives. *Global Media Journal. German Edition* 3 (1): 1–12.

Lotan, Gilad, Erhardt Graeff, Mike Ananny, Devin Gaffney, Ian Pearce, and danah boyd. 2011. "The Revolutions Were Tweeted: Information Flows During the 2011 Tunisian and Egyptian Revolutions." *International Journal of Communication* 1: 31–54.

Maireder, Axel, Brian E. Weeks, Homero Gil de Zúñiga, and Stephan Schlögl. 2017. "Big Data and Political Social Networks." *Social Science Computer Review* 35 (1): 126–141.

McNair, Brian. 2009. "Journalism and Society. Journalism and Democracy." In *The Handbook of Journalism Studies*, edited by Karin Wahl-Jorgensen, and Thomas Hanitzsch, 237–250. London: Routledge.

Mellado, Claudia. 2015. "Professional Roles in News Content: Six Dimensions of Journalistic Role Performance." *Journalism Studies* 16 (4): 596–614.

Mellado, Claudia, and Claudia Lagos. 2014. "Professional Roles in News Content: Analyzing Journalistic Performance in the Chilean National Press." *International Journal of Communication* 8: 2090–2112.

Mellado, Claudia, and Arjen van Dalen. 2014. "Between Rhetoric and Practice." *Journalism Studies* 15 (6): 859–878.

Norris, Pippa. 2000. *A Virtuous Circle: Political Communication in Postindustrial Societies*. Cambridge: Cambridge University Press.

Nygren, Gunnar, and Bogusława Dobek-Ostrowska. 2015. *Journalism in Change*. Bern: Peter Lang.

Olausson, Ulrika. 2017. "The Reinvented Journalist: The Discursive Construction of Professional Identity on Twitter." *Digital Journalism* 5 (1): 61–81.

Papacharissi, Zizi. 2015. *Affective Publics: Sentiment, Technology, and Politics*. Oxford Studies in Digital Politics series. Oxford: Oxford University Press.

Papacharissi, Zizi, and Maria de Fatima Oliveira. 2012. "Affective News and Networked Publics: The Rhythms of News Storytelling on #Egypt." *Journal of Communication* 62 (2): 266–282.

Patterson, Kerry, Joseph Grenny, David Maxfield, and Ron McMillan. 2007. *Influencer: The Power to Change Anything*. Highbridge: Tata McGraw-Hill Education.

Paulussen, Steve, and Pieter Ugille. 2008. "User Generated Content in the Newsroom: Professional and Organisational Constraints on Participatory Journalism." *Westminster Papers in Communication and Culture* 5 (2): 24–41.

Paulussen, Steve, and Raymond A. Harder. 2014. "Social Media References in Newspapers: Facebook, Twitter and YouTube as Sources in Newspaper Journalism." *Journalism Practice* 8 (5): 542–551.
Pavlik, John. 2000. "The Impact of Technology on Journalism." *Journalism Studies* 1 (2): 229–237.
Reese, Stephen D. 2010. "Journalism and Globalization." *Sociology Compass* 4 (6): 344–353.
Sajuria, Javier, Jennifer van Heerde-Hudson, David Hudson, Niheer Dasandi, and Yannis Theocharis. 2015. "Tweeting Alone? An Analysis of Bridging and Bonding Social Capital in Online Networks." *American Politics Research* 43 (4): 708–738.
Saldaña, Magdalena, Vanessa d. M. Higgins Joyce, Amy Schmitz Weiss, and Rosental C. Alves. 2017. "Sharing the Stage." *Journalism Practice* 11 (4): 396–416.
Schudson, Michael, and Chris Anderson. 2009. "Objectivity, Professionalism, and Truth Seeking in Journalism." In *The handbook of journalism studies*, edited by Karin Wahl-Jorgensen, and Thomas Hanitzsch, 88–101. London: Routledge.
Singer, Jane B. 2005. "The Political J-Blogger." *Journalism: Theory, Practice & Criticism* 6 (2): 173–198.
Skogerbø, Eli, and Arne H. Krumsvik. 2015. "Newspapers, Facebook and Twitter." *Journalism Practice* 9 (3): 350–366.
Tandoc, Edson C., Lea Hellmueller, and Tim P. Vos. 2013. "Mind the Gap." *Journalism Practice* 7 (5): 539–554.
Tandoc, Edson C., and Tim P. Vos. 2016. "The Journalist Is Marketing the News." *Journalism Practice* 10 (8): 950–966.
van Dalen, Arjen, Claes H. de Vreese, and Erik Albæk. 2012. "Different Roles, Different Content? A Four-Country Comparison of the Role Conceptions and Reporting Style of Political Journalists." *Journalism: Theory, Practice & Criticism* 13 (7): 903–922.
Vis, Farida. 2013. "Twitter as a Reporting Tool for Breaking News." *Digital Journalism* 1 (1): 27–47.
Waisbord, Silvio. 2013. *Reinventing Professionalism: Journalism and News in Global Perspective*. New York: John Wiley & Sons.
Weaver, David H., and G. Cleveland Wilhoit. 1986. *The American Journalist: A Portrait of U.S. News People and Their Work*. Bloomington: Indiana University Press.
Weaver, David H., and G. Cleveland Wilhoit. 1996. *The American Journalist in the 1990s: U.S. News People at the End of an Era*. Mahwah, NJ: Erlbaum.
Weaver, David H., and Lars Willnat. 2016. "Changes in U.S. Journalism." *Journalism Practice* 10 (7): 844–855.
Willnat, Lars, David H. Weaver, and Jihyang Choi. 2013. "The Global Journalist in the Twenty-First Century." *Journalism Practice* 7 (2): 163–183.

iD http://orcid.org/0000-0003-0740-561X
iD http://orcid.org/0000-0002-4029-0829
iD http://orcid.org/0000-0002-7305-1429

AND DELIVER US TO SEGMENTATION
The growing appeal of the niche news audience

Jacob L. Nelson

Non-profit news publishers, a small but growing piece of the news media environment, often explicitly attempt to build strong ties with their audiences. Many assume this approach differs from that of legacy newsrooms, which have historically kept the audience at arm's length. In this article, I argue that this distinction has blurred. In-depth interviews with reporters and editors at a daily newspaper (The Chicago Tribune) *and a local news non-profit (City Bureau) reveal that: (1) both organizations are pursuing a more collaborative relationship with their audiences; and (2) this pursuit is ill-suited for the traditional mass audience approach to news production. I conclude that journalists aspiring to work more closely with the audience find greater success when that audience is narrow to begin with.*

Introduction

For the past two decades, the news industry has struggled to overcome profound financial instability. Local newspapers in particular have faced huge drops in print advertising and subscription revenues, leading to staff cuts and closures (Nielsen 2015; Siles and Boczkowski 2012). In light of these circumstances, journalism researchers and stakeholders are turning their focus to news non-profits, an increasingly popular alternative to local news production (Ferrucci 2015c, 2017; Konieczna and Powers 2016; Mitchell et al. 2013; Rosentiel et al. 2016). News non-profits have rapidly spread across the United States (Mitchell et al. 2013), and most are only a few years old (Rosentiel et al. 2016). Though the future of the news industry remains marked with uncertainty, it appears likely that the non-profit news model will be a part of it.

Many believe that a world where journalism stems from news non-profits rather than commercial newspapers would look very different from the present. Non-profit journalism combines aspects of traditional reporting (e.g., professional editors and reporters working to publish original content) with collaborations between foundations, community activists, and data scientists (Konieczna and Robinson 2014; Robinson 2011, 2014; Robinson and DeShano 2011). News non-profits tend to embrace "public service journalism" (Ferrucci 2017), an approach to news production that explicitly embraces strong, collaborative ties with the news audience. Public service journalists privilege direct communication with their audiences (e.g., in-person events, online conversations via social media platforms) in hopes of shifting news production from one-way lectures to two-way dialogues. This runs counter to legacy news organizations, which have historically been uninterested in interacting with or hearing from their readers (Gans 2004). Yet, as journalism's economic crisis continues, even traditional news publishers have begun altering their approach in order to survive. Might this include a similar attempt to improve the journalist/audience relationship? If so, how might this attempt differ from that of a non-profit news publisher?

What follows is an investigation of these questions based on in-depth interviews with reporters and editors at two local news organizations in Chicago: a traditional newspaper (*The Chicago Tribune*), and a news non-profit (*City Bureau*). Findings reveal that, contrary to expectations about legacy newsrooms, both organizations are pursuing stronger, more collaborative relationships with the news audience. However, this pursuit occurs differently, and with different levels of success, depending on how each news organization conceptualizes the audience in the first place. *City Bureau* editors see Chicago as comprising multiple audiences separated by geography and socioeconomic conditions, and focus specifically on cultivating close ties with several of these groups. *Tribune* editors and reporters, on the other hand, generally conceive of their readers as one loosely collected mass of people that likely live in the Chicago area but can also include anyone with an internet connection. The paper's larger, more varied readership makes pursuing a more participatory relationship with the audience less intuitive and often more frustrating.

These findings suggest that journalism's shift from ignoring to embracing audience input is not relegated to one type of news organization, but is instead occurring throughout the profession as a whole. More importantly, they indicate that the pursuit of a more collaborative relationship with the news audience is ill-suited for a traditional mass audience approach to news production. While *City Bureau* editors described encouraging interactions with their limited, carefully chosen audience, *Tribune* editors and reporters described exasperating and alienating experiences with a much broader group of people. In light of these findings, I conclude that journalists pursuing a more collaborative relationship with the news audience find greater success when they focus on narrower audiences to begin with. Doing so, however, increases audience fragmentation at a moment when many fear the news media environment is already hopelessly torn apart.

News Production and the Audience

Throughout the twentieth century, journalists working for commercial news publishers (e.g., daily newspapers, broadcast news stations) were relatively unconcerned with their audience "and rejected feedback from it" (Gans 2004, 230). Instead, journalists decided which stories to cover based on their professional judgment, and aspired to impress their editors rather than their readers (Boczkowski 2013). This indifference stems from the fact that, in a much more limited media environment, journalists working for well-known news brands could rightly assume their reporting would be widely received (Webster 2014). As a result, reporters and editors in commercial news organizations rarely considered their audience's preferences or backgrounds when making editorial decisions.

As the twentieth century came to a close, this approach became untenable. First, the arrival of cable brought with it a much larger array of television options, fragmenting the broadcast news audience (Nadler 2016). Then, the advent of the internet led to drastic losses in print journalism advertising and subscription revenues (McChesney and Pickard 2011; Prior 2007; Seamans and Zhu 2014; Siles and Boczkowski 2012). Commercial news media suddenly had a financial incentive to question its detached attitude toward the audience, and to seek out an approach that would bring those audiences back (Nadler 2016; Williams and Delli Carpini 2011).

It is within this current media environment that many journalism stakeholders and researchers have begun to argue that the news industry should take a stronger interest in the audience (Batsell 2015; Lewis, Holton, and Coddington 2014; Loosen and Schmidt 2012; McCollough, Crowell, and Napoli 2017; Mersey 2010). Advocates of this strategy believe that when journalists know more about how audiences interact with the news, they can more effectively create content that meets the audience's preferences and expectations. They argue that news publishers should begin identifying and keeping the audience in mind throughout the news production process, rather than simply publishing news and assuming that the audience will show up. One increasingly popular type of news production has aggressively taken up this approach: the non-profit news model.

Non-Profit Journalism

News non-profits seek funding from grants and donations rather than ad revenue, frequently partner with a variety of civic organizations in addition to more conventional newsrooms, and actively court audience participation (Felle 2016; Ferrucci 2015c; Konieczna and Robinson 2014; Ognyanova et al. 2013; Pickard and Stearns 2011; Rosentiel et al. 2016; Wenzel, Gerson, and Moreno 2016). Though non-profit journalism precedes the digital era, in the past few years it has begun to play a more prominent role in the news media landscape. Some news non-profits focus on specific subjects (e.g., criminal justice, climate change); many, however, seek to fill the local news void left by traditional, daily newspapers (Ferrucci 2015a, 2015b; Mitchell et al. 2013; Patel and McLellan 2012; Rosentiel et al. 2016). Local news non-profits have grown increasingly common, leading researchers to investigate their impact on the news environment and the communities they cover (Coates Nee 2013; Coates Nee 2013; Ferrucci 2015c; Konieczna and Powers 2016).

These studies have found that the philosophy behind news non-profits bears a strong resemblance to public journalism, a failed movement in the 1990s where commercial news publishers attempted to improve their ties with their audiences (Ferrucci 2015c, 2017). Public journalism efforts attempted to engage communities, give citizens the power to shape the news agenda, present the news in an easily understood format, and galvanize readers (Charity 1995; Ferrucci 2015c; Glasser 1999; Rosen 1996). The news non-profit approach is similarly focused on better understanding and connecting with specific audiences in an attempt to empower citizens, which is why it has been recently dubbed *public service journalism* (Ferrucci 2015c). News non-profit journalists often aspire to engage marginalized communities, and they do so by attempting to not only report stories *about* these communities, but *to* them as well.

From One, Many

Public service journalism's emphasis on improving news coverage of and for specific communities speaks to an important development in news production more generally: the division of the news audience into multiple audiences. Commercial journalism has historically taken a "mass audience" approach to news production, where reporters and editors assumed a neutral, detached tone in order to appeal to as many people as possible (Webster 2014; Williams and Delli Carpini 2011). This resulted in reporters and editors focusing predominantly on their own demographic: educated, white, middle-class males (Epstein 1974; Fishman 1980; Tuchman 1978). As a result, news organizations have struggled to address women, minorities, lower-income groups, and those "on the fringes of society" (Clarke 2014; Hess 2015; McChesney and Pickard 2011; Mersey 2010, 129; Nadler 2016; Richards 2013). News ethnographies throughout the twentieth century portray this oversight not as a malicious attempt to exclude specific populations, but as an unintended consequence of the news industry comprising a mostly homogenous group of people and treating its audience as a similarly homogenous mass (Fishman 1980; Gans 2004; Tuchman 1978).

Non-profit news journalists, on the other hand, often explicitly acknowledge the existence of distinct audiences. Doing so allows them to focus primarily on improving their relationship with specific groups they believe have been underrepresented or left out by traditional news media. For example, the news non-profit One River, Many Stories focused specifically on engaging with citizens living near the St. Louis River in an attempt to "build an alliance among the region's professional journalists, educators and citizen storytellers" ("About"). This approach stems from the assumption that confining the audience to a small subsection of the total population makes it easier to pursue a more collaborative relationship with them. When a publication focuses on a specific demographic, it increases the likelihood of garnering more members from that group, but also of alienating anyone outside of it. As a result, this approach comes with a cost—it limits the size of the potential audience. A smaller audience is incompatible with a media environment dependent on advertising dollars, but fits more naturally within the news industry's ongoing shift towards subscription and donation-based revenue models (Pfauth 2016; Vernon 2016; Williams 2016).

More importantly, the pursuit distinct audiences instead of one mass audience might adversely affect democratic society by diminishing the ability for people to come together and discuss issues in shared public spaces (Katz 1996). Katz referred to this as "audience segmentation," which he lamented would occur with the arrival of multiple broadcast channels (1996, 23). Within such a news media environment, audiences would grow more extreme in their views because they would not be exposed to conflicting viewpoints. Many fear that this is already occurring, and that the advent of partisan news that began with cable channels like Fox and MSNBC and has continued with websites like The Huffington Post and Drudge Report has allowed liberals and conservatives to confine themselves to news sources that align with their ideologies, while ignoring everything else (Jamieson and Cappella 2009; Pariser 2011; Stroud 2010, 2011). Currently, it seems this fear has not panned out (Gentzkow and Shapiro 2011; Napoli 2016; Nelson and Webster Forthcoming; Weeks, Ksiazek, and Holbert 2016). Even in a media environment of seemingly infinite choice, audiences continue to congregate among a few well-known brands like *The New York Times*, *The Washington Post*, CNN, and ABC that have continued to publish news intended for a mass audience. However, assuming the desire to build stronger ties with the audience extends to the news industry as whole, this might very well change.

In light of these circumstances, this project seeks to answer two questions. First, is the pursuit of a stronger relationship with the news audience confined solely to news non-profits, or has it spread to more traditional outlets as well? And is a small, niche audience necessary for a more collaborative journalist/audience relationship to be successful?

With that, my research question is as follows:

How do a news non-profit and a traditional newspaper conceptualize and pursue their audiences?

Method

My analysis draws on data collected through 29 in depth interviews with reporters and editors from both *City Bureau* and *The Chicago Tribune*. During the interviews, I asked a variety of questions to better understand how my subjects conceptualized and pursued their audiences. The interviews were recorded, and ranged in length from one to two hours. The recordings were transcribed, and the transcriptions were analyzed using grounded theory to find recurring themes and patterns (Fleming 2014; Nelson and Lewis 2015). All but one subject agreed to allow me to me to use their name and title. Northwestern's Institutional Review Board (IRB) exempted all research involving human subjects in this study.

The Chicago Tribune

The Chicago Tribune is the eleventh largest daily paper in the country (Lipinski 2016). The *Tribune* was chosen because, as a renowned news institution, it exemplifies a traditional, commercial newspaper. I interviewed 25 *Tribune* employees, including its associate editor, digital editors, section editors, columnists, and investigative and beat reporters. I also interviewed two members of the *Tribune*'s marketing team, which conducts internal audience research to persuade advertisers to partner with the paper.

City Bureau

The local news non-profit *City Bureau* is a collective of news professionals that seeks to provide "responsible" and "responsive" reporting to minority communities in Chicago ("About"). *City Bureau* began in early 2016 with a grant from the McCormick Foundation. Its model involves a core staff that oversees a rotating group of reporters as they produce investigative stories focused primarily on Chicago's South and West Side communities — areas that comprise an overwhelming portion of Chicago's black and Hispanic citizens (the South Side is over 90 percent black, and the West Side is 80 percent black or Hispanic) and that *City Bureau's* founders believe to be underreported by bigger name Chicago presses like the *Tribune*. *City Bureau* editors then partner with other outlets to co-publish these stories. *City Bureau's* reporting has appeared in traditional news publications like *The Chicago Reader* and *The Guardian*, as well as smaller, community presses like the *Chicago Defender* and the *Chicago Reporter*.

I chose *City Bureau* because of its stated interest in redefining "what local media means to a community" ("About"), its focus on the city's minority neighborhoods, and its success thus far. Since it was founded, *City Bureau* has won prestigious journalism awards, and has been profiled in journalism blogs like *Niemanlab*, *Columbia Journalism Review*, and *Mediashift* (Dalton 2015; Lichterman 2016; Spinner 2016). Most recently, the staff successfully raised over $10,000 to build a "public newsroom" on Chicago's South Side and expand its operations, and received a $50,000 grant from Democracy Fund.

As a small non-profit, *City Bureau* has only four principal staff members, all of whom are also founders. Two work for *City Bureau* full-time—Editorial Director Darryl Holliday and Community Director Andrea Hart—and two are part-time—Editor Bettina Chang and the Operations Manager Harry Backlund. All four worked in local journalism prior to starting *City Bureau*: Hart covered suburban Chicago for Patch.com, Holliday covered Chicago for the *Chicago Sun-Times* and *DNAinfo Chicago*, Backlund is the founding publisher of a community newspaper on the city's south side, and Chang still works fulltime as a web editor for *Chicago Magazine*. I interviewed all four.

Results

What follows are interview excerpts collected from both news organizations that explore how journalists from each conceptualize and pursue their audiences. The results are divided into two sections: the first focuses on data collected from *The Chicago Tribune*, and the second on *City Bureau*.

The Chicago Tribune

Writing for everyone, thinking of no one. Interviews with *Tribune* reporters revealed that they generally do not write with a specific audience in mind, but instead with the hope of reaching as wide an audience as possible. The paper's reporters and editors see their potential audience as incredibly broad, so they focus more on reaching as many people as possible than they do on determining who might be excluded in that pursuit. When pressed to visualize their audience, reporters and editors frequently observed that *Tribune* readers comprise both urban and suburban residents of the Chicagoland area, as well as a portion of residents flung throughout the state of the Illinois. However, as Deputy Editorial Page Editor Marie Dillon points out, the audience might also include anyone who stumbles onto a Tribune article online, including people who live outside of the Midwest:

> You used to think it was your subscribers—the people who paid for your paper and wanted to read what you had. But it's so much broader than that now. Almost anyone who sees a link to anything in your paper is going to react to it, and engage with it, and maybe share it.

The fact that the *Tribune's* audience included such a wide range of demographics seemed to discourage reporters from conceptualizing their readers as any group in particular. Instead, reporters and editors described drawing on their own preferences and news judgment to determine what and how to report. As Travel Reporter Josh Noel said, "To me it's just like, is it a good story? Tell me a good story. As a consumer of news that's what I look for."

Who the mass audience approach leaves out. The *Tribune's* focus on reaching a mass audience was evident in the way its reporters and editors discussed online audience measurement data. In general, *Tribune* journalists said they draw on these data to understand *how many* people their content is reaching, as opposed to *who* those people are. Consistent with prior research (Clarke 2014; Mersey 2010; Nadler 2016), this focus on measures of audience size rather than any other category sometimes led editors to overlook the interests of minority communities in Chicago. Digital News Editor Randi Shaffer touched on this while discussing how the *Tribune* approaches coverage of Englewood, a South Side, mostly black neighborhood:

> For us on the web team, metrics are huge. They let us know what people are interested in, they let us know what we should report more on. And we're not on the ground. We're not out talking with the community. And I think it's interesting, because my boyfriend is a photographer for the *Tribune*. And so he has an entirely different perspective than me, because he's the one that's down in Englewood. He's the one that is taking photos of crying moms on the sides and I'm the one that's counting all of the clicks as people report it. And so ... he'll see this is a big deal, this is important news. And I'm staring at my numbers and I say, "Well, you think it's important, because you're there, but the people don't think it's important, because they're not clicking on it."

Shaffer's observation suggests that, by prioritizing content that will appeal to a large audience, *Tribune* editors sometimes overlook the preferences of a subset of that audience.

The Pitfalls of Interacting with a Mass Audience

Interviews with *Tribune* reporters and editors revealed that the paper has an inconsistent approach to its relationship with its audience. While some at the paper believe they should communicate with and listen to the audience, others consider that outside of their responsibilities. There is little guidance from managers about what the ideal journalist/audience relationship should look like and how it should or should not be pursued. As a result, some described taking steps to communicate with readers via in-person events or social media platforms, while others were so discouraged by the vitriol they found in online comments to their articles that they admitted they rarely even looked at them. The uncertainty with which editors and reporters defined and discussed their relationship with their audience revealed an underlying tension between the *Tribune* staff's desire to not seem stuck in traditional ways of approaching the audience and an inability to reinvent the paper as a fundamentally different and much more audience-focused news organization.

Those who did describe routinely communicating with readers, including education reporter Dawn Rhodes and columnist Heidi Stevens, who said they do so to answer questions about how stories were reported, or to clarify a point they feel has been lost on readers. As Stevens explained:

> It's a waste of the potential to tweet your stuff and Facebook post your stuff and then not go in there and answer for people's comments and questions. It's like having a room full of people who just listened to your conversation and then being like, "I have nothing else to say to you people." It's like you're saying stuff to me. Now I'm going to say stuff back. My Facebook page, under any of my columns, it's a conversation.

Yet the same *Tribune* journalists who discussed taking steps to interact with the audience also volunteered examples where the audience angered or scared them. In a digital media environment, the ease with anyone can find a piece of content and then reach out to its author can have frightening consequences, as columnist Rex Huppke learned first-hand. He described how a political column he'd written inspired the ire of right-wing extremists who came across the article when it was relinked on an extremist blog. They responded by aggressively bombarding Huppke with threats and vitriol. It was clear during the interview that he was still grappling with the lingering effects of the experience:

> It can make you gun shy sometimes. Because you're like, "Do I want to walk into this shit storm? This is going to suck." … I don't know that you had to consider that before when you were writing, and only *The Chicago Tribune* audience was reading you. I don't think you had to worry quite so much. There are always nuts, but there's not a nation full of nuts. … And it's still like a tiny number of people in total. But when they all come after you at once … it kind of gives you the chills a little bit.

This anecdote gets at a disconcerting and often overlooked consequence of what happens when news organizations make it easier for the audience to contact journalists, and a reason why journalists writing for publications with a large, widespread readership may not want to interact with the audiences who are reading their work. As Rhodes explained, drawing on her own experience interacting with angry readers via Twitter, "We're kind of fighting this, almost like fighting a mob in a way."

Even when the audience is not threatening, it can still be crude or vile enough to discourage further interaction. Both Stevens and Huppke mentioned feeling ambivalent about reading comments to their articles or responding to readers because they so often were discouraged by just how angry people were. Huppke touched on this topic while explaining his reluctance to converse more with readers on social media platforms like Facebook or Twitter:

> I'm not tremendously interactive on social media. I am a little bit, but more only with people that I kind of have gotten to know who are funny and whatever. Like I don't reply a lot, for a couple of reasons. One, I don't have time. That's the number one reason, really. Because I could do that, but I would literally—that could consume my every waking moment. Two, because I think it can lead down some really bad roads. It's very difficult to engage in any kind of actual cogent or sensible or thoughtful conversation like that, because stuff is misinterpreted and it just becomes hell on earth. And because a lot of times you're just dealing with assholes who are trolls, so it's not worth acknowledging them.

Interviews with reporters and editors revealed that those who did make efforts to interact with the audience felt better about interactions that occurred in more intimate or offline venues. For instance, Huppke said emails tended to be less crude than Facebook and Twitter comments, and Stevens said small, public events tended to be where the most civil audience engagement took place. Huppke called both Facebook and the *Tribune's* commenting pages places "for abuse and hatred and meanness," and said he's been encouraging his bosses to disable the ability for readers to comment. Stevens was more open to continuing correspondence via social media, but said the best interactions occurred in person:

> I do conversations a lot on comments and stories and Twitter. But the best way is really in person. I do a fair number of speaking engagements so a lot of women's groups will ask me to come and talk. … That, honestly, is the best way to hear what's on people's minds.

Targeting the tech crowd. Interactions with the audience were less stressful for *Tribune* staff when confined to specific, niche audiences. For example, editors described one recently launched section called Blue Sky, which targets Chicago's growing community of tech entrepreneurs. The staff involved with this section regularly host or attend events in Chicago where they interact with Blue Sky readers, who comprise people in the Chicago startup community. They also use an audience engagement platform called Hearken to solicit questions about what stories to cover from the audience. Blue Sky Editor Andrea Hanis put her audience strategy simply: "We talk to people … all the time." And unlike Huppke and Stevens, Hanis seemed to have only positive things to say about these sorts of audience exchanges. Most notably, she described using social media to hear from or communicate with her audience with much less ambivalence than the *Tribune* columnists writing for much larger audiences:

> I actually use Twitter a lot for ideas. I think when you're covering a niche audience, it's a fantastic way to find out what they're talking about and what they care about, so I find that to be a really good source of ideas.

In short, *The Chicago Tribune* generally maintains a mass audience approach to the news audience, which leads to the privileging of stories that appeal to a large audience, rather than a specific audience. This has frustrating and sometimes frightening consequences for *Tribune* writers attempting a more collaborative or interactive relationship with the audience, especially when faced with angry or threatening readers expressing their rage via social media. However, *Tribune* staff working for sections that deviate from the mass audience approach to target niche audiences (e.g., Blue Sky) report a more communicative, less disdainful relationship between themselves and the small, intentionally chosen audience they are pursuing.

City Bureau

Writing about and for minority audiences. *City Bureau's* core staff explicitly and frequently discussed how they target distinct audiences with their content. *City Bureau's* founders described their potential news audience as split between the minority South and West Side communities that tend to be overlooked by Chicago's established news outlets, and the political elites whose attention must sometimes be summoned so that wrongs within these communities can be corrected. Holliday put this separation bluntly by referring to Chicago's media ecosystem as "a segregated industry."

Because of *City Bureau's* unique publishing and non-profit structure, it has the ability to partner with different publications without considering which will bring in larger audiences or more revenue. Instead, these decisions are made primarily in terms of which community should the story reach. As Holliday explained, while there are some instances where *City Bureau* editors would like a story to reach the global, mass audience pursued by a publication like *The Guardian*, there are other instances where they would prefer a story to reach a narrower community of people more easily reached by a small community press like *The Chicago Defender*:

> We did a story about West Side churches moving into West Side streets … you can't make a commercial corridor if you have like 15 churches on a block. … That story is not a *Guardian* story. … It's a story that like people in the neighborhood pick up and they say like, "Oh, this is my block. … Now we can talk about this." That wouldn't work in *The Guardian*. It wouldn't be the same impact. … And there are some times where we're trying to like call the mayor, the police chief to attention, you know, like we're trying to call accountability for people to leverage whatever power they have. … Those stories, that's a *Guardian* story.

In other words, *City Bureau* editors are quick to acknowledge that the news audience within these communities differs from the news audience outside of them. As a result, their reporting and publication decisions are based on first finding underreported stories about the South and West Sides of Chicago, and then determining if those stories should be directed at the people who live in these areas, or the people who live outside those areas. In short, *City Bureau's* unconventional approach to publishing allows it the unique flexibility to choose its intended audience on a story-by-story basis.

Because *City Bureau* editors are so focused on reaching specific audiences, it is important that they know which local news publications reach which Chicago communities. This knowledge stems from a combination of intuition, personal experience, and audience data. For instance, *City Bureau* editors have seen Chicago Public Radio's audience research, so they know that outlet can be tapped to reach a mostly white, North Side audience. When *City Bureau* editors want to target Chicago's political elites, they partner with the *Chicago Reader* because, as Holliday explained, "We know that in the mayor's press box every day he gets the *Reader*." When they want to reach the city's South Side, they publish in the *South Side Weekly*, a print, non-profit newspaper that is distributed on the South Side. And when they want to reach a mass audience, they partner with Chicago Public Radio or *The Guardian*. More often than not, however, *City Bureau* focuses on smaller, community presses like *South Side Weekly*, *The Chicago Defender*, and *Austin Weekly News*.

Engaging underreported communities. *City Bureau* draws on a number of means of building strong, collaborative relationships with its South and West Side audiences. First, and most notably, the organization hosts events, like its weekly Public Newsrooms, that invite community members to hear from and interact with *City Bureau* journalists as well as other news media professionals. Because *City Bureau's* newsroom is located in the South Side neighborhood Hyde Park, these events occur within one of the communities that *City Bureau* is attempting to engage with and report on. Furthermore, when *City Bureau* publishes an article, its staff also works with the reporters of the story to coordinate events within the community the story is focused in an attempt to oversee an in-person conversation about the story's topic. Holliday summarized *City Bureau's* community focus in this way:

> What stories look like when they involve the community I think is—it involves being in person and it involves having a meeting, a workshop, an event and say, like, "Please come. Here's what we're doing, but how can you affect that? How can you influence it? Who do you know that we should be talking to? Should we be talking to you, your neighbor, the guy who's a complete—no journalist has ever spoken to, but like who everybody on the block knows?" ... How can you really bring people into the process as opposed to just laying out the agenda and saying, "Well, this is what we're going to do in perpetuity.'

City Bureau's Public Newsrooms are intended to reach out to and empower community members who feel disconnected from the stories told about them and their neighborhoods by other news organizations. *City Bureau* staff described their hopes that these events would lure out South and West Side residents who had previously been disengaged with civic life and were interested in changing that. However, as Editor Bettina Chang pointed out, so far this has not been the case. Instead, attendees tend to be people who are already very engaged in public life on behalf of these communities:

> We definitely right now get the people who are hyper-engaged. We get a lot of people who work for nonprofits or in the social/public sector kind of stuff. Every once in a while we do get someone who is like, "I just came. Somebody told me to come. My sorority sister told me to come, so I'm here.' We're really hoping to get those people involved. We've gotten really good feedback from those people because I think they expected the least, but they got the most.

In other words, for now it seems that *City Bureau's* attempt to build a more collaborative relationship with its audience is more likely to succeed with those already invested in *City Bureau's* mission and the communities it has chosen to focus on. Expanding the audience to include disengaged citizens poses a more difficult challenge.

In addition to these public events, *City Bureau* also offers two training initiatives meant to both increase community awareness of the organization and teach aspiring journalists how to contribute to the news production process. The first of these initiatives partners *City Bureau* reporters with a non-profit that offers media production education to South and West side young people. The second, called Documenters, offers community members basic journalism training needed for them to attend public meetings (e.g., school board meetings, police board meetings, city council meetings), and live tweet or blog about them. As Community Director Andrea Hart explained, "It's really true to the sort of public journalism school model of like, 'Okay, you have an interest in civic issues in your neighborhood—let's help you build that out.'"

Finally, *City Bureau* maintains an online presence and communicates with its audience via social media platforms like Facebook and Twitter. Taken together, these efforts reveal *City Bureau* to be primarily focused on explicitly building a strong, collaborative relationship with a small subset of Chicago residents. Editors at *City Bureau* believe that a disconnect exists between Chicago's traditional, established journalism brands and its minority communities, and seek to address this disconnect by reporting on issues that affect these communities specifically, and then utilizing a novel publishing model to point these stories either at the audiences within these communities or at audiences outside of them. However, publishing stories is only one piece of *City Bureau's* audience outreach. The other, equally laborious pieces of this process include live events, journalism training, and online interactions. Because *City Bureau* is not a daily news operation, its staff is able to devote much of its time to planning and executing these more audience-focused initiatives. And because *City Bureau* is so explicitly focused on specific communities within Chicago, determining who its staff should target with both their news coverage and audience interactions is a relatively straightforward process.

Discussion

These results reveal that a stronger journalist/audience relationship is a goal that is being pursued not just by news non-profits, but by more traditional news brands as well. Though *The Chicago Tribune* and *City Bureau* are drastically different in many key ways—including size, age, circulation, and mission—employees within both expressed a desire to communicate with audiences in order to improve both the quality of news each organization provides, as well as to benefit those for whom these news stories are provided. These findings suggest that the distinction between how innovative news non-profits and more traditional news organizations pursue and consider the audience has begun to blur. Though the *Tribune* historically kept the audience at arm's length, its reporters and editors described an increasing interest in using live events and digital technology to establish a more conversational relationship between news provider and consumer.

The *Tribune* is not alone. Many newsrooms now encourage their reporters to interact with readers via social media platforms or live events. In fact, a growing number employ "engagement editors" tasked with corresponding with readers on social media platforms (Powers 2015). Furthermore, traditional news outlets like the *The Washington Post*, the BBC, and NPR are also increasingly adopting audience engagement tools like Hearken, Groundsource, and Coral Project, which allow these organizations to solicit questions and comments from readers to help determine what stories get reported. The motivations for this pursuit may vary: organizations like *City Bureau* focus on increasing collaboration with minority communities in order to improve their agency in the stories told about them, while *Tribune* editors and reporters in some cases seek to make their own reporting more comprehensible to readers, and in other cases to cultivate a sense of community among Chicagoans working in a similar industry.

These findings also show that, regardless of the underlying motivations, pursuing a more collaborative relationship with the news audience is ill-suited with a mass audience approach to news production. *Tribune* columnists and reporters complained about the vitriol and mob mentality they faced when attempting to engage with audience members online, while the *Tribune's* Blue Sky team and *City Bureau*'s founders reported no such qualms. This project is limited in that neither the *Tribune* nor *City Bureau* seemed entirely sure how to describe what the ideal journalism/audience relationship would look like, making it impossible to determine whether or not either organization had achieved this goal. However, that does not diminish the two main findings of this project: first, that both traditional and public service journalism organizations are making attempts to listen to and interact with news audiences, and second, that those tasked with targeting niche audiences were more encouraged by their attempts than those focused on reaching a much wider readership.

Two decades ago, Katz sounded the alarm for what audience segmentation would do to democratic society. He worried that increasing media choice would lead to the disappearance of a shared cultural space where citizens could gather to hear and discuss the same information (Katz 1996). Yet, my findings suggest that segmentation might be the key to building strong bonds between news media providers and the audience. *Tribune* columnists and reporters writing for the paper's general readership faced disappointments and frustrations when attempting to interact with a mass audience, while both the *Tribune's* Blue Sky and *City Bureau* editors reported positive exchanges of story ideas and information when communication was confined to specific, niche groups. Furthermore, confining conceptualizations of the audience to narrowly determined communities freed *City Bureau* and Blue Sky journalists to pursue story ideas that would most likely resonate with these distinct groups without worrying if others would find them interesting. Assuming the goal of building stronger bonds with the audience continues to grow, news publishers pursuing this goal will find more incentive to segment their audience into distinct groups rather than pursue the audience as one loosely connected mass.

This raises an important question: What will civil society lose when journalism's understanding of the public changes to one that is narrower, involved, and community focused? On the one hand, there are some who believe this change will restore public trust in journalism and give agency to marginalized communities who until now have felt excluded from their own news stories. Doing so, however, might further polarize society by leaving citizens no opportunity to interact with those of differing backgrounds or perspectives. Extreme political polarization already exists within the United States and across the globe, with liberals and conservatives disagreeing not just about policies, but about "basic facts" (Bump 2016; Doherty, Kiley, and Johnson 2016), despite the fact that a few news brands still comprise an overwhelming majority of the news audience. If all news media becomes targeted at specific groups, will public life grow even more fragmented and polarized? Many assume that improving the relationship between journalism and the audience will have nothing but positive consequences for civic engagement and democracy. The truth may be more complicated.

DISCLOSURE STATEMENT

No potential conflict of interest was reported by the author.

FUNDING

This work was supported by Northwestern University and the Tow Center for Digital Journalism.

REFERENCES

About. *City Bureau*. Accessed July 18. http://citybureau.org/

About. *One River, Many Stories*. Accessed August 17. http://onerivermn.com/front-page/about/

Batsell, Jake. 2015. *Engaged Journalism : Connecting with Digitally Empowered News Audiences*. Columbia University Press.

Boczkowski, Pablo J. 2013. *The News Gap : When the Information Preferences of the Media and the Public Diverge*. The MIT Press.

Bump, Philip. 2016, April 9. Political Polarization is Getting Worse. Everywhere. *The Washington Post*. https://www.washingtonpost.com/news/the-fix/wp/2016/04/09/polarization-is-getting-worse-in-every-part-of-politics/?utm_term=.233cc3242d91

Charity, Arthur. 1995. *Doing Public Journalism*. New York: Guilford Press.

Clarke, Debra M. 2014. *Journalism and Political Exclusion : Social Conditions of News Production and Reception*. Montréal and Kingston: McGill-Queen's University Press.

Coates Nee, Rebecca. 2013. "Creative Destruction: An Exploratory Study of How Digitally Native News Nonprofits are Innovating Online Journalism Practices." *International Journal on Media Management* 15 (1): 3–22. doi:10.1080/14241277.2012.732153.

Coates Nee, Rebecca. 2014. "Social Responsibility Theory and the Digital Nonprofits: Should the Government aid Online News Startups?" *Journalism: Theory, Practice & Criticism* 15 (3): 326–343. doi:10.1177/1464884913482553.

Dalton, Meg. 2015, December 13. QandA: How Will City Bureau Regenerate Civic Media in Chicago? *Mediashift*. Accessed August 12. http://mediashift.org/2015/12/qa-how-will-city-bureau-regenerate-civic-media-in-chicago/

Doherty, Carroll, Jocelyn Kiley, and Bridget Johnson. 2016. *In Presidential Contest, Voters Say "Basic Facts," Not Just Policies, Are in Dispute*. Pew Research Center: http://www.people-press.org/2016/10/14/in-presidential-contest-voters-say-basic-facts-not-just-policies-are-in-dispute/?utm_source=adaptivemailerandutm_medium=emailandutm_campaign=16-10-14 panel election reportandorg=982andlvl=100andite=413andlea=66827

Epstein, Edward Jay. 1974. *News From Nowhere: Television and the News*. New York: Vintage Books.

Felle, Tom. 2016. "Digital Watchdogs? Data Reporting and the News Media's Traditional 'Fourth Estate' Function." *Journalism: Theory, Practice & Criticism* 17 (1): 85–96.

Ferrucci, Patrick. 2015a. "Murder Incorporated: Market Orientation and Coverage of the Annie le Investigation." *Electronic News* 9 (2): 108–121.

Ferrucci, Patrick. 2015b. "Primary Differences: How Market Orientation can Influence Content." *Journal of Media Practice* 16 (3): 195–210.

Ferrucci, Patrick. 2015c. "Public Journalism no More: The Digitally Native News Nonprofit and Public Service Journalism." *Journalism: Theory, Practice & Criticism* 16 (7): 904–919.

Ferrucci, Patrick. 2017. "Exploring Public Service Journalism: Digitally Native News Nonprofits and Engagement." *Journalism and Mass Communication Quarterly* 94 (1): 355–370.

Fishman, Mark. 1980. *Manufacturing the News*. Austin: University of Texas Press.

Fleming, Jennifer. 2014. "Media Literacy, News Literacy, or News Appreciation? A Case Study of the News Literacy Program at Stony Brook University." *Journalism and Mass Communication Educator* 69: 146–165.

Gans, Herbert J. 2004. *Deciding What's News*. Evanston, IL: Northwestern University Press.

Gentzkow, Matthew, and Jesse M. Shapiro. 2011. "Ideological Segregation Online and Offline*." *Quarterly Journal of Economics* 126 (4): 1799–1839.

Glasser, Theodore L. 1999. *The Idea of Public Journalism*. New York: Guilford Press.

Hess, Kristy. 2015. "Making Connections." *Journalism Studies* 16 (4): 482–496. doi:10.1080/1461670X.2014.922293.

Jamieson, Kathleen Hall, and Joseph N. Cappella. 2009. *Echo Chamber: Rush Limbaugh and the Conservative Media Establishment*. Oxford: Oxford University Press.

Katz, Elihu. 1996. "And Deliver us From Segmentation." *Annals of the American Academy of Political and Social Science* 546: 22–33. <Go to ISI>://A1996UR82700003.

Konieczna, Magda, and Elia Powers. 2016. "What can Nonprofit Journalists Actually do for Democracy?" *Journalism Studies* 3: 1–17. doi:10.1080/1461670x.2015.1134273.

Konieczna, Magda, and Sue Robinson. 2014. "Emerging News Non-Profits: A Case Study for Rebuilding Community Trust?" *Journalism: Theory, Practice & Criticism* 15: 968–986. doi:10.1177/1464884913505997.

Lewis, Seth C., Avery E. Holton, and Mark Coddington. 2014. "Reciprocal Journalism." *Journalism Practice* 8 (2): 229–241. doi:10.1080/17512786.2013.859840.

Lichterman, Joseph. 2016, January 14. Working with Young Reporters, City Bureau is Telling the Story of Police Misconduct in Chicago. *Nieman Lab*. Accessed March 9. http://www.niemanlab.org/2016/01/working-with-young-reporters-city-bureau-is-telling-the-story-of-police-misconduct-in-chicago/

Lipinski, Ann Marie. 2016, April 1. Chicago Tribune. *Encyclo*. Accessed August 12. http://www.niemanlab.org/encyclo/chicago-tribune/?=fromembed

Loosen, Wiebke, and Jan-Hinrik Schmidt. 2012. "(Re-)Discovering the Audience." *Information, Communication and Society* 15 (6): 867–887. doi:10.1080/1369118x.2012.665467.

McChesney, Robert W., and Victor W. Pickard. 2011. *Will the Last Reporter Please Turn out the Lights: The Collapse of Journalism and What can be Done to Fix it*. New York: New Press: Distributed by Perseus Distribution.

McCollough, Kathleen, Jessica K. Crowell, and Philip M. Napoli. 2017. "Portrait of the Online Local News Audience." *Digital Journalism* 5: 100–118. doi:10.1080/21670811.2016.1152160.

Mersey, Rachel Davis. 2010. *Can Journalism be Saved?: Rediscovering America's Appetite for News.* Santa Barbara, Calif.: Praeger.

Mitchell, Amy, Mark Jurkowitz, Jesse Holcomb, Jodi Enda, and Monica Anderson. 2013. *Nonprofit Journalism: A Growing but Fragile Part of the U.S. News System.* Pew Research Center. http://www.journalism.org/2013/06/10/nonprofit-journalism/

Nadler, Anthony M. 2016. *Making the News Popular: Mobilizing U.S. News Audiences.* Springfield, IL: University of Illinois Press.

Napoli, Philip M. 2016. "Requiem for the Long Tail: Towards a Political Economy of Content Aggregation and Fragmentation." *International Journal of Media and Cultural Politics* 12 (3): 341–356.

Nelson, Jacob L., and Dan A. Lewis. 2015. "Training Social Justice Journalists: A Case Study." *Journalism and Mass Communication Educator* 70 (4): 394–406.

Nelson, Jacob L., and James G. Webster. 2017. "The Myth of Partisan Selective Exposure: A Portrait of the Online Political News Audience." *Social Media + Society* 3 (3). doi:10.1177/2056305117729314.

Nielsen, Rasmus Kleis. 2015. *Local Journalism: The Decline of Newspapers and the Rise of Digital Media.* London: Tauris Academic Studies.

Ognyanova, Katherine, Nien-Tsu Nancy Chen, Sandra Ball-Rokeach, Zheng An, Minhee Son, Michael Parks, and Daniella Gerson. 2013. "Online Participation in a Community Context: Civic Engagement and Connections to Local Communication Resources." *International Journal of Communication* 7: 2433–2456. doi:1932–8036/20130005.

Pariser, Eli. 2011. *The Filter Bubble: What the Internet is Hiding From You.* New York: Penguin Press.

Patel, Mayur, and Michele McLellan. 2012. *Getting Local: How Nonprofit News Ventures Seek Sustainability.* http://www.knightfoundation.org/publications/getting-local-how-nonprofit-news-ventures-seek-sus

Pfauth, Ernst-Jan. 2016, March 14. Why Subscriptions are the Future of Journalism. *Editor and Publisher.* Accessed April 14. http://www.editorandpublisher.com/feature/why-subscriptions-are-the-future-of-journalism/

Pickard, Victor, and Josh Stearns. 2011. "New Models Emerge For Community Press." *Newspaper Research Journal* 32 (1): 46–62.

Powers, Elia. 2015, August 19. The Rise of the Engagement Editor and What It Means. *Mediashift.* http://mediashift.org/2015/08/the-rise-of-the-engagement-editor-and-what-it-means/

Prior, Markus. 2007. *Post-Broadcast Democracy: How Media Choice Increases Inequality in Political Involvement and Polarizes Elections.* Cambridge: Cambridge University Press.

Richards, Ian. 2013. "Beyond City Limits: Regional Journalism and Social Capital." *Journalism: Theory, Practice & Criticism* 14 (5): 627–642. doi:10.1177/1464884912453280.

Robinson, Sue. 2011. "'Journalism as Process': The Organizational Implications of Participatory Online News." *Journalism & Communication Monographs* 13 (3): 137–210.

Robinson, Sue. 2014. "The Active Citizen's Information Media Repertoire: An Exploration of Community News Habits During the Digital Age." *Mass Communication and Society* 17: 509–530.

Robinson, Sue, and Cathy DeShano. 2011. "'Anyone can Know': Citizen Journalism and the Interpretive Community of the Mainstream Press." *Journalism: Theory, Practice & Criticism* 12 (8): 963–982.

Rosen, Jay. 1996. *Getting the Connections Right: Public Journalism and the Troubles in the Press.* New York: Twentieth Century Fund.

Rosentiel, Tom, William Buzenberg, Marjorie Connelly, and Kevin Loker. 2016. *Charting New Ground: The Ethical Terrain of Nonprofit Journalism*. American Press Institute. https://www.americanpressinstitute.org/publications/reports/nonprofit-news/

Seamans, R., and Feng Zhu. 2014. "Responses to Entry in Multi-Sided Markets: The Impact of Craigslist on Local Newspapers." *Management Science* 60 (2): 476–493. doi:10.1287/mnsc.2013.1785.

Siles, Ignacio, and Pablo J. Boczkowski. 2012. "Making Sense of the Newspaper Crisis: A Critical Assessment of Existing Research and an Agenda for Future Work." *New Media and Society* 14 (8): 1375–1394.

Spinner, Jackie. 2016, March 25. With Partnerships and Young Reporters, Chicago's City Bureau Builds a Collaborative Community Newsroom. *Columbia Journalism Review*. Accessed June 3. http://www.cjr.org/united_states_project/chicago_city_bureau.php

Stroud, Natalie Jomini. 2010. "Polarization and Partisan Selective Exposure." *Journal of Communication* 60 (3): 556–576.

Stroud, Natalie Jomini. 2011. *Niche News: The Politics of News Choice*. Oxford: Oxford University Press.

Tuchman, Gaye. 1978. *Making News: A Study in the Construction of Reality*. New York: Free Press.

Vernon, Pete. 2016, December 6. Subscription Surges and Record Audiences Follow Trump's Election. *Columbia Journalism Review*. Accessed April 14. http://www.cjr.org/business_of_news/trump_journalism_subscription_surge.php

Webster, James G. 2014. *The Marketplace of Attention: How Audiences Take Shape in a Digital Age*. Cambridge: The MIT Press.

Weeks, Brian E., Thomas B. Ksiazek, and R. Lance Holbert. 2016. "Partisan Enclaves or Shared Media Experiences? A Network Approach to Understanding Citizens' Political News Environments." *Journal of Broadcasting and Electronic Media* 60 (2): 248–268.

Wenzel, Andrea, Daniella Gerson, and Evelyn Moreno. 2016. "Engaging Communities Through Solutions Journalism." *Columbia Journalism Review*, April 26. https://www.cjr.org/tow_center_reports/engaging_communities_through_solutions_journalism.php

Williams, Alex T. 2016. *Paying for Digital News: The Rapid Adoption and Current Landscape of Digital Subscriptions at U.S. Newspapers*. American Press Institute. https://www.americanpressinstitute.org/publications/reports/digital-subscriptions/single-page/

Williams, Bruce A., and Michael X. Delli Carpini. 2011. *After Broadcast News: Media Regimes, Democracy, and the New Information Environment / Bruce A. Williams, Michael X. Delli Carpini*. New York: Cambridge University Press.

NURTURING AUTHORITY

Reassessing the social role of local television news

Tanya Muscat

When considering the role of local journalism in a networked media environment, it is crucial to examine how audiences attribute news with the power to define social knowledge. In particular, television news programs need to appeal to audiences by reinforcing a sense of local journalistic authority to assert the parameters of who and what is worthy of coverage. This article presents the findings from interviews with a range of commercial television news viewers in Sydney, Australia. It positions viewership in the context of people's wider engagement with news, and in relation to their interpersonal and digital social interactions. The paper argues that local audiences have conflicting attitudes to the role of television news, both contesting and re-inscribing the programs with the power to demarcate social, political, and cultural knowledge. It traces how local audiences challenge the ability of news to convey boundaries within the community through processes of exclusion, connecting the contestations to the lived experiences of the individuals. It identifies that television news programs nurture journalistic authority in terms of their local relevance, and it contributes insights on the significance of local news by engaging with the means by which audiences themselves attach social power to journalism.

Introduction

As the digital networked media environment alters patterns of news production and consumption, traditional forms of journalism need to reaffirm connections with local audiences. One of the concerns raised is whether local news can adequately engage citizens in community matters, facilitating participation in civic and democratic life (Allan 2010; Fenton 2011; Firmstone and Coleman 2014; Nielsen 2015). At the same time, scholars have begun to consider how local news can perform a civic role and be seen as central to the function of society, in order to maintain capital amongst a vast range of news media choices (Carson et al. 2016; Hess 2016). In a changing news media landscape, recent research on local journalism has turned toward audiences to understand the ways in which people conceive of the role of news in relation to their everyday experiences. With an abundance of news possibilities, engaging with localized audiences is essential to come to terms with the diverse factors that influence how traditional news outlets sustain relevance and convey social, political, or cultural knowledge.

This article investigates how commercial television news outlets nurture a sense of local journalistic authority among news audiences from a range of social backgrounds. It draws on research regarding social capital (Hess 2015; Rojas, Shah, and Friedland 2011) and civic culture (Dahlgren 2009, 2005, 2003), to consider the broader communicative interactions that influence how certain news outlets reinforce notions of social order and reinscribe power relations through contested processes. I argue that local commercial television news outlets have an unrealized capacity in relation to audiences' wider engagement with news across platforms, lived experiences, and their interpersonal and digital social interactions. Based on interviews with diverse local audiences, the findings suggest that viewers assign value to what news outlets do, but also in terms of what they could do. This article points to the ways in which journalistic practices could be realigned in the local context, through the audiences' perspectives, in order to reach this unfulfilled potential.

Conceptualizing Social Capital and Civic Culture

Traditional journalistic expectations relate to the democratic function of news (Schudson 2008; Schultz 1998); however, recent studies have called for a reassessment of this role (Eldridge and Steel 2016; Hess 2015). One of the proposed means for better understanding the function of news is through the theory of social capital (Putnam 2000). In reviewing existing research in journalism studies, Hess (2013, 2015) argues for a reconceptualization of social capital to more explicitly acknowledge power relations. Mediated social capital recognizes the power that can be utilized by media outlets in being able to facilitate communal bonds, bridge connections, or link ordinary individuals to elites in society (Hess 2015). Another approach to social capital is through a communicative framework. In their study, Rojas, Shah, and Friedland (2011) stress that social capital emerges through the communicative interactions between personal networks, institutional influences, news use, and political talk. Considering the interplay between people's communicative frameworks and mediated social capital is useful as patterns of news consumption and discussion evolve. For some individuals, interpersonal news shared informally in online or offline contexts constitutes a form of "local" news (Eldridge and Steel 2016; Swart, Peters, and Broersma 2016). As people participate in everyday talk, they share news but also make use of their social contexts within communities to generate locally informed meanings that can differ to those produced by journalists (Bird 2010; McCallum 2010). Audiences can contest the authority of news to demarcate social knowledge where it does not align with their lived experiences, but how news outlets maintain capital in these instances requires further consideration.

In order to discuss how news outlets might sustain capital with localized audiences in contradictory circumstances, this article draws on the concept of civic culture (Dahlgren 2009, 2005, 2003). As a term, civic culture "is a framework intended to help analyze the conditions that are necessary for – that promote or hinder – civic engagement" (Dahlgren 2009, 103). Television programs, and more specifically public and commercial broadcast journalism, are one of the many cultural resources that people can utilize to partake in political life. There is much existing research on the relationship between news and civic society, demonstrating that commercially produced news does not tend to promote civic engagement (Cushion 2012; Tiffen et al. 2017), and news consumption does not often lead to civic action (Couldry, Livingstone, and Markham 2007). Yet, civic also relates to the ability of certain news outlets to be seen as acting in the common good, and the power that comes with constituting the boundaries of communities through inclusions and exclusions (Hess 2016). The attempts to reinforce social order through exclusionary reporting can intertwine with ethnic and race relations, religious or cultural values, as well as through spatial and socio-economic factors. Scholars have found a strong relationship between commercial news reporting and the problematic or criminalized representation of ethnic diversity (Jakubowicz et al. 1994; Liu 2004; Poynting and Noble 2003; Nunn 2010). Another line of research on minorities and media has found how mainstream news systematically excludes Indigenous Australians, as connected to a history of race and power relations (see McCallum and Waller 2017). Commercial television news coverage rearticulates relations of exclusion across cultural values, as individuals from diverse ethnic or religious backgrounds are often positioned as being incompatible with the predominant culture (Muscat 2015; Phillips 2011, 2009; Rane, Ewart, and Martinkus 2014). Exclusion also intersects with spatial dynamics, whereby ethnic minority audiences in lower socio-economic areas express how negative mainstream televisual representations can restrict them from feeling a sense of belonging (Dreher 2000). Conceptualizing capital as connected to civic potential might further reveal how news outlets maintain local journalistic authority to demarcate social knowledge among audiences who are simultaneously subject to a greater degree of mediated surveillance or exclusion. The conditions of civic potential could explain how news outlets convey social value where people do not recognize journalism as meeting an idealized civic function in society. Ewart and Beard (2017) have called for greater academic knowledge regarding ethnic minority news habits, as disengagement from mainstream news poses significant implications to both civic society and the journalism industry. This article provides insights detailing how audiences from different suburbs, socio-economic, and cultural backgrounds understand the civic potential of local commercial television news as part of their everyday lived experiences.

When examining the relationship between local news and audiences, research has concentrated on towns or rural and regional areas (Carson et al. 2016; Hess 2015; Nielsen 2016), and also within urban areas or metropolitan cities (Coleman, Thumim, and Moss 2016; Costera Meijer and Bijleveld 2016; Firmstone 2016). There is an ongoing discussion within journalism literature regarding the terms "local," "community," and "metropolitan" (Franklin 2006; Hanusch 2015; Hess and Waller 2017; Kramp 2016; Sjøvaag 2015), with a prevalent focus on print journalism. "Local" most often refers to print and broadcast journalism outside metropolitan cities, whereas news produced in major cities is metropolitan. Hess and Waller (2017, 7) note that the terms "'local' and 'community' can be multi-layered," as used by residents in a city to describe a range of socio-spatial formations relating to municipalities, suburbs, neighborhoods, or cultural groups. A multi-layered use of "local" is echoed in this research, with participants employing the term "local" to refer to their city, as well as the municipalities, suburbs, and diverse communities existing within Sydney. The metropolitan city of Sydney provides a unique case study to consider how news outlets sustain local journalistic authority, as broadcast journalism has to serve the needs of a broad and diverse population. As the most populous city in Australia, metropolitan Sydney covers 4775 square miles and contains an estimated population of 5 million (Australian Bureau of Statistics 2017). The city has a high proportion of migration with 41.9 percent of individuals born overseas, and 63.8 percent of the population have one or more of their parents born overseas (ABS 2016). The majority of the population is located in Western Sydney,[1] an area that is of importance for news outlets as it contains 45.59 percent of the city's residents (ABS 2016). Patterns of urban segregation also result in a concentration of ethnically diverse individuals and those from Muslim backgrounds in Western Sydney (Jakubowicz et al. 2014). As news practices continue to shift, commercial television news is faced with the challenge of resonating with the expectations of diverse localized audiences in order to maintain relevance.

This article illuminates how the social capital of commercial television news outlets in the city of Sydney is connected to an ability to be perceived of as authoritative forms of local news. In terms of media habits within Australia, television remains the main source of offline news, with commercial news on the Seven and Nine Networks among the most popular (Fisher, Watkins, and Breen 2017). As part of a mixed-model regulatory approach, the commercial Seven, Nine, and Ten Networks provide localized news services broadcast from the main metropolitan cities. It must be noted that these commercial television news outlets are metropolitan in the sense that they encompass a vast urban area and provide local, national, and international coverage. This article discusses commercial television news in Sydney as local broadcast journalism rather than metropolitan, by utilizing the participants' understanding of these television news programs as being local news outlets, which is further elaborated in the findings. Within the major metropolitan cities, television news is also supplied through the national public service broadcasters the Australian Broadcasting Corporation (ABC) and Special Broadcasting Service (SBS).[2] A number of regional commercial television news services are provided through WIN, Prime, and Southern Cross outside metropolitan areas; however, this research solely concentrates on broadcast journalism within the city of Sydney.

Research Design

This article draws on the findings from interviews conducted during 2013 and 2014 with a range of 40 commercial television news viewers, located across the city of Sydney. The research undertook purposive sampling for age (18–30, 31–45, 46–60, and 61–80) and gender. It canvassed educational background and employment to contextualize the participants' responses and inform the socio-economic status in relation to news viewership; however, this did not form part of the purposive sampling. Commercial television news viewers in Australia tend to be from "working-class" backgrounds, whereas public broadcast audiences more often hold university degrees (Bean 2005, 49). Within this research, the commercial news viewers comprised a variety of educational backgrounds including 42.5 percent with some secondary, completed secondary, or vocational education qualification; 32.5 percent hold a university degree or diploma; and 25 percent have a post-graduate university qualification. The interview sampling endeavored to achieve diversity across a range of cultural groups; but no emphasis was placed on a representative sample of cultural perspectives nor on the experiences of one diasporic group. The majority of interviews took place in Western Sydney, an area often misrepresented in mainstream news media (Dreher 2000; Gannon 2009), but that also contains the largest possible audience for commercial television news based on population figures. The interviews were tape-recorded, ranging in duration from 20 minutes to 80 minutes, and were transcribed and analyzed in NVivo. Interviews were conducted using a semi-structured interview schedule, inviting participants to discuss how their local commercial television news viewership fit into a broader cross-media news landscape including traditional, digital, and alternative forms of journalism. Participants were encouraged to recall news reports of interest, to reflect on news reporting, and to elaborate on their online and offline participation in everyday discussions regarding issues of interest. The analysis qualitatively identified thematic similarities and differences across the audiences' experiences and these findings are discussed in the following sections.

Findings

The findings show that from the perspectives of audiences, commercial television news occupies an unrealized position of local journalistic authority to nurture social connections in comparison to other news outlets. First, I outline how audiences locate these news sources in relation to their cross-media news use, as well as their interpersonal and digital social interactions. Second, I demonstrate that audiences have contradictory attitudes to the role of commercial television news based on their embodied experiences within and across communities. I establish that even though audiences contest the ways in which commercial news programs attempt to reinforce social order through processes of exclusion, participants also re-inscribe the local news outlets with a power to maintain social order through the ability to foster social cohesion. Audiences ascribe certain news outlets with capital based on the relationship between civic practice and civic potential, namely how they could better use their authority in the local context to resonate with their diverse viewers.

Local Sources and Networks of News

Living with news. Across all age groups, participants delineated how their preferences for commercial news linked to their everyday routines. Although the technological means existed for shifted viewing across platforms, 92.5 percent of participants viewed news programs as they were broadcast. Daily domestic routines delimited the time participants were willing to dedicate to cross-media news consumption, which increased the perceived value of local television news. Jenny (46–60) identified how individuals without children might have different news practices: "It's not that it's not important ... if you're a single person on your own, I think you have that time."[3] While patterns of news consumption can connect to gendered variations in domestic labor (Gauntlett and Hill 1999), both males and females in this research emphasized parenting commitments as a factor limiting their allocated time for news consumption. In addition to time constraints, commercial television news preferences were also formed through an extended period of viewership. There was a link between childhood news viewing and parent's preferences for 12.5 percent of participants (aged 18–45), and 20 percent of people mentioned a prolonged personal history of viewing the same news program (aged 31–80). Swart, Peters, and Broersma (2016) observe that news outlets are of greater importance if they are able to reaffirm a viewer's identity, but news outlets also foster bonds with audiences through key local news personalities. Nine News achieved prominence in viewers' news preferences through the trusted news anchor Brian Henderson, who continuously presented either the weekday or the weekend bulletins from 1957 until 2002. James (31–45, South Sydney) stressed the importance of fitting a 30-minute broadcast into his everyday routine, but further associated Nine News with his identity: "Mum and Dad always preferred Nine News with Brian Henderson ... it's just one of those ingrained things in your personality."

Younger participants also valued efficient information, but contextualized commercial viewership in relation to professional commitments and recreational activities. Previous findings indicate that younger audiences are less likely to have routinized television news viewership (Bird and Dardenne 2009; Costera Meijer 2013), and that young users often multitask while engaged in viewership (Costera Meijer 2007). The results in this research suggest that participants aged 18–30 conceptualize habitual televisual news practices as a strategic form of information management. Vicky (18–30) worked as an emergency room doctor and explained: "I'm just so busy. … I guess my 30 minutes of commercial news is how I keep in touch with current affairs." When compared to public broadcast, commercial news provided pertinent local information in a salient manner. Lisa (31–45) clarified her Nine News preference: "The local news that I watch is simple to watch, it's quick with information … and if there is some major world event, only then I'll go to SBS or ABC." News users across all age ranges appreciated the ability to multitask, and local commercial news was more readily comprehensible in comparison to public broadcast news. Toward the end of the interviewing period, Seven News and Nine News switched from a 30-minute to an hour-long bulletin. The prolonged format did not resonate with participants (Stuart, 46–60 and Tom, 61–80), as information was repetitive and draw out which detracted from the particular appeal of commercial news.

Networks of news media and news talk. When situated in relation to other news outlets across platforms, commercial television news occupies an important role in providing local information. In this research, 12.5 percent of participants indicated that their respective commercial television news preferences constituted their sole form of news. For 75 percent of participants, commercial television news fit into an Australian repertoire consisting of radio, print, or television news accessed across traditional, digital, and social media. Varying news outlets provided different affordances, as James explained in relation to television broadcast: "SBS you get more world news. … Channel 2 you get more Australian news, and Channel 9 and Channel 10 you get more Sydney-based news." While most participants utilized Australian sources of news across platforms, a further 12.5 percent of participants also used international mainstream or alternative news (BBC, CNN, Deutsche Welle, Al Jazeera, Russia Today, Haaretz, and The Young Turks). These news users were mostly either migrants or from diasporic backgrounds, and only Kate (31–45) developed international news preferences through her professional context which required her to live abroad.

Participants outlined that social media functioned as a digital extension of their individual lives, but generally not as a platform for news discussion or political talk. In this research, people aged 46–80 did not use online and social media platforms for news discussion. As a Turkish migrant, Rob (46–60) was an exception: "Facebook [has] nothing to do with the Australian news. … I use it just for what's happening in Turkey." Younger participants employed social media to share news or view shared content but avoided online discussions. Rather, social media enabled news users to undertake an advocacy role related to the social, cultural, professional, or political dimensions of their particular lives. Although there is an aversion to engaging in online discussions and commenting, interpersonal talk enables people to more easily apply filtering practices. Previous studies find the domestic context is the preferred space for political talk as it minimizes conflict (Madianou 2010), and workplace conversations take place generally with colleagues with similar viewpoints (Wyatt, Elihu Katz, and Kim 2000). This research extends these findings, as participants identified that they would filter discussions with family members, or were aware of other family members filtering in order to prevent conflict. The temporal dimensions to interacting were significant, where discussions functioned as an extension of ritualized family viewing practices (Lull 1988): "If we're sitting there and watching together, then I'll discuss it, but otherwise I don't really discuss it" (Anita 18–30). Participants also pointed to the natural constriction of social information shared in their personal and professional networks. Albert (46–60, Western Sydney) noted that often colleagues shared the same information, "We all pretty much tend to watch the same thing ... with my work, I mix a lot with men of my own age, and a lot of them are blue collar." One exception was Pratima (46–60) whose workplace interactions with an Indigenous Australian provided her with a different social perspective outside her personal network. Only three participants deliberately sought to participate in news talk for a range of different social, political, or cultural perspectives (Jim, 31–45, Lesley, 46–60, and Barbara, 61–80). Even then, the significance of avoiding conflict underscored interpersonal interactions as Barbara stated, "you talk about it and if they disagree strongly you change the subject."

The practices of filtering news talk also characterized how participants discussed their cross-media Australian news habits. Accessing different news sources linked to issues of partisan reporting, as 35 percent of participants perceived that political agendas influenced the production of news content. Greg (18–30) elaborated, "You don't get a range of opinions on some of the big issues of the day on commercial television, you do across mediums." Like Newman et al. (2016), this research found that participants were likely to feel news was more trustworthy if it aligned with their particular perspective. Mike (31–45) explicitly reflected on how this shaped his news preferences, "I've often thought to myself, whether I'm choosing them because I feel that there's a particular bias that's more to my worldview? ... I would say, yes I probably am guilty of that." Certain news outlets are able to sustain capital by fostering connections among those with similar political views, which further influences how people apply filtering in their interpersonal interactions. Gary (46–60) watched both Seven News and ABC News, as commercial news was useful for local information viewed while multitasking, whereas public broadcast was more broad and in-depth. He identified Seven News as more being more politically conservative (Liberal Party) and ABC News as left leaning (Labor Party). These political orientations influenced his interpersonal interactions:

> You ask them do you watch ABC and you get a no. So you know straight away, okay they're informed basically on what Channel 7, 9 and 10 have done. So therefore, they're going to be biased to that side. ... I don't tend to go any further because I think it's going to be one-sided.

The perception that certain news outlets were more objective if they aligned with the viewer's worldview underscores the ways in which news outlets are able to facilitate links with potentially likeminded people beyond geographic associations. Yet, it also highlights how news programs that do not align with viewer's political orientations can be mobilized as a resource to survey alternate political perspectives and apply mediated filters to manage localized interpersonal connections.

Social Power and Civic Potential

Cultivating capital. Throughout the interviews, participants articulated that the social importance of commercial television news was established through suburban links. Although local news media can generate feelings of community through collective interests (Anderson 1983; Carey 1989; Cottle and Rai 2006; Hess 2015), this occurs as a complex negotiation of uneven spatial-power relations. In mainstream media, Western Sydney is often portrayed in a negative manner, which has led to a number of successful alternative community media interventions aimed at shifting representations (Couldry and Dreher 2007; Dreher 2010; Gannon 2009; Ho 2012; Salazar 2010). Nonetheless, Western Sydney has become a crucial component of contemporary commercial news attempts to nurture social capital. At the time of interviewing, Seven News actively cultivated their position as an authoritative outlet for local reporting through the following promotion:

Voiceover: Seven News knows Sydney, because everyday we're just around the corner. Our people don't just work in Sydney.

News Anchor: We live here. I grew up here [South Wentworthville] and went to school right here.

Voiceover: With more people on the ground and more resources across the country, we're everywhere you need us to be. Seven News, first for Sydney.

The names of select suburbs accompanied visual footage, screened in the following order (suburbs from the West are italicized): *Liverpool*, *Blacktown*, *Castle Hill*, *Campbelltown*, Hornsby, *Cabramatta*, *South Wentworthville*, Chatswood, Mona Vale, *Parramatta*, Cronulla, *Bankstown*, Strathfield, and Mt. Colah. While this might suggest increased negative surveillance, the advertisement promoted positive interactions between the news anchor and culturally diverse individuals in the different suburbs. Although the Nine News 2013 promotion emphasized experience and immediacy, previous advertisements from 2011 also contained a similar emphasis on Sydney suburbia. Both Seven News and Nine News built capital by fostering affective connections with local viewers across Sydney, enabling the outlets to be seen as forms of "local" or "community" focused journalism:

> Channel 7 tries to be a lot more community based. In the promotions they say, well we're from Campbelltown, they name suburbs in Sydney that make you feel like you're relevant (Vicky, Inner City).

> If there's a big local event on I find that the commercial stations will have better coverage than ABC or SBS … that's what appeals to their audience, the local Sydney content (Dianne, Western Sydney, 61–80).

Local television news programs are a valuable form of social knowledge for participants, enabling them to cultivate relations with others in and beyond their networks. In their four-country case study including Australia, Cottle and Rai (2006, 177) find that the frame of "collective interest" appears more frequently in commercial news compared to public broadcast reporting. For the participants in this research, commercial news equips them to maintain shared local interests with others throughout the city. Lisa (31–45), an Anglo-Australian living in North Sydney, said, "It's always good to stay connected … keeping a common interest with people." Conversely, the ability to perform a central civic role and generate collective interest also had a negative dimension in exacerbating potential exclusion if participants did not watch commercial news programs. Altan (31–45) was part of the Turkish diaspora living in Western Sydney and predominantly favored international and public broadcast news outlets. He was highly critical of commercial television news coverage, but explained he would watch, "because it gives me a great opinion on what the 60 percent of people that I'm going to meet the next day have an opinion on." Local television news outlets have social capital not only by contributing to a sense of "community," but by enabling audiences to survey what others in their professional or personal networks might discuss.

Strategic surveillance. Local news outlets are associated as covering all aspects of suburban Sydney, but participants also identified a greater degree of social surveillance focused on Western Sydney. Ellen (61–80) was from an Anglo-Australian background, living in Western Sydney, and her sole source of news was Nine News because "they go all over." Yet, television news outlets developed social capital through the frequent localized surveillance that concentrated upon certain cultural minorities, lower socio-economic suburbs, and the conflations with crime: "you've got your shootings, and your gangs, if there's something happening in Cabramatta which is very much Vietnamese people out there now" (Ellen). These mainstream representations can further reproduce feelings of social exclusion as experienced by culturally diverse residents in Western Sydney (Dreher 2000; Salazar 2010). Local journalistic authority that is developed through surveillance can become amplified when participants are disconnected from the socio-spatial or racial contexts of reporting. Emma (31–45) was a migrant from the United Kingdom, and like Ellen, her only source of news was Nine News. She drew upon mediated knowledge when reflecting on the importance of commercial broadcast:

> They highlight a lot of social problems … quite often they show problems in lower economic areas. … I think this place in Campbelltown is really bad … there's higher crime, that sort of stuff does need to be highlighted, but on the other hand I suppose if they're put on the TV like that they get more of a bad name.

Despite contemplating the negative ramifications of overexposed surveillance, local television news had a role in sustaining a sense of social order, as she stated, "people need to be aware of these things as well." For some viewers, these news outlets performed a civic role by scrutinizing criminalized behavior, yet this did not resonate with a number of people living in Western Sydney.

In the research, 20 percent of participants drew upon their experiences living in Western Sydney to contest the ways in which local news outlets attempted to assert a civic function by reinforcing social order through surveillance and polarization. For these viewers, spatial dynamics intersected with the representations of cultural, racial, and religious minority groups. Two Western Sydney residents observed:

> I don't feel intimidated in going to a place like Mount Druitt [Western Sydney] or Hurstville [South Sydney], places that are heavily populated with negative media attention. … If there's an offence, or a crime's occurred in Granville [Western Sydney] … we know a Middle Eastern man allegedly did this. … You don't ever hear an Anglo-Australian crashed into a car. (Priya, 18–30)

> They love to say its South-West Sydney … when something happens up in the North Shore, they'll go to the exact suburb. … There's a lot more ethnic people out in the

> Western suburbs and I honestly think it's a racially motivated thing ... where [the] North Shore, it's more white Anglo-Saxon. (Galvyn, 18–30)

However, the oversaturated news coverage on certain minority groups also shapes how participants frame their discussions of surveillance. Participants predominantly reflected on depictions of specific minorities in Western Sydney, and they also emphasized how commercial television news excessively scrutinized the borders of the nation. Throughout the research, 37.5 percent of viewers considered the politicized coverage concentrating on asylum seeker movements and refugees. Jennifer (31–45) was a Lebanese migrant living in Western Sydney. She felt commercial television news programs reinforced negative perspectives, as "they have portrayed a particular image with refugees ... they haven't portrayed it in a neutral way." Through coverage, certain news outlets can further perpetuate existing social inequalities through the systematic exclusion or banishment of certain social groups (Gutsche 2015; Hess 2015). Notably, only two viewers living outside the West drew on their professional interactions to contest the exclusion or stereotyped representation of Indigenous Australians in local television news (Nick, 18–30, South Sydney, and Pratima). As an Indian migrant living in North Sydney, Pratima had little exposure to individuals from Indigenous communities. She reflected on her local news viewership and her professional network:

> We have an Aboriginal worker, only after she started we came to know a lot of Aboriginal stories. ... But the TV, the media doesn't portray all those things ... they drink and they don't go to work ... but it is not like that.

Pratima further elaborated that local television news needed to exercise an interest in supporting Indigenous Australians. If viewers are critical of the exclusions that manifest in local television news coverage, they also simultaneously draw attention to the power of the news outlets to encourage cohesion. In this regard, the exclusionary or stereotyped representations functioned as limitations to local news in realizing civic potential, which might be overcome through mechanisms of positive "surveillance."

Capturing the Capacity of Local Television

Participants evaluated the mixed capacity of local broadcast journalism to disrupt ingrained socio-cultural misconceptions and mediate civic engagement. One of the ways this could be achieved is through more inclusive and detailed reporting, as local news is positioned to popularly reach a range of viewers and dispel polarization in society. Vicky was from a Chinese diasporic background and recalled a specific Seven News crime report that reconciled concerns she might have regarding Islamic values and social cohesion:

> They'll get the Bankstown leader of this religion to comment ... saying that this was absolutely not an act of love to anyone who believes in this God. I would have thought, oh is this really part of believing in the Qur'an, is it accepted? But it helps clarify other religions which I'm not familiar with, and I guess it helps build support that this is not accepted behavior, in any way, regardless of your beliefs.

The distinct, albeit commercial, connection to the local context provides certain news outlets with a civic potential that is a partially or completely unrealized asset. Although realizing civic potential might not traditionally be associated with the role of commercial news, particularly when compared to public broadcast, there are advantages in utilizing this capacity to resonate with viewers. Unexpectedly, it was mostly the younger participants aged 18–45 who discussed the civic function and potential of the local news outlets. Bill (18–30) stated Seven News and Nine News "might do a [local] goodwill story, for example. You won't see that on SBS." Commercial television news outlets are in a position in the media landscape that equipped the programs to undertake civic action, in ways that public broadcast or other news outlets across platforms are unable to do. Andrew (18–30) also identified this civic function as significant factor in viewership, where commercial news and current affairs programs achieved capital by promoting civic interests:

> The other thing is Channel 9 they also seek out ways to help ... and inform people of how to help ... me as a viewer, was also interested in that and how I could help, if there was anything that I could do.

A number of areas were identified where commercial television news programs could further build capital in Sydney through goodwill reports, facilitating community engagement, and by providing better information on actions relating to a range of marginalized and minority groups. In this regard, local news outlets could better resonate with viewers by balancing negative surveillance with positive "surveillance" of community initiatives, civic engagement, and social cohesion. Yet, in discussing civic practice and allocating civic potential to these particular commercial television news programs over other news outlets, participants further concentrated the existing power these news outlets already had.

Across the research, 40 percent of viewers felt that local television news did not realize its potential in supporting cultural, suburban, Sydney, or national "communities." Jane (46–60, Anglo-Australian) drew upon her interactions with residents who were part of the Muslim community in Campbelltown, where she had lived across the road from a Mosque: "you never hear the good side of the stories, what they're doing in the communities ... to say this group is doing all this community work." Kate also discussed the capacity for commercial television news to report on community initiatives in order to realize civic potential across Sydney. As an Anglo-Australian living in the Inner West, Kate received news about the community initiative, "The Welcoming Dinner Project" through her interpersonal interactions. This project connects eight locally established residents to eight migrants (asylum seekers, refugees, or international students) to share a meal, form social connections, and enable community participation. Kate discussed the existent religious and racial power dynamics present within Sydney, indicating how local news programs were not meeting their civic potential through:

> Ways of building communities rather than talking about the ways the community is failing, or is fearful, or is excluding, because there are amazing things happening. ... I'd like to see more good news about that and about ways that you could get engaged with things.

Altan echoed these comments, and he underscored that it could involve simple measures, by refocusing local news coverage on positive attempts at social cohesion. These perspectives are of further significance in light of recent research, which indicates that over half of the Australians surveyed avoid the news and attribute the avoidance to a negative impact of news on their mood (Fisher, Watkins, and Breen 2017). Realigning local commercial broadcast journalism to promote community building and civic practice is one way to provide younger viewers with news that makes them feel good, while overcoming the limitations that are associated with exclusionary or polarized coverage of certain groups. Although most viewers concentrated on religious, cultural, and racial minorities, two individuals contemplated the commercial news coverage of homeless individuals in Sydney. Aiko (18–30) drew upon her personal experiences of being homeless to discuss civic potential. She stressed commercial television news programs could promote engagement, providing local audiences with information on ways to assist. While Greg generally felt television news programs could do more to reach their civic potential, he identified how reporting on the homeless within Sydney generated action. His particular motivations to buy a "Backpack Bed," with all profits donated to local homeless charities in Sydney, stemmed from a local commercial news report. Even if information in television news might not always translate into civic engagement, viewers still expressed a desire for local news outlets to take a greater social role in realizing their civic potential.

Conclusion

As people's news practices continue to fragment, this article has sought to understand how diverse audiences attribute certain news outlets with the power to demarcate social knowledge within the broader news landscape. In order to maximize viewership, commercial television news outlets cultivate a sense of local journalistic authority by promoting connections to key suburbs and communities in Sydney. This localized focus also creates conflicting attitudes among viewers as the news outlets generate mediated social capital through mechanisms of surveillance or exclusion that often do not resonate with their lived experiences. Yet, commercial television news outlets have a distinct relevance in the media landscape through the efficient provision of pertinent local information. While facilitating community building and civic practice are associated with the function of public broadcast journalism, these news outlets are perceived as being disconnected from the localized context. This affords commercial broadcast with a central civic role, which oscillates between promoting or hindering engagement and community building.

Local commercial broadcast journalism has an untapped reservoir where it can better resonate with diverse audiences by refocusing the ways in which it undertakes "surveillance" on certain communities or marginalized groups. First, participants indicated that commercial television news should provide expedient knowledge on how people could take civic action. Second, the news outlets should also take a more active role to realize civic potential by supporting a range of communities through their unique connection to the local context. At the same time, these measures would further concentrate the existing capital that the commercial news outlets already have, and one aspect that needs to be considered is how public broadcast journalism can also better resonate with local viewers. This article provides an important update to research on localized audiences and news media representations in Sydney, demonstrating how being "local" fundamentally links to the civic and social capital of commercial broadcast. It also shows that this occurs as a conflicted process, and it is necessary to further explore how the authority to be perceived of as local is nurtured or inhibited through journalistic practices. In addition, analyzing the spatial–temporal dimensions to news use is important in future research, given the ongoing changes in patterns of news media production, consumption, and disrupted news routines. To do so might necessitate the use of ethnographic approaches, beyond interviewing, in order to contribute to knowledge of how people attach meaning to varied news practices as well as to the diversity of circumstances in which these meanings and practices are constituted.

ACKNOWLEDGEMENTS

The author would like to thank Dr Maya Ranganathan and the anonymous reviewers for comments on earlier versions of this work.

DISCLOSURE STATEMENT

No potential conflict of interest was reported by the authors.

NOTES

1. Western Sydney consists of the local government areas of Blacktown, Camden, Campbelltown, Canterbury-Bankstown, Cumberland, Fairfield, The Hills, Liverpool, Parramatta, Penrith, and Wollondilly.
2. Within the city of Sydney, the traditional news landscape also includes two daily city-based newspapers, one daily national newspaper, one daily national finance newspaper, 28 community-based newspapers, 49 migrant newspapers; as well as community, commercial, and public broadcast radio stations.
3. Pseudonyms are used for participants to protect their identities, and ages are provided within in the ranges that were used for the sampling criteria. The age range is included in the first instance where the participant is mentioned. The participant's location in Sydney, cultural or migratory background, level of education, or occupation are provided where relevant to give context to specific responses.

REFERENCES

Allan, Stuart. 2010. *The Routledge Companion to News and Journalism*. London: Routledge.

Anderson, Benedict. 1983. *Imagined Communities*. London: Verso.

Australian Bureau of Statistics. 2016. "2011 Census: Data and Analysis QuickStats" http://www.abs.gov.au/websitedbs/censushome.nsf/home/quickstats?opendocument&navpos=220.

Australian Bureau of Statistics. 2017. "Regional Population Growth, Australia, 2015-16." http://www.abs.gov.au/AUSSTATS/abs@.nsf/mf/3218.0.

Bean, Clive. 2005. "How the Political Audiences of Australian Public and Commercial Television Channels Differ." *Australian Journal of Communication* 32 (2): 41–55.

Bird, S. Elizabeth. 2010. "News Practices in Everyday Life." In *The Routledge Companion to News and Journalism*, edited by Stuart Allan, 417–427. London: Routledge.

Bird, S. Elizabeth, and Robert W. Dardenne. 2009. "Rethinking News as Myth and Storytelling." In *The Handbook of Journalism Studies*, edited by Karin Wahl-Jorgensen and Thomas Hanitzsch, 201–217. New York: Routledge.

Carey, James. 1989. *Communication as Culture*. London: Unwin Hyman.

Carson, Andrea, Denis Muller, Jennifer Martin, and Margaret Simons. 2016. "A New Symbiosis? Opportunities and Challenges to Hyperlocal Journalism in the Digital Age." *Media International Australia* 161 (1): 132–146. doi:10.1177/1329878X16648390.

Coleman, Stephen, Nancy Thumim, and Giles Moss. 2016. "Researching Local News in a Big City." *International Journal of Communication* 10: 1351–1365.

Costera Meijer, Irene. 2007. "The Paradox of Popularity: How Young People Experience the News." *Journalism Studies* 8 (1): 96–116. doi:10.1080/14616700601056874.

Costera Meijer, Irene. 2013. "Valuable Journalism: A Search for Quality From the Vantage Point of the User." *Journalism: Theory, Practice & Criticism* 14 (6): 754–770. doi:10.1177/1464884912455899.

Costera Meijer, Irene, and Hildebrand P. Bijleveld. 2016. "Valuable Journalism: Measuring News Quality From a User's Perspective." *Journalism Studies* 17 (7): 827–839. doi:10.1080/1461670X.2016.1175963.

Cottle, Simon, and Mugdha Rai. 2006. "Between Display and Deliberation: Analyzing TV News as Communicative Architecture." *Media, Culture & Society* 29 (2): 163–189. doi:10.1177/0163443706061680.

Couldry, Nick, and Tanja Dreher. 2007. "Globalization and the Public Sphere: Exploring the Space of Community Media in Sydney." *Global Media and Communication* 3 (1): 79–100. doi:10.1177/1742766507074360.

Couldry, Nick, Sonia Livingstone, and Tim Markham. 2007. *Media Consumption and Public Engagement: Beyond the Presumption of Attention*. 2nd ed. Basingstoke: Palgrave Macmillan.

Cushion, Stephen. 2012. *The Democratic Value of News: Why Public Service Media Matter*. Basingstoke: Palgrave Macmillan.

Dahlgren, Peter. 2003. "Reconfiguring Civic Culture in a New Media Milieu." In *Media and the Restyling of Politics*, edited by John Corner and Dick Pels, 151–170. London: Sage.

Dahlgren, Peter. 2005. "Television, Public Spheres, and Civic Cultures." In *A Companion To Television*, edited by Janet Wasko, 411–432. Malden, MA: Blackwell Publishing.

Dahlgren, Peter. 2009. *Media and Political Engagement: Citizens, Communication and Democracy*. Cambridge: Cambridge University Press.

Dreher, Tanja. 2000. "Home Invasion: Television, Identity and Belonging in Sydney's Western Suburbs." *Media International Australia* 94 (1): 131–145. doi:10.1177/1329878X0009400113.

Dreher, Tanja. 2010. "Speaking up or Being Heard? Community media Interventions and the Politics of Listening." *Media, Culture & Society* 32 (1): 85–103. doi:10.1177/0163443709350099.

Eldridge II, Scott, and John Steel. 2016. "Normative Expectations: Employing 'Communities of Practice' Models for Assessing Journalism's Normative Claims." *Journalism Studies* 17 (7): 817–826. doi:10.1080/1461670X.2016.1154795.

Ewart, Jacqueline, and Jillian Beard. 2017. "Poor Relations: Australian News Media Representations of Ethnic Minorities, Implications and Responses." In *Minorities and Media: Producers, Industries, Audiences*, edited by John Budarick and Gil-Soo Han, 165–192. London: Palgrave Macmillan.

Fenton, Natalie. 2011. "Deregulation or Democracy? New Media, News, Neoliberalism and the Public Interest." *Continuum* 25 (1): 63–72. doi:10.1080/10304312.2011.539159.

Firmstone, Julie. 2016. "Mapping Changes in Local News." *Journalism Practice* 10 (7): 928–938. doi:10.1080/17512786.2016.1165136.

Firmstone, Julie, and Stephen Coleman. 2014. "The Changing Role of the Local News Media in Enabling Citizens to Engage in Local Democracies." *Journalism Practice* 8 (5): 596–606. doi:10.1080/17512786.2014.895516.

Fisher, Caroline, Jerry Watkins, and Michelle Dunne Breen. 2017. *Reuters Institute Digital News Report 2017: Australia*. http://www.digitalnewsreport.org/survey/2017/australia-2017/.

Franklin, Bob. 2006. "Preface: Local Journalism and Local Media: Contested Perceptions, Rocket Science and Parallel Universes." In *Local Journalism and Local Media: Making the Local News*, edited by Bob Franklin, xvii–xxii. London: Routledge.

Gannon, Susanne. 2009. "Rewriting 'the Road to Nowhere': Place Pedagogies in Western Sydney." *Urban Education* 44 (5): 608–624. doi:10.1177/0042085909339377.

Gauntlett, David, and Annette Hill. 1999. *TV Living: Television, Culture and Everyday Life*. London: Routledge.

Gutsche, Robert E. 2015. "Boosterism as Banishment: Identifying the Power Function of Local, Business News and Coverage of City Spaces." *Journalism Studies* 16 (4): 497–512. doi:10.1080/1461670X.2014.924730.

Hanusch, Folker. 2015. "A Different Breed Altogether?" *Journalism Studies* 16 (6): 816–833. doi:10.1080/1461670X.2014.950880.

Hess, Kristy. 2013. "Tertius Tactics: Mediated Social Capital as a Resource of Power for Traditional News media." *Communication Theory* 23 (2): 112–130.

Hess, Kristy. 2015. "Making Connections: 'Mediated' Social Capital and the Small-Town Press." *Journalism Studies* 16 (4): 482–496. doi:10.1080/1461670X.2014.922293.

Hess, Kristy. 2016. "Power to the Virtuous: Civic Culture in the Changing Digital Terrain." *Journalism Studies* 17 (7): 925–934. doi:10.1080/1461670X.2016.1154796.

Hess, Kristy, and Lisa Waller. 2017. *Local Journalism in a Digital World*. London: Palgrave Macmillan.

Ho, Christina. 2012. "Western Sydney is Hot! Community Arts and Changing Perceptions of the West." *Gateways: International Journal of Community and Research and Engagement* 5: 35–55.

Jakubowicz, Andrew, Jock Collins, Carol Reid, and Wafa Chafic. 2014. "Minority Youth and Social Transformation in Australia: Identities, Belonging and Cultural Capital." *Social Inclusion* 2 (2): 5–16.

Jakubowicz, Andrew, Heather Goodall, Jeannie Martin, Tony Mitchell, Lois Randall, and Kalinga Seneviratne. 1994. *Racism, Ethnicity and the Media*. St Leonards: Allen and Unwin.

Kramp, Leif. 2016. "Conceptualizing Metropolitan Journalism." In *Politics, Civil Society and Participation*, edited by Leif Kramp, Nico Carpentier, Andreas Hepp, Richard Kilborn, Risto Kunelius, Hannu Nieminen, Tobias Olsson, Pille Pruulmann-Vengerfeldt, Ilija Tomanić Trivundža and Simone Tosoni, 151–183. Bremen: Edition Lumière.

Liu, Shuang. 2004. "Social Categorisation of Chinese Ethnic Groups and its Influence on Intergroup Relations in Australia." *Australian Journalism Review* 26 (1): 69–82.

Lull, James. 1988. "Constructing Rituals of Extension Through Family Television Viewing." In *World Families Watch Television Edited by James Lull*, 237–260. Newbury Park, CA: Sage.

Madianou, Mirca. 2010. "Living with News: Ethnographies of News Consumption." In *The Routledge Companion to News and Journalism*, edited by Stuart Allan, 428–438. London: Routledge.

McCallum, Kerry. 2010. "News and Local Talk: Conversations About the Crisis of Indigenous Violence in Australia." In *The Anthropology of News and Journalism: Global Perspectives*, edited by S. Elizabeth Bird, 151–167. Bloomington: Indiana Press.

McCallum, Kerry, and Lisa Waller. 2017. "Indigenous Media Studies in Australia." In *Minorities and Media: Producers, Industries, Audiences*, edited by John Budarick and Gil-Soo Han, 105–124. London: Palgrave Macmillan.

Muscat, Tanya. 2015. "Constructing the Nation Every Night: Hegemonic Formations in Today Tonight and A Current Affair." *Media International Australia* 155 (1): 16–27. doi:10.1177/1329878X1515500104.

Newman, Nic, with Richard Fletcher, David A. Levy, and Rasmus Kleis Nielsen. 2016. *Reuters Institute Digital News Report 2016*. http://www.digitalnewsreport.org/.

Nielsen, Rasmus Kleis. 2015. "Introduction: The Uncertain Future of Local Journalism." In *Local Journalism: The Decline of Newspapers and the Rise of Digital Media*, edited by Rasmus Kleis Nielsen, 1–30. London: I.B. Tauris.

Nielsen, Rasmus Kleis. 2016. "Folk Theories of Journalism: The Many Faces of a Local Newspaper." *Journalism Studies* 17 (7): 840–848. doi:10.1080/1461670X.2016.1165140.

Nunn, Caitlin. 2010. "Spaces to Speak: Challenging Representations of Sudanese Australians." *Journal of Intercultural Studies* 31 (2): 183–198. doi:10.1080/07256861003606366.

Phillips, Gail. 2009. "Ethnic Minorities in Australia's Television News: A Second Snapshot." *Australian Journalism Review* 31 (1): 19–32.

Phillips, Gail. 2011. "Reporting Diversity: The Representation of Ethnic Minorities in Australia's Television Current Affairs Programs." *Media International Australia* 139 (1): 23–31. doi:10.1177/1329878X1113900105.

Poynting, Scott, and Greg Noble. 2003. "'Dog-Whistle' Journalism and Muslim Australians Since 2001." *Media International Australia* 109 (1): 41–49.

Putnam, Robert. 2000. *Bowling Alone: The Collapse and Revival of American Community*. New York: Simon and Schuster.

Rane, Halim, Jacqueline Ewart, and John Martinkus. 2014. *Media Framing of the Muslim World: Conflict, Crises and Contexts*. Houndmills: Palgrave.

Rojas, Hernando, Dhavan V. Shah, and Lewis A. Friedland. 2011. "A Communicative Approach to Social Capital." *Journal of Communication* 61 (4): 689–712. doi:10.1111/j.1460-2466.2011.01571.x.

Salazar, Juan. 2010. "Digital Stories and Emerging Citizens: Media Practices by Migrant Youth in Western Sydney." *3CMedia: Journal of Community, Citizen's and Third Sector Media and Communication* 6: 54–70.

Schudson, Michael. 2008. *Why Democracies Need an Unlovable Press*. Cambridge: Polity Press.

Schultz, Julianne. 1998. *Reviving the Fourth Estate*. Cambridge: Cambridge University Press.

Sjøvaag, Helle. 2015. "The Emergence of Metropolitan News: Shifting Concepts of Localism in Norwegian Regional Newspapers." *Nordicom Review* 36 (2): 17–32.

Swart, Joëlle, Chris Peters, and Marcel Broersma. 2016. "Navigating Cross-Media News Use: Media Repertoires and the Value of News in Everyday Life." *Journalism Studies*. doi:10.1080/1461670X.2015.1129285.

Tiffen, Rodney, David Rowe, Sharon Coen, and James Curran. 2017. "News Consumption, Political Knowledge and Political Efficacy." In *Public Opinion, Campaign Politics and Media Audiences: New Australian Perspectives*, edited by Bridget Griffen-Foley and Sean Scalmer, 208–242. Carlton: Melbourne University Publishing.

Wyatt, Robert, O. Elihu Katz, and Joohan Kim. 2000. "Bridging the Spheres: Political and Personal Conversation in Public and Private Spaces." *Journal of Communication* 50 (1): 71–92. doi:10.1111/j.1460-2466.2000.tb02834.x.

"TIGHTENING THE KNOTS" OF THE INTERNATIONAL DRUGS TRADE IN BRAZIL

Possibilities and challenges for news media to acquire social capital through in-depth reporting

Alice Baroni and **Andrea Mayr**

Much academic analysis of media representations of drugs-related violence in Brazil has focused on their role in perpetuating violence and societal divisions. There is less research on how the country's traditional news media can shape information in order to foster dialogue between people and potentially resolve conflict. This article aims to address this gap by exploring the possibilities and challenges for printed news media to acquire "mediated" social capital. The concept is understood here as a specific resource of power that has the potential to connect people from diverse social, cultural and economic backgrounds. In order to do so, we analyse how a popular Rio newspaper has used its symbolic power to produce social capital with an investigative series about Brazil's involvement in the international drugs trade. It is argued here that the series paints a complex picture of its causes and consequences and is an important step towards a deliberative process about possible solutions to drugs-related violence in Rio and beyond.

Introduction

In 2000, Brazilian anthropologist Alba Zaluar wrote that fear of drug-related dangers in Brazil is not merely a media creation but, to a degree, justified (Zaluar 2000). This is borne out by the high numbers of people who are killed in a costly "war on drugs" that has been waged by the state and its police force against the urban poor who live in favelas and other peripheral neighbourhoods of the city.[1]

Rio's mainstream media has defined this recurring scenario of drugs-related violence as an urban "war", a metaphor which not only justifies largely futile and lethal police tactics, but also suppresses the complexity of the issue and stifles debate (Leu 2004). The press has portrayed favelas as spaces of "exception" (Leu 2008) and cast their residents as urban others who pose a threat to social order and to the citizens living in Rio's "formal city".[2] These media discourses have therefore contributed to widening the gap between different groups of people based on class and the spatial divisions (Ramos and Paiva 2007; Varjão 2009).

In this article, however, we will discuss a piece of journalism that avoids this "spectacle of violence" (Leu 2004) with an investigative series that addresses the drugs trade as a transnational problem. Written by Fabio Gusmão and Guilherme Amado, two journalists from Rio newspaper *Extra*, it exposes the corruption of public officials and the lack of border control and co-operation between the judicial systems of Brazil, Paraguay, Peru and Bolivia. The series, which bears the title *"Os embaixadores do Narcosul"* (The *Narcosul*'s ambassadors), clearly links Brazil, the largest consumer market for marijuana and cocaine in the South Cone, to the other three producing countries. Importantly, *Narcosul* questions the common-sense argument that locates drug trafficking exclusively within Rio's favelas. It thereby avoids stereotyping media images about favela residents which exonerate society and its institutions of the responsibility to deal with the problem in a meaningful way. What this article aims to show then is how the series' production processes may function as "mediated social capital", that is, a resource of power that offers citizens and policy makers ways to deal with drugs-related violence that go beyond the "war on drugs".

In what follows, we first contextualise our research on the *Narcosul* series by providing a brief overview of Brazil's print mediascape and some of its working practices, set against the backdrop of urban violence. After introducing *Extra*, we discuss social capital in relation to news media and (investigative) journalism. Going beyond Bourdieu, we adopt Hess' concept of "mediated social capital" to address the following questions: how journalists' *habitus* and social connections can reinforce their position within the journalistic field and how journalists' social capital functions as a resource of power through in-depth reporting. In other words, how do they engage elites in discussions that in the long run may inform policy-making on the drugs problem. The *Narcosul* series presents a useful case study for exploring these issues.

(Investigative) Journalism in Brazil

Brazil has one of the largest and well-developed press systems in Latin America. There are about 300 newspapers in Brazil. Only four dailies, however, have the circulation to influence national opinion and politics significantly. They are *O Estado de S. Paulo, Folha de S. Paulo, Jornal do Brasil and O Globo,* the last two being located in Rio de Janeiro. While the country's elite and the middle class read these newspapers, most of the population get their news from television and radio (Herscovitz 2004).

Although Brazil is the world's fourth largest democracy, notions that come with democracy, such as press freedom and the protection of media workers, are relatively new in many parts of Brazil. Nevertheless, the democratisation process following the end of the dictatorship in 1985 allowed investigative journalism to establish itself as a practice in Brazil's newsrooms (Souza 1988; Porto 1996; Waisbord 2000; Fortes 2005). Earlier examples of investigative journalism do exist, but are rare (see Magno 2006; Baroni 2012).

Brazil is one of the most dangerous places in the world for journalists, who often become targets of aggression, intimidation and judicial censorship. Journalists who expose corruption and crime do so at great risk to their lives. In 2002, a turning-point in this crisis of violence was reached in the aftermath of the killing of the well-known journalist Tim Lopes who was killed by drug traffickers in a favela of Rio de Janeiro while conducting investigative reporting there.

Lopes' case brought about important changes in journalists' working practices. Bulletproof vests and cars were adopted and journalists underwent special training to work in areas of high risk, while others were no longer allowed by their media companies to enter these areas (see Moretzsohn 2003). These procedures reinforced divisions and consolidated the symbolic and real boundaries between the "asphalt" (formal city) and the "hill" (favela).

Brazilian journalism faces the same dramatic industry restructuring as other countries, such as declining advertising revenue and staff reductions. According to Amado (interview, April 1, 2017), Infoglobo (which *Extra* belongs to) dismissed about two-thirds of its newsroom staff within a two-year period. These factors, coupled with dangerous working conditions, are clearly not conducive to investigative reporting, which depends to a large extent on reporters' ability to collect a huge amount of material from different sources. In Bourdieu's terms, it depends on the reporters' habitus and on their social capital, including the relationship with their sources.

There is an extensive literature on the complex interplay between ethics and the impact of sources on journalism practice in Brazil. Schmitz and Karam (2013), Chaparro (2016) and Kucinski (2002), for instance, argue that the increasing proactivity and specialisation of sources combined with the decline of investigative journalism in Brazilian newsrooms have imposed themselves as a threat to independent newsgathering by journalists. According to Kucinski (2002, 59), "the journalist no longer goes after sources. The sources bring them what they [sources] want to see published". By contrast, the *Narcosul* series can be seen as an example of journalists using their social capital and social connections on behalf of a more in-depth form of journalism, which depends on sources' willingness to co-operate in the news production process. Amado therefore had to build relationships of trust with a wide range of sources across borders in order to be able to collect and analyse a large amount of data for his transnational investigative research.

Journalism of this kind needs to reach beyond local contexts. That is why transnational networks of investigative journalism and platforms have sprung up in Brazil and the rest of Latin America, which allow journalists from the region to share knowledge about investigative techniques and information of public interest that is key to the development of the Americas. The main topics of the work published typically have to do with governance, human rights or things of high political impact for the Americas (see Mioli and Nafría 2017).

Background and Context: Socio-economic and Cultural Roots of Violence in Rio de Janeiro

Media and sociological analysis of urban violence in Rio de Janeiro indicates that it is historically associated with "irregular armed groups" that control the territories in which they operate, which are typically favelas and other low-income communities (e.g. Cano 1997; Leu 2004, 2008; Cano and Ribeiro 2016). Local drug dealers are the most common groups to fulfil that role and are often linked to wider networks, known as *facções* ("factions") or *comandos* ("commands"). Here they establish a certain kind of social order and impose rules that govern the daily lives of favela residents.

The origins of these *comandos* go back to the 1980s and have been documented by various researchers, often with diverging viewpoints (Amorim 1993; Lima 1991; Penglase 2008). Brazil's two main drug cartels, the Comando Vermelho ("Red Command") and the Primeiro Comando da Capital ("First Capital Command") were originally formed by prisoners as self-protection groups in Brazil's brutal prison system, but have since moved into cocaine trafficking, particularly from the 1980s onwards, abandoning any political ideology there may have been. The First Command is now the largest and best organised drug cartel in

Brazil. It is believed to have members in two-thirds of the country's states, and operates drug-trafficking routes between Brazil, Bolivia and Paraguay.

Both cartels have managed to establish deep roots in poor communities with a system of "forced reciprocity" (Penglase 2008), whereby they provide security in return for complicity from favela residents. According to some (e.g. Goldstein 2007), it is the abandonment of favela communities by the state for over a century that lay the foundation for the increasing influence of drug traffickers as a "parallel state" across Brazil's poor areas. Arias (2006, 293–294), on the other hand, argues that networks in Rio's favelas connect drug traffickers with politicians, civic leaders and the police. Instead of creating parallel powers inside favelas, these networks allow drug gangs to engage in political activities, and to "appropriate state power and social capital that make their ongoing criminal activities possible". Whatever the case, Penglase (2008) argues that these drug cartels are more than mere criminal associations that seek profit from the sales of drugs. Rather, they are very much the "unintended or undesired" offspring of the dictatorship and should be situated within Brazil's rampant socio-economic inequality and a corrupt political system that shows disregard for the human rights of many of its (poor) citizens. This contextualisation of urban violence is precisely what is missing from news reports, which present mostly factual or sensationalist information, without offering much background analysis (see Ramos and Paiva 2007; Biazoto 2011; Patterson 2013). The *Narcosul* series does acknowledge that both cartels now have established networks to Bolivia and Paraguay, but significantly, demonstrates that it is powerful independent distributors who really dominate and control the international drugs trade.

Extra and its *Narcosul* Series

Extra belongs to Brazil's largest news conglomerate O Globo and is a popular newspaper for the lower middle classes ("Class B and C"). The paper has a strong commitment to addressing urban violence and human rights abuses, perhaps more so than other newspapers in Rio (Gusmão, interview, April 12, 2017; see also Mayr, forthcoming). The idea for the *Narcosul* investigative series, which was published in May 2014 over a nine-day period, arose from Gusmão and Amado's wish to produce an in-depth and analytical coverage of the complexities of the drugs trade in Brazil with a view to exposing the root causes of the violence that goes with it. A six-month journalistic investigation took Amado and a photographer to 16 cities in Bolivia, Paraguay, Peru and Brazil. After interviewing 79 people and analysing 4300 pages of public and confidential information in the four countries and the United States, Amado was in a position to "tighten the knots of the international drugs trade", as he put it, and reveal the names of eight major drug traffickers and their operations in these countries. To aid the production process, editor Gusmão used WhatsApp to create "Rede Narcosul", a network to connect reporters on the entire continent to facilitate exchange of information and ideas, and seek help on stories about drug trafficking, money laundering, human trafficking and border evasions. The series was given the Brazilian *Esso* Journalism award for best reportage in the Southeast Region category.

Extra has encountered strong criticism from the public for championing human rights issues. This is because many people in Brazil still see human rights as a Trojan horse,[3] which are felt to have no place in what they perceive as war-like conditions. It has become part of the national discourse to say that defending human rights amounts to granting privileges to criminals (Holston 2008). However, *Extra*'s continued emphasis on respect for human rights and its avoidance of polarisation and confrontation when reporting on the sensitive topic of drug trafficking is an important step for conflict-sensitive reporting. Amado told us that he deliberately did not use the word "favela" in the *Narcosul* reports so as to avoid the "othering" of segments of Rio's population who are already stigmatised.

Theory and Method

This study is guided by Bourdieu's theory of social capital and some of the key literature that examines social capital in relation to news media (Bourdieu 1986; Coleman 1988; Putnam 2000; Hess 2013). Bourdieu defines social capital as "the aggregate of the actual or potential resources which are linked to possession of a durable network of more or less institutionalised relationships of mutual acquaintance or recognition" (Bourdieu 1986, 248). The concept captures the idea of interaction in social networks, which enables individuals to develop norms of trust and reciprocity, which are necessary for successful engagement in collective activities. Bourdieu made the important point that these collective activities and transformations in culture are rarely revolutionary; instead, they are dependent on the possibilities present in the positions inscribed in the field. "In such fields, and in the struggles which take place in them, every agent acts according to his position (that is, according to the capital he or she possesses) and his *habitus*, related to his personal history" (Bourdieu 2005, 47). Habitus is a synergy between cultural capital, an individual agent's life history (prior disposition and heredity) and social conditions.

Bourdieu's original term has been reconceptualised by Hess's (2013) notion of "mediated social capital". She defines this term as "a resource of power available to traditional, commercial news media through its ability to connect people, consciously and unconsciously, across various social, economic, and cultural spaces and to link people with those in positions of power" (Hess 2013, 113). Hess's concept is useful for the present study in that it allows us to explore how journalists' social connections and habitus reinforce their position in the world. It also allows us to make claims about the role of in-depth reporting in connecting different groups of people as it acknowledges the importance of social, political and cultural content in the communication process. The concept is also in synergy with Bourdieu's notion to change the world through "symbolic power", that is through the ways in which the world is represented (Bourdieu 1989, 23).

The way the media uses symbolic forms such as language to present a topic can alter the perception of audiences and have very practical social, economic and political implications (see, e.g., Hall 1980; Mayr and Machin 2012). In order to assess this potential, we conducted a qualitative textual analysis of the nine articles of the series, focusing on Biazoto's (2011) "de-escalation-oriented" form of conflict news coverage.

Apart from analysing the nine articles of the series for its use of language, we conducted three one-hour interviews with Amado and two one-hour interviews with *Narcosul* editor Gusmão, using extracts from these interviews to offer an insight into their ability to conduct this type of investigative journalism. The interviews provided us with information on journalists' working practices, which led us to focus on three main questions: (1) the role key sources play in the success of the journalists' venture and their safety; (2) the challenges Rio's journalists face in reporting on drugs-related violence, crime control and human rights in a society where citizens are easily seduced by the idea of taking justice into their own hands; and (3) the potential the *Narcosul* series has to engage policy makers, thereby functioning as linking social capital to (transnational) government policy on drugs-related violence.

The *Narcosul* Series: Analysis of Themes and Patterns

The *Narcosul* series is the result of the enterprise teamwork and habitus of *Extra* journalists and their colleagues in Paraguay, Peru and Bolivia. Gusmão emphasised the need for journalists to acquire specific knowledge about public security because of the complexity of societal and armed conflicts in Brazil. For him, one needs to understand a fact beyond its singularity, that is, in a longitudinal sense. Gusmão and Amado wanted to let the public know about the transnationalisation process of criminal activities and traffickers' efficiency in expanding their business beyond national borders. They therefore practised a form of transnational journalism, a practice that is rapidly gaining ground in South America:

> the *Narcosul* series was born from our attempts to understand … why narco-traffickers are more efficient than sovereign nations in sharing information and collaborating with each other. The problem isn't just a drug problem, but [involves] everything that is related to it. (Gusmão, interview, April 12, 2017)

The *Narcosul* series was published in 2014 as nine news articles and resulted in the building of a profile of eight "*Narcosul* ambassadors", consisting of a list of the most prolific traffickers in South America. An online platform was created[4] which "showcases" the 170 most wanted narco-traffickers from Brazil, Paraguay, Peru and Bolivia. The production process consisted of

- 79 interviews with former state presidents, members of Congress, diplomats, prosecutors, judges, police officers, lawyers, representatives to the United Nations, researchers and drug traffickers from four countries: Brazil, Paraguay, Peru and Bolivia.
- An analysis of 4300 pages of secret and public documents collected from the following institutions: United Nations Office on Drugs and Crime; Peru's National Commission for Development and Life Without Drugs (DEVIDA); Bolivia's Special Force Against Drug Trafficking (FELCN); Paraguay's National Anti-drug Secretariat (SENAD); the Federal Police (PF) in Brazil; and the Office of National Drug Control Police (ONDCP) in the United States.
- A 15,654-kilometre road trip through 16 different cities in Brazil, Paraguay, Peru and Bolivia, to conduct interviews and collect, verify and produce data.

As for "de-escalation-oriented aspects" (Biazoto 2011) in the news coverage, the nine newspaper articles clearly reveal a sensitivity to the use of language in that they refrain from using polarising labels. The words *favela* and *guerra* ("war") and other militaristic metaphors, which are common in the Brazilian mainstream press, are avoided. Instead of the word *bandido* ("bandit", "thug"), a very loaded term in Brazilian discourses to describe drug dealers, the more neutral terms *traficante* ("trafficker") and *criminoso* ("criminal") are used throughout to describe drug dealers. In so doing, the series clearly deconstructs popular clichés and "common sense" knowledge about the drugs trade. The way the media uses symbolic forms such as language to present a topic can alter the perception of audiences and have very practical social, economic and political implications (Hall

1980; Mayr and Machin 2012). The creation of a novel narrative through symbolic content that goes beyond the usual war rhetoric is therefore an important step towards shaping media and societal discourses on drugs and violence (symbolic capital).

However, whether its choice of themes inspires reflexivity and critical thinking in the reader cannot be answered conclusively. Apart from using neutral labels to describe social actors and events in the series, there is also clear contextualisation and embedding of the drugs trade in its wider social, cultural and historical roots, although the series focuses more on the corruption of public officials. What may be missing from the articles is a detailed discussion of drugs policy, although the final article of the series does address the decriminalisation of drugs.

One of the three research questions concerns the challenges for the series to function as mediated social capital that would in the long run have an effect on transnational drug-related violence. During the *Narcosul* production process, Amado realised that there was a lack of collaboration among journalists. He commented that he "showed in the series that there was a lack of articulation and official collaboration to combat organised crime and drug trafficking in particular, [as much as I realised] a lack of collaboration among journalists to produce effective transnational journalism" (Amado, interview, July 18, 2017). However, Amado and Gusmão succeeded in engaging journalists from the four countries to make the *Narcosul* investigation possible. Gusmão said:

> We created a co-operative [journalistic] group. The Ipys [Instituto Prensa y Sociedad or Press and Society Institute], which co-finance the *Narcosul* series played a very important role in this process. Guilherme had contact with other reporters who in turn had access to other sources. He also needed the help of colleagues to [have access to] telephone interceptions ... [where the Spanish language was difficult to translate] he contacted his [Latin American] colleagues. Soon after we created the Narcosul Network, a network of collaborators using WhatsApp. (Gusmão, interview, August 7, 2017)

The *Narcosul* series can be said to function as bonding social capital in that Gusmão and Amando created a network of journalistic collaborators across different locations. Bonding social capital refers to relationships amongst members of a network who are similar in some form (Putnam 2000). Although the "Rede Narcosul" ("Narcosul Network") mentioned above was active for only two years, it laid the foundation for transnational journalism in South America and beyond. For example, in 2014 Gusmão and Amado were invited by investigative journalist Paul Radu, Director of the Organized Crime and Corruption Reporting Project, to attend a conference in Senegal entitled, "Investigating and Reporting Corruption on Organized Crime in the Sahel" in a clear to attempt replicate "Rede Narcosul" in Africa (Amado, interview, April 1, 2017). Since 2017, Amado has also been collaborating with an expanded network of journalists to report on Brazil's *Lava Jato* ("Operation Car Wash") corruption scandal[5]:

> I am currently working in association with Latin American journalists on a joint report on *Lava Jato*. So if I get a document from Peru, for instance, I forward it to a colleague in Ecuador, Chile, Mexico, Panama ... This kind of articulation is missing. My idea is to create an exclusive social network of transnational journalists ... from anywhere in the world.[6] (Amado, interview, July 18, 2017)

Amado and Gusmão's *rede de fontes* ("net of sources") across wider social spaces also played a role in facilitating their work and keeping them safe during the investigation.

Reporting on organised crime requires relationships of trust with sources, who play an important part in providing journalists' access to information and further key sources. In addition, sources in a position of power use their own social capital to ensure the safety of journalists during the investigation process. Amado (interview, July 18, 2017) said: "If I didn't have a strong net of sources I could have been murdered or wouldn't have had access to qualified information". In addition, his social connections were essential for him to have access to key sources from the four countries. Amado commented that, while in Brazil, he had to use his own social capital and habitus, demonstrating to sources that he was knowledgeable about the drugs trade and organised crime. This earned him the trust and respect of informants while in Paraguay, Peru and Bolivia. He only had to use the name of the well-known Globo Group to gain access to sources of information in these countries.

Gusmão and Amado's habitus is a fundamental attribute to be considered for the success of the *Narcosul* series, which reinforces their position in the journalistic field. Gusmão has reported on disputes between drug gangs and societal conflicts in Rio for the past 22 years, which has given him extensive knowledge about the complex interplay of crime, state power, and police and gang violence. He grew up in the North Zone of Rio, where he witnessed all sorts of violations perpetrated by what became known as *Cavalos Corredores* ("Running Horses"), a death squad formed by Military Police officers. Gusmão (interview, April 12, 2017) said: "When I was a teenager, I lived on the corner of "Cavalos Corredores", where the Vigário Geral massacre[7] took place; they were loved by the residents because they executed [robbers] in front of everybody". Therefore, as a reporter he has managed to build a vast archive of news articles and photographs, which he then used to create the criminal profiles of Rio's drug gang leaders. Gusmão's upbringing put him in a position to produce in-depth journalism, unlike journalists from more privileged and safer areas of the city. In this respect, Ramos and Paiva (2007) stress the need for mainstream newsrooms to become more socially diverse in order to improve the quality of journalistic insight into Brazil's favelas. As for Amado, he had the combination of enterprise and team-work skills required to conduct independent newsgathering and to build a network of collaborators in Brazil, Peru, Paraguay and Bolivia who contributed to the success of the reportage. What is more, being awarded the Esso Journalism Award in 2014 strengthened the position of *Extra* journalists in the field, as the prize committee is formed by renowned journalists who acknowledged the excellence in the *Narcosul* series.

Our interviews and informal conversations with Amado also shed light on how these journalists use their own symbolic capital, in this case the power to construct a novel account of Rio's drug-related problems and crime control to engage elites with their stories. Importantly, the series not only resulted in bridging social capital, but linking social capital also. Linking social capital is the extent to which individuals build relationships with institutions and individuals who have relative power over them (Szreter and Woolcock 2004). The journalists managed to do so by building complex connections between authorities from interrelated fields. The *Narcosul* investigation process included a mass of informants who approach organised crime from their own specialism (e.g. law enforcement, policing, diplomacy, public affairs, affairs of states). Amado put it the following way:

> At the time I built a net of sources I was able to access strategic authorities … I engaged them in debate and made them read my material [*Narcosul* series] and by doing so they could understand which policy changes were needed. (Amado, interview, July 18, 2017)

Both journalists used their own social capital not only to connect these authorities, but also make them think about questions and exploration of the international drugs trade in South America. Amado said: "To interview and bring them into the discussion … to a certain extent I make them reflect on their own actions and, consequently, [to think about] the public policy as a whole" (Amado, interview, July 18, 2017).

In this way, the *Narcosul* series functions as linking mediated social capital, or in other words, as a resource of power to connect elites in several ways: the reportage was adopted by the Federal Police Academy and included in its curriculum to train police officers; it was also disseminated by José Eduardo Cardoso, Brazil's former Minister of Justice among the secretaries of the Ministry of Justice; and it was also requested by Ambassador Nelson Antonio Tabajara, Director of the Department of Defence and Security Affairs. In addition, Joaquim Araújo, a Brazilian diplomat who was based in Lima when the *Narcosul* series was published in 2014, said that the reportage succinctly expressed his understanding of drug trafficking in the region. He could not indicate a direct impact of the series on the (inter)-national debate on illegal drug markets, although he pointed out that there has been an effort to tackle transnational crimes due to the worrying indexes for public security and health in South America. For him, the South Cone Ministerial Meeting on Border Security at the Itamaraty Palace, in Brasilia on November 16, 2016, reflected this concern (Joaquim Araújo, personal communication, May 8, 2017). Internationally, the investigation series was published in *El Pais Uruguay* and was reviewed by Insight Crime, a non-profit journalism and investigative organisation dedicated to the study of organised crime in Latin America. Furthermore, Amado and Gusmão publicised the *Narcosul* series at conferences and seminars on investigative journalism and organised crime in Brazil, Argentina, Peru and Senegal.

The third research question sought to assess the difficulties journalists face in reporting on drugs-related violence and crime control in Rio. Both Amado and Gusmão said that *Extra* journalists are usually "beaten up" on social media by readers who are resistant to the notion that human rights and crime control can go together. Regarding news media reporting on drugs-related violence and human rights, Amado said:

> Nowadays, Rio's common-sense attitude is "an eye for an eye". Human rights are losing out in Rio de Janeiro. "An eye for an eye" is winning. Journalism may bend towards one side or another. Journalism, again, I always say it, journalism isn't made on Mars, it's made on Earth, in Brazil, in Rio de Janeiro, where people are assaulted. But [considering] the power we have for change, we must not allow ourselves to be easily seduced by the discourse of taking justice into our own hands. (Amado, interview, July 18, 2017)

As for journalism and social order in Rio, Gusmão self-critically observed the following:

> Journalism in Rio … I think we practise, we still take the point of view of the authorities. Although we might be critical … It's natural to accept the official version much more than the critical one. This seems like a contradiction, but it is not. Because it is practically impossible to criticise all aspects of all police actions in Rio de Janeiro. But what we propose to report we try to balance these [features]. News media in general,

particularly, the moment we are living in, sees favelas only as spaces of violence; we only forget this during carnival when you have in favelas that vigorous energy—because they [favela residents] are the ones who make the party happen. (Gusmão, interview, August 7, 2017)

However, *Extra* journalists do criticise Rio's social order, particularly the "eye for an eye" attitude of many citizens who approve of brutal police interventions in favelas. They are often criticised on social media for questioning the "politics of fear and hate", which is gaining ground in Rio. This fear, as we said at the beginning of the article, is to some extent justified. After falling steadily for a number of years, lethal violence in Rio is again on the rise, especially following the 2016 Olympics and Michel Temer's (illegal) rise to power (O'Boyle 2017). Military police have resumed their operations in favelas as drug gangs have begun to reassert themselves. So what is journalism's potential, if at all, to bridge the divide between people living in and outside favelas, in other words to function as bridging capital?

To begin with, the *Narcosul* series strongly argues that local drug dealers and favela residents are not the main culprits in the drugs trade. This in itself is a major advance on the way drugs-related violence is usually reported in news media in Brazil (see Biazoto 2011). In order to convey to readers the complexity of the drugs trade, Amado wrote in the first article of the series that "[the *Narcosul*'s ambassadors] are more like businessmen than favela criminals". Here Amado benefits from *Extra*'s concentration of symbolic power (Couldry 2003) to break with established media discourses about favelas as places of violence and their residents as criminals.

The last article of the series, in addition, addresses the controversial issue of decriminalisation of drugs in Brazil and other countries, featuring extracts of interviews with the former president of Brazil and Bolivia, Fernando Henrique Cardoso and Jorge Quiroga, respectively, who have opposing views on drug legalisation. Unlike *Extra*, mainstream media tend to obscure the connections between social problems and the actions (or non-actions) of political leaders.

Second, the production process and the networks that have to be built to produce investigative news articles in themselves function as a resource of power, not only because they connect people, but also because they build spaces for dialogue. *Extra* did this with a Question & Answer session via Twitter in which Amado answered readers' questions and listened to their comments on the *Narcosul* series. Amado (interview, July 18, 2017) spoke with about 30 readers and was impressed they had read the whole series. For him, this is a first step towards "deliberation", a process in which people take part before making a decision related to issues that affect their lives (Romano 2010). This is perhaps the best example of bridging capital in the series.

The idea that a newspaper and journalists use their social capital and position to connect with its readership deliberately across a range of fields and spaces may clash with journalistic norms of objectivity. However, as Lesage and Hackett (2014, 46) argue, "Objectivity in journalism is not a single, fixed thing but can include a range of meanings amongst different journalists". Objectivity in the *Narcosul* case should refer to *Extra*'s journalists' proactivity to conduct independent newsgathering in order to ensure a fair representation of opposing sides in the debate about Brazil's involvement in the international drugs trade.

Conclusion

This study has investigated the conditions in which news media can produce investigative/in-depth reporting which functions to build mediated social capital in order to connect people and communities to overcome the "favela–asphalt" dichotomy and lead to an end of the "war" on drugs in its poor communities through policy change. We suggested at the outset that this form of journalism could lead to a constructive societal dialogue and ultimately serve to protect human rights for all of Rio's citizens. However, our analysis suggests that this form of bridging social capital, which refers to relationships amongst people who are dissimilar in a demonstrable fashion, such as age, socio-economic status and race/ethnicity (Szreter and Woolcock 2004), will be the most difficult to achieve, given the deep rifts in Brazilian society.

However, the *Narcosul* series clearly functions as linking social capital in that it has managed to disseminate the findings of its transnational investigative journalism to authorities who have influence on policy making. *Narcosul* denounces the inability or unwillingness of four countries to tackle their domestic and international problems, such as the systemic corruption of government officials and the illegal arms and drugs trade which crosses borders. By emphasising the weakness of state institutions in these respects and by calling on authorities to find new ways of addressing their drugs-related problems, *Narcosul* clearly functions as mediated social capital that engages elites in debate who have the power to conceive and execute public security policies.

Furthermore, our analysis has also shown that *Narcosul* resulted in the building of an expanded network of journalistic collaborators fostering transnational journalism in South America, hence its bonding capital (Szreter and Woolcock 2004). A transnational drugs trade requires transnational investigative journalism that transcends national boundaries. The local aspect still defines news output but importantly is "shaped by a transnational flow of information" (Helmueller 2017, 8).[8] As the burgeoning literature on the theory and practice of transnational journalism (e.g. Kraidy 2011; Esser 2013; Hellmueller 2014, 2017; Reese 2015) shows, these transnational networks not only tackle serious problems, they also indicate a shift in the conceptualisation of journalism culture, which has traditionally been discussed within a national system. Further research should be undertaken in this area. The replication of "Rede Narcosul" in Africa, for instance, is a very promising development that should be taken up in future research on transnational journalism.

Brazil's ill-conceived "war" on drugs and mainstream media coverage thereof has proven incapable of containing drug sales and disrupting drug markets. Instead it has been characterised by lethal violence and human rights abuses committed by the state and its police forces against the poor. An investigative series such as the one reported here with its evidence of connecting to people in positions of power through mediated social capital is a first step towards a more enlightened approach to the transnational drugs problem. The *Narcosul* series is an important example of a newspaper developing bonding, bridging and linking strategies though its mediated social capital, that may result in a more effective system of political and media communication. As Silverstone (2007, 5) says, the media are the principal means of connection and disconnection, of symbolic inclusion and exclusion by the "boundary work" they perform, defining distance and closeness between "us" and "them". According to Silverstone, this requires imagination, understanding and duty of care. *Extra* has taken an important step in that direction.

ACKNOWLEDGEMENTS

We would like to express our gratitude to Guilherme Amado for all his help throughout the project. We are also indebted to Fábio Gusmão and Joaquim Araújo, who generously offered their time to be interviewed.

DISCLOSURE STATEMENT

No potential conflict of interest was reported by the authors.

FUNDING

This work was supported by the Coordination for the Improvement of Higher Education Personnel (CAPES), under the National Post-doctoral Programme.

NOTES

1. Homicide rates are highly influenced by race, gender and age. According to Human Rights Watch (2016), "police in the state of Rio de Janeiro alone have killed more than 8000 people in the past decade, including at least 645 people in 2015. One fifth of all homicides in the city of Rio last year were police killings, many of which drug-related. Among those killed by police, three quarters were black men".
2. The term "formal city" is used in opposition to favelas, which are neither regarded as centralised formal suburbs nor the outer peripheries. The latter are "equally "formal" in the sense that they are actually part of the city, paying their taxes and participating in the formal economy" (Veloso 2010, 254). Favelas, on the other hand, are characterised by informal economies and do not pay taxes.
3. A recent survey by the Centre for Studies on Public Security and Citizenship found that for 73 per cent of the 2353 interviewees human rights are incompatible with crime control and 56 per cent believed that human rights protection just benefits criminals (Lemgruber, Cano, and Musumeci 2017).
4. The online platform of the most wanted Narcosul traffickers can be retrieved at https://extra.globo.com/noticias/mundo/foragidos-narcosul/.
5. Concerning Brazil's Lava Jato corruption scandal, see https://gijn.org/2017/08/01/lava-jato-a-case-study-in-cross-border-investigation/.
6. Guilherme Amado was among the 18 journalists awarded the John S. Knight Journalism Fellowships for the 2017–2018 academic year at Stanford University. His project was on the role played by a social network in transnational journalism.
7. The Vigário Geral massacre occurred on August 29, 1993 at the favela of Vigário Geral, located in the north of Rio de Janeiro city. A death squad composed of Rio Military Police killed 21 residents, supposedly out of revenge for the killing of four police officers two days prior, who were allegedly involved in the extortion of drug traffickers.
8. Transnational journalism is different from global journalism, which is more concerned with establishing consensual norms that allow journalistic organisations to function globally.

REFERENCES

Amorim, Carlos. 1993. *Comando Vermelho: A história secreta do crime organizado [Comando Vermelho: a secret history of organized crime]*. 1st ed. Rio de Janeiro: Record.

Arias, Enrique Desmond. 2006. "The Dynamics of Criminal Governance: Networks and Social Order in Rio de Janeiro." *Journal of Latin American Studies* 38 (2): 293–325.

Baroni, Alice. 2012. *Os efeitos de verdade em Os Sertões e Abusado [The truth-effect in "Rebellion in the Backlands" and "Abused"]*. São Paulo: Annablume.

Biazoto, Joice. 2011. "Peace Journalism Where There is no War. Conflict-Sensitive Reporting on Urban Violence and Public Security in Brazil and its Potential Role in Conflict Transformation." *Conflict&Communication Online* 10 (2): 1–19.

Bourdieu, Pierre. 1986. "The Forms of Capital." In *Handbook of Theory and Research for the Sociology of Education*, edited by J. G. Richardson, 241–258. New York: Greenwood.

Bourdieu, Pierre. 1989. "Social Space and Symbolic Power." *Sociological Theory* 7 (1): 14–25.

Bourdieu, Pierre. 2005. "Habitus." In *Habitus: A Sense of Place*, edited by Jean Hillier, and Emma Rooksby, 43–49. Burlington, VT: Ashgate.

Cano, Ignacio. 1997. *Lethal Police Action in Rio de Janeiro*. Rio de Janeiro: ISER.

Cano, Ignacio, and Eduardo Ribeiro. 2016. "Old Strategies and New Approaches Towards Policing Drug Markets in Rio de Janeiro." *Police Practice and Research* 17 (4): 364–375.

Chaparro, Manuel Carlos. 2016. Iniciação a uma teoria das fontes: tipificação das fontes [Starting a theory on sources: Typification of sources]. Accessed November 13, 2017. http://oxisdaquestao.provisorio.ws/artigos/iniciacao-uma-teoria-das-fontes/

Coleman, James S. 1988. "Social Capital in the Creation of Human Capital." *The American Journal of Sociology* 94: S95–S120.

Couldry, Nick. 2003. "Media, symbolic power and the limits of Bourdieu's field theory." In Media@LSE electronic working papers, 2. Department of Media and Communications, London School of Economics and Political Science, London, UK.

Esser, Frank. 2013. "The emerging paradigm of comparative communication enquiry: advancing cross-national research in times of globalization." *International Journal of Communication* 7: 113–128.

Fortes, Leandro. 2005. *Jornalismo investigativo [Investigative Journalism]*. São Paulo: Contexto.

Goldstein, Donna. 2007. *Laughter out of Place: Race, Class, Violence and Sexuality in a Rio Shantytown*. Berkeley: University of California Press.

Hall, Stuart. 1980. "Encoding / Decoding." In *Culture, Media, Language: Working Papers in Cultural Studies, 1972–79*, edited by D. Hobson Hall, A. Lowe, and P. Willis, 128–138. London: Hutchinson.

Hellmueller, Lea. 2014. "The Analytical Model of Transnational Journalism Culture." In *The Washington, DC Media Corps in the 21st Century*. New York: Palgrave Macmillan.

Helmueller, Lea. 2017. "Gatekeeping Beyond Geographical Borders: Developing an Analytical Model of Transnational Journalism Cultures." *International Communication Gazette* 79 (1): 3–25.

Herscovitz, Heloiza G. 2004. "Brazilian Journalists' Perceptions of media Roles, Ethics and Foreign Influences on Brazilian Journalism." *Journalism Studies* 5 (1): 71–86.

Hess, Kristy. 2013. "Tertius Tactics: "Mediated Social Capital" as a Resource of Power for Traditional Commercial News Media." *Communication Theory* 23: 112–130. doi:10.1111/comt.12005.

Holston, James. 2008. "Dangerous Spaces of Citizenship: Gang Talk, Rights Talk, and the Rule of Law in Brazil." Working Paper 21, Center for Latin American Studies, University of California, Berkeley.

Human Rights Watch. 2016. *"Good Cops Are Afraid": The Toll of Unchecked Police Violence in Rio de Janeiro*. New York: Human Rights Watch.

Kraidy, Marwan M. 2011. "The Rise of Transnational media Systems: Implications of pan-Arab media for Comparative Research." In *Comparing Media Systems Beyond the Western World*, edited by D. C. Hallin and P. Mancini, 177–201. Cambridge, UK: Cambridge University Press.

Kucinski, Bernardo. 2002. *A pauta econômica e a agenda das assessorias de imprensa [The economic and public relations agenda]*. In Alberto Dines (Org.). a mídia e os dilemas da transparência[The media and the dilemma of transparency], 55–59. Brasília: Banco do Brasil.

Lemgruber, Julita, Ignacio Cano, and Leonarda Musumeci. 2017. *Olho por olho? O que pensam os cariocas sobre "bandido bom é bandido morto" [An eye for an eye? What do Rio's citizens think of "only a dead bandit is good bandit"]*. Rio de Janeiro: CESeC.

Lesage, Frédérik, and Robert A. Hackett. 2014. "Between Objectivity and Openness—The Mediality of Data for Journalism." *Media and Communication* 2 (2): 42–54.

Leu, Lorraine. 2004. "The Press and the Spectacle of Violence in Contemporary Rio de Janeiro." *Journal of Latin American Cultural Studies* 13 (3): 343–355. doi.org/10.1080/1356932042000287062.

Leu, Lorraine. 2008. "Drug Traffickers and the Contestation of City Space in Rio de Janeiro." *Revista da Associação Nacional dos Programas de Pós-Graduação em Comunicação* 11 (1): 1–16.

Lima, William da Silva. 1991. *400 contra 1: História do Comando Vermelho [400 against 1: Comando Vermelho history]*. (1st ed.). Petrópolis: Vozes.

Magno, Ana B. 2006. A agonia da reportagem – das grandes aventuras da imprensa brasileira à crise do mais fascinante dos gêneros jornalísticos: uma análise das matérias vencedoras do Prêmio Esso de Jornalismo [the agony of reporting – from the great adventures of the Brazilian press to the crisis of the most delightful journalism genres: An analysis of Esso award-winning journalism reporting]. Dissertação (Programa de Pós-graduação em Comunicação Social – Universidade de Brasília.

Mayr, Andrea. in press. "'Eu não Mereço morrer assassinado': Social media Activism by Favela Youth in Rio de Janeiro and its Representation in a Newspaper." In *Discourses of Disorder*, edited by Chris Hart. Edinburgh University Press.

Mayr, Andrea, and David Machin. 2012. *The Language of Crime and Deviance: An Introduction to Critical Linguistic Analysis in Media and Popular Culture*. London: Continuum.

Mioli, Teresa, and Ismael Nafría. 2017. *Innovative Journalism in Latin America*. Knight Centre for Journalism in the Americas. Accessed November 13, 2017. https://knightcenter.utexas.edu/books/IJENGLISH1.pdf

Moretzsohn, Sylvia. 2003. "O caso Tim Lopes: o mito da "mídia cidadã" [The Tim Lopes case: The myth of citizens' media]. Accessed November 13, 2017. www.bocc.ubi.pt/pag/moretzsohn-sylvia-tim-lopes.pdf

O'Boyle, Brendan. 2017. "Violence in Rio: "We Have to Look for a Collective Solution"." Americas Quarterly. Accessed August 11, 2017. http://americasquarterly.org/content/violence-rio-we-have-look-collective-solution?utm_content=bufferdc06c&utm_medium=social&utm_source=facebook.com&utm_campaign=buffer

Patterson, Thomas E. 2013. *Informing the News: The Need for Knowledge-Based Journalism*. New York: Vintage Books.

Penglase, Ben. 2008. "The Bastard Child of the Dictatorship: The Comando Vermelho and the Birth of "Narco-Culture" in Rio de Janeiro." *Luso-Brazilian Review* 45: 118–145. http://doi.org/10.1353/lbr.0.0001

Porto, Mauro P. 1996. A crise de confiança política e suas instituições: os mídia e a legitimidade da democracia [Political trust crisis and its institutions: Media and legitimacy in democracy]. In *Condicionantes da consolidação democrática: ética, mídia e cultura política,* M. Baquero (Org.), 41–64. Porto Alegre: Ed.Universidade/UFRGS.

Putnam, Robert D. 2000. *Bowling Alone: The Collapse and Revival of American Community.* New York: Simon & Schuster.

Ramos, Silvia, and Anabela Paiva. 2007. *Mídia e violência: novas tendências na cobertura de criminalidade e segurança no Brasil [Media and Violence: new Trends in the Coverage of Crime and Security In Brazil].* Rio de Janeiro: IUPERJ.

Reese, Stephen D. 2015. "Globalization of Mediated Spaces: The Case of Transnational Environmentalism in China." *International Journal of Communication* 9 (19): 2263–2281.

Romano, Angela. 2010. *International Journalism and Democracy: Civic Engagement Models From Around the World.* New York: Routledge.

Schmitz, Aldo, and Francisco Karam. 2013. "Os Spin Doctors and as Fontes das Notícias." [The spin doctors and the news sources]. *Brazilian Journalism Research* 9 (1): 98–115.

Silverstone, Roger. 2007. *Media and Morality: On the Rise of the Mediapolis.* Cambridge: Polity Press.

Souza, Maria do C. C. 1988. A Nova República brasileira: sob a espada de Dâmocles [The new Brazilian republic: Under the sword of Damocles]. In *Democratizando o Brasil,* A. Stepan (Org.), 563–627. Rio de Janeiro: Paz e Terra.

Szreter, S., and M. Woolcock. 2004. "Health by Association? Social Capital, Social Theory, and the Political Economy of Public Health." *International Journal of Epidemiology* 33 (4): 650–667.

Varjão, Suzana. 2009. *Micropoderes, Macroviolências: Um estudo sobre a palavra e a construção da ordem social [Micro-powers, macro-violence: A study of the word and the construction of social order].* Cadernos Temáticos da CONSEG, 41–46. Brasília: Mídia e Segurança Pública.

Veloso, Leticia. 2010. "Governing Heterogeneity in the Context of "Compulsory Closeness": the "Pacification"of Favelas in Rio de Janeiro." *Suburbanization in Global Society* 10: 253–272.

Waisbord, Siilvio. 2000. *Watchdog Journalism in South America.* New York: Columbia University Press.

Zaluar, Alba. 2000. "Perverse Integration: Drug Trafficking and Youth in the Favelas of Rio de Janeiro." *Journal of International Affairs* 53 (2): 653–671.

Index

Note: **Bold** page numbers indicate tables, *italic* numbers indicate figures.